THE INDIAN HOSPITALITY INDUSTRY

Dynamics and Future Trends

Advances in Hospitality and Tourism

THE INDIAN HOSPITALITY INDUSTRY

Dynamics and Future Trends

Edited by
Sandeep Munjal
Sudhanshu Bhushan

Apple Academic Press Inc.
3333 Mistwell Crescent
Oakville, ON L6L 0A2 Canada

Apple Academic Press Inc.
9 Spinnaker Way
Waretown, NJ 08758 USA

© 2017 by Apple Academic Press, Inc.

First issued in paperback 2021

No claim to original U.S. Government works

ISBN 13: 978-1-77-463651-0 (pbk)
ISBN 13: 978-1-77-188579-9 (hbk)

Library and Archives Canada Cataloguing in Publication

The Indian hospitality industry : dynamics and future trends / edited by Sandeep Munjal, Sudhanshu Bhushan.

Includes bibliographical references and index.
Issued in print and electronic formats.
ISBN 978-1-77188-579-9 (hardcover).--ISBN 978-1-315-22544-9 (PDF)
1. Hospitality industry--India. 2. Tourism--India. I. Munjal, Sandeep, editor II. Bhushan, Sudhanshu, 1964-, editor

TX910.I53I53 2017   338.4'7910954   C2017-902589-9   C2017-902590-2

Library of Congress Cataloging-in-Publication Data

Names: Munjal, Sandeep, editor. | Bhushan, Sudhanshu (Education analyst), editor.
Title: The Indian hospitality industry : dynamics and future trends / [edited by] Sandeep Munjal, Sudhanshu Bhushan.
Description: Oakville, ON, Canada ; Waretown, NJ, USA : Apple Academic Press, 2017. | Series: Advances in hospitality and tourism | Includes bibliographical references and index.
Identifiers: LCCN 2017017449 (print) | LCCN 2017022120 (ebook) | ISBN 9781315225449 (ebook) | ISBN 9781771885799 (hardcover : alk. paper)
Subjects: LCSH: Hospitality industry--India. | Hotels--India. | Food service--India.
Classification: LCC TX910.I5 (ebook) | LCC TX910.I5 I5585 2017 (print) | DDC 647.940954--dc23
LC record available at https://lccn.loc.gov/2017017449

Apple Academic Press also publishes its books in a variety of electronic formats. Some content that appears in print may not be available in electronic format. For information about Apple Academic Press products, visit our website at **www.appleacademicpress.com** and the CRC Press website at **www.crcpress.com**

ABOUT THE EDITORS

Sandeep Munjal

Prof. Sandeep Munjal is a Director at the Vedatya Institute, Gurgaon, in the National Capital Region (NCR Delhi), India. Prof. Munjal brings a unique combination of extensive industry and academic experience spanning over 22 years. Having worked with industry leaders such as the Taj Group of Hotels in India and ARAMARK Corp. in the United States, he offers a global perspective. He has also been engaged in a range of consultancy assignments in the hospitality and retail sectors in India. An IHM–Auragabad alumni, awarded the "best all round performance" medal, Prof. Munjal also pursued higher education in United States, in hospitality management at Widener University, Chester, PA. He is an avid researcher and has published widely in the area of hospitality management and heritage tourism in international and national journals. Throughout his career journey, he has received numerous awards and certifications.

Sudhanshu Bhushan

Sudhanshu Bhushan is currently Professor at the Vedatya Institute, Gurgaon, India. He is Ex-Vice Chancellor of Shri Venkateshwara University, Gajrola, UP, India. He is also Director at Convergence Management Advisors, Gurgaon. Earlier he was Associate Dean, at the GD Goenka World Institute and Founder Director of the J.K. Padampat Singhania Institute of Management and Technology, Gurgaon. Dr. Bhushan completed his PhD from Boston University, USA, and has an extensive teaching and corporate experience in the United States and Europe. He was an economist with FICCI and an advisor for development programs at ADB, Manila. He has authored papers in various areas of retail, services, hospitality, and economics.

CONTENTS

List of Contributors .... *ix*

List of Abbreviations .... *xi*

Advances in Hospitality and Tourism Book Series .... *xiii*

About the Series Editor .... *xv*

Preface .... *xvii*

1. **Economics of the Indian Hotel Industry—An Overview: A Global Benchmarking Across Different Segments of Hotel Offerings and Mapping the Growth Trajectory of the Industry** 1
   Sudhanshu Bhushan

2. **The Growth Story of Hotels in India: Looking Beyond the Rhetoric** 17
   Sandeep Munjal and Anmole Singh

3. **Corporate Social Responsibility: An Important Aspect of the Indian Hospitality Industry** 43
   Savita Sharma

4. **The Indian Hospitality Sector Is in a Flux: Changing Trends That Respond to the New Customer** 61
   Arvind K. Birdie

5. **Competing for Profitability: The Role of Revenue Management as a Strategic Choice for Indian Hotels** 85
   Anjana Singh

6. **Skilling India Initiative: Responding to the Critical Need for Skilled, Trained Manpower for the Indian Hospitality Industry** 105
   Shweta Tiwari

7. **Leadership Development in the Hospitality Industry: Perspectives from India** 125
   Sonia Bharwani

8. **Arts-Informed Leadership in Family-Run Business: Arts in Play** 155
   Vimal Babu and Amirul Hasan Ansari

9. **Service Quality and Customer Experience: The Key to Building**

Sustainable Competitive Advantage in Fine Dine Restaurants..............195

Gaurav Tripathi and Kartik Dave

10. Push for the Food and Beverages Segment to Drive Revenue
    Growth in Indian Hotels..227

    Debpriya De and Sandeep Munjal

11. Culinary Innovation in Indian Hotels and Building Cost
    Efficiencies That Spur Profitability Growth...251

    Sanjay Sharma

12. Events and Catering Business: Shift from Unorganized to
    Organized..275

    Kaveri Vij

13. Generation Z and Specialist Coffee Shops in India: A Perspective
    of the Needs, Motives, and Issues of Generation Z 299

    Durgamohan Musunuri

14. Epilogue and Future Trends of the Indian Tourism and
    Hospitality Industry...325

    Sudhanshu Bhushan

Index...363

LIST OF CONTRIBUTORS

Amirul Hasan Ansari
Centre for Management Studies, Jamia Millia Islamia Central University, New Delhi, India.
E-mail: ahansari@jmi.ac.in

Vimal Babu
School of Business, Auro University, Hazira Road, Opp. ONGC, Surat, Gujarat, India.
E-mail: vimalsairam@gmail.com

Sonia Bharwani
Associate Dean, Indian School of Management and Entrepreneurship, Mumbai, Maharashtra, India.
E-mail: sbharwaniphd@gmail.com

Sudhanshu Bhushan
School of Management and Entrepreneurship, Vedatya Institute, Gurgaon, India. E-mail: sudhanshusb@gmail.com

Arvind K. Birdie
Associate Professor,Department of PG Studies,Vedatya Institute, Gurgaon, India. E-mail: arvindgagan@gmail.com

Kartik Dave
Associate Professor, Marketing School of Business, Public Policy and Social Entrepreneurship, Ambedkar University, Delhi, India. E-mail: davekartik123@gmail.com

Debpriya De
Associate Professor, School of Hospitality and Tourism Management, Vedatya Institute, Gurgaon, India. E-mail: debpriya.de@vedatya.ac.in

Sandeep Munjal
Director, Vedatya Institute, Gurgaon, India. E-mail: sandeep.munjal@vedatya.ac.in

Durgamohan Musunuri, MBA, PGDIT, PhD
Director, Bhavan's Usha & Lakshmi Mittal Institute of Management, New Delhi, India.
E-mail: durgamohan27@gmail.com

Sanjay Sharma
Associate Professor, School of Hospitality and Tourism Management (SHTM), Vedatya Institute, Gurgaon, India. E-mail: sanjayihm@yahoo.co.in

Savita Sharma
Assistant Professor, School of Tourism and Hospitality Management, Ansal University, Gurgaon, India.
E-mail: savitasharma@ansaluniversity.edu.in

Anjana Singh
Associate Professor, School of Hospitality and Tourism, School of Hospitality and Tourism Management, Vedatya Institute, Gurgaon, India. E-mail: singhanjana@gmail.com

Anmole Singh
Assistant Professor, School of Hospitality and Tourism Management, Vedatya Institute, Gurgaon, India.
E-mail: anmole.singh@vedatya.ac.in

Shweta Tiwari
Vedatya Institute, Gurgaon, India. E-mail: shweta.amit@rediffmail.com

Gaurav Tripathi
Assistant Professor, Marketing Area, Birla Institute of Management and Technology, Greater Noida, India. E-mail:tripathi_gaurav@hotmail.com

Kaveri Vij
Co-Founder and Partner, Designer Events Inc., New Delhi, India. E-mail: kaverivij26@gmail.com

LIST OF ABBREVIATIONS

AIRIS	Artists in Residence
ARI	average rate index
ARR	average room rate
BoP	bottom of the pyramid
BRIC	Brazil, Russia, India, China
CBTL	Coffee Bean and Tea Leaf
CFA	confirmatory factor analysis
CRM	customer relationship management
CSR	corporate social responsibility
EIH	East India Hotels
EY-EEMA	Event and Entertainment Management Association
FDI	foreign direct investment
FG	focus group
FHRAI	Federation of Hotel and Restaurant Association of India
FSI	floor space index
FSSAI	Food Safety and Standards Authority of India
FTA	foreign tourist arrival
GDP	gross domestic product
HAI	Hotel Association of India
HMCs	hotel management contract
HRIDAY	Heritage City Development and Augmentation Yojana
IDIs	in-depth interviews
IHCL	Indian Hotels Company Limited
JV	joint venture
LLP	limited liability partnership
MPI	market penetration index
MT	metric tons
NCR	National Capital Region
NPD	new product development
NSP	new service development
NVQF	National Vocational Qualification Framework
OTAs	online travel agents
PMKVY	Pradhan Mantri Kaushal Vikas Yojana
REITs	Real Estate Investment Trusts

RevPar	revenue per available room
RGI	revenue growth index
RMSI	revenue market share index
THSC	Tourism and Hospitality Skills Council
VAT	value added tax

ADVANCES IN HOSPITALITY AND TOURISM BOOK SERIES BY APPLE ACADEMIC PRESS, INC.

Editor-in-Chief:
Mahmood A. Khan, PhD
Professor, Department of Hospitality and Tourism Management, Pamplin College of Business, Virginia Polytechnic Institute and State University, Falls Church, Virginia, USA
Email: mahmood@vt.edu

Books in the Series:

Food Safety: Researching the Hazard in Hazardous Foods
Editors: Barbara Almanza, PhD, RD, and Richard Ghiselli, PhD

Strategic Winery Tourism and Management: Building Competitive Winery Tourism and Winery Management Strategy
Editor: Kyuho Lee, PhD

Sustainability, Social Responsibility and Innovations in the Hospitality Industry
Editor: H. G. Parsa, PhD
Consulting Editor: Vivaja "Vi" Narapareddy, PhD
Associate Editors: SooCheong (Shawn) Jang, PhD,
Marival Segarra-Oña, PhD, and Rachel J. C. Chen, PhD, CHE

Managing Sustainability in the Hospitality and Tourism Industry: Paradigms and Directions for the Future
Editor: Vinnie Jauhari, PhD

Management Science in Hospitality and Tourism: Theory, Practice, and Applications
Editors: Muzaffer Uysal, PhD, Zvi Schwartz, PhD, and
Ercan Sirakaya-Turk, PhD

Tourism in Central Asia: Issues and Challenges
Editors: Kemal Kantarci, PhD, Muzaffer Uysal, PhD, and
Vincent Magnini, PhD

Poverty Alleviation through Tourism Development: A Comprehensive and Integrated Approach
Robertico Croes, PhD, and Manuel Rivera, PhD

Chinese Outbound Tourism 2.0
Editor: Xiang (Robert) Li, PhD

Hospitality Marketing and Consumer Behavior: Creating Memorable Experiences
Editor: Vinnie Jauhari, PhD

Women and Travel: Historical and Contemporary Perspectives
Editors: Catheryn Khoo-Lattimore, PhD, and Erica Wilson, PhD

Wilderness of Wildlife Tourism
Editor: Johra Kayeser Fatima, PhD

Medical Tourism and Wellness: Hospitality Bridging Healthcare (H2H)©
Editor: Frederick J. DeMicco, PhD, RD

Sustainable Viticulture: The Vines and Wines of Burgundy
Claude Chapuis

The Indian Hospitality Industry: Dynamics and Future Trends
Editors: Sandeep Munjal and Sudhanshu Bhushan

Tourism Development and Destination Branding through Content Marketing Strategies and Social Media
Editor: Anukrati Sharma, PhD

Evolving Paradigms in Tourism and Hospitality in Developing Countries: A Case Study of India
Editor: Bindi Varghese, PhD

The Hospitality and Tourism Industry in China: New Growth, Trends, and Developments
Editor: Jinlin Zhao, PhD

ABOUT THE SERIES EDITOR

Mahmood A. Khan, PhD, is a Professor in the Department of Hospitality and Tourism Management, Pamplin College of Business at Virginia Tech's National Capital Region campus. He has served in teaching, research, and administrative positions for the past 35 years, working at major U.S. universities. Dr. Khan is the author of seven books and has traveled extensively for teaching and consulting on management issues and franchising. He has been invited by national and international corporations to serve as a speaker, keynote speaker, and seminar presenter on different topics related to franchising and services management. He is the author of *Restaurant Franchising: Concepts, Regulations, and Practices, Third Edition, Revised and Updated*, published by Apple Academic Press, Inc.

Dr. Khan has received the Steven Fletcher Award for his outstanding contribution to hospitality education and research. He is also a recipient of the John Wiley & Sons Award for lifetime contribution to outstanding research and scholarship; the Donald K. Tressler Award for scholarship; and the Cesar Ritz Award for scholarly contribution. He also received the Outstanding Doctoral Faculty Award from Pamplin College of Business.

He has served on the Board of Governors of the Educational Foundation of the International Franchise Association, on the Board of Directors of the Virginia Hospitality and Tourism Association, as a Trustee of the International College of Hospitality Management, and as a Trustee on the Foundation of the Hospitality Sales and Marketing Association's International Association. He is also a member of several professional associations.

PREFACE

The purpose in commissioning this book is to track the evolution and the status of the hospitality industry of India in the post-liberalization era of the Indian economy. India has been in a period of change and transition for the last two decades, moving from a mixed economy toward a market economy model. The Indian hospitality industry is metamorphosing into a mature industry, and we are witnessing these changes in transition, which are volatile, complex, controversial, and challenging within the hospitality world comprised of academia and practitioners. In this context, the commission of this book was a difficult challenge for getting the authors to track the above-mentioned changes of the past two decades in the dynamics of the hospitality industry and developing the thematic base of the book.

Various authors and experts in hospitality management have provided critical analysis of key thematic areas as they are evolving in the context of the economic change in India. The book, thus, is a kaleidoscope of diverse thematic ideas and thoughts and frameworks, which are evolving in hospitality management in India for the lost two decades. In our editorial capacity, we guided authors on the convergence and divergence of these thematic areas so that an overall macro-perspective can be discerned by the reader. We hope we have done justice with our contribution of this book, and the documentation and analysis of the context of the current state of hospitality management. The book covers and develops a unique academic framework that is not axiomatic in flavor but prescriptive in nature. We hope both academia and the practicing world of hospitality management will find it interesting.

THE KALEIDOSCOPE

The hospitality industry in India has come a long way since the first wave of economic liberalization that swept the nation in the early 1990s, given the presence of every major hotel brand in India today. The economic liberalization and an impressive GDP (gross domestic product) growth resulted in many socioeconomic changes that has created a positive consumption climate for the hospitality industry (food retail, business travel, leisure travel) at a domestic level and also created an international interest in business and leisure travel to India. The combined impact was the spiraling demand for hospitality services and products, including hotels, restaurants, catering, event management services, and retail. The socioeconomic changes included an increase in spending power and discretionary income, along with a better understanding of the quality and standards that hospitality brands had to offer internationally. The discerning customer wanted the best in class, at the best price (value offering), and was willing to spend provided the expectations were met. From a demographic significance, this constituted a large middle class along with the equally significant upper-class elite. Given the sheer size, comprising about 200–300 million people, this was a market no hospitality group could ignore, an opportunity that no brand could sit out.

For nearly two decades, the hospitality industry in India charted growth that was marked by the arrival and growth of international brands like Marriott, IHG, Carlson Rezidor, Hyatt, Accor, and Starwoods in the hotel space. These brands are today offering products and services to a wide range of segments and have presence in not just the major Indian cities but a host of Tier-II and III cities in the country. In the restaurant space, again the same pattern is visible, especially in the QSR (quick service restaurant) segment, with the growth of international brands like Dominos, Pizza Hut, KFC, Johnny Rocket, Subway, Taco Bell, Papa John, Burger King, etc., to name a few. The fine-dining restaurant segment too is now finding both international brand interest and investment. Other segments that constitute the hospitality industry like food retail, or event management and contract food services too, are in a phase of growth and development. These may not have reached the same level of penetration or growth as the hotels but are surely on a growth trajectory. The presence of a large unorganized sector with respect to these components of the hospitality industry is a factor, but the maturity process has commenced and the years to come will see a shift toward an organized format, with a strong presence of international brands.

It is time that the India story from the hospitality industry perspective is told. This book is an effort to tell that story, one defined by the industry's push for growth in revenues and struggle to match the revenue growth with profitability. The editors and contributing authors for the specific chapters in the book offer an industry-informed take on the ground reality and the way forward with respect to the facet or segment of the industry that they are looking at. The authors are either practitioners themselves or bring their viewpoint through their research effort. It is highly likely that there is no published commentary on the state of the hospitality sector in India of the depth and width that this book attempts to offer. It is important that stakeholders—which include domestic and international hospitality professionals, business leaders, investors, and those in governmental positions especially in the tourism ministry—to be informed of the issues and challenges that the hospitality industry in India is up against. The book attempts to look at the dilemma of an industry that responded to the demand growth promise by ramping up supply, only to find that the investments made were received by an actual growth that was way shy of forecasts and left investors with unexpected losses on their profit and loss statements and bloodied balance sheets. In their defense, to those who predicted handsome returns for the hotel industry through impressive ARRs (average room rates) and occupancy predictions, the shift in macroeconomic fundamentals of the economy may have been the reason for the not so robust growth in demand on the ground.

It is important to visit the ground reality and to understand the issues and challenges alongside the growth potential that the Indian economy stands for, given that is likely to be christened the fastest growing economy in the world. The book is an attempt in that direction with the findings presented by the authors as they examine wide-ranging aspects. The segments of the hospitality industry in India should help readers build a better understanding of the hospitality business in the local as well as global economic context.

The 14 chapters that constitute this book offer an insight into the multiple dimensions of the Indian hospitality industry. While the hotels segment remains in focus, the book recognizes that the hospitality sector includes other segments as well, like the events and catering businesses, the restaurants, and coffee shops. The opening chapters set the tone for providing an overarching perspective on the status of the industry in terms of the macroeconomic variables and how they may have impacted the health of hospitality businesses in India. The second chapter digs into the heart of the current dilemma, where further capacity addition by hotel brands is on hold, given the poor financial returns that investors have to deal with in the current economic scenario. The chapter brings out the differing views of brand managements and investor representatives on the reasons behind the mess. The authors share their findings and provide a perspective on how the industry needs to find a way to bring the brands and asset ownerships together to jointly find solutions, close the trust deficit, and move forward.

The revenue management capacity and approach that is being deployed by the industry in India is discussed, and the strategic role that adherence to contemporary revenue management practices can play is highlighted by the author. In a marketplace where "distribution" is largely on visible digital platforms, revenue management is a strategic tool that is a must for effective decision-making. Another chapter looks at the significance of "corporate social responsibility" in view of the changes in Indian company law through a recently passed legislation that makes it mandatory for businesses to spend a given percent of their profits for a listed number of socially important causes. For an industry that is often seen as being on the wrong side of the sustainability and environmental impact debate, the author charts the current landscape of "CSR" with respect to Indian hotels and offers recommendations for initiatives that will create a positive impact.

The hospitality sector has for decades identified the shortage of skilled, trained manpower as the single biggest challenge to its growth. The new "Skill India" initiative under the aegis of the Ministry of Urban Affairs, Government of India, there is an opportunity to build a training infrastructure that can meet the needs of the industry. This is discussed in another chapter, which offers a clear perspective on the human resource challenge at the line level and how the new initiative may be able to play a role. The human resource challenge is not restricted only to the need for skilled labor; for a growing industry, there is need for professionals in leadership roles. This is an emerging issue, especially for the luxury segment of the hotel industry. Another author offers an interesting take on "leadership skills" with respect to family-run hospitality businesses in India, by recognizing the leadership skill as an art form.

The book has more to offer. There is a chapter that analyzes the status of "F&B"-driven revenue growth in Indian hotels, given that occupancy levels have remained below par. The chapter documents best practices of key hotel brands and also discusses how the industry innovated and responded to the challenge of revenue growth, such as by deploying their food and beverage offerings as a differentiator. Another chapter probes the efforts by the industry toward "culinary innovation," such that the revenue growth is also supported by profit maximization through effective cost management. The emergence of coffee shop chains that are patronized by the "generation Z" is observed as a cultural phenomenon, and the segment is discussed in a separate chapter in the book.

The restaurant segment is a high growth segment of the Indian hospitality landscape. Aspects around services quality that will determine the performance of the sector are discussed in a chapter wherein the author clearly identifies the "service quality" and "service experience" as critical success factors for creating sustainable competitive advantage. Another chapter offers a broader commentary on consumer trends that are defining their expectations from the hospitality industry, guided by behavior shifts that have sociocultural moorings.

CONCLUSION

All in all, the book attempts to bring to the discussion table aspects that are relevant to building a better understanding of the Indian hospitality industry and will allow readers to get a 360 degree view, factoring in multiple viewpoints, and hopefully to understand the dilemma and the opportunity that the industry is looking at in the coming decade or so. It is a good read for professionals from the service industry globally, students looking for careers in the business, entrepreneurs and investors, government representatives, policymakers, and other stakeholders.

Hospitality management is characterized by "generic" elements, derived from business management disciplines and also elements of "specialism," developed from a very specific context in the hospitality industry. Though this is a global pattern of hospitality education, it is magnified in the case of Indian hospitality management education. In India, hospitality industry management, theory, and practice have almost 90% indigenous elements. It is a home-grown theory and practice and therefore is unique. It is also unique because the industry is characterized by fragmentation, eclecticism, lack of methodological approach and documentation, and pluralism in terms of culture and management. Thus, we hope the book would be a unique read for the readers.

In the end, a very special expression of gratitude to Mr. Amit Kapur, Managing Promoter at Vedatya Institute, for enabling a culture and work environment that facilitates research efforts like these. Without his support this research would not have been possible. We would also like to take this opportunity to thank Dr. Mahmood A. Khan for having given us an opportunity to work on this book.

Wishing the readers an enjoyable read!

Editors
—**Sandeep Munjal**
—**Sudhanshu Bhushan**

CHAPTER 1

ECONOMICS OF THE INDIAN HOTEL INDUSTRY—AN OVERVIEW: A GLOBAL BENCHMARKING ACROSS DIFFERENT SEGMENTS OF HOTEL OFFERINGS AND MAPPING THE GROWTH TRAJECTORY OF THE INDUSTRY

SUDHANSHU BHUSHAN*

School of Management and Entrepreneurship, Vedatya Institute, Gurgaon, India

*E-mail: sudhanshusb@gmail.com

CONTENTS

Abstract 2
1.1   Introduction...2
1.2   The Dynamics of Industry 3
1.3   The Initiatives 4
1.4   The Trends 4
1.5   The Future Scenario..14
Keywords 15
References...15

ABSTRACT

This chapter traces the significant impact of the hospitality industry across the globe. Special focus has been given to the changing demands of customers in India, and the emerging trends exhibited by hotel providers, to meet the changing needs of the industry as a whole. The author compares the developed hospitality markets of the United States and Europe and their prevailing trends, with the emerging market in India. The Indian tourism and hospitality industry has materialized as one of the key drivers of growth among the services sectors in India. It contributes to 6.23% to the national gross domestic product and 8.78% of the total employment in the country. Constant transformation, functional growth, and improving standards have gained the hospitality industry of India approval all over the world. The chapter concludes with pointing out the opportunities available in India, both in terms of hospitality service offerings and financing options to create sustainable brand value. The chapter sets the tone of the book in considering the various critical aspects of Indian hospitality industry in an emerging market of India, from an academic and most importantly from a practitioner's perspective.

1.1   INTRODUCTION

The impact of hospitality on the global economy is significant across the world. The travel and tourism industry encompasses 266 million jobs and contributes 9.5% to the gross domestic product (GDP) globally. With the travel and tourism sector growth forecasted to expand by 3.9% during 2016, the sector will be increasingly recognized as a key driver of economic growth at the local, regional, and global level as quoted by the Economic Impact Analysis, developed by the World Travel and Tourism Council.

Tourism in India demonstrates a high potential based on our rich cultural and historical heritage, variety in ecology, terrains, and places of natural beauty spread across the country. The tourism industry is a large employment generator, besides being a significant source of foreign exchange earnings for the country. In 2014, approximately 12.8 million domestic travelers and 7.7 million foreign tourists comprised the tourist traffic in India. The foreign exchange earnings generated from overseas tourists in 2014 equaled US$ 20.24 billion, indicating an annual growth rate of 9.7%.

1.2   THE DYNAMICS OF INDUSTRY

The hotel industry has a direct impact on both the overall economic growth and in improving employability in the country. In India, the industry contributes 6.88% to the GDP, employing a population of 8.7% (36,695,000 direct and indirect jobs) in 2014, expected to rise by 1.8% in 2015–2016 to 37,365,000 jobs, and rise by 2% per annum to 45,566,000 jobs in 2025 (9.0% of the total jobs) as per the World Travel and Tourism Council. The tourism and hospitality sector's direct contribution to GDP aggregated to US\$ 44.2 billion in 2015 and is expected to register a CAGR of 10.5%. The direct contribution of travel and tourism to GDP is expected to grow to 7.3% per annum to US\$ 88.6 billion (i.e., 2.5% of GDP) by 2025.

During the period April 2000–May 2015, this sector attracted around US\$ 8.1 billion of foreign direct investments, according to the Department of Industrial Policy and Promotion. Some of the recent investments in this sector are as follows:

- Fairfax-owned Thomas Cook has acquired Swiss tour operator Kuoni Group's business in India and Hong Kong, for about Rs. 535 crores (US\$ 85.6 million) in order to scale up the in-bound tour business.
- US-based Vantage Hospitality Group has signed a franchise agreement with India-based Miraya Hotel Management to establish its mid-market brands in the country.
- Thai firm Onyx Hospitality and Kingsbridge India asset management firm have set up a joint venture (JV) to open seven hotels in the country by 2018, for which the JV will raise US\$ 100 million.
- ITC is planning to invest about Rs. 9000 crores (US\$ 1.42 billion) in the next 3–4 years to expand its hotel portfolio to 150 hotels. ITC will launch five other hotels in Mahabalipuram, Kolkata, Ahmedabad, Hyderabad, and Colombo by 2018.
- Goldman Sachs, the New York based multinational investment banking fund, has invested Rs. 255 crores (US\$ 40.37 million) in Vatika Hotels.
- Japanese conglomerate Soft Bank will lead the Rs. 630 crores (US\$ 95.6 million) funding round in Gurgaon-based OYO Rooms.
- MakeMyTrip will acquire the travel planning website Mygola and its assets for an undisclosed sum and will focus on innovating in the online travel segment.

1.3   THE INITIATIVES

Some of the major initiatives taken by the Government of India to give a boost to the tourism and hospitality sector are as follows:

- The Government of India plans to cover 150 countries under the e-visa scheme by the end of 2015, besides opening an airport in the NCR region to ease the pressure on Delhi airport.
- The Tourist Visa on Arrival scheme enabled by Electronic Travel Authorization, launched by the Government of India on November 27, 2014 for 43 countries has led to sharp growth in usage of the facility. During the month of July, 2015, a total of 21,476 tourist arrived on e-Tourist Visa as compared to 2462 during the month of July, 2014, registering a growth of 772.3%. During January–July 2015, a total of 147,690 tourist arrived on e-Tourist Visa as compared to 14,415 during January–July 2014, registering a growth of 924.6%.
- The Government of India has set aside Rs. 500 crores (US$ 79.17 million) for the first phase of the National Heritage City Development and Augmentation Yojana (HRIDAY). The 12 cities in the first phase are Varanasi, Amritsar, Ajmer, Mathura, Gaya, Kanchipuram, Vellankani, Badami, Amaravati, Warangal, Puri, and Dwarka.
- Under "Project Mausam," the Government of India has proposed to establish cross-cultural linkages and to revive historic maritime cultural and economic ties with 39 Indian Ocean countries.

Given the current fast paced socioeconomic ecosystem, Indians are on the move like never before. The interesting question to be asked is, where do these travelers stay when they reside overnight outside their hometowns? We do not have any comprehensive and coherent data on the subject yet, nor do we quite understand the price, product, and service combinations which could induce each segment of these travelers to patronize new alternatives of short-term accommodation.

1.4   THE TRENDS

The Indian hotel industry comprises three subsets of consistent players:

- the real estate asset investors who own the hotel properties,
- hotel management companies who operate the hotel, and

•   brand owning companies who "flag" or provide the brand for the
    hotel.

Hotels broadly operate across four different price, product, and service
points. Luxury and deluxe hotels equivalent to the 5-star category and
above, upscale and up-market hotels equivalent to the 4-star category, mid-
scale and mid-market hotels equivalent to the 3-star category, and budget or
economy hotels equivalent to the 2- or 1-star category of available assets.
Although there are subcategories reflecting entry and exit points in each
of the four broad categories, the supply of rooms, in general, increases in
a pyramid shape as one goes down the price scale, that is, there are more
upscale rooms than deluxe rooms, more mid-scale rooms than upscale
rooms, and so on.

The United States has the most developed hotel market in the world
today. It has about 4.9 million hotel rooms in 52,887 properties serving
about 318 million population. The US hotel industry generates a revenue of
US$ 163 billion with an average occupancy of 62%. The main differentia-
tion across the categories lies in the services offered, due to extremely high
payroll costs. The cost of product is relatively low, due to easy financing
(high leverage, long repayment tenures, and low interest rates), available
and cheap infrastructure (power, water, public transport, sanitation, etc.),
and a relatively quick and transparent government approval process. The
low barriers to entry for hotel development have led to hotel assets being
commoditized, and with the large supply of rooms available; the power
resides with the brand-owning companies who alone can ensure a strong
topline with their loyal customer base. The brands focus on customer satisfaction, by ensuring that hotels are built and services provided, according to
their specifications and standards.

The Indian market, in contrast, is underdeveloped and lies at the opposite
end of the spectrum. The numbers of member hotels at FHRAI (Federation
of Hotel and Restaurant Associations of India) as on March 31, 2014 were
3681 and increased to 3938 as on March 31, 2015. It has increased to 3990
as on August 22, 2015. The details of the members of FHRAI are as under.
The pan-India membership of FHRAI accounted for a little over 166,077
rooms (Table 1.1).

The occupancy for 2013–2014 remained unchanged at 60.4% as compared
to that in 2012–2013. The average room rate (ARR) was the highest in the
last 5 years, increasing by 4.9% to close at Rs. 4729. It is important to note
that the increase in ARR was recorded across all star categories (except the
Heritage category) (Exhibit 1.1).

TABLE 1.1   Hotel Rooms in India (August 2015).

Category	Total	
	Nos.	**Rooms**
5 Star deluxe	153	32,996
5 Star	156	20,740
4 Star	167	15,297
Heritage	58	2101
3 Star	335	18,636
2 Star	49	2010
1 Star	7	192
Unclassified	1700	74,105
Total	2625	166,077

Source: Adapted from Federation of Hotel and Restaurants Association of India, 2015.

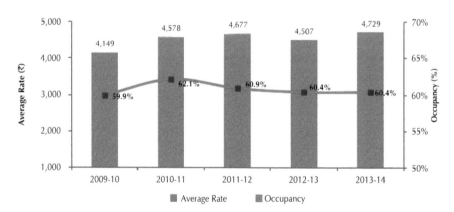

EXHIBIT 1.1   Occupancy and Average Rates (2009–2010 to 2013–2014).

Source: FHRAI, HVS, and Ecotel: Indian Hotel Industry Survey 2013–2014.

Table 1.2 illustrates the average occupancy and ARRs for 30 cities/ regions across the country over the last 5 years, as quoted from the FHRAI Survey results.

MKG Hospitality's global ranking of hotel groups in terms of number of rooms clearly illustrates the supremacy of the Anglo-American groups. The Inter Continental Hotel Group remains in the first place, with Hilton

TABLE 1.2 Average Occupancy and Average Room Rates across 30 Cities (2009–2014).

City	Occupancy					Average room rate				
	2009/2010	2010/2011	2011/2012	2012/2013	2013/2014	2009/2010	2010/2011	2011/2012	2012/2013	2013/2014
All India	59.9%	62.1%	60.9%	60.4%	60.4%	4149	4578	4677	4507	4729
Agra	57.0%	63.2%	68.3%	60.3%	57.7%	2482	3968	3974	4381	3988
Ahmedabad	65.7%	67.6%	65.1%	63.0%	60.4%	3367	3234	3650	3902	3106
Aurangabad	57.9%	59.5%	ID	49.0%	ID	2850	2612	ID	3203	ID
Bengaluru	52.6%	53.8%	58.7%	56.6%	59.7%	6766	5838	6849	5533	6300
Bhopal	66.1%	ID	78.0%	72.4%	67.7%	3110	ID	3827	4300	3366
Chandigarh	69.1%	70.4%	ID	65.4%	54.9%	4780	4544	ID	3639	4396
Chennai	65.6%	64.8%	69.1%	69.8%	68.2%	4083	5508	4365	4345	4043
Coimbatore	75.5%	72.8%	66.5%	61.3%	59.3%	3236	3968	4100	3655	2987
Delhi-NCR[a]	64.6%	59.0%	61.4%	57.1%	57.7%	6985	6763	7319	7455	8282
Goa	63.1%	64.4%	69.5%	67.7%	69.9%	4757	7807	5856	5749	5643
Hyderabad	58.8%	53.3%	55.4%	55.7%	56.9%	5137	4152	4020	3856	3367
Indore	65.2%	65.4%	57.9%	61.4%	55.8%	1814	1869	2590	2631	2032
Jaipur	57.7%	64.0%	59.4%	58.6%	57.3%	4059	3071	3447	3490	3878
Jodhpur	43.2%	49.2%	48.8%	46.3%	45.0%	4552	5519	7005	8431	11,350
Kochi	64.4%	74.2%	81.1%	71.5%	68.4%	2806	1528	1536	2882	2186
Kolkata	64.5%	65.4%	67.1%	67.1%	70.1%	4880	4788	5302	5461	5230
Lucknow	58.7%	59.8%	63.3%	65.0%	68.8%	5109	2393	2966	3047	3426

TABLE 1.2 *(Continued)*

City	Occupancy					Average room rate				
	2009/2010	2010/2011	2011/2012	2012/2013	2013/2014	2009/2010	2010/2011	2011/2012	2012/2013	2013/2014
Mount Abu	67.5%	63.0%	ID	ID	ID	2159	2821	ID	ID	ID
Mumbai	67.2%	69.0%	73.5%	71.5%	72.9%	5833	5087	6063	5971	5397
Mussoorie	45.9%	52.5%	39.4%	ID	ID	6078	5817	4807	ID	ID
Mysore	67.7%	71.4%	62.4%	65.7%	ID	2637	4634	1973	3738	ID
Nagpur	61.5%	76.6%	ID	54.1%	60.9%	3132	2314	ID	3018	1654
Pune	53.2%	53.3%	53.2%	57.8%	58.3%	3921	3140	3293	2724	2963
Raipur	39.0%	ID	ID	ID	ID	1521	ID	ID	ID	ID
Shimla	48.0%	42.7%	47.8%	56.5%	53.1%	1790	2267	1904	2636	2139
Thiruvananthapuram	55.3%	61.8%	60.9%	57.1%	53.6%	1422	1380	2330	1474	2590
Udaipur	47.0%	55.2%	52.1%	59.5%	50.9%	3543	7406	2081	4449	9698
Vadodara	65.6%	77.8%	71.7%	68.0%	60.6%	4360	3703	3901	3698	3454
Visakhapatnam	62.1%	76.3%	ID	63.3%	59.0%	2809	5431	ID	3367	4371
Gurgaon[b]			65.5%	61.0%	58.2%			8122	7776	7691

ID, insufficient data.

[a]Delhi-NCR data including Faridabad, Ghaziabad, Gurgaon, and Noida (Shaded Portion), rest excluding Gurgaon data.

[b]Gurgaon included with Delhi-NCR for 2009/2010 and 2010/2011.

(Reprinted from Federation of Hotel & Restaurant Associations of India (FHRAI), Indian Hotel Industry Survey 2013–2014. With permission.)

Worldwide ranked second, Marriott International at the third position, and Wyndham Hotel Group at the fourth position close behind. Each of the top four groups worldwide has more than 645,000 rooms in operation. It is especially significant that all the groups in the Top 10 showed growth in their supply. Georges Panayotis, CEO and founder of MKG Group, explains: "Major hotel groups are in a race for growth to resist growing pressure from tech and web giants, with respect to which they must reach a critical size."

With some 19.5 million rooms on January 1, 2014, the global hotel supply slowed with a growth of 3% in recent years. Overall, the global hotel supply (branded and independent supply) grew by close to 200,000 rooms.

Growth in the branded supply was supported by the dynamism of leading hotel groups on the international scene, where they are diversifying geographically to balance risk. Given the maturity of most developed countries, emerging markets continue to be the key markets, with Asia-Pacific in the forefront (+11.5% growth in its chain supply). In 2015, the Middle East and Africa region (+7.2%) was also a focus of international attention, alongside Latin America (+3.8%) with Brazil as a focal point. While together they still account for close to 70% of the chain supply, North American and European continents continue to lose market share on a year on year basis.

Contrary to the developed market scenario as existing in the United States, there is no significant variation in the range of services offered across the 4-star hotel category in India, although the quality of these services varies enormously. Even the unorganized guest-house segment often offers a full suite of services.

The main differentiation across Indian categories lies in the quality of product. This is because the cost of product is very high, primarily due to a combination of exorbitantly high land cost (with low floor space index [FSI], referring to the ratio of built-up or constructed area to the land area), expensive debt (low leverage, short repayment tenures, and high interest rates), an absence of basic infrastructure (most hotels have to provide their own power back-up, water supply/treatment, sanitation, and transport), and perhaps the world's slowest and most opaque government approval process. According to ICRA, starting a new hotel in India requires clearances from roughly 40 central and state agencies and 110 licenses, many of which have to be applied for sequentially!

The relatively few rooms and the enormous barriers to hotel asset creation have led to some uniquely Indian anomalies:

- The majority of hotels in India are built by local high net worth individuals or real estate developers, who can manage the land acquisition and local government approval process effectively.
- The balance of power resides with the hotel owners who have established a management brand leading to a branded commoditization.

The individual developers without any consolidated hospitality expertise generally build their hotels according to their own desires and without adhering to any specific brand's product and service standards. Since land costs are high (as a percentage of total asset cost, often exceeding 50% in the metros unlike the United States where this is generally less than 30%), many asset owners opt to build deluxe and upscale hotels rather than mid-scale and budget hotels due to both prestige reasons and because the incremental cost between a 5-, 4-, or 3-star hotel is not very significant. The shortage in supply of lower category rooms is further exaggerated by the absence of a good public transport and price conscious hotel guests, who are unwilling to trade location for price, as the saving in room rates is effectively annulled by the increase in the cost of transport and in the time spent traveling.

As a result, about 50% of the classified hotels in the FHRAI's membership list are deluxe, leading to an inverted pyramid of supply meeting the needs of a regular pyramid of demand (Table 1.1). It is clear that there is enormous latent demand in India for appropriately priced mid-market and budget hotel products, as has already been demonstrated in the transportation and automobile sectors, with the advent and success of low-cost carriers and economically priced cars. Before attempting to assess the likely evolution of the Indian hotel sector in the medium to long term (5–10 years), it would be worthwhile to evaluate the current and likely future growth of the Indian economy.

The Indian economy should nearly quadruple from a GDP of $2.30 trillion currently to $3.9 trillion by 2020. This is primarily because gross capital formation at around 31% of GDP and an incremental capital output ratio of 4% should lead to a GDP growth rate of about 9%. This growth rate should continue through 2020 and be accompanied by a number of connected and independent developments:

- With population growing at 1.2% annually, an expected increase in adult literacy from % (530 million) at present to 78% (790 million) by 2020 and the median age increasing from 26 to 29 years by 2020; the working population (20–59 years old) will increase by 20%, that is, 600 million to about 730 million by 2020. The increase in literacy will improve both employability and productivity in the country.

- Total households will increase from 260 million currently to 300 million by 2020, with the consuming segment (earning Rs. 90,000 or more annually) increasing from 125 to 200 million. This increase in the educated middle class, with expanding disposable incomes and consequent discretionary spending, will lead to extraordinary opportunities in some sectors of the economy.
- The composition of the GDP (57% services, 26% manufacturing, and 17% agriculture) will continue to shift in favor of the services sector. Total private consumption will continue to remain at 60% of GDP in 2020.
- With increased tax revenues, there will be increased government spending on the infrastructure and social sectors, as is already evident in the outlay of the central budgets over the past decade.

Taking these factors into account, the sectors that should witness extraordinary growth (12% or more annually) over the next decade, and which will drive the demand for hotel rooms are

- financial services (banking, capital markets, life insurance);
- infrastructure (power, roads, railways, irrigation, water supply, and sanitation);
- education;
- pharmaceuticals and healthcare;
- media and entertainment;
- organized retail and logistics; and
- automobiles and auto components.

Typically, growth in demand for hotel rooms is directly linked to growth in the services and manufacturing sectors for the business travel segment, and to growth in discretionary income for the leisure travel segment. The World Travel and Tourism Council estimates that while India's travel and tourism sector will grow at 8.2% annually, leisure travel will grow at 7.1% annually, and business travel by 6.6% annually through 2025. Significant latent demand will also arise due to the creation of a large inventory of low-priced rooms, quite similar to what occurred in the aviation sector with the introduction of low cost air travel.

Rating agency ICRA has stated that the Indian hotel industry revenue growth is expected to strengthen to 9–11% in 2015–2016, driven by a modest increase in occupancy and small increase in rates. Industry wide revenues are expected to grow by 5–8% in 2014–2015. Over the next 12 months, ICRA expects RevPAR (revenue per available room) to improve by 7–8% driven by up to 5% pickup in occupancies and 2–3% growth in ARRs. "Further, margins are expected to remain largely flat for 2014–15 while a moderate sub-par expansion is expected in 2015–16. While occupancies pan India are showing signs of improvement during 2014–15, this appears to be driven by a few pockets such as Mumbai, where occupancies grew by 15% year-to-date in December 2014 supported by traffic for large conferences and weddings," stated ICRA's analysis.

As the momentum in domestic demand gathers steam, the Indian hotel sector's dynamics will witness significant changes, including the following:

- Development of new business models will emerge to cater to the explosive demand in the upscale, mid-scale, and economy segments. Though initially the upscale segment will witness maximum growth as relatively low hanging fruit, the largest opportunity will lie in the mid-scale and budget segments in the long term. Success in the latter categories will depend entirely on innovative ways to overcome the high cost of asset formation, in order to offer acceptable price, product, and service trade-offs to consumers, to induce them to move down from the and deluxe upscale segment or move up from the guest houses offerings. Nearly, every hotel company operating in India will want to move into these segments, as the one lesson learnt from the economic crisis of 2008–2010 was that the value conscious domestic hotel guest represents the only relatively stable source of demand in the downturn.

- Although initially it will be necessary for many domestic and international brands to own and operate their hotels in order to provide a consistent brand experience, successful brands will over time be able to divest their assets wholly or partially, to move into brand-cum-operator or pure brand players. By 2020, the separation of asset, management, and brand into distinct business segments will be the rule of the thumb rather than the exception. Thus, power will shift back to the brands, due to the superior topline results they can deliver in an increasingly cluttered and competitive environment, with their brand loyal customers, reservation and distribution systems, and alliances and loyalty programs.

- Hotel companies will increasingly reduce, and even exit, capital investment in assets by entering into partnerships, JVs, leasing models, and public–private partnerships.

- Asset investors will expect hotel operators and brands to design, develop, and lease their hotels on a long-term basis and offer the owners a combination of a minimum guaranteed return and a revenue share profitability model. Capital appreciation will also accrue to the hotel owners. Life insurance companies, pension funds, and real estate investment trusts would find such long-term asset investment opportunities ideal, as would hotel companies looking to rapidly develop hotels to their brand specifications in an asset light manner.
- The central and state governments will also begin to offer a variety of incentives to encourage hotel development, once they recognize that the hotel sector can contribute significantly to local economies through tax revenues, improving employability with vocational and on-the-job training, and by offering employment to the locals.

Incentives offered are likely to include the following:

(a) Infrastructure status (Section 80IA) to the hotel industry, leading to a friendlier debt financing and tax incentives. As an initial step in this direction, the 2010–2011 budget has included hotels under Section 35 AD where any capital expenditure, excluding land, goodwill, and financial instruments, incurred after April 1, 2010 will be eligible for 100% deduction as an investment-linked tax incentive in the year of expenditure;

(b) Under the infrastructure lending scheme of the RBI, hotels having a capex of Rs. 20 crores (without land cost) and hotels with a star rating of 1 star and above anywhere in India, will became eligible for infrastructure financing under the RBI harmonized list for infrastructure sub sectors. Currently, hotels of 200 crores capex (without land cost) and hotels with a star rating of 3 star and above are eligible.

(c) By classifying the hospitality sector as a permissible infrastructure activity under Section 54 EC, hotel will be able to raise tax-free bonds through notified financial institutions thereby saving on capital gains tax.

(d) Higher built-up areas (FSI) for hotels leading to lower land cost. Incidentally, Manhattan offers 15 FSI as compared to 1.5–5.0 in India;

(e) Single window clearance for hotel projects leading to reduced time to market costs;

(f) Provision of land on a long-term lease on a revenue sharing basis for setting up of lower category hotels;

(g) Guaranteeing availability of appropriate infrastructure such as uninterrupted power, treated water, access to public transport, sanitation and effluent treatment, etc.

1.5   THE FUTURE SCENARIO

The Indian travel market continues to change with the advent of online aggregated budget accommodation providers. The market leaders are OYO Rooms and Zo Rooms based on the level of investments raised. Both are at the Series B stage with OYO, bringing its total funds raised to $125 million. Zo reportedly received a $30 million Series B injection quickly after a $15 million Series A fund infusion. Treebo is looking at aggregating hostels under a single brand and platform, raised $6 million in June 2015. Vista Rooms is another startup and has already built up a portfolio of 450 Vista-branded properties in a matter of months.

Pranav Maheshwari the founder of Vista states: "Most hoteliers don't understand how to digitally enable their business. They struggle with online bookings, automated check in and checkout never mind the situation around managing reviews. We talk with our partners on a constant basis and believe we can make a difference. It's not just about the price. The market is huge. We think there are around 150,000 properties in India which could move over to this branded sector. The major players have got say 2,500 between them so we've just scratched the surface."

Stayzilla is a startup which specializes in alternative stays like homestays, houseboats, and hostels and picked up $15 million Series B funding this February 2015. Yatra.com has joined the race with the biggest selection of budget properties, with more than 40,000 3-star and below properties on its books. It wants to get this number up to 60,000 by the end of the year. The emergence of this concept over the past few months highlights the massive potential that exists within the budget segment hotel space in India. The growing awareness among travelers for well-maintained budget is increasing exponentially. From the guest perspective, it is going to be a buyers' market over a sellers' market.

According to a report by HVS and The World Travel and Tourism Council, the travel industry in India is expected to reach 1747 million travelers by 2021, which will require 188,500 additional hotel rooms. Mid-market hotels will be the driving force because they usually have more rooms per hotel than a 5-star or luxury hotel and can be built faster and more cost-effectively in multiple micro-markets as well as in most tier I, II, and III cities, the report said. The demand for hotel rooms in India will grow between 9% and 11% annually over this decade, with the greatest growth lying at the middle and bottom of the price pyramid, that is, in the mid-scale and economy segments. The winners in this race will be those who find innovative ways to overcome the structural barriers to hotel asset creation in India. These will include partnerships with the government and financial investors. They will build powerful brands by addressing the high quality yet low priced needs of millions of Indian travelers, at a profit. These brands of tomorrow will be global in size, yet focused exclusively on the Indian market.

KEYWORDS

- **hospitality industry**
- **changing demands**
- **hotel providers**
- **practitioner's perspective**
- **global economy**

REFERENCES

E&Y. *Global Hospitality Insights*, E&Y, 2015.

EIH. *Annual Report*. EIH, 2014–2015.

Federation of Hotel and Restaurants Association of India. *59th Annual Report*. Federation of Hotel and Restaurants Association of India, 2014–2015.

FHRAI; HVS; Ecotel. *Indian Hotel Industry Survey*. FHRAI, HVS and Ecotel, 2013–2014.

Hospitality. *Game Changers or Spectators*, Deloitte, 2015.

Hotel Leela Venture Ltd. *Annual Report*. Hotel Leela Venture Ltd., 2014–2015.

Indian Hotel Industry. *Weaker than Expected Supply Addition during 2014–2015 Supporting Occupancies*. ICRA Research Services, 2015.

Ministry of Tourism, Government of India. *Annual Report (2014–2015)*. Ministry of Tourism, Government of India.

Ministry of Tourism, Government of India. *India Tourism Statistics at a Glance*. Ministry of Tourism, Government of India, 2014.

The Indian Hotel Company Ltd. *Annual Report (2014–2015): 114th Hotels in India, Trends and Opportunities*, 2015, HVS.

World Travel and Tourism Council. *Travel and Tourism Economic Impact 2015 India*. World Travel and Tourism Council, 2015.

www.businesstoday.in. *Mid Market Blues*, March 1, 2015, Retrieved from: http://www.businesstoday.in/magazine/features/budget-hotels-have-lost-the-shine-in-hospitality-industry/story/215482.html.

www.Economictimes. Indiatimes.com. *Hotel Aggregators Reach Out to Hotel Chains to Acquire Unsold Inventory*, September 23, 2015. Retrieved from: http://economictimes.indiatimes.com/topic/budget-hotel-segment-business.

www.hotel-online.com. *2014 Global Hotel Rankings: The Leaders Grow Stronger: IHG Retains Top Spot.* June 23, 2014. Retrieved from http://www.hotel-online.com/press_releases/release/global-hotel-rankings-the-leaders-grow-stronger-ihg-retains-top-spot.

www.ibef.org. *Tourism and Hospitality Industry in India*, September, 2015, Retrieved from http://www.ibef.org/industry/tourism-hospitality-india.aspx.

CHAPTER 2

THE GROWTH STORY OF HOTELS IN INDIA: LOOKING BEYOND THE RHETORIC

SANDEEP MUNJAL* and ANMOLE SINGH

School of Hospitality and Tourism Management, Vedatya Institute, Gurgaon, India

*Corresponding author. E-mail: sandeep.munjal@vedatya.ac.in

CONTENTS

Abstract 18

2.1 Introduction 19

2.2 Methodology 21

2.3 Macro-environment at a Glance 21

2.4 Implications 38

Keywords 40

References 41

ABSTRACT

Much has been said and written about the Indian growth story, with respect to the hospitality sector in general and the hotels space in particular. It is a capital intensive business. One look at the major hotel brands like Intercontinental Hotel Group, Carlson Rezidor, Accor, Marriott, and Hyatt, and it becomes apparent that they are managing hotel assets for others. Aside from the brand name and the specifications that go with it, these corporations are managing hotel portfolios running into 2500 plus hotels each across the globe. The Indian growth story led by the entry of these brands a decade or so ago is no different.

Capacity addition across a range of hotel segments has and will continue to be guided by the demand push that macroeconomic fundamentals will provide, but having said that, investment in new hotels, greenfield or otherwise, will require investor confidence, wherein they find investment in hotel assets attractive. It is important to analyze the business approaches that have found favor in the Indian marketplace, to comment on their success so far and any challenges that need to be addressed.

Some key questions to be asked are as follows:

- What is the status of hotel room inventory in India and where is the capacity expansion headed?
- What is the profile of the investors in the Indian hotel space and what are the key challenges that they face?
- What types of business partnerships or contractual arrangements are finding interest?
- Are investors achieving acceptable returns on their investment? Are hotel brands as custodians of these investments ensuring that the investor's interest is being protected?
- Are the owners of hotel assets relying on debt or is it a mix of debt as well as equity? Is servicing of debt an issue?

Answers to the above questions will have implications on the growth of the hotel sector in India. Profitable investments by hotel owners will encourage more investments (including significant amount of foreign capital); it is critical to assess the success of key brands in ensuring that they deliver the promised returns on investment to the owners of the hotel assets they manage.

2.1 INTRODUCTION

The chapter attempts to take a hard look at the business approaches that are driving the growth of the hotel industry in India. The macroeconomic indicators have been largely supportive of growth, especially when seen in the context of a pessimistic global economic scenario. The Indian economy continues to chart a healthy growth trajectory, with a GDP growth rate ranging from a low of 5.5% to a high of close to 8% through the past decade. A purposeful government is enabling legislative support to policy level changes, aimed at improving India's credentials both as a country to do business with as well as a destination for tourism purposes. A weak crude oil price has resulted in substantial savings for the government, enabling it to not only manage the fiscal deficit but also fund big ticket infrastructure enhancement projects across the country. In short, the macro-environmental factors seem to be quite well placed for the hotel sector to thrive and grow.

The financial performance of some of the bell weather Indian hotel companies over the last few years is however in sharp contrast, to the above mentioned positive environmental construct. With IHCL (Indian Hotels Company Limited) popularly known as the "Taj Group" posting losses for the last 4 years (The Indian Hotel Company, 2013; 2014; 2015), Leela Hotels in severe losses (Leela Palaces and Resorts Limited, 2015), and the EIH (East India Hotels) popularly known as the "Oberoi Group" reporting a below par net profit margin of 4–6% over the last 5 years (EIH Limited, 2013; 2014; 2015); there is clearly something not adding up. While a deeper analysis of financial performance of the mentioned Indian hotel chains may offer a rational explanation for their individual fiscal troubles, the general gloom does throw open a discussion on the potential returns that investors can expect in the Indian market given the challenges on the ground.

The capacity expansion and arrival of new brands (international and domestic) in the Indian hotel industry has been a game changer. The intense competition is here to stay; the supply side however is expected to respond to the demand as well as the cost of capital of investments being made. This chapter will offer a holistic perspective on the current status and also evaluate the business approaches that are finding acceptance in the Indian market (Fig. 2.1).

FIGURE 2.1 Fiscal performance of key Indian hotel companies at a glance.

	2012–2013			2013–2014			2014–2015		
	IHCL	EIH	Leela	IHCL	EIH	Leela	IHCL	EIH	Leela
Revenue	37,433.60	14,684.80	6447.00	40,661.90	15,465.70	7184.00	41,886.40	16,682.70	7549.00
Gross profit	33,618.10 89.81%	12,733.90 86.71%	5936.90 92.09%	36,391.20 89.50%	13,395.50 86.61%	6565.70 91.39%	37,455.50 89.42%	14,468.60 86.73%	6879.50 91.13%
Operating profit	−2917.90 −7.79%	739.9 5.04%	−4214.00 −65.36%	−4121.60 −10.14%	1824.80 11.80%	−4873.80 −67.84%	−2324.80 −5.55%	1450.60 8.70%	−4701.30 −62.28%
Net profit	−4302.40 −11.49%	417.7 2.84%	−4334.90 −67.24%	−5538.50 −13.62%	1071.20 6.93%	−4415.10 −61.46%	−3781.00 −9.03%	631.00 3.78%	−4158.40 −55.09%
Return on equity	−0.14	0.01	−0.35	−0.21	0.04	−0.51	−0.16	0.02	−0.99

Source: Company (EIH Limited, Leela Palaces and Resorts Limited, The Indian Hotel Company) Annual Reports and MSN Money, (2016a–c).

2.2 METHODOLOGY

The research outlined in this chapter is based on secondary sources like sector reports, newspaper briefs, and feedback offered by reputed analysts. Primary research is conducted in the form of personal interviews with the leadership team at hotels, personal, and telephonic interviews with few prominent hotel owners (or their representatives) to get their perspectives. The inputs are documented and presented in the findings.

2.3 MACRO-ENVIRONMENT AT A GLANCE

The Government of India has recognized the travel and tourism industry as one of the key contributors to the economy of the country, demonstrating a high growth potential. The industry's total contribution to GDP in 2015 was around INR 8300 billion (6.3% of GDP), a number which is expected to grow to 7.2% (contribution to GDP) by 2026 (INR 18,000 billion). The country is ranked No. 3 amongst 184 countries when it comes to forecasted growth from 2016 to 2026 (WTTC, 2016). These forecasts are guided by expected increase in the footfall of the domestic and the international travelers resulting from a few key initiatives, like Visa on Arrival, Incredible India marketing campaigns, state tourism marketing campaigns, etc. Primarily driven by the influx of business and leisure travels, the Indian hospitality sector is expected to grow further with the support of the earlier mentioned policy changes and government initiatives. India has witnessed a rise in the number of travelers since the launch of the Incredible India campaign (FICCI, 2013). In 2015, from January to July, more than 1 lakh visitors used the e-Tourist on Arrival Visa service against a mere 40,000 in the complete year of 2014. Foreign tourist arrival (FTA) numbers in India took a leap of 4.4% in 2015 to 80 lakhs, against 76 lakhs in 2014 (The Financial Express, 2016). FTAs are expected to continue growth at a steady pace to 13.43 million by 2024 (CCI, 2015). Domestic tourist visit figures have also demonstrated strength as it grew by 12% in 2014(Ministry of Tourism, 2015). These numbers are further expected to grow at a respectable rate considering the forecasted rise in GDP contribution by WTTC (CCI, 2015).

All the above-cited statistics support the belief that the Indian hotel sector will continue to grow in terms of market size in both the short and medium term. The international markets have responded to the positive fundamentals of the Indian market, resulting in hotel companies like IHG (Intercontinental Hotel Group), Marriott, Hilton, Dusit Deverana, Shangrila, Accor, and Hyatt, scaling up their presence in the Indian market. All the above brands operate under varied business models. Irrespective of the mode of entry and growth strategy, what is apparent is the fact that India is central to their growth plans.

2.3.1 STATUS OF ROOM SUPPLY IN THE INDIAN MARKET

The forecasted growth in travel and tourism, coupled with the improvement in the socioeconomic status and strengthening of the Indian middle class, indicates a need for added room supply to ensure the availability of a comprehensive tourism product. The average all India occupancy stood at 61.3% for the year 2014–2015 as compared to 60.4% in the previous financial year. The same upward trend (though the movement was quite marginal) was observed with another key performance indicator, average room rate (ARR) (FHRAI, 2015). Though this is not sufficient information to comment on the impact of the macroeconomic forces at play, it does pin down a fact that growth in demand has outpaced the growth in supply pipeline in 2014–2015. It is equally important to mention here that the additional room supply that materialized was only 50% of the forecasted capacity that was expected to arrive downstream. It is a common knowledge that many projects were deliberately slowed to respond to a weakening demand growth in 2009–2010, ensuring that occupancies across existing hotels across multiple segments remained above the threshold of 60%.

According to a research conducted by Khanna and Bhandari (2015), India witnessed a stark increase in the number of branded hotel rooms. Over the past 10 years, the supply has almost tripled in absolute numbers, leaping from 39,285 in 2006–2007 to 112,284 in 2014–2015, at a compounded average growth rate (CAGR) of 14%. Tier II cities like Noida, Gurgaon (both part of the NCR region), and Pune have witnessed the strongest growth in terms of overall supply. It is important to also recognize that the report only covers branded inventory. The stand-alone hotels, B&Bs and Homestays, also added to the total room supply.

Khanna and Bhandari (2015) forecast a 30% increase in branded room inventory in the next 5 years, increasing from 112,284 units in 2014–2015 to 146,485 in 2019–2020. Of the indicated proposed supply, it is clear that there is a slight shift in the business orientation. While Indian hotel sector has traditionally been dominated by Indian hotel companies primarily operating luxury properties, the changing dynamics of the economy and the entry of international hotel operators have changed the hotel segmentation landscape.

More than 65% of the branded hotel rooms in the proposed supply pipeline are for the mid-scale and budget segment (Fig. 2.2). Hotel operators are now focusing on the less expensive (with regards to development costs) segments across all regions. The luxury hotels are mostly concentrated on the Tier I regions, like Bengaluru, Kolkata, Mumbai, and Delhi/NCR (National Capital Region—includes Gurgaon and Noida). The trend has been similar over the past 3 years where there has been a studied and informed effort to expand the portfolio through development of mid-scale and budget properties (Fig. 2.3; Table 2.1).

It is important to recognize that the hotel sector is not comprised by the branded hotels alone, which are affiliated to globally recognized companies like IHG, Marriott, Hyatt, Taj, Oberoi, etc. Moreover, adding significantly to the inventory are the independent standalone hotels. These hotels constitute a large and significant part of the unorganized hotel market. Riding on the back of technological advancement brands like OYO Rooms, ZO Rooms, and FabHotels have offered a marketing and distribution platform to many of these standalone hotels, which are now available to potential customers to view, search, and book. The app- and web-based companies also provide quality assessments on the services and product quality of the standalones, thus communicating their reliability and quality assurance to the potential booker, domestic as well as international. As this trend continues a huge supply of "accommodation units" in the form of single room, two rooms or similar capacities from individual home owners, apartment owners, and small hotels will get consolidated through a brand identity. The challenge will be to standardize these as per established brand standards and ensure that the same are made available to customers as they experience the product. Brands like OYO Rooms and others are facing the challenge of managing exponential growth, without dilution in the quality of service delivery that was promised. Nonetheless, the supply impact is dramatic and a game changer.

Traditionally, Indian hotel market has been dominated by the independent unaffiliated hotels, considering the existence of only a handful of Indian hotel operators like IHCL, EIH Ltd., and ITDC. In 1998–1999, only 25% of the hotels were branded properties. This branded to unbranded ratio stood at 44% in 2010–2011, with a CAGR of 4.9%. This number is expected to grow at a CAGR of 4.0% by 2020–2021 and is expected to reach 65% (HVS, 2012a). The effect is an implication of the entry and growth of several multinational hotel companies, like IHG, Marriott, Hyatt, Carlson Rezidor, Starwoods, Hilton, etc. entering the market with an aggressive approach to setup multiple hotels in an attempt to achieve higher guest loyalty and recognition,

FIGURE 2.2 Existing supply across major cities.

	2006/2007	2007/2008	2008/2009	2009/2010	2010/2011	2011/2012	2012/2013	2013/2014	2014/2015	12-month change (%)	Compounded growth (%)
Agra	1336	1336	1419	1439	1439	1739	1299	1293	1719	32.9	3.2
Ahmedabad	519	675	800	1521	1785	1975	2477	2777	2991	7.7	24.5
Bengaluru	2414	3456	3889	5597	5947	7713	8536	10,162	11,317	11.4	21.3
Chennai	2442	2826	3307	3806	4066	4904	6330	7105	7464	5.1	15.0
New Delhi	7990	9019	8625	8129	9111	10,697	11,338	12,370	13,277	7.3	6.6
Gurgaon				1980	3246	3782	4559	5190	6088	17.3	25.2
NOIDA				300	351	527	841	1239	1322	6.7	34.5
Goa	2450	2768	2795	3288	3375	3885	4406	4703	4909	4.4	9.1
Hyderabad	1868	2554	2761	3782	4036	4797	5411	5734	5875	2.5	15.4
Jaipur	1388	1556	1683	2472	2554	3054	4129	4523	5018	10.9	17.4
Kolkata	1354	1396	1373	1520	1588	1787	2163	2243	2530	12.8	8.1
Mumbai	7402	8454	7948	9877	11,303	12,052	12,807	13,022	12,731	-2.2	7.0
Pune	777	1346	1518	2672	4691	5672	5317	6159	6197	0.6	29.6
Other	9345	11,596	12,357	15,412	18,039	21,729	24,642	24,657	30,846	25.1	16.1
Total	39,285	46,982	48,475	61,795	71,531	84,313	94,255	101,177	112,284	11.0	14.0

(Reprinted from Khanna, A.; Bhandari, H. Hotels in India Trends & Opportunities, 2015 [Online]. Available athttp://www.hospitalitybizindia. com/Images/HVS_2015_Hotels_India_Trends_Opportunities.pdf [last accessed 13 May 2016]. Used with permission.)

FIGURE 2.3 Proposed branded hotels (2014/2015–2019/2020).

	Existing supply 2014/2015	Proposed supply	Increase in future supply (%)	Active development of supply (%)	Luxury (%)	Upscale (%)	Mid-market (%)	Budget (%)	Extended stay (%)
Agra	1719	503	29	43.0	0.0	0.0	56.3	43.7	0.0
Ahmedabad	2991	1026	34	64.0	0.0	57.0	25.4	0.0	17.5
Bengaluru	11,317	5317	47	52.0	20.9	35.2	19.2	19.4	5.3
Chennai	7464	3311	44	83.0	3.2	0.0	47.2	41.4	8.1
New Delhi	13,277	2502	19	87.0	0.0	34.7	58.2	7.1	0.0
Gurgaon	6088	2084	34	10.0	0.0	11.5	52.4	24.6	11.5
NOIDA	1322	1873	142	13.0	13.3	35.2	35.0	5.2	11.2
Goa	4909	1743	36	50.0	6.0	13.5	53.5	27.0	0.0
Hyderabad	5875	2474	42	61.0	0.0	13.9	44.9	24.3	16.9
Jaipur	5018	1119	22	92.0	0.0	45.9	41.8	12.2	0.0
Kolkata	2530	2870	113	70.0	15.7	42.5	30.8	11.0	0.0
Mumbai	12,731	5561	44	33.0	16.3	24.8	39.8	18.7	0.4
Pune	6197	2005	32	64.0	25.5	19.5	35.8	19.3	0.0
Other	30,846	23,882	77	70.0	1.8	21.0	49.8	25.6	1.8
Total	112,284	56,270	50	61.0	6.9	23.7	43.6	22.2	3.6

(Reprinted from Khanna, A.; Bhandari, H. Hotels in India Trends & Opportunities, 2015 [Online]. Available at http://www.hospitalitybizindia.com/Images/HVS_2015_Hotels_India_Trends_Opportunities.pdf [last accessed 13 May 2016]. Used with permission.)

TABLE 2.1 Proposed Branded Hotel across Various Segments.

	Luxury (%)	Upscale (%)	Mid-scale (%)	Budget (%)	Extended stays (%)
2012/2013	14.50	29.20	35.30	18.00	3.00
2013/2014	9.30	20.80	39.70	26.40	3.60
2014/2015	6.90	23.70	43.60	22.20	3.60

(Reprinted from Khanna, A.; Bhandari, H. Hotels in India Trends & Opportunities, 2015 [Online]. Available at http://www.hospitalitybizindia.com/Images/HVS_2015_Hotels_India_Trends_Opportunities.pdf [last accessed 13 May 2016]. Used with permission.)

and eventually a larger presence in India. As mentioned earlier, an India-focused growth strategy of many of the mentioned brands adds another interesting dimension to the growth of the internationally branded rooms supply. In fact in continuation with the above discussed trends in 2016, Marriott became the brand with the highest room inventory in India post its acquisition of Starwoods Hotels, edging out IHCL. Carlson Rezidor, another high impact international hotel brand in India, is facing potential acquisition, by a Chinese brand; this is likely to impact the Indian market as well.

Guided by global cues, consolidation among global brands through mergers and acquisitions underway, as well as because of the unique opportunities that India presents, the next few years will continue to witness a dynamic Indian hotel space with expanding room inventory across multiple segments. What will be interesting to watch is whether the market delivers on the demand growth promise that is forecasted by many analysts.

2.3.2 COST OF ADDITIONAL ROOM INVENTORY

The supply line projection and number of projects signed and planned have always been positive, but not all came into existence in the stipulated time period. According to *Trends and Opportunities* report of Khanna and Bhandari (2015), traditionally, the Indian market has seen just 60% of the proposed supply under active development with 2014–2015 (61%) exhibiting slower active development, as compared to the previous fiscal year (69%).

According to HVS, a popular hotel consulting and asset evaluation firm, it takes around US$317,000 per room key to build a luxury property, which is threefold of what is takes to develop a mid-scale property (US$98,000 per room key). Meanwhile, a budget hotel requires US$55,000 (Wij & Khanna, 2012). It is important to note that these numbers don't include cost of land, which can typically be around 30% of the total cost of development.

Developers and operators face a number of challenges as they try to develop the required infrastructure. These can be pertaining to high finance costs, lack of investor interest due to unimpressive exit options, lack of professionalism on part of the owners, and the tedious nature of the approval process (it can take as long as 2 years to procure the necessary licenses). But one challenge that constitutes the biggest hurdle is the availability of land and the inflated real estate prices (Jaiswal, 2012). Given the size of capital investment required to build a hotel, in an economy which is already growing at a pace much slower than what was projected or expected, the key question to ask is whether the expected returns on investment will come through. Land costs alone account for 30% of the total project cost which is under further pressure; due to increase in real estate prices (Jaiswal, 2012; HVS, 2012a), Amitabh Devender (formerly, National Head—Hospitality and Leisure Services, Chesterton Meghraj Property Consultants) suggests that if this land cost component breaches another 15% increase, consequential ramifications will be witnessed with regards to the gestation periods, tariff structures, break-even period extension, and the finance cost servicing issues (Mansukhani, 2005).

With nonavailability of land at a feasible rate, poor civic infrastructure availability to set up hotels in the city outskirts and inflated cost of construction material and labor, the sector is facing multiple challenges. It is the compounded impact of these challenges along with the demand–supply cues that led to a shortfall in the projected supply). The year 2014–2015 experienced an increase in the number of conversion of existing hotels, therefore not limiting themselves to just development of new properties to stimulate expansion (Khanna & Bhandari, 2015). This could also be identified as one of the factors that could have led to diminishing development activity of the proposed new hotels, which fell by 10%. In fact, many hotels moved from one brand identity to another; for example, the Pullman, Gurgaon (Accor) became Le Meridien, Gurgaon (Starwoods). The high cost of greenfield development seems to have pushed many a brands to look for capacity expansion via the inorganic route, translating into the practice of the competition trying to win management contracts (from competition) and convert unbranded, standalones into branded hotels.

2.3.3 WHERE IS THE INVESTMENT COMING FROM?

The growth of the Indian hotel industry over the last decade or so has been supported largely by domestic investment. The real estate sector in India till more recently has been operating in a rather unregulated business environment. Real estate companies, big and small, saw investments into hotels as the natural diversification. Though hard to prove empirically, the investments into the "hard asset" that hotels represented provided an opportunity to park "black money," evading the tax net or government scrutiny. Most of them already owned land banks at locations that were appropriate for development into hotels, resorts, or serviced apartments. The experience of this investor group in the real estate sector brought to the table an experiential curve around facilitating land acquisitions with or without government involvement and an understanding of the laws, regulations that needed to be followed or circumvented as the case may be. From required licenses to any environmental clearance to quintessential political connect, the group was well placed to manage most aspects that a local participant can be expected to enable, in terms of ease of doing business in India.

Their project implementation experience too was a valuable asset for greenfield hotel projects. While it is true that most of the actual construction activity is outsourced by the real estate companies, the ability to mobilize contractors, architects, and other experts required to implement a "hotel construction" project was far more easier for those coming from a real estate background. Thus, it is of no surprise that nearly every real estate business in India is invested heavily in hotels. The below-cited list is a case that proves the above statement:

List of Indian Real Estate Companies with hotel investments:

- Eros Group (Shangrila Delhi and Radisson Blu Faridabad)
- Unitech (Courtyard by Marriot, Gurgaon, Kolkata, and Noida)
- Today Group (Crowne Plaza, Delhi and Gurgaon)
- K. Raheja Corp (JW Marriott Sahar, Mumbai, Renaissance Mumbai, Marriott Bengaluru, Four Points Vashi, Westin Hyderabad, JW Marriott JUHU, Lakeside Chalet, Mumbai)
- Nitesh Estates (Ritz Carlton, Bengaluru)
- Adarsh Developers (Shangri-la, Bengaluru)
- Poddar Group (Multiple Hyatt Hotels pan India)
- ABIL Group (Westin Pune, St. Regis Mumbai, Sun-n-sand Pune, Le Meridien Nagpur)
- Oberoi Realty (The Westin, Mumbai), Ambience Group (Leela, Gurgaon and Kempinski Ambience, Delhi)
- Mahagun Developers (Park Plaza, Shahdara and Sarovar Portico, Vaishali)
- Mantri Developers (Hyatt Regency, Kormangalam)
- Prestige Group (Aloft Bengaluru, Angsana Bengaluru)
- Brigade Group (The Sheraton, Bengaluru)
- Supertech (Radisson Blu Rudrapur, Country Inn & Suites, Meerut)
- Emaar MGF (Boulder Hills Golf and Country resort, Hyderabad and Fortune Park Metropolitan, Jaipur)
- Ansal API (Multiple hotels including the Sheraton, Saket, Delhi)
- Bestech (Multiple Carlson Hotels including Park Plaza and Country Inn Brands)
- Amrapalli Group (Holiday Inn Greater Noida, Clarks Inn, Bareilly and Deogarh).

The above-cited list is by no means a complete picture but clearly validates the discussion that the bulk of greenfield development in room capacity in India has been through investments from the real estate sector. With the real estate regulatory bill being passed in 2016, it will be interesting to see if there is any impact on investments from the sector toward hospitality-related projects. The bill not only supports the cause of home buyers but also changes the landscape of regulatory focus on the real estate sector in India.

2.3.4 BUSINESS PARTNERSHIPS AND APPROACHES THAT ARE DRIVING THE GROWTH STORY

Beyond the discussion on the real estate sector driven investments into new hotel projects, the other important aspect that deserves attention is the role of domestic and international hotel companies or brands. While some of the prominent Indian hotel companies like IHCL, EIH, ITC Hotels, etc. have recognized that the only route to build a larger footprint in terms of number of hotels as well as overall room inventory is through partnerships, their overall growth has been quite limited when compared to that of some of the International brands like Carlson Rezidor and IHG in particular. Another interesting facet is the growth of the mid-segment to budget hotel space. The big players in the Indian market were slow to move in on this opportunity, which was the focus of international brands as well as some of the home grown hotel chains like the Sarovar Hotels, Lemon Tree Hotels, and Golden Tulip, to name a few. With more than 100 plus functional hotels a piece, Sarovar and Lemon Tree have made a mark in the 3- and 4-star hotel categories in India.

The hotel companies managing these hotels often lend not only their brand name and operating specifications but are also active in managing the performance of the hotels, responsible for their day-to-day functioning, with a clear mandate to deliver strong returns to the hotel ownerships as well as the parent hotel brand company. The hotel brands are generally averse to making capital investments to set up new hotel projects (though exceptions are there), their investments are largely focused on building their management teams and training capacities to ensure that they can deliver on the quality and efficiency promise that wins them management rights to run these hotels owned by third parties.

There is broad range of arrangements or partnerships that have allowed hotel brands to manage and operate hotels that are owned by a range of promoters or investors. Some of the prominent models that are popular in India are discussed below:

2.3.5   MANAGEMENT CONTRACTS

Under management contracts, the owner of the asset or hotel is brought into agreement with the operator. The agreement defines the relationship between the two parties, the owner and the operator, driven primarily by the contract and not the asset. The key aspects covered in a hotel management contract (HMCs) are (JLL, 2014) as follows:

- *Term period*: Initial term period, the extension period, and number of extensions. A hotel management contract survey, conducted by HVS, reported that an average length of contract of APAC-based hotels was 18.3 years, which is higher than the prevailing trending in a more mature market like the United States (Thadani & Mobar, 2014).
- *Fee payable*: There are multiple natures of fees payable to the operator by the owner: base fee, incentive fee, sale and marketing fee, loyalty program fee, technical services fee, and reserve for FF&E (furniture, fixture, and equipment). The fees structure is very variable and varies depending upon the region of operations, the hotel segment, and the room inventory.
- Operating budget (defines the operating terms of reference in financial terms).
- Performance clause, which is based on benchmarks set for GOP (gross operating profit) and RevPar (revenue per available room).
- Restrictions (owners and operators).
- The termination clause.
- Operator contributor clause.

Most of the popular International hotel operators like Marriott, IHG, and Hilton conduct the major portion of their business through this model. Marriott, one of the world's most popular hotel groups, operates 40% of their properties under management contract (Marriott International Inc., 2015). Operators earn through management fees charged to manage operations at the asset. This mostly consists of base management fee, which is mostly a portion of the revenues generated and can be around 2–4%, and additionally the incentive fee which is based on the profits made. The fee component for the long-term leased model can vary. The model has proven to work for these companies and is a lesson that the Indian counterparts can draw from.

Many hotels in India are operated under the management contract across all segments. The concept was introduced and injected into the Indian hotel business scenario only with the entry of international operators. An HVS survey depicted the growing popularity of HMCs with the hotel owners (HVS, 2013). The report covers the sentiments of the Indian hotel owner and identified certain issues between the "owner" and "operator" outlook. Lack of alignment between the owner's objectives and the brand's standards, and the development assurances not matching operative deliveries and the contracts being too pro-operator focused, are some of the issues that are predominant. The relationship between the owner and operator is not always the smoothest. Recent past has witnessed a lot of relationships going sour between the operator/hotel company and the owners. This can be attributed to the inability of the HMCs to be true to the Indian business environment, no surprise that the Indian owners feel that the terms of these contracts are less favorable as compared to what their western counterparts enjoy (Thadani &Mobar, 2013).

One clause that is very unpopular with the "Operator" is the performance test clause. It is so for the obvious reasons. The operators try and escape without mentioning them in the contracts and if asked about it, it is heavily negotiated (Dar & Bhardwaj, 2014). It is supposed to be the owners' protection against poor performance by the operator but Indian owners have shed light on their grievance that it typically protects the brands' interests. The "performance clause" constitutes the most important part of the contract from an owner's perspective and needs to be negotiated well. However, all in all the hotel owners have exhibited a general sense of satisfaction with their contracted operators (HVS, 2013). Recently, India has seen the emergence of many hotel operators and has witnessed a stark rise in competition. This increased competition has swung the balance a little more toward the owners, who can now negotiate for better terms in regards to the fees, duration, and exit options.

2.3.6 FRANCHISE AND JOINT VENTURES

Not the most unique idea, the franchise model exists in an array of industries. The franchisee (or the buyer) pays to acquire the rights of franchisor (the provider) to use the name, product, and processes independently. The models are beneficial to both the parties, as the small businessman get the freedom to operate independently but yet enjoy the benefits of membership, while the franchisor get to have his flag at the asset. The franchisor does not own or manage the property, the franchisee does. The franchisor receives multiple varieties of fees from the franchisee, apart from the initial application fee and fee per room night. He pays for adopting the brand and logo to access the reservation system and per reservation fee for every booking received. The list doesn't stop here. The franchisee has to pay for mandatory trainings and guest loyalty programs (Vallen & Vallen, 2009). It is probably also the most profitable model for any hotel company and financially viable for the owner as well. The operator does not have to block valuable monetary fund in developing capital intensive assets, instead gets sustainable returns for the defined processes and brand value. In addition, the company also gets their flag established at a new location.

The franchisee model is thus the most popular model in the global hotel business. Marriott's portfolio is build upon 57% franchisee agreements and 2% of joint venture holdings. While IHG, the world's biggest hotel company, has more than 80% hotel properties franchised to owners (Intercontinental Hotels Group, 2016). Indian budget and economy hotel brands like Ginger (a subsidiary of IHCL) and Berggruen Hotels have planned to expand in India through the similar model, where they plan to franchise their key brands to diverse ownerships (Sathyanarayanan, 2014).

Yet, the model is not the easiest to choose, as it has immediate financial implications for the owner/operator. They have to pay a variety of fees up front (as mentioned earlier). These franchisee fees make up for a huge portion of the operating cost. It can account for almost 8% of the total sales from all sources (Vallen & Vallen, 2009). Thus, eating into the profits sometimes in nominal margins is earned, which stood at around 13% in 2016 Q1 for the global Hotel and Leisure Industry. Nevertheless, on the other hand, the services received for the fees add substantially to the average occupancy and average daily rates. The dilemma of "fee"-related dilution to profitability against "services" support toward profits has the owners/operators in split. Though the "number" looks heavy, but when compared to the management contract model, some owners believe that it is more financially viable. The hotel chain only makes 40% of what it does from HMCs but the onus of performance lies with the asset owner, leading to less finger pointing, and also helps the hotel chain in cutting operating costs. Companies have also started converting their management contracts into franchise models, with an understanding that they may present a superior option in the Indian context (Sathyanarayanan, 2014).

2.3.7 BRAND OWNED/LEASED AND OPERATED

The owner in this style of business model is responsible for setting up the hotel in terms of the hard asset and also the operational management. The owner, through various tools of funding and investment, may build the property or buys an existing one. The owner has the liability to bear the financial and legal responsibilities attached. Leasing is not very different to ownership. The only difference is that the hotel operating company takes the building on rent from the developer and pays rent.

Traditionally, until the introduction of the multi-branded international hotel chains setup in India, the Indian hotel sector was dominated by hotel companies like IHCL, EIH, Leela, and ITC in the private sector. These hotel companies setup their own hotels with their own standards and benchmarks. The companies dealt mostly in the luxury segment, as the market was dominated by international business visitors, diplomats, and leisure travelers. They continue to work on the same model and prefer to develop their own asset or lease it (e.g., Taj Mansingh, New Delhi, India). The model requires a lot of investment which needs to have the right balance of different funding instruments. Funding is available through multiples sources, like individuals, banks, government agencies, and REITs (Real Estate Investment Trusts). REITs work very similar to equity stocks. The investors purchase portions of the real estate being developed and are paid returns in accordance. REITs perform an investment-raising function, though quite popular in the west for over two decades, they have been recently explored in India and are yet to achieve the western reputation of being an efficient tool for funding projects.

This approach is profitable yet very risky, probably the riskiest. The mandatory rent and debt servicing burden, even during the downturn, make it avoidable. They are "asset-heavy" models, slow to induce growth, and are generally quite costly as well. Due to its capital intensive nature, hotel companies cannot develop a large portfolio. A company, with too many leased and owned hotels in its portfolio, makes the balance sheet too heavy.

It is not a very popular model for many international hotel companies like Marriott (own and lease only 1% of their properties) (Marriott International Inc., 2015) and IHG, who own and lease only 9 of their 5000+ hotels (Intercontinental Hotels Group, 2015). They primarily operate on an "asset light" model. Many other companies like Accor and Hilton too have recently adopted the strategy as they continue to sell their properties to developers, and signing them back on management contracts. In the times of consolidation, this seems to be the best way to progress.

2.3.8   FINDINGS FROM INTERVIEWS WITH HOTEL OWNERS AND REPRESENTATIVES

As mentioned in Section 2.2 earlier, in order to capture the perspective of the "ownership" on multiple aspects around the growth story of the hospitality industry in India, interviews were conducted in person or in some cases through Skype. In all 12 cases, representatives (or owners themselves) were contacted for this research. A semi-structured approach was followed to elicit responses on key themes around the "management" of the hotels, the returns expected versus those realized, and the nature of relationship with hotel brands in terms of ensuring that the "ownership" views are heard and their interests protected. With the exception of one owner who was also running the property, the rest of the respondents had either management contracts or franchise arrangements in place to operate the hotel assets owned by them.

2.3.8.1   RETURN ON INVESTMENT

While none of the respondents shared any detailed financial input in terms of the fiscal performance (for obvious reasons), they did comment that the prevailing occupancy scenario was not what the forecasts shared with them by managing brands indicated. Though they expressed an understanding that the 60% plus occupancy will not drive acceptable returns, the challenge for many of them has been to service debt and also explain the sub-par returns to investors behind them. Only one respondent expressed that the "returns were good and the potential for growth is inspiring." While no actual financials were shared nearly half of the owners mentioned the business had accumulated losses, others stated that the ROI (return on investment) was less than their cost of capital.

The respondents were candid in expressing that the projections made by the hotel companies (management or operator) were quite misleading and not founded on the factual situation on the ground. They were also unanimous in expressing that the management brands had failed to deliver performance on cited ARR or occupancy parameters, while they had ensured that their (hotel brands) interests were protected. It was quite apparent that the investments made to adhere to brand standards, and quality specifications only caused financial stress, the impact on operating performance was quite dismal in their view.

Four players had changed partners due to poor returns, but for one, the rest felt that the struggle for returns is likely to continue in the immediate future and were not really optimistic. Those in Tier II cities cited that the expected tourism growth has not come through, those in metro cities cited an oversupply in room inventory as the key factor, resulting in poor ROI. When asked about any plan to expand their hotel portfolio, only two respondents stated that they were willing to invest more, the rest wanted to wait out the downturn, before making any further investments.

A typical 100 room hotel in a Tier I city would cost anywhere between Rs. 150 and Rs. 200 crores, for a 4/5 star property, a Tier II city would bring down the cost range between Rs. 80 and Rs. 120 crores. For the investment to yield returns is a tall order, given the fact that the most hotels operating at ARRs that are 30–35% lower than what would be required for generating a double digit ROI, given an average occupancy pegged at 70% or more.

2.3.8.2   SOURCES OF FUNDING

On the issue of the nature of funding, the general response was that it was through a group of investors or debt raised by sister concerns of business entities owned by them. There is no validated data on the quantum of invest-ment made by the investors, neither were the respondents eager to provide any clear input on the size of the investments made. The ball park numbers stated earlier however do provide a perspective on the potential size of investments required, to build greenfield hotel projects.

2.3.8.3   RELATIONSHIPS WITH MANAGING HOTEL BRANDS

Despite the earlier mentioned discomfort with poor returns and inability of the managing hotel brands to deliver on promised results, the respondents recognized that the "self-op" option was not a viable option. They were cate-gorical in stating that operating the hotels (taking over the role of the hotel management partner) was not the solution to their fiscal woes.

Those who had experience more than one partnership were candid that there was little difference in terms of experience from one brand to another. Most of the respondents mentioned that the hotel brands are becoming more sensitive to the concerns of "owners" and are willing to offer better contrac-tual terms, as well as help in finding cost saving solutions without compro-mising with brand specifications. "Phased fit outs" that allow the capital investment to be staggered with the demand cycle are finding acceptance. Few of the interviewed owners mentioned that even after being open for business for 2–3 years, they are still delaying room inventory fit outs due to sluggish demand growth.

The owners generally felt that the "entrepreneurial" approach to running business was found lacking among the management teams that the hotel brands brought to the table. Lack of focus on innovation that brings operating efficiencies was another pet peeve that came through. The owners expect the hotel brands to be more forthcoming in terms of sharing the "downside" rather than hedging their financial risk through contractual terms that do not penalize poor operating results, irrespective of whether the reasons are macroeconomic or a result of managerial performance.

A large number of respondents mentioned that one of the persistent issues of contention between them and hotel brands is their focus, on strengthening their brand presence often at the cost of the "owners." From marketing to training of teams to spending on "CSR" activities, the expenses always find their way to the "ownership" account. The owners are increasingly vigilant of what they end up paying for and are willing to question costs that they feel are outside the scope of their contractual arrangement, and in some cases question the contract itself, in case the same is biased toward the hotel brand (Management Company).

Most owners felt that their relationships with hotel brands that manage their assets are for most part "transactional" in nature. What this implies is that brand loyalty or tenure-based associations are not quite the norm. The recent churn in hotel assets moving from one brand to another is a clear indication of the way forward.

2.3.9 HOTEL MANAGEMENT VIEWPOINT AT A GLANCE

The perspective from the leadership of hotel brands (domestic and International brands) was indicative of a clear gap in understanding of each other's perspectives.

Many business leaders acknowledged that there is a trust deficit between the hotels "owners" and the brand management players. The owners often feel they are being victimized, and their views not given required attention. Given the phase of weak occupancies and ARRs, the relationships are on the edge due to financial pressure, especially where contracts were negotiated with "forecasts" that are quite distant from the reality of the day. The owners feel misled and cheated, often not buying the argument that it is the macroeconomic shift, that is, the bane of the poor financial returns on their investment.

Brand leadership from multiple hotel companies argued that "owners" did not understand the cyclic nature of hotel business, do not recognize the value that brands bring, and are usually dismissive of the operational efficiencies that the management teams bring to the table. They also stated that "owners" fail to see the challenges and operate with a tunnel vision. A case in point is the usual apathy to any spending on training and motivation of staff, not recognizing that the "human resource" is a critical success factor that deserves attention and investment. The managers from leading brands were synonymous in stating that "owners" who are quite eager to invest in "hard assets" are quite hesitant to invest when it comes to the "soft assets," often ignoring the direct impact that this may have.

Few managers also expressed that ownership interference in the day-to-day functioning of hotels too was a challenge. Over a period of time, based on some understanding of hotel operations, owners tend to step in, influence, or make decisions that managers are expected to follow. This often results in breach in the spirit of the contractual relationship, often leading to an impasse where a brand may take a decision to exit the relationship.

2.4 IMPLICATIONS

The findings have implications for the industry at large. The feedback from both the management and leadership that represent the hotel brands and from the representation from the hotel ownerships is indicative of a need for communication to achieve a clear perspective of each other's pain points, and hopefully find middle ground. Hotel brands need to see themselves as "custodians" of hotel assets, making sure that they put the interests of the owners first, which will also ensure that the brand thrives. The trust deficit that was apparent from the interviews with representation from both sides needs to be closed. The management of hotels under their ownership is not what the owners or investors seek; they do however want healthy returns on their investments, and a confidence that the hotel brands will protect their interests as their own. The management teams representing hotel brands look for autonomy, independent functionality, and non-interference from owners. They recognize that lack of returns in a sluggish economy puts financial pressure and generates a level of unease but maintains that that is the cost of doing business (business risk) that any investor must remain alive to.

All in all, the downturn provides the Indian hotel industry an opportunity to mature, build a understanding between the investment side and the operating side wherein; they see themselves as being on the same side of the fence and not in conflict. The future growth of the industry will depend to a large extent on this maturation process. With economic growth strengthening, the upside in demand will bring growth in ARRs and occupancies. What is critical is that there is a state of readiness from both the investor base as well as the brand's bench strength.

Some recommendations to sort this dilemma are

- Joint bodies to discuss, argue, and close contentious issues that are general in nature. While an over-arching industry bodies exist, these can be more specific to purpose.
- Formation of working groups to align interests of both hotel brands and ownerships. These can be limited to hotel brands and the group of owners or more broad based.
- Brands to consider "indigenization" to ensure that the local context is responded to in all decisions around the "brand standards" and operational elements.
- Hotel brands are seen to drive "brand specifications" in terms of room sizes, décor, F&B facilities beyond the levels at which they operate in their home countries, this indulgence is mostly at the cost of ownerships, without clarity on any incremental returns. This approach must be avoided.
- Contractual terms should maintain parity such that mutual interests are protected. Hotel brands, third part consultants, should resist from using financial projections that create distrust going forward. Terms of reference must be sensitive to "economic duress" and follow the example of revising "vendor contracts" during inflationary times, in spirit of ensuring coexistence.
- Investors and owners should conduct due diligence to ensure they understand the business risks involved; more effectively, this activity is performed, the higher the level of understanding and confidence of ownerships. This is especially critical in the Tier II and III cities in India.
- Efforts should be made by the industry to seek more diversified investment; the current status of being "real estate" centric is not a healthy scenario. Moreover, a shift away from "black money"-driven asset development will allow financial transparency to come in.
- Build an "entrepreneurial" approach to managing hotel assets such that efficient deployment of resources, innovation in operational aspects thrives, enabling best ROI. Any apathy toward the financial goals of the investor and ownership is ill advised.

- The "operator" and "owner" should clearly define their respective role and responsibilities and recognize that more often than not it is because of a trust deficit that results ultimately in severance of business relationships.

The growth story of the hotel industry in India is just unfolding, it has its twists and turns, but it is for real. The next decade will see more maturity, better understanding of approaches that succeed, and more value being created for hotel brands, owners, and off course the customers. As India takes its position of the driver of global economic growth, the positive impact on its own economy in general and the hotel sector in particular are given.

Multiple challenges remain, but a stable political climate, and a pro-growth government at the center, should make a difference in resolving some of the macro, policy level issues. The learning curve of international hotel brands and that of some of the domestic hotel chains will allow them to take the hotel industry in India to the next level. Despite the issues, it must be recognized that the industry has come a long way. From just three to four key players, with hardly any segment width in the early 1990s, the industry today boasts the presence of every major global hotel brand, with many layers of segments being made available to the customer. It's a dynamic business space, with new products, services being offered to a discerning global customer. The Indian hotels are alive to that requirement and are finding mention among the "leading hotels" of the world. Nearly every lodging format (hotels, resorts, heritage hotels, service apartments, B&Bs, etc.) will see growth in the years to come. As the expected demand growth across segments gets realized, the profitability challenge will also find resolution and investments made in the sector will attract financial returns that will be competitive globally.

KEYWORDS

- revenue growth
- management contracts
- investment
- return on investment
- room inventory

REFERENCES

CCI. *A Brief Report on Tourism of India*, 2015 [Online]. Available at http://www.cci.in/pdfs/ surveys-reports/Tourism-in-India.pdf (last accessed 13 May 2016).

Dar, A.; Bhardwaj, P. *Measuring Performance in a Hotel Management Agreement: Owner's Anxiety*, 2014 [Online]. Induslaw.com. Available at http://induslaw.com/publications/pdf/ alerts-2015/USIndiaBusiness_book.pdf (last accessed 13 February 2017).

EIH Limited. *Annual Report 2012–2013*, 2013 [Online]. Available at http://www.eihltd.com/ investor_relations/EIHLimited_AR2012-2013.pdf (last accessed 14 February 2017).

EIH Limited. *Annual Report 2013–2014*, 2014 [Online]. Available at http://www.eihltd.com/ EIHLimited_AR2013-2014.pdf (last accessed 14 February 2017).

EIH Limited. *Annual Report 2014–2015*, 2015 [Online]. Available at http://www.eihltd.com/ eihlimited_ar2014-2015.pdf (last accessed 14 February 2017).

FHRAI. *Indian Hotel Industry Survey 2014–2015*, 2015 [Online]. Federation of Hotel & Restaurant Associations of India: New Delhi. Available at http://www.hotelnewsresource. com/pdf16/HVS0118162.pdf (last accessed 23 May 2016).

FICCI. *India as a Hotspot for Inbound Tourism*, 2013 [Online]. Available at http://ficci.in/ spdocument/20236/india-as-a-hotspot-for-inbound-tourism.pdf (last accessed 13 May 2016).

HVS. *Hotels in India Trends & Opportunities*, 2011 [Online]. Available at http://www.hvs. com/Content/3185.pdf (last accessed 23 May 2016).

HVS. *Hotel Room Supply, Capital Investment and Manpower Requirement by 2021*, 2012a [Online]. Gurgaon. Available at http://rss.hsyndicate.com/file/152004848.pdf (last accessed 27 May 2016).

HVS. *Hotels in India Trends and Opportunities*, 2012b [Online]. Available at http://www.hvs. com/Content/3311.pdf (last accessed 23 May 2016).

HVS. *The Indian Owner Speaks*, 2013.

HVS. *2014 Hotels in India Trends and Opportunities*, 2014 [Online]. Available at http:// www.hospitalitynet.org/file/152005460.pdf (last accessed 13 February 2017).

Intercontinental Hotel Group. *Annual Report and Form 20-F 2015*, 2016 [Online]. Available at https://www.ihgplc.com/files/reports/ar2015/files/pdf/annual_report_2015.pdf (last accessed 13 February 2017).

Jaiswal, K. *Budget Hotels: Will The Business of Economy Pick Up in India?*, 2012 [Online]. Times of India–Economic Times. Available at http://articles.economictimes.indiatimes. com/2012-02-19/news/31075285_1_budget-hotels-economy-hotel-hotel-chain   (last accessed 26 May 2016).

JLL. *Management Contract Trends—A Review*, 2014 [Online]. Available at http://fhrai.com/ PDF/Management%20Contracts%20Trends%20-%20eVersion.pdf (last accessed 15 June 2016).

Khanna, A.; Bhandari, H. *Hotels in India Trends & Opportunities*, 2015 [Online]. Available athttp://www.hospitalitybizindia.com/Images/HVS_2015_Hotels_India_Trends_Opportunities.pdf (last accessed 13 May 2016).

Leela Palaces and Resorts Limited. *Annual Report 2014–2015*, 2015 [Online]. Available at https://www.theleela.com/img/brand/investor-relations/subsidiary-companies/2014-15/ Leela%20Palace%20and%20Resorts%20Limited.pdf (last accessed 14 February 2017).

Mansukhani, B. *Budget Hotels: Will the Business of Economy Pick Up in India?*, 2005 [Online]. Times of India–Economic Times. Available at http://articles.economictimes. indiatimes.com/2012-02-19/news/31075285_1_budget-hotels-economy-hotel-hotel-chain (last accessed 26 May 2016).

Marriott International. *2015 Annual Report*, 2015 [Online]. Available at http://investor.share-holder.com/mar/marriottAR15/pdfs/Marriott_2015_Annual_Report.pdf (last accessed 13 February 2017).

Ministry of Tourism. *India Tourism Statistics at a Glance 2014*, 2015 [Online]. Available at http://tourism.nic.in/writereaddata/CMSPagePicture/file/marketresearch/statisticalsur-veys/India%20Tourism%20Statistics%20at%20a%20Glance%202014.pdf (last accessed 13 May 2016).

MSN. *EIHOTEL—Stock Quote for EIH Ltd.—MSN Money*, 2016a [Online]. Available at http://www.msn.com/en-us/money/stockdetails/fi-138.1.EIHOTEL.NSE?symbol=EIHOTEL&form=PRFISH.

MSN. *HOTELEELA—Financial Reports for Hotel Leela Venture Ltd.—MSN Money*, 2016b [Online]. Available at http://www.msn.com/en-in/money/stockdetails/financials/fi-138.1.HOTELEELA.NSE (last accessed 20 June 2016).

MSN. *INDHOTEL—Stock Quote for Indian Hotels Co Ltd—MSN Money*, 2016c [Online]. Available at http://www.msn.com/en-us/money/stockdetails/fi-138.1.INDHOTEL.NSE?symbol=INDHOTEL&form=PRFISH (last accessed 20 June 2016).

Sathyanarayanan, D. *Hotel Chains Warm Up to Franchise Model*, 2014 [Online]. Times of India–Economic Times. Available at http://articles.economictimes.indiatimes.com/2014-08-21/news/53073146_1_ginger-hotels-roots-corporation-berggruen-hotels (last accessed 17 June 2016).

Thadani, M.; Mobar, J. *Critical Challenges Faced by Hotel Owners in India*, 2013 [Online]. Available at http://www.hvs.com/Jump/Article/Download.aspx?id=6568 (last accessed 17 June 2016).

Thadani, M.; Mobar, J. *HVS Hotel Management Contract Survey*, 2014.

The Financial Express. *Foreign Tourist Arrivals Grow By 4.4 Pc in 2015*, 2016 [Online]. Available at http://www.financialexpress.com/article/economy/foreign-tourist-arrivals-grow-by-4-4-pc-in-2015/190929/ (last accessed 13 May 2016).

The Indian Hotel Company. *112th Annual Report*, 2013 [Online]. Available at https://www.tajhotels.com/content/dam/thrp/financial-report/annual-reports/2012/The%20Indian%20Hotels%20Company%20Limited%20(IHCL)%20Results/ihcl_annual_report_2012_13.pdf (last accessed 14 February 2017).

The Indian Hotel Company Limited. *113th Annual Report*, 2014 [Online]. Available at https://www.tajhotels.com/content/dam/thrp/financial-report/annual-reports/2013/The%20Indian%20Hotels%20Company%20Limited%20(IHCL)%20Results/TAJ-AR-2013-14-For-Web.pdf (last accessed 14 February 2017).

The Indian Hotels Company Limited. *114th Annual Report 2014–2015*, 2015 [Online]. Available at https://www.tajhotels.com/content/dam/thrp/financial-report/annual-reports/2014/The%20Indian%20Hotels%20Company%20Limited%20(IHCL)%20Results/IHCL-AR-2014-15.pdf (last accessed 13 February 2017).

Vallen, G.; Vallen, J. *Check-In Check-Out*, 8th ed. Pearson/Prentice Hall: Upper Saddle River, NJ, 2009; pp 31–72.

Wij, I.; Khanna, A. *HVS—Hotel Development Cost Trends in India*, 2012 [Online]. Hvs.com. Available at http://www.hvs.com/article/4912/hotel-development-cost-trends-in-india/ (last accessed 27 May 2016).

WTTC. *Travel & Tourism Economic Impact 2016 India*, 2016 [Online]. Available at https://www.wttc.org/-/media/files/reports/economic%20impact%20research/countries%202016/india2016.pdf (last accessed 13 May 2016).

CHAPTER 3

CORPORATE SOCIAL RESPONSIBILITY: AN IMPORTANT ASPECT OF THE INDIAN HOSPITALITY INDUSTRY

SAVITA SHARMA*

School of Tourism and Hospitality Management, Ansal University, Gurgaon, India

*E-mail: savitasharma@ansaluniversity.edu.in

CONTENTS

Abstract 44

3.1   Introduction 44

3.2   The Denotation of CSR 45

3.3   CSR in Hospitality 49

3.4   CSR Performance at a Glance 52

3.5   CSR and Corporate Performance 56

3.6   Conclusion and Suggestions 58

Keywords 59

References 59

ABSTRACT

The aim of this chapter is to understand and debate the meaning of corporate social responsibility (CSR) with respect to the hospitality industry in India. The concept of CSR was debated insistently in the early 1990s, but it was not reason enough for the companies to follow the same practices. In recent years, CSR has become one of the cornerstones of success, for many Indian companies as the government has mandated them to spend at least 2% of their net profits on CSR for companies with at least Rs. 5 crores net profits or Rs. 1000 crores turnover or Rs. 500 crores net worth under the new Companies Act 2013. Therefore, companies have started contributing to the requisite areas. It's been followed aggressively across sectors including the hospitality industry. Most of the luxury chain hotels fall under the categories which have to spend on CSR. Therefore, this chapter helps to understand the range of activities and their benefits to various companies and suggests that getting involved into the CSR activities provides a better platform and reputation for them. The present study is also an effort to identify various policies and activities, followed by the hotels with respect to CSR, and how new policies and activities can be merged strategically with the existing structure of organizations.

3.1 INTRODUCTION

Globalization has made the world smaller and business expansion is taking place in high growth economies like India, despite the global slump. Companies are expanding their operations and crossing geographical boundaries. There was a time when people used to feel happy to learn about opening up of new companies, because it would provide better jobs to people, and they didn't have to continue with the customary low paying work. There are a lot of prospects to start up new projects because of the possible opportunity and the massive development, also equally valid is the emerging threat to the environment due to rapid economic growth. Environmental issues, emanating from economic growth, provide a tremendous challenge for today's society. The business atmosphere has undergone enormous change in recent years in terms of both globalization and sensitivity toward nature, and there is a renewed push to safeguard natural resources and the cultural heritage. World of business has become so completive that it has become important for companies to stand out from their competition. Corporate social responsibility (CSR) is being recognized as a differentiator and is seen as a fundamental principle that should be central to the business strategy. Business has a critical role to play toward its direct and indirect stakeholders. It is a known fact that a company can flourish and have sustainability only when it takes into account the well-being of all the stakeholders involved seriously. A company's work schedule reflects the thought process of the business to engage in action concerning key sustainable development issues, which leads to responsible behavior. It is noteworthy to realize that consumer behavior in the past half-a-decade has taken a major shift. It is indeed interesting to study the storyline of recent blockbuster movies and television commercials nowadays, having more of an appeal for random acts of kindness and the feel good factor, by helping someone without any expectations of return. A shift in the paradigm of the customers' awareness has made corporates to turn green and ethical to gain better acceptability by the customers. People have become more observant while buying any product nowadays and evaluate multiple products of the same category, before going for any decision to select a particular product. Therefore, developing a CSR policy could be a way to highlight the company's integrity, which may establish trust and a long-term bond with the company. A topic of significant research interest has been to study the impact of CSR-related activities of a business as a differentiator in the competitive marketplace.

3.2 THE DENOTATION OF CSR

The concept of CSR is much broader than philanthropic activities alone. It requires special attention by the companies to act beyond mere legal obligations and to integrate the social, environmental, and ethical aspects as a fundamental responsibility into the company's business process. Doing things in a positive, responsible manner can be referred to as CSR in the simplest way. The main objective of CSR is that a corporate or business entity should realize their responsibility beyond a mere economic role in society. The key components of CSR may at least include the following.

3.2.1 CORPORATE GOVERNANCE

This refers to major issues like accountability, transparency, and legal conduct in compliance. An excellent corporate governance policy would help a company to comprehend its broader objectives, protect shareholder rights, fulfill legal responsibilities and create transparency for the stakeholders.

3.2.2 BUSINESS ETHICS

Business ethics refer to value-based and ethical business practices. A company has to be honest, truthful, and fair in terms of its policies, practices, and decision-making to be sustainable in the market. It also includes the company's compliance with legal standards and adherence to rules, by both internal and external stakeholders.

3.2.3 THE WORKPLACE AND LABOR RELATIONS

Workplace and labor relation refer to the necessary working conditions and policies required like health and safety, employee relations, which leads to a healthy balance between work and nonwork aspects of the life of its employees. Basically, it relates to human resource which is very critical for any company, it makes recruitment less challenging and also improves employee retention, eventually reducing the cost of recruitment and retention.

3.2.4 THE AFFIRMATIVE ACTION

Affirmative action refers to providing equal opportunity for all employable people, including those with disability, candidates from the local community, etc. Fair gender policies, stern guidelines on prevention of sexual harassment at workplace, and support toward employee volunteering are few of the good practices which reflect a strong CSR approach communicated by the company.

3.2.5 THE SUPPLY CHAIN

Business is not a secluded process and companies should use its strategic intent to influence the entire supply chain (social, environmental, human rights, and other aspects) to positively impact the stakeholders. If a company neglects the supply chain, then it may reflect badly on the company which may affect the business adversely.

3.2.6 THE CUSTOMERS

Customers are the main focus for any company because all products and services are aimed at providing customers with convenience, satisfaction, and a positive perception. With increased awareness and means of communication, the cost and quality of products are not the only concern, but customers are also taking interest in the company's procedures and practices linked to the delivery of the goods and services, considering the supply chain and other aspects closely related to delivery.

3.2.7 THE NATURAL ENVIRONMENT

Environment refers to all the natural resources which are available on the earth and are very important for each and every individual on this earth. Excess use of natural resource has become one of the major concerns for everyone, especially for companies to run its operations. Thus, it becomes important for companies to get engaged in mandatory requirements as well find suitable solutions to reduce the use of natural resources. Many of the companies are producing environment friendly goods, which will help reduce the adverse effects of their activities on the environment.

3.2.8 THE COMMUNITY

Community is one of the stakeholders of any company, which has a direct impact on the company's procedures and conduct of business. A company should always asses the issues and risks faced by the local community. Involvement of the community is necessary to avoid repercussions, make a positive change, and improve the brand image of the company. Association with community could also be integrated with the overall business strategy and community-focused CSR activities can be planned and implemented effectively.

CSR is inferred as a sense of willingness to accept more than just company policy driven actions, and their impact on society and the natural environment, which is supported by Wood (1991) in his statement "The basic idea of CSR is that business and society are interwoven rather than distinct entities." Basically, it is about how a company's existence affects the stakeholders beyond insular interests, knowing the impact that business processes have on the community at large. It relates to what can be arbitrated ethically and morally. There are a number of definitions suggested by various authors to describe the meaning of CSR, but till now, there is no universally accepted definition for CSR. That is the reason people are still debating the list of actions, which could be recognized as components of CSR. CSR, which is an acronym of Corporate Social Responsibility, is associated with many other terms such as corporate citizenship, responsible business, corporate social responsiveness, corporate sustainability, corporate social investment, and stake holder management (Carroll, 1979; Clarkson, 1995; Griffin & Mahon, 1997; Maignan & Ferrel, 2001; Shropshire & Hillman, 2007; Standwick & Standwich, 1998; Turban & Greening, 1996; Waddock & Graves, 1997). Out of all the above acronyms and meanings, Carroll (1979) has gained the maximum popularity, which refers to CSR as a multidimensional concept that consists of majorly four types of responsibilities: economical, legal ethical, and discretionary. Economic responsibilities include the commitments of a company to maintain economic growth and to meet up with their consumption needs. Legal responsibilities include the economic mission within the framework of legal requirements. Ethical responsibilities include the company's moral rules, which define appropriate behavior in society. Discretionary responsibilities are equivalent to philanthropic activities, which reflect the society's desire to see a company contributing to its development. Regardless of the vocabulary, the main objective is that any business should think about more than just earning profit in the society. This will come into play only when there is willingness to accept responsibilities beyond business driven actions, toward a wider responsibility encompassing society and the environment. It is about the way businesses operate and exist to produce a positive impact on society. A number of commissions and authors have twisted and formed many statements for a better understanding regarding CSR, which includes the World Business Council for Sustainable Development. It has provided a statement that helps the business community realize its obligation toward the principles of sustainability in business as "The continuing commitment by business to behave ethically and contribute to economic development, while improving the quality of life of the workforce and their families as well as of the local community and society at large" (WBCSD, 1999). The Commission of the European Communities (2001) has issued a statement that explains CSR as "a concept whereby companies integrate social and environmental concerns in their business operations and in their interactions with their stakeholders on a voluntary basis." In the Indian scenario, CSR has become more visible with the government embedding it into the new Companies Act 2013. If we look beyond India, then CSR became "the talk of the town in corporate circles" in 1960 (Mees & Bonham, 2004). It is indeed a self-regulatory mechanism to encourage corporate entities toward more "responsible business" that encourages a positive impact in society and within the organization as well. The concept of CSR gained popularity in 1960s and now has taken the shape of a law with mandatory compliance guidelines. Altogether, there are many thoughts and definitions shared on CSR, but in simple words, it can be summarized as activities undertaken by companies beyond their economic activities to make the world a better and sustainable place.

3.3   CSR IN HOSPITALITY

Some of the organizations across the globe had been contributing toward CSR, even much before introduction of formal CSR regulations including in the hospitality industry. Corporate behavior toward social responsibility and a sensitive approach toward sustainability are finding new vigor in the Indian business environment. However, the same has occupied an intense platform internationally for quite some time. There was a time when the service industry was not much concerned about their actions and their effect on the environment, but in the present scenario, it has been observed that the tourism industry and hotel organizations have shown a significant interest in CSR. Hotels have started recognizing that besides trust building with the community, CSR practices attract customers and employees which help the business grow and remain profitable. The tourism industry would seem to have particular and identifiable duties outside the business arena due to its very close relationship with destination environments and societies which are facets of its products (Henderson, 2007). If we observe the day-to-day activities of hotels, then it would be obvious that there is a huge consumption of natural resources by them to perform their routine operations. For example, the laundering procedure consumes a lot of water resources, which leads to wastage of water in large quantities. To reduce water wastages, hotels are promoting various kinds of procedures, where guests are requested to reuse their towels and linen in an effort to reduce water consumption. In fact, hotels which are implementing towel and linen reuse programs are ostensibly reducing water usage and also showcasing themselves to be a socially responsible hotel to their customers. These programs can help reduce environmental degradation, enhance public relations, and reduce the operational costs of the hotel. Individuals worldwide are becoming increasingly savvy about expressing environmental preferences. Hotels recognize that an eco-friendly reputation can enable them to target environmentally conscious customers, gain differentiation advantages, and yield premium prices for their services (Rivera, 2002). Most of the researchers, who have investigated the impact of CSR on tourism and on other service industries, have found that CSR activities lead to a positive effect. People have revealed their willingness to work for a company that cares about customers, employees, and society for the sense of being valued and respected. Green and Pelazo (2011) examined that CSR demonstrates a relatively consistent level of positive support by consumers and it enhances the overall value proposition for consumers in three forms: emotionally, socially, and functionally. Consumers have also revealed a willingness to spend 20–50% more for organically produced food (Barkley, 2002) and $3000–8000 more for hybrid cars over comparable non-hybrid models (Walters, 2005). Smith (1996) has observed in a survey that about 88% of customers are likely to purchase from companies, which are socially responsible and demonstrate a respect for the environment, which helps the financial performance of hotels implying that CSR may be used as marketing tool. On the other side, Maignan et al. (1999) have observed that CSR helps attract more talented and committed employees which helps the companies to hire and retain loyal and efficient employees. It is important because the hotel organization's rapport with the employees can directly sway the customers' reactions to it and impacts its profitability. It has been observed by many authors that CSR initiatives are often the reflection of the firm's values and norms, and if the employees get motivated by the thought behind the strategies, then the employees attitudinal and behavioral support can help to achieve the firm's goal (Bartel, 2001; Dutton et al., 1994; Mael & Tetrick, 1992), which further helps to attract customers.

The hospitality industry is considered to be a manpower-driven, people-focused, and service-oriented industry, in which the role of the service providers (employees) becomes quite important. They are the ones who serve and interact with the customers and are thus best placed to understand the way customers evaluate service quality. In fact, CSR results in multidimensional gain to a company, in terms of adding value to customers, leading with a positive vision, inspiration, and integrity, hence attracting quality workforce and team members. CSR while enhancing a positive reputation also builds good and stable partnerships. Day-by-day consumer awareness is rising toward social responsibility; therefore, it becomes important for the hospitality industry to begin strengthening their efforts on CSR as part of their overall corporate and business strategies. Strategic CSR may be used to attract good quality employees in the hospitality industry because both internal and external stakeholders are people and can be influenced positively by sharing the CSR initiatives. It has also been observed that customers are not only aware of CSR practices and choose the companies, which have a positive CSR orientation, but also willing to participate in these kinds of activities. But during this study, it was found that hospitality industry in India is still lacking behind and has had not much visibility or initiative to take on CSR activities as compared to other business sectors.

3.3.1 METHODOLOGY

The present study has gathered information from secondary data. Secondary data were collected through journals, articles, and annual reports. The Indian hotel industry is well known for its hospitality and presently, there are a number of hotel brand competing in the Indian market. It has been observed that embedding CSR practices in the company's policy has become very common in the corporate world globally. Therefore, this study is an effort to identify the level of involvement of the Indian hotel companies, with respect to offering policy-driven support to CSR initiatives. Activities performed by the top two chain hotels of India (The Taj Group and The Oberoi Group) and a young Indian hotel company (Lemon Tree) are documented and discussed with reference to the new Companies Act, 2013 under Section 135 which makes financial contribution toward CSR mandatory. These research findings can be used by practicing business leaders, to improve on their efforts toward CSR.

3.3.2 THE NEW COMPANIES ACT, 2013 AND THE INDIAN HOTEL INDUSTRY

The Indian government through an amendment to the Companies Act, 2013, on August 29, 2013, initiated reforms aimed at improving corporate governance, streamlining regulations and enhancing the visibility of minor investors. The legislation has given a broader mandate to the 60-year-old Companies Act announced in 1956. According to Section 135 of the 2013 Companies Act, each company which has "a net worth of Rs. 500 crores or more, or turnover of Rs. 1000 crores or more, or net profits of Rs. 5 crores or more during any financial year shall constitute a Corporate Social Responsibility Committee reporting to the Board. The company should comprise of three or more directors, out of which at least one director shall be an independent director." The Act has very clearly defined the responsibly of the board members and provided guidelines for CSR activities, which states that CSR activities could include

- eradicating extreme hunger and poverty,
- promotion of education,
- promoting gender equality and empowering women,
- reducing child mortality and improving maternal health,
- combating human immunodeficiency virus, acquired immune deficiency syndrome, malaria, and other diseases,
- ensuring environmental sustainability,
- employment enhancing vocational skills,
- social business projects,
- contribution to the Prime Minister's National Relief Fund or any other fund set up by the Central Government or the State Governments, for socioeconomic development and relief and funds for the welfare of the Scheduled Castes, the Scheduled Tribes, other backward classes, minorities, and women,
- such other matters as may be prescribed, and
- it also states that the company shall give preference to the local area and areas around it where it operates.

The present act offers an opportunity to make businesses more responsible and provides corporate regulations that offer a direction through which we can change the way Indian corporate do business, looking beyond just fiscal targets and the bottom line.

It has been observed that some of the companies have been contributing toward CSR initiatives but the same was not under any framework and thus difficult to formally acknowledge. The Indian hospitality companies too have taken initiatives to demonstrate that they care for the society, environment, and customers. That said there is clearly potential to do much more.

3.4   CSR PERFORMANCE AT A GLANCE

3.4.1   THE TAJ HOTELS RESORTS AND PALACES

The Indian Hotels Company Limited and its subsidiaries are collectively known as Taj Hotels Resorts and Palaces and is one of the oldest and largest Indian hotel company started in 1903. The group is very well known for its contribution toward the well-being of society. Taj has initiated CSR activities under the program EARTH, elaborated as Environment Awareness and Renewal at Taj Hotels which is responsible for a conscious effort to commit to conserve energy and includes other sustainability focused strategies. Other initiatives are distributing food to local charities and orphanages, providing support and training to less privileged and marginalized youth across India along with setting up centers for skilled training, contributing to maintain public gardens, public areas, supporting environmental issues, promoting local and traditional art, and protection of heritage along with donations made for education and other miscellaneous requirements of community. Other than this, they have always extended their hands to support their employees and customers.

3.4.2 LUXURY CHAIN HOTEL: THE OBEROI GROUP OF HOTELS

It is a public limited company established under the Indian Companies Act, 1913. It is a marquee Indian Hotel group. The company is already engaged in a number of community development and social service efforts, as a part of their CSR practice. The Oberoi Hotels Private Limited has a vision to take up "education for the underprivileged children." The CSR policy of the group focuses on addressing the critical social, economic, and educational needs of the marginalized underprivileged children of society, where the company gives attention to educational, nutritional, health, and psychological development needs. In addition to this, the CSR policy also offers contribution toward the Swacch Bharat Kosh set up by the central government, for the promotion of sanitation, contribution to the Prime Minister's National Relief Fund along with focus on environmental sustainability issues. The company encourages its employees to participate in all CSR projects. The hotel group has a vision to enhance hospitality skills amongst the youth and provides opportunities to deserving candidates through employment in the company itself.

3.4.3 YOUNG RESPONSIBLE HOTEL COMPANY: LEMON TREE

Lemon Tree Hotel Company was started in the year 2002 and is a growing chain that works on the concept of "refreshing" which provides high quality accommodation spread in many cities of India. Even though being a small and young organization, Lemon Tree Hotel feels proud to take the responsibility of planet, people, and profits. Hotel management believes that the brand should stand for more than "just profit." Many of the environmental efforts are incorporated in the daily operational procedures like use of CNG instead of LPG, plantation of trees and shrubs on hotel premises, use of green building materials as relevant, designing new buildings in accordance with Universal Design concepts, etc. to provide better accessibility for differently abled people. There are many future investments planned like extensive use of LED light fittings, solar photo voltaic system for lighting, alternative sources of energy, and many more like this. Lemon Tree Hotels exclusively focuses on an initiative to hire people with disabilities and defined the goal as mainstreaming "Opportunity Deprived Indians" for the workforce. In fact, presently about 15% of their total staffing across India falls under employees with disabilities. As per their capabilities, they are deployed in different departments like housekeeping, kitchen stewarding, and few even in the food and beverage services. Future planning is to increase the percentage gradually across the chain in India over next 10 years. Hiring employees with disabilities is imbibed in the hotel's human resource policy, instead of recognizing the initiative as a CSR practice. As far as profitability is concerned, the hotel practices best-in-class cost structure both in building and operating hotels. The Lemon Tree Hotel company has been ranked as one of the top 100 great places to work in India for 5 continuous years.

It has been observed that Indian hotels have historically been involved in various philanthropic activities based on their understanding and ways. Because they were self-driven, now, after the announcement of the New Companies Act, 2013 amendment, hotels have segregated their initiatives under various sections of the mandate, which gives a clear picture of areas which needs to be focused upon. It is very clear in the Table 3.1 that CSR initiatives are practiced irrespective of the category of hotel. Lemon Tree is a relatively young hotel group as compared to the big giants of the Indian hotel industry like The Taj and The Oberoi; but they are very clear and focused on providing employment for disabled people along with few initiatives for environmental sustainability. It has been witnessed that there is a lack of contribution toward the promotion of gender equality and empowering women and some of the other areas which need attention are eradicating extreme hunger and poverty, emphasis on education, to name a few that need immediate support. It is difficult to verify facts, but companies are now sharing more in this respect either through their websites or through public statements released to the media. Hotel businesses are contributing in various areas and sometimes they don't even publicize because they feel that it is their duty to at least return something to the society. The New Company Act, 2013, has provided clear guidelines about the areas which need special attention and the hotel industry can improve their social and environmental performance further.

TABLE 3.1 CSR Initiatives by Key Indian Hotel Companies.

CSR guidelines	Taj	Oberoi	Lemon Tree
Eradicating extreme hunger and poverty	Distribute food to local charities and orphanages	–	–
Promotion of education	Donations made for education and other miscellaneous requirements of community	–	–
Promoting gender equality and empowering women	–	–	–
Reducing child mortality and improving maternal health	–	Promoting social, economic, and educational needs of the marginalized under-privileged children of the society	–
Combating human immunodeficiency virus, acquired immune deficiency syndrome, malaria, and other diseases	–	–	Very high focus on disabled people, their needs, providing training, and making them employable at their own hotels
Ensuring environmental sustainability	Committed to conserve energy and other sustainability strategies	Contribution toward environmental sustainability	Focused toward energy and water conservation, use of green material
Employment enhancing vocational skills	Provide training to less privileged and marginalized youth	–	Provide training to disabled people to get the employment
Contribute to the Prime Minister's National Relief Fund	–	Contribution toward Prime Minister's National Relief Fund	–
Give preference to the local area	Contribute to maintaining public garden, public areas, and the surrounding environment	Swacch Bharat Abhiyan sanitation program	–
Other	Local and traditional art, and protection of heritage	–	–

3.5　CSR AND CORPORATE PERFORMANCE

Globally, the hospitality industry is beginning to recognize the benefits from undertaking proactive environmental efforts. The connection between social and financial performance of a company plays an important role in the analysis of socially responsible investment. Though the legitimacy and value of CSR has never been a point of concern, but CSR implementation is still a "dream-come-true" for the society and regulatory bodies, as the fact cannot be ignored that many companies still view CSR as "window dressing" than actual responsible business. The concern of CSR professionals and policy makers is over the fact that, CSR should not get restricted to the manipulation of balance sheets and operating statements, with the corporate starting up their own non-profit entity merely to route CSR compliance budget back in the organization through other manipulations. A firm should now be attentive to the bottom line or profitability expectations and also be a good corporate citizen. CSR refers to as its premise that corporations must justify their existence in terms of service to the community rather than just profit (Crook, 2005). CSR orientation allows businesses to pursue long-term sustainability by balancing of economic, environmental, and social imperatives which also symbolizes a triple bottom line (TBL) expectation. Hospitality businesses must learn to deal with the expectations of both internal and external stakeholders simultaneously. The TBL approach is used as framework to measure and report corporate performance equally in terms of economic, social, and environmental performance. Indian government has announced a mandate to spend at least 2% of their net profit on CSR, for companies with at least Rs. 5 crores net profit or Rs. 1000 crores turnover or Rs. 500 crores net worth under New Companies Act 2013, which is an attempt to align private enterprise to the goal of global sustainable development by providing the companies with a broader set of working objectives rather than just counting profitability figures. The TBL framework integrates financial goals along with the social, ecological, and cultural context. There are many companies which have adopted the TBL section in their financial reporting, to evaluate their business performance in terms of a broader perspective to create better business visibility. A company's investment in socially acknowledged activities leads to the satisfaction of their stakeholders (McWilliams & Siegel, 2001). Studies have revealed that most customers agree to the fact that companies engaged in charity and CSR activities automatically climb-up the customer priority chart and also act as a cementing agent in customer and company loyalty relationship, besides enjoying an overall goodwill in market.

Some of the latest studies in CSR have indicated that the customers are ready to boycott companies that do not behave socially responsible, hence, directly affecting the performance of the company. On the other side, the competitor behaving responsibly takes away those customers who boycotted previous company. The recent example in Indian context is Maggie noodles versus Patanjali Atta noodles that defines the statement very well. This way, the "value-linking chain" of business has directly impacted the "CSR-performance chain." Also, socially responsible companies have gained or enhanced their brand image and positive reputation, which has not only attracted customers but also impacted employee perception and made them decide for a longer work tenure, which in turn has allowed the responsible companies to grow in an ethical and profitable manner. CSR initially seen as an expense or financial drain does eventually lead to stronger profits through enhanced public image and improved overall financial performance. A strategic decision toward supporting society environment helps the corporate to contribute to both corporate wealth and as well as overall societal wealth. It is important for corporate to get sensitive toward CSR to fill up the gap amongst people, environment and business to achieve sustainable performance at a holistic level. CSR is getting aligned with the core business strategies because of the swift change in the social and environmental context. A progressive approach to business definitely has a spirited advantage by being more receptive to societal signals. It is prospering by helping the society prosper. In today's scenario, it has become important for any company to showcase their name in the list of companies, which are ethical and responsive toward the environment for their economic sustainability. Embedding social responsibility in the corporate policies will benefit the organizations in many forms where few are as follows:

- better capacity to manage environmental risks,
- greater use of renewable resources,
- improved financial performance,
- lowering operating costs,
- better and competitive quality of services,
- better product durability and functionality,
- enhanced brand image and reputation,
- increased sales and customer loyalty,
- increased ability to attract and retain employees,
- publicity at no cost, and
- sustainable business prospects.

3.6 CONCLUSION AND SUGGESTIONS

It has been observed that Indian hospitality companies have started realizing the importance of CSR, in terms of their accountability toward the environment, society, and the profit maximization motive. Although the ancestry of CSR lies in the philanthropic activities of the corporate, the concept is getting merged with the regulatory compliance aspects, especially in the Indian scenario. It has also been observed that there may be an initial fiscal burden on the companies but over a longer term, it would be advantageous to achieve balance of economic, environmental, and social imperatives. In the long run, the costs and profits of socially responsible conduct will compensate each other along with sustainable business and environment. The corporate world indeed cannot ignore the shifting interest in the consumer behavior space as it directly affects the choice and preference of the customer, hence, directly affecting the corporate performance, positively or negatively. Therefore, to evade the negative impact on the customers, it becomes important for companies including the hospitality industry to come forward and be participative to promote and implement CSR initiatives. It also increases the commitment and morale of employees with the organizations and leads to a higher job satisfaction and retention rate. The employees' organizational commitment has a strong influence on the organizational performance. The present study has observed that hotels are involved in various philanthropic activities from years back as per their understanding and ways because they were self-driven. It has been witnessed that there is a lack of contribution toward promoting gender equality and empowering women. Other areas which need attention are eradicating extreme hunger and poverty, emphasis on education, to name a few. Problems like economic backwardness and poverty in India are complex issues and need a holistic approach. Though the Indian government has various policies which support the poor, it is not sufficient for such a populous country which needs additional support from the corporate world. Corporate requires the society to carry on business and the society needs to be nourished to allow businesses to prosper. For a sustainable business growth to happen, the hospitality industry must seek common ground where their CSR principles and actions satisfy the demands of the environment, stakeholders, and the society at large. The industry must work to create a platform, where maximum number of participants can contribute toward a sustainable future irrespective of their size and business presence. Further continued research in this area can assist the hospitality industry to measure the impact of their efforts, as well as their overall CSR footprint in India.

KEYWORDS

- CSR
- sustainability
- environment
- Indian company law
- triple bottom line

REFERENCES

Barkley, A. Organic Food Growth: Producer Profits and Corporate Farming, In: Paper Presented at the *Risk and Profit Conference*, Department of Agricultural Economics, Kansas State University: Manhattan, KS, 15–16 August 2002.

Bartel, C. Social Comparisons in Boundary-spanning Work: Effects of Community Outreach on Members' Organizational Identity and Identification. *Adm. Sci. Q.* **2001,** *46*(3), 379–413.

Carroll, A. B. A Three-dimensional Conceptual Model of Corporate Performance. *Acad. Manage. Rev.* **1979,** *4*(4), 497–505.

Clarkson, M. A Stakeholder Framework for Analyzing and Evaluating Corporate Social Performance. *Acad. Manage. Rev.* **1995,** 20(1), 92–117.

Commission of the European Communities. *Promoting a European Framework for Corporate Social Responsibility*, 2001. Available at.

Crook, C. The Good Company. *Economist* **2005,** *8410*, 3–18.

Dutton, J.; Dukerich, J.; Harquail, C. Organizational Image and Member Identification. *Adm. Sci. Q.* **1994,** *39*(2), 239–263.

Green, T.; Pelazo, J. How Does Corporate Social Responsibility Create Value for Customers? *J. Consum. Mark.* **2011,** *28*(1), 48–56.

Griffin, J. J.; Mahon, J. F. The Corporate Social Performance and Corporate Financial Performance Debate. *Bus. Soc.* **1997,** *36*(1), 5–31.

Henderson, J. C. Corporate Social Responsibility and Tourism: Hotel Companies in Phuket, Thailand, after the Indian Ocean tsunami. *Int. J. Hospitality Manage.* **2007,** *26*(1), 228–239.

Mael, F.; Tetrick, L. Identifying Organizational Identification. *Educ. Psychol. Meas.* **1992,** *52*(4), 813–824.

Maignan, I.; Ferrell. O. C. Corporate Citizenship as a Marketing Instrument—Concepts, Evidence and Research Directions. *Eur. J. Mark.* **2001,** *35*(3/4), 457–484.

Maignan, I.; Ferrell, O. C.; Hult, G. T. M. Corporate Citizenship: Cultural Antecedents and Business Benefits. *J. Acad. Mark. Sci.* **1999,** 27(4), 455.

McWilliams, A.; Siegal, D. Corporate Social Responsibility: A Theory of the Firm Perspective. *Acad. Manage. Rev.* **2001,** *26*, 117–127.

Mees, A.; Bonham, J. Corporate Social Responsibility Belongs with HR. *Can. HR Rep.* **2004,** *17*(7), 11 (retrieved 22 June 2006, from Proquest database).

Rivera, J. Assessing a Voluntary Environmental Initiative in the Developing World: The Costa Rican Certification for Sustainable Tourism. *Policy Sci.* **2002,** *35*(4), 333–360.

Shropshire, C.; Hillman, A. J. A Longitudinal Study of Significant Change in Stakeholder Management. *Bus. Soc.* **2007,** *46*(1), 63–87.

Smith, C. Corporate Citizens and their Critics. *New York Times* 8 September 1996, p. 11.

Standwick, P. A.; Standwich, S. D. The Relationship between Corporate Social Performance and Organizational Size, Financial Performance, and Environmental Performance: an Empirical Examination. *J. Bus. Ethics* **1998,** *17*(3), 195–204.

Turban, D. B.; Greening, D. W. Corporate Social Performance and Organizational Attractiveness to Prospective Employees. *Acad. Manage. J.* **1996,** *40*(3), 658–672.

Waddock, S. E.; Graves, S. B. The Corporate Social Performance—Financial Performance Link. *Strat. Manage. J.* **1997,** *18*(4), 303–319.

Walters, P. *Cities Question the Costs of Hybrid Cars.* Philadelphia Associated Press, 9 December 2005.

WBCSD (World Business Council for Sustainable Development). *Corporate Social Responsibility: Meeting Changing Expectations*, 1999. http://www.wbcsd.ch.

Wood, D. J. Corporate Social Performance Revisited. *Acad. Manage. Rev.* **1991,** *16*, 691–718.

CHAPTER 4

THE INDIAN HOSPITALITY SECTOR IS IN A FLUX: CHANGING TRENDS THAT RESPOND TO THE NEW CUSTOMER

ARVIND K. BIRDIE*

Department of PG Studies, Vedatya Institute, Gurgaon, India

E-mail: arvindgagan@gmail.com

CONTENTS

Abstract 62

4.1 Introduction 62

4.2 Hospitality Segment in the Indian Economy and the Indian Culture 68

4.3 Development of the Fast-Food Industry in India 76

4.4 Foreign Versus Domestic Tourists 77

4.5 The World Online 77

4.6 Conclusion 78

4.7 Recommendations That Will Help Hospitality Industry Respond to Changing Trends 79

Keywords 82

References 82

ABSTRACT

In recent years, the Indian hospitality industry has emerged as one of the key industries driving growth of the services sector in India. Globalization and technological advancements have revolutionized the service sector. This chapter focuses on the factors governing behavior of today's Indian consumer such as aging, economy, social change, mass media, changing perceptions, lifestyle changes, and access to more disposable income which has brought about a change in the profile of today's consumer. The effects on the industry are discussed given that it is sensitive to the needs and desires of consumers, with a wide range of options available for the consumers. Concepts like homestays in Kerala, spa resorts, ecotourism, medical tourism, family packages with advanced services like online booking, etc. are catching up fast. The author discusses the same from the context of consumer-driven response from the hospitality sector. The chapter also draws insights from practitioners for providing services and satisfaction to today's more aware consumers. It also examines how the hospitality industry is creating innovation in services. The chapter also brings in a perspective from various stakeholders such as hoteliers, consumers, and researchers on changing consumer behavior and its impact on the industry recommendations and implications for future are also to conclude these discussions.

4.1   INTRODUCTION

The hospitality industry is defined as "hosts offering service to guests," which includes reception, entertainment, and other services provided to travelers and tourists. Hospitality is a long-running tradition in India. From the majestic Himalayas and the stark deserts of Rajasthan, over beautiful beaches and lush tropical forests, to idyllic villages and bustling cities, India offers unique opportunities for every individual preference.

The last quarter of the 20th century has seen an increasing international movement of goods, services, people, funds, and information. The hospitality industry, traditionally more focused on the physical product, is waking up to a consumer who is demanding consistent delivery of the brand promise and, in the upscale to luxury segments, the experiential dimension will define a successful brand as much as the finer points of product design. In emerging markets such as India and China, there is a significant rise of the middle class, generating an increase in demand for both business and leisure travel.

The buying behavior of consumers in India has changed, and education, age, income, economic scenario, media, and technology play a predominant role in shaping the way people shop, according to the 2014 report on consumer behavior by the Retailers Association of India and consultancy firm KPMG.

The Indian populace has been evolving steadily and pockets of disposable income have been shifting to accommodate leisure travel. The Millennials are dictating the spending habits in the market and are not averse to spending a little extra on small creature comforts. That being the domestic scenario, the travel and tourism sector is doing quite well, roping in foreign tourists as well as investments. Between April 2000 and August 2014, the sector attracted US\$ 7.4 billion of FDI and the foreign tourist arrivals witnessed a growth of 12.9% between July 2013 and July 2014.

While the numbers depict a solid growth in the sector, the paradigm shift that should be expected in the coming years is the rise of the consumer-led brand focus. The coming years mark a change in the perception of luxury from product design to experience, making it all the more important for industry operators to identify and leverage consumer behavior trends in the hospitality market for the coming years.

By now, accommodation options throughout India have become extremely diverse, from cozy home stays and tribal huts to stunning heritage mansions and Maharaja Palaces. From Kashmir to Kanyakumari, from Gujarat to Assam, there are different cultures, languages, lifestyles, and cuisines in play. This variety is increasingly reflected by the many forms of accommodation available in India, ranging from the simplicity of local guest houses and government bungalows to the opulent luxury of royal palaces and 5-star deluxe hotel suites.

Indian tourists featured in the global top 10 list of nationalities that spend the most on hotel rooms abroad. Jaisalmer, Wayanad, Rishikesh, and Amritsar have featured in the top 100 list of high-quality services in hotels, in terms of giving the best value for money according to a study spearheaded by the leading global hotel search website *trivago*. In the fourth edition of *trivago's* Best Value Index, Wayanad, located on the Western Ghats in Kerala, has secured ninth position in the world with a score of 96.36%.

4.1.1 FACTORS AFFECTING CONSUMER BEHAVIOR

A number of authors have charted the rise of consumption, including Benson(1994), Miles (1998), Ritzer (1999), and Gabriel and Lang (1995).

Most authors argue that growth of consumption can be explained by a number of key factors, which are as follows:

1. *The economy*—Recent movements in the economies of some developed and most developing countries have led to upturns in stock market prices and lower unemployment, leaving people with unprecedented levels of disposable income. It has led to growth in the number of people able to take advantage of early retirement opportunities. The result is that people want and can afford more goods and services, such as hospitality has become a major form of recreation. From a supply perspective, companies, especially those quoted on the world's stock markets, recognize that in order to be seen to be doing well, it is necessary to show substantial profit increases year on year. Economic growth has also got significant political implications which governments are keen to exploit as they recognize the social benefits of consumption (Miles, 1998). The country has witnessed a change in consumption patterns. The middle-class population with higher disposable incomes has caused a shift in the spending pattern, with discretionary purchases forming a substantial part of total consumer spending. Increased affordability and affinity for leisure travel are driving tourism in India and in turn aiding growth of the hospitality industry in India. Emergence of the credit culture, easier availability of personal loans, has also aided the growth in the travel and tourism industry and thus the hospitality industry in the country.

2. *The growth of the youth market*—The youth of today are experienced consumers, and companies market directly to them, recognizing their role in the family decision-making unit. As Goodman (1997) argues, "The marketplace has turned kids into short consumers." This is increasingly true within the hospitality industry. Consider fast food restaurants and theme parks, for example, children and young people have become consumers of hospitality services. In the United Kingdom, the growth of child-friendly public houses has been a dominant feature of the sector since the late 1980s. All the major public house retailers have a version of the public house as the child activity center, for example, Greenalls'-based original Jungle Bungle concept. **Millennials** have become the fastest growing customer segment within the hospitality industry. Exploration, interaction, and experience are the major focus of the Millennials, who are willing to pay more for a superior experience. Many of them are looking for an overall gourmet experience for a reasonable price

and this has produced new lobby designs in the hotel sector. Lobby bars and hotel restaurants are wide open with combination work, play, eat, and drink spaces designed with this Millennial customer in mind, one who is a "party of one" but "hanging out together." They are looking for a unique and novel experience and this has and will continue to influence change within the market. Moreover, this customer segment is interested in utilizing technology to do things that many others have become accustomed to doing manually: checking in at hotels, paying their restaurant and bar bills, and looking up places to eat, shop, and play to name a few. In addition to wanting technology, Millennials have no problems speaking up. If what they are seeking is not handled to their liking, they will turn to Twitter, Facebook, Yelp, or TripAdvisor to voice their complaints. And last but not least, 59% of Millennials stayed at independent hotels last year, 20% more than boomers and double those 70% and over, according to MMGY Global Company. They currently represent 32% of all US travelers and by 2025 will represent over 50% of all travelers.

3. *Technological change*—Ritzer (1999) suggests that technological change is probably the most important factor in the growth of consumption, citing the development of transportation links such as cars, motorways, and jet travel as being of prime importance in this growth. Innovative technology, mobile check-ins, and seamless connectivity across platforms and devices are no longer the future, they are the present. Today, mobile apps are being used as everything from a digital concierge to accessing big data. Geo-location can make it easy to sell guests something that is literally right in front of them. In a recent survey by Software Advice, guests desired local restaurant and hotel restaurant discounts when looking for deals as well as maps with coupons for other deals. Hotels are using 1App, which sends guests deals to do everything related to eating, playing, and shopping. Additionally, monitoring guest use of the internet relative to bandwidth can provide a different data set, perhaps one that will drive down the ever increasing costs of providing ridiculous levels of said bandwidth. Most importantly, when looking at the face of a changing consumer today, technology innovation is paramount. Also included are developments such as television and delivery technology, which are necessary to expedite mass advertising. If we consider the typical hotel stay, for example, computers will be used by both the consumer and the supplier at all stages of

the stay. In India, Reliance Jio has offered a game-changing plan that puts a smart phone with 4G features and unlimited data for 3 months at a price of USD 35.0, making fast internet accessible to millions of young users at an amazingly affordable price.

4. *Social change*—Contemporary society is characterized by consumption rather than production, as was previously the case. All aspects of contemporary are the focus of consumption, including most relationships and encounters we undertake. Mass market tourism is a growing industry worldwide which has seen major growth from less than 100 million worldwide arrivals in the 1950s, to an expected excess of 1.6 billion arrivals by 2020, and estimated to be as high as 2.6 billion by 2050

5. *The mass media*—Marketing is an important aspect for any company involved in business. As such, it is a competitive world out there, and social media marketing is the "new kid in town" and it can reach out to the people accessing these social media platforms regularly. Communication is essential for any corporation and business, therefore either they change the way information is conveyed or be prepared to lose some of the audience. It is imperative for marketing managers to continuously find a solution to appeal, keep new and current consumers (Schneider, 2009).

   Whatever the arguments about the power of advertising, however, companies such as McDonald's, KFC, and Burger King spend billions of pounds every year seeking to convert consumers to the one. Social network is the ideal platform for communication that applies perfectly with marketing in the virtual world. Social networks are groups of individuals who prefer to communicate with one another through a preferred site based on the profile created for themselves (Laudon & Traver, 2007).

6. *Facilitating means*—The growth of sophisticated means for exchange is seen as one key factor in the growth of consumption, as it removes a natural barrier for growth at the individual level. Growth of credit cards, store cards, etc. allows one the freedom to consume. Today's consumer operate on the "buy now, pay later" principle, made a reality by available credit. The growth of mail order, television shopping channels, and internet has fueled the growth in consumption; products are more available and in age of mass media are more advertised. These new facilitators of travel consumption have done much for huge growth in hospitality, often paid for using credit cards.

7. *Globalization*—Major changes highlighted above are accompanied by increased globalization, "A process whereby the common currency of consumption plays a key role most evidently through the influence of multinational companies" (Miles, 1998). Growth is clearly visible within the hospitality industry, where companies such as McDonald's have grown at a rapid rate. The first McDonald's opened in 1955 and by 2000, McDonald's had over 30,000 stores in more than 100 countries including India, Russia, China, and Israel. In an interesting reversal to the more often seen American-led globalization of markets, Preta Manger, a UK-based "sandwich" company, has recently opened a store in New York's Time Square. The fast food industry is growing at an ever-increasing speed throughout the world. The expansion of American fast food comes with much more than it appears, the restaurants initially expected. The restaurants went into countries with the expectation of just serving food to customers at a fast pace and low price. However, they have slowly changed the diets in countries, impacted social lives, and economic positions. They have done a great job at adapting to their local markets, yet they remain the closest things to America that many of their customers have experienced. For this reason, the impact that the restaurants have on people goes far beyond the food being served. People go to KFC, McDonald's, and Pizza Hut for the experience rather than the food. Young children in East Asia have begun incorporating French Fries into their diet, which is very different from their typical diet of rice and vegetables. People center their social lives around McDonald's such as having birthday parties there and even getting married. In January, McDonald's added wedding packages to its Hong Kong menu. This is the only city in the world where McDonald's offers the service, prompted by frequent inquiries about fast food weddings from customers in recent years. The influence of soft power that fast food restaurants bring with them can be noticed just by looking at the foreign populations that consume the food. The information-technology imperative shows us that the universalizing of the fast food markets around the world is growing. Fast food has become a staple in the lives of people all across the world, and the more that restaurants adapt to their local markets the less cultural homogenization we will see. The global markets have witnessed major shifts in consumer's behavior that have been much influenced by

the change of technology, innovation, research, and development. The consumers' needs thus dynamically change in order to respond to the change in the social and business environment. The corporate and business strategies of companies are thus being developed in the light of "market potential" but, however, how the customer would react to the products and services of companies in new and existing markets remains a major question. The analysis of consumer behavior thus became the inevitable and critical part of the overall planning and decision-making function in the organization that helps to match the core competencies and capabilities of the organization with the needs of the customers that are largely influenced by a number of sociodemographic and psychological factors.

4.2 HOSPITALITY SEGMENT IN THE INDIAN ECONOMY AND THE INDIAN CULTURE

The contribution of the entire travel and tourism sector in India to gross domestic product is estimated to rise from 8.6% (USD 117.9 billion) in 2010 to 9.0% (USD 330.1 billion) by 2020. Between 2010 and 2019, the demand for travel and tourism in India is expected to grow annually by 8.2%, which will place India at the third position in the world. Travel and tourism in India also accounts for 49,086,000 jobs in 2010 (about 10% of the total employment) and is expected to rise to 58,141,000 jobs (10.4% of total employment) by 2020 (World Travel and Tourism Council, 2009).

India has a great tradition of accommodating people of other origins and tolerance toward cultural differences, lifestyle, habits, and religion. Indian culture stories are abound of hosts who lovingly cook up the best foods available to them for their guests, way beyond what they can afford, going hungry themselves rather than not being able to satisfy their guests. This element of Indian culture is based on the philosophy of "Atithi Devo Bhava," meaning "the guest is God" in the Sanskrit language. From this stems the Indian generosity toward guests whether at home or elsewhere.

The hotel industry in India expanded in the mid-1970s with the growth of the three prominent chains of hotels IHCL, EIL, and ITC. They largely represented the luxury segment of the hotel industry. Large part of the industry otherwise remained unorganized and unbranded. Only during the last decade did the mid-segment gradually develop beyond non-chain properties, with entrants into the field such as Hilton Garden Inns and Taj Group's Ginger Hotels, Sarovar Hotels, Lemon Tree, and Tulip Hotels to name a few. Other prospective entrants consider the mid-market segment most promising as well. Since 2000, India has also experienced the rapid emergence of unconventional and innovative hospitality service providers, be it far off eco-lodges in the jungles or NGOs offering accommodation in tribal villages. After many years of obscurity, the Indian hospitality industry is suddenly now in the limelight of the global hospitality industry. The trade press is full of features on the potential of the Indian hospitality sector and presents ever new stories of successful innovations in the industry.

4.2.1   UPCOMING TRENDS IN INDIA

4.2.1.1   NEW ENTRANTS FROM OUTSIDE OF THE INDUSTRY

New entrants to the Indian hospitality industry also come from other segments of the economy. While real estate companies invest in the sector to leverage their properties, financial service providers such as ICICI Bank and Citi Bank have teamed up with major Indian tourism players like Thomas Cook and Cox & Kings to offer personal travel loans and "holiday now, pay later" schemes. Strong companies from other industrial backgrounds also diversify into the hospitality business in order to take advantage of their brand equity. For example, Reliance Industries and the Mahindra Group successfully entered the hospitality industry. Others engage with the hospitality industry to increase their bargaining power, such as eminent IT companies, who count among the biggest clients of hospitality services in India. This heavy dependence coupled with expected increase in hotel room rates prompts them to buy stakes in hospitality ventures and even maintain their own accommodation facilities.

4.2.1.2   BASED ON LOCATION

Locations of hospitality service providers can be divided into three main categories: urban settings, rural settings, and special locations. Among these three categories, metropolitan cities dominate the industry, accounting for 75–80% of total revenues, with Delhi and Mumbai leading the field.

4.2.1.2.1   Rural Tourism and Home Stays

Increasingly, hospitality services are offered in India's rural areas. Private persons convert their country homes into home stays, villagers too offer home stays, and agriculturalists as well as farmers open their farms to visitors.

Notably, it is not only foreign tourists who demand these services. More and more Indian families as well as corporate clients are tempted to the countryside with the advent of quality amenities and improved facilities. Many new and innovative leisure destinations are being developed in the remote corners of India. Beaches, mountains, agricultural estates, wildlife sanctuaries, and religious pilgrimage places, among others, have played a key role in putting rural India on the hospitality map. This trend has the potential to change the face of rural India.

4.2.1.2.2   Based on Theme

Beach resorts, diving resorts, river resorts, mountain resorts, ski resorts, family resorts, golf resorts, etc., the list of hotel themes in the hospitality industry in India is ever more diversified. Themes such as cultural tourism, religious tourism, ecotourism, medical tourism, adventure tourism, beach holidays, and wellness vacations offer prospective customers many more value propositions. Whether guests visit diving resorts from Goa in the west, to the Andaman Islands in the far east, riverside camps catering especially to canoeing and kayaking, mountain, and jungle lodges focusing on trekking enthusiasts, ski resorts in the Himalayas for fans of snow sports, or royal tents during camel, horse, and elephant safaris, all these options tremendously widen the experiences the Indian hospitality industry is able to offer. Other emerging forms of accommodation in India take a rather unique theme. For example, recently the first futuristic themed hotels emerged in India. A prominent example here is the brand new Chrome Hotel in Kolkata, with its experimental architecture and high-tech facilities.

4.2.1.2.3   Authenticity

Based on the belief that it depends heavily on the type of accommodation how guests will experience local culture, a rising amount of hospitality service providers focus on the cultural content, for example, accommodations that mirror the authentic architecture, flair, and lifestyle of the respective destinations. New hospitality ventures such as New Delhi-based "Travel Must" go a step further and take tourists to fascinating places that are not always easy to navigate on their own, trying to strike a balance between cultural immersion, vivid history, sheer natural beauty, and enjoyment. They offer exposure to the local culture and heritage by offering deep insights into the local culture such as local trades, customs, art, architecture, religion, food, and music. These kind of authentic cultural experiences are tailored according to the demands and needs of the clients and can be as diverse as a tribal village stay in the jungle-clad mountains of Alwar; or an urban homestay run by a university professor and her scientist husband.

"Travel Must" has emerged as an example of a trusted intermediary between local communities and the interested consumer, it ensures that a meaningful exchange results between guests and hosts. Guests are welcomed into private homes, attend fascinating ceremonies, and gain invaluable insights into ancient, complex cultures often unknown and inaccessible to outsiders. Intricate local networks coupled with unique cultural setting guarantee that guests learn about and participate in the rich traditions that make India such a vibrant destination.

4.2.1.2.4 *Ecotourism*

Ecotourism can be defined as responsible travel to natural areas that conserves the environment and improves the well-being of native cultures, thereby contributing to the preservation of the diversity of our world's natural and cultural environment. According to the World Tourism Organization, ecotourism is the fastest growing market in the entire tourism industry. From the 1990s, the global ecotourism sector has experienced an annual growth rate of between 20% and 34%, thereby growing three times as fast as the tourism industry as a whole. Until 2014, the ecotourism industry is expected to grow up to a quarter of the world's total travel market (Pandey, 2009).

India had initially been a laggard regarding ecological hospitality models rather following the old trodden path of mass tourism. However, the ugly face of mass tourism in India was soon visible and eco-sensitive tourism emerged as a popular concept in the hospitality industry, striking a balance between business interests and sustainability. Given the massive potential, Indian hoteliers have jumped on the bandwagon and are gradually harnessing the potential of some of the most outstanding ecosystems in the world, such as in the Himalayas and the Western Ghats.

An excellent example here is Kerala, a state on the tropical Malabar Coast of southwestern India that is nicknamed as "God's own country." It is famous especially for its houseboats traveling the extensive backwaters, Ayurveda retreats, jungle lodges in the Western Ghats, pristine beach resorts, eco-lodges, and other Ecotourism initiatives. Its unique culture and traditions, coupled with its varied geography, has made it one of the success stories in India. An increasing number of tour operators in India make it a point to minimize the negative environmental impacts caused by their customers and make positive contributions to the conservation of biodiversity. So, when their customers chance upon a Red Panda in the Himalayas or witness the hatching of sea turtles on the Bay of Bengal, they have improved the chances of preserving their habitat by providing a realistic economic alternative to exploiting local natural resources.

The environment is becoming more and more of a priority in the Indian hospitality industry. Statutory compliances are already in place regarding sewage, energy, products, and water usage. Upcoming properties often have programs to save water and energy and reduce solid waste in place. Besides the obvious cost advantages of energy conservation and product recycling, the potential to market Ecotels is massive.

To be certified as an Ecotel, a hotel must adhere to at least two of the following five factors:

- energy efficiency,
- water conservation,
- employee education and community involvement,
- solid waste management, and
- environmental commitment.

Rainwater harvesting, tree plantation drives, and converting wet waste to energy through biogas plants are some of the many strategies Indian hoteliers go with nowadays in the above context. Ecologically sensitive hotels can also be found in the high end luxury market, such as the 5-star-rated Orchid Hotel in Mumbai, which is Asia's first certified eco-friendly 5-star hotel and the world's only Ecotel to be certified as ISO 14001 (Environmental Management Standard).

4.2.1.2.5 *Agricultural Tourism*

Agricultural tourism is widely acknowledged as an instrument for economic development and employment generation, particularly in the remote and backward areas. It creates opportunities to generate additional revenue, makes a case for economic diversity, and improves the understanding about farmers in society. The Indian government collaborates with the United Nations Development Program to promote rural tourism and has also sanctioned more than 100 rural tourism infrastructure projects to spread tourism and socioeconomic benefits to identified rural sites. Guests in India can stay on farms ranging from stud farms, dairy farms up to full-fledged agricultural farms. They are perfect for urbanites looking to unwind and get back to nature, but with a bit of comfort and the chance to freely choose the activities in what the guests want to engage in, whether they want to milk the cows, wash the buffalos, learn to grind wheat, pick vegetables, or go fishing. Besides, guests experience the natural, cultural, and heritage aspects of the region, such as the local geography, cuisine, and handicrafts.

4.2.1.2.6   Unconventional Accommodations

Today's travelers are enthusiastic about traveling in different ways to widen their experiences. This is also reflected in their choice of unconventional accommodation options. In India, religious centers, ashrams, and monasteries are among the popular alternatives to the usual choices of accommodation. Given that the cleanliness and hygiene aspects of these accommodations are improved, due to their unique cultural content, this segment offers a huge potential. Organizations such as the Krishnamurti Foundation, Bharat Sevashram Sangha, Ramakrishna Mission, ISKCON, and Aurobindo Ashram are among the popular religious institutions that offer accommodation options across India.

4.2.1.2.7   Spas/Wellness

Even before the Beatles went on their famous pilgrimage to Rishikesh with Maharishi Mahesh Yogi in 1969, India has been a popular travel destination for American tourists seeking serenity and spiritual growth. But in recent years, wellness travel to India has exploded. Mia Farrow, Steve Jobs, and Oprah are just a few of the many Westerners who have flocked to India for life-changing trips to visit meditation retreats and spiritual sites. Now, the southeast-Asian countries are the fastest growing wellness travel destinations, with a projected 22% annual growth rate. In comparison, the United

States, the leading country for wellness travel, has an average annual growth rate of 5.8%.

Wellness travel or any tourism associated with the goal of maintaining or enhancing one's personal well-being is now a $439 billion industry world-wide within the $3.2 trillion global tourism industry, representing 14% of all tourism spending. It's estimated to have a trillion dollars worth of economic impact.

"As more people embrace overall healthier lifestyles at home, we are now seeing those behaviors translate and be integrated into their travel and vaca-tion habits," Susie Ellis, Chairman and CEO of the Global Spa and Wellness Summit, said in a statement. "For others, vacation provides an escape from the non-stop activities of their daily lives. As these two trends converge, we are seeing many people commit their vacation time and dollars to wellness travel, as evidenced by their increased spending and specific global destina-tion choices." Spa experiences, healthy eating, opportunities for personal growth, yoga and meditation, fitness, stress reduction, and holistic health are among the experiences sought by wellness travelers, according to the 2013 Global Wellness Tourism Economy Report.

Ellis explains that the recent mindfulness boom may be playing a part in attracting more visitors to India.

"India's wellness offerings are very understandable, they have yoga, meditation and Ayurveda," Ellis tells the Huffington Post. "Right now, those are things that are really resonating with people … the kind of things that people want and need are the things that India is offering."

Since the 2002, "Incredible India" tourism ad campaign, travel to the country, has been on a fairly steady rise. The campaign sought to bring higher quality and quantity tourists to India, the country had long been attracting hikers and travelers staying at low-cost ashrams, but the tourism board knew that if they attracted wealthier tourists, the rest would follow.

Visitors going to India for wellness-based trips will often spend a fair amount of time visiting there, learning about the ancient arts of yoga and meditation, as well as Ayurveda (the Indian "science of life," a system of traditional medicine) on an extended week or two long trip, according to Ellis. "To go to India and detox and spend a week and really feel what it's like to be in a state of mindfulness, that's life-changing," says Ellis. "And it would attract the people who have the time and resources to do that."

Several upscale destination spas in India that have become popular among such travelers are Ananda in the Himalayas (a palace that was formerly home to the Maharajah of Tehri Garhwal) and the Soukya Holistic Health Center in Bangalore, says Ellis.

A growing number of wellness retreats and spas are cropping up across India, from Dharamsala to Mysore, to accommodate the growing demand for holistic health-based travel. Lonely Planet event ranked Sikkim, India as one of the top 10 travel destinations for 2014.

Along with India, China, South Korea, Russia, and Germany are some of the other top wellness tourism destinations. Still, the United States remains the top destination for wellness travel, with $167.1 billion in expenditures and a total of 141.4 million wellness trips taken annually followed by Germany at 49.3 million.

4.2.1.2.8 Medical Tourism

With the introduction of a new category of visa, the "Medical Visa," the Indian government seeks to promote medical tourism in India. Afghans, Arabs, Southeast Asians, and Westerners arrive in droves in India for access to cheap, yet quality medical, services. Hospitals like the Apollo Group maintain information center's abroad and team up with tour companies to attract medical tourists to India. While patients recuperate in hospital, their relatives enjoy the tourist sights and go shopping. The ITC Group even opened a hotel, sharing its premises with a hospital in Thane near Mumbai in order to service medical tourists.

The expertise of Indian doctors in modern medicine from heart surgery to cataract removal has put India on the world health-care map. This cutting edge medical expertise coupled with affordable prices makes this value proposition hard to resist, and consequently there is an increased flow of people to India for medical services. India received 1.1 million medical tourists in 2009, registering a growth of 17% (India Brand Equity Foundation, 2010). The market for medical tourism in India is estimated at half a billion USD and is expected to grow to USD 3.29 billion by 2018 (Kumar et al., 2009).

4.2.1.2.9 Technology and Emergence of e-Services

The Indian hospitality industry has changed tremendously in recent years. Technological innovations might very well be the biggest driver behind this change. Speeding up decision-making, facilitating guest reservations, widening information access, improving payment options, and managing outsourcing processes, technological innovations have led to ever higher efficiency levels. Technology adoption by new hotels is increasingly giving them a cutting edge over their competition. Rooms become multi-functionary and can be used flexibly, as an entertainment center or as an office. Existing hotels face the choice of huge modernization costs or being left behind.

The advent of the internet has opened up many avenues for the hotel industry, most importantly the ability to conduct client bookings. It is reported that by now, 25% of all reservations are made online in India, thus making it a key tool in room occupancy fulfillment. The internet also has revolutionized the marketing of hospitality services, which is especially evident in the increased marketing potential of niche products, such as NGOs offering accommodation in tribal villages or spiritual retreats deep inside the Himalayas.

With the advent of third-party travel websites like Hotels.com and Expedia.com as well as the many home grown platforms such as Make-mytrip.com and Yatra.com, information flows between hospitality service providers and their potential clients have improved massively. These distribution channels have quickly gained importance given the pace at which they have grown over the last few years. Independent hospitality review and opinion websites like TripAdvisor have also become immensely popular, offering users the opportunity to see photos and read actual guest comments, etc., while the hotels themselves are able to showcase their products and services to a wider audience. Engaging customers in a two-way communication via social networking websites such as Facebook allows the hospitality industry to quickly react to customer needs and wants.

4.3 DEVELOPMENT OF THE FAST-FOOD INDUSTRY IN INDIA

The Indian fast-food habits and the customer perception toward fast food has noticed a gradual shift in the recent years, as the significant portion of the population is spending more money on eating fast food from the domestic and international retailers in the market. The sector was once unnoticed and had diluted existence in the food and hospitality industry; but recent findings suggested that there is huge potential in the sector as the growth rate was recorded above 30% in the recent years. The liberalization and globalization of industries backed by the Government in 1991 was also one of the reasons for the development of the fast food industry, as a number of international retailers entered the market thereafter. The major international players including Kentucky Fried Chicken, McDonalds, Pizza Hut, and Dominos entered the Indian market in the last decade. In the presence of overseas companies in the market, the domestic players too changed their business strategies in terms of offering new menus at revised prices and many other services including entertainment, change in store formats, opening of stores at a number of locations, and providing food and services with the influence of the western culture.

4.4   FOREIGN VERSUS DOMESTIC TOURISTS

Earlier foreign tourist arrivals to India were highly lopsided, with a few countries such as the United States and the United Kingdom accounting for the bulk of arrivals in India. In recent years, foreign tourist arrival figures have been diversifying. More and more people from Afghanistan, Bangladesh, Sri Lanka, and Nepal visit India now, as visitors from Southeast Asian countries, South America, and Africa also prefer it as an exotic travel destination.

The guests of the future will become increasingly unpredictable. Social status and wealth will no longer be good predictors of the needs and objectives of the guests. That is why flexibility is becoming the key advantage in a highly volatile hospitality industry. In addition, technology will play an increasingly important role in the hospitality equation. Web-savvy India is in a good position to engage its international competition with search engine optimization, web advertising, and e-marketing. Many innovative concepts developed in the Indian market can also be easily adapted by other nations such as Nepal, Pakistan, China, and Brazil. One interesting innovation export might very well turn out to be the quality budget hotels that are mushrooming in India.

4.5   THE WORLD ONLINE

There are currently more than 1.5 billion people around the globe with access to the internet. With this number forecast to increase by around 50% by 2015, operators need to embrace the world online and ensure that they deliver their brand through multiple (and ever-changing) channels. The social media frenzy has taken the world by storm over the last few years. By 2015, this will become truly integrated within the travel and hospitality decision-making process, representing both threats and opportunities for the industry. The transparency of social media can highlight any inconsistencies between the brand pledge and its execution across geographic boundaries. Websites such as TripAdvisor are often the new customer's first point of call. While this represents a real challenge for brand owners, it also offers unparalleled opportunities for consumer feedback and opens new channels of communication between the brand and its customers.

Rapid urbanization and lifestyle changes have increased time-starved consumers exponentially and the segment that values convenience has grown. Buying behavior of the BoP (bottom of the pyramid) consumers who have an average household income below Rs. 100,000 a year has also changed, thanks to impact of government schemes. The segment, however, still remains largely untapped, and local influencers seem to determine the purchasing habits when it comes to the BoP segment in smaller cities in India.

The report also reveals that the youth constitutes a considerable proportion of the online users, and growth in online retail has been driven by increased value consciousness, small city aspirations, and growing importance of convenience. Retailers are focusing on satisfaction on key service parameters and loyalty, which can be driven by strengthening front end operations.

Urban markets, which refers to locations apart from top tier cities that are vastly untapped, are home to the majority of the Indian market and consist of a large number of heterogonous subgroups that remain largely underserved and are characterized by increased brand consciousness. The urban segment has consumers adopting newer channels of purchase to overcome inherent purchase barriers. Online players have also stepped in to fill the demand–supply gap created by the lack of physical stores in these cities. Amid growing brand consciousness, companies may also need to cater to strong local tastes of urban consumers, which may involve tweaking the product, marketing, and supply chain as well.

4.6 CONCLUSION

Innovation and diversification hold the key to survival in the hospitality industry in the long run. Fierce competition has led to innovative ideas being implemented by hotel majors in India, thereby delivering impressive hospitality products and services. Exotic spas, gorgeous golf courses, multicuisine fine dining, spacious conference, and convention facilities are all among the growing list of facilities found in leading hotels across India. Hotels are also adapting to innovate with operating models by bringing in external brands of restaurants, spas, and lounges on lease or management contracts, to capitalize on proven concepts that generate substantial revenue by attracting hotel guests and local residents. Cafes and bars which have high profit margins are increasing their presence in hotels and are quickly developing into core profit centers. A prominent example is Café Coffee Day found at Ginger Hotels.

Taking the example of India's most famous spa, Ananda Spa, one can feel the extent of diversification in the industry. Renovating the erstwhile palace of a local Maharaja in the Himalayas, Ananda Spa has created a spa resort that heavily draws on India's spirituality. Inviting "resident masters," such as those who teach Yoga and heal using Ayurveda, and combining and packaging spiritual wares with pure luxury, offers a promising revenue model.

By now, however, any new trend that emerges in any part of the world rapidly spreads to India, such as the latest fads of ice bars and ethnic lounges. With well-traveled upwardly mobile consumers, new and trendy food concepts find an increasing following in India. The resulting manifold opportunities entice famed international chefs to move to India. At the same time, foreign tourists increasingly dare to sample the diversity of local food. Even many domestic guests seek opportunities to dine on quality local delicacies, drink traditional beverages, and learn something of the culinary traditions of the locale.

4.7 RECOMMENDATIONS THAT WILL HELP HOSPITALITY INDUSTRY RESPOND TO CHANGING TRENDS

The next 5 years will herald the era of a consumer-led brand focus for the hospitality industry. Consumers are changing faster than ever before in both attitude and behaviors. Hospitality groups should review their global expansion plans and consider:

1. *The World Online*

   There is no doubt that the hotel's overall competitiveness today is determined by how well it manages its internet market.
   —Max Starkov, President and Chief Executive Officer,
   e-Business Strategist

   The future of the gaming experience will be dependent on social networking and social media channels. The consumer or video game player will crave increased communications with interactive gaming technology; that simulates reality and delivers more choices and preferences.
   —Gavin Isaacs, Executive Vice President and
   Chief Operating Officer, Bally Technologies

As social media websites expand and access to the internet and online distribution channels becomes more accessible, a new breed of confident, empowered and savvy travelers is emerging. Gone are the days when everyone walks into a high-street travel agent and flicks through brochures to book their flights and hotel as a package in one transaction. Savvy consumers are now "unbundling" the whole booking experience, self-booking directly with suppliers or through new channels such as network carrier websites. In recent years, online consumers have also become increasingly value conscious, with the internet providing unlimited scope for price comparison and greater transparency of guest experience on a global scale. The use of technology is also changing and this needs to be addressed throughout the consumer's journey. Mobile technology will increasingly be at the heart of the consumer–brand interaction and offers a plethora of opportunities for customization, communication, promotion, and loyalty. However, the overall spend on technology in the sector still lags behind other sectors.

2. Consumers are increasingly environmentally aware which will pose further challenges for the industry. By 2015, regulatory, economic and stakeholder pressures are likely to create a virtuous circle that will begin to shape new expectations amongst both leisure and business consumers. Few will be prepared to pay a premium for green hotels but value plus value is likely to become a growing consumer mantra. Develop an environmentally responsible brand and embed a 360 degree view of sustainability within the business model. Price, quality, brand, and convenience will continue to drive consumer spending but sustainability be part of the decision-making process.

IHG views sustainability as a business issue and it is core to the company's five year strategic plan.
—David Jerome, Senior Vice President,
Social Corporate Responsibility, InterContinental Hotels Group

It is the domestic traveler who is the key driver of sustainable hospitality growth in many of the largest hospitality markets.
—Baumgarten, President and CEO,
World Travel Council, 2015.

Committing greater resources to the Indian markets. The steady increase in demand from Western travelers is supporting the hospitality industry in emerging markets; however, it is not the key driver. By focusing their strategies on the business and international leisure travelers, hospitality groups are ignoring the largest market segment the domestic traveler. Chinese and Indian domestic traveler numbers far exceed their international arrivals. India has over 563 million domestic travelers, compared to inbound arrivals of five million; in China, there are 1.9 billion domestic travelers compared to inbound arrivals of 52 million. These domestic travelers are the most important factor in the expansion of the emerging hospitality markets. The increase in their numbers and spending power is being driven by the strength of the underlying economic development and prosperity in China and in India. One effect of this is a rise in business travel, whilst the US business travel market is expected to stagnate over the next 5 years, growing at 0.3% per year, China's business travel spending will grow 6.5% annually to 2013. More importantly, economic development coupled with a rapidly growing population results in the proliferation of the "middle classes." In China, rising disposable income amongst the local populace has led to a greater appetite for travel, with the greatest impact being felt in domestic and inter-regional tourism markets. India is going to be no different.

New property development by 2015 will increasingly be impacted by regulations and codes requiring buildings to be built more sustainably. It is already happening in Europe.
—Taylor, F., Corporate Vice President,
Sustainability and Innovation, Wyndham Worldwide.

3. Understand different generational needs and values. The boomers are a key segment and should be targeted with "experiential" life-enhancing products, designed to appeal to their "forever young" attitudes.
4. Consider "lifestyle" brand opportunities. If done well, this segment can deliver a strong return on investment. However, the challenge is to keep lifestyle brands current and relevant.
5. Embrace rather than resist the influence of social media. Engage consumers in a dialogue that builds awareness and community increases web traffic and search rankings and draws in potential new guests.
6. Develop a multichannel approach with increasing use of mobile smart phone technology. Developing this capacity will enable hoteliers to create a greater degree of loyalty, by ensuring their services fit the quick response needs of today's "on-the-move" consumer.
7. Invest in talent management. Engage employees with the brand and deliver consistent standards of customer service across global portfolios. Develop innovative talent programs and redesign operating models to effectively execute the talent strategy.

8. Develop and invest in research and development (R&D). The industry needs to adopt more of an R&D focus to have a chance of staying ahead of their consumer's needs and desires.

9. Understanding the boomer mindset. Despite the growth of travel and hospitality companies specifically targeted at the boomer generation, the market is far from flooded and the scale of opportunity is large. The key to unlocking the boomer generation is understanding and appealing to its "forever young" attitude. Boomers are reluctant to consider themselves as senior citizens and are adopting travel habits previously associated with younger generations. Experiential travel is an important dimension. Retired boomers have more time to explore their interests and passions. "Voluntourism," hobby-based or educational travel such as painting holidays or archaeological digs will appeal to this demographic. Boomers are also more experienced, confident travelers than the older generations of the past and will be searching for "off the beaten track," authentic and adventurous travel experiences that countries like India offer.

10. The global population is evolving and the pockets of disposable income available for travel are shifting. Affluent baby boomers in the Western world are moving into retirement, living longer, and are hungry for travel experiences. The middle classes in emerging markets are expanding and most of the new entrants will come from China and India. Despite disposable income lagging behind the current developed world, international tourism from these two source markets will accelerate over the next few years. Products and services should be targeted to the attitude of "agelessness" and interest in experiential travel shown by the boomers, appealing to their sense of adventure, independent spirit, and desire to explore off the beaten tourist track.

KEYWORDS

- **consumer behavior**
- **hospitality trends**
- **Indian consumer**
- **India story**
- **homestays**

REFERENCES

Benson, J. *The Rise of Consumer Society in Britain*. Heinemann: London, 1994.

Gabriel, Y.; Lang, T. *The Unmanageable Consumer*. Sage: London, 1995.

Goodman, E. Zapping Xmas. *Washington Post*, 20 December 1997, p 14.

India Brand Equity Foundation. *Tourism & Hospitality*. India Brand Equity Foundation: Gurgaon, 2010. Retrieved from http://www.ibef.org/artdispview.aspx?in=74&art_id=26026&cat_id=120&page=3.

Kumar, L.; Singh, T.; Saigal, N.; Cebula, B. Dissecting the Indian Hospitality Industry. In: *Perspective Volume 1*. Technopak: Gurgaon, 2009.

Laudon, K. C.; Traver, G. C. *E-commerce*. Pearson-Prentice Hall: New Jersey, 2007.

Miles, S. *Consumerism as a Way of life*. Sage: London, 1998.

Pandey, T. *Agri-tourism—Elixir for Rural India*. Yes Bank and ASSOCHAM: New Delhi, 2009. Retrieved from http://www.assocham.org/events/recent/event_418/Tushar_Pandey.pdf.

Ritzer, G. *Enchanting a Disenchanted World*. Sage: London, 1999.

Schneider, G. P. *Electronic Commerce*. Cengage Learning: Course Technology: Singapore, 2009.

World Travel and Tourism Council. *WTTC Tourism Economic Research 2009—India*. World Travel and Tourism Council: London, 2009. Retrieved from https://www.wttc.org/-/media/files/reports/economic%20impact%20research/countries%202015/india2015.pdf.

CHAPTER 5

COMPETING FOR PROFITABILITY: THE ROLE OF REVENUE MANAGEMENT AS A STRATEGIC CHOICE FOR INDIAN HOTELS

ANJANA SINGH*

School of Hospitality and Tourism, Vedatya Institute, Gurgaon, India

*E-mail: anjana.singh@vedatya.ac.in

CONTENTS

Abstract 86

5.1   Introduction 86

5.2   Challenges 89

5.4   Findings 92

5.5   Discussion and Conclusion 101

Keywords 103

References 103

ABSTRACT

In today's competitive business eco-system, the management of 5-star hotels requires a culture of flexibility and innovation, in working with a new set of conventions and strategies to achieve a competitive edge and enhanced profits. Hotels represent significant investment for both investors and the national economy and need long-term strategic planning and effective management to be successful. Improved customer service, better quality, operational effectiveness, sustained bottom line profitability, and ability to engage with customers are most important to survive in an extremely competitive market place. Revenue management has been one of the key contributors toward business profitability, and its wide adoption by most service organizations, especially hotels, is evidence of its success and strong future as a strategic tool. There has been little research in the Indian context to examine the adoption of revenue management practices in India, due to issues around its acceptance by customers. The purpose of this research was to explore the existing revenue management practices, emerging opportunities, and the challenges in the luxury segment from the hotel operator's perspective. A qualitative approach was adopted for the investigation through personal in-depth interviews with revenue managers and general managers (in absence of revenue manager) of 5-star luxury hotels. This study aimed to explore the revenue management practices and the challenges faced by Indian revenue managers of 5-star luxury hotel categories. This research is helpful in identifying the level of achievement of 5-star luxury hotels in applying revenue management practices and also throws light on the knowledge and awareness level of revenue managers. This study also uncovered the challenges faced by Indian hospitality managers while implementing revenue management in 5-star hotels of India. The practical implication of this study was to suggest strategies that Indian hotel managers can adopt to overcome challenges and help current revenue management practice to evolve into "responsible revenue management."

5.1 INTRODUCTION

The oldest sport is competition and the relevant field here is the global business environment, with many national and international players offering their services. Those who recognize this fact and learn the sport will survive and others will fail. Competition communicates and impacts the effectiveness of the organization in the market, in comparisons to other organizations offering similar products and services. Operations and marketing are the two predominant factors that are directly related to addressing competitiveness. Operation usually represents baseline strategies that are particularly important for effectiveness and productivity.

Dev (1989) states that strategies are the blueprints of the decisions made on how to conduct and compete for the product or service in the market. It may be the most misunderstood concept but yet has to be understood at all levels of the organization. The strategic management process helps individual businesses to focus their everyday actions on the core objectives and achieve performance. See et al. (2003) in a study found that the most important leadership competency is strategic positioning for future leaders and then industry knowledge. Revenue management has been a great source of profitability for the hospitality sector. There are many researches that highlight the positive effects of applying revenue management strategies to achieve an organization's profitability goals. It has been proved that when compared to any other information management systems, revenue management systems and strategies can increase your return on investment by 200% (Cross, 1998). Smith et al. (1992) quoted in their article that Robert Crandall, the head of American Airlines estimated that yield management techniques have contributed marginal revenue of $1.4 billion in last 3 years. The discipline of revenue management started with the airline industry and was adopted by hotels in the late 1980s. Marriott and Cross (2000) mentioned that "The Marriott International" was a pioneer in adapting revenue management in hotels. They had managed to increase their incremental revenue by $150–200 million. Chiang et al. (2007) defined revenue management as "an integrated, continuous and organized approach to maximize room revenue, through the manipulation of room rates in response to forecasted patterns of demand." Kimes and Wirtz (2003) stated that revenue management is effective only, with certain characteristics, which are the fixed capacity, segmented market according to similar characteristics, perishable inventory, fluctuating demand, high fixed cost, and advance bookings. Schwartz (1998) argued in his research that only one condition is required, and that is perishable inventory, and rest of the characteristics may be or may not be present. To add further, Kimes (2003) suggested that the elementary elements like ability to segment the markets according to consumer behavior and its spending capacity, detailed information on historical demand and booking patterns, well-defined policies on pricing and overbooking, and robust information system to implement revenue management strategies effectively increase revenues not only from rooms but the overall hotel revenue earnings. As against airlines, hotels look for ancillary revenues from other revenue center departments as well, like restaurants, function space, and spas. Accurate forecasting and controlling inventory for those guests who gives you overall holistic maximum revenue, rather than accepting reservation that is paying a higher price only for one night, can add significant profits to hotels.

Due to frequent changes in the global economy, the position of revenue management has changed from short-term tactics to a long-term strategy. Kimes (2009) stated that strategy should help in not just managing demand but creating demand for the hotel as well. It includes the overall management of all revenue streams and selling strategies. Kimes (2010) in her recent study confirmed that most of the hotel managers believe that in future, revenue management will cover all revenue streams in the hotel and will get integrated into marketing, operations, and the finance functions of the hotel itself. Information technology has been playing a vital role in execution of strategies. Connolly and Olsen (2000) concluded in their research that integration of IT with strategy is the way forward. It plays an incredible role in the areas of productivity and revenue enhancement and helps in gaining competitive advantage. Technology would simplify complex strategic decisions and would help in making better effective long-term profit decisions for the entire hotel. Apart from technology, the role of social media has opened opportunities to directly interact with customers. The swift acceptance of social media worldwide gives effective information and a platform to implement strategic revenue management strategies, which eventually will help hotels to be more customers centric and expand their brand presence. Noone et al. (2011) confirmed that this medium can help in pushing pricing and promotions, with the long-term objective of identifying customer behavior and new target markets.

Kimes (2008) has mentioned in her study that the move from the tactical to a strategic approach has extended the role of revenue management in other parts of the hotel, like function space, restaurants, and spas. Next to the rooms division, for hotel substantial revenue comes from food and beverage services. It seems to be very important that with equal attention, the revenue management strategies should also encompass these revenue centers as well. This holistic approach focuses on total hotel revenues rather than only room revenues.

Since the role of revenue management is becoming more strategic and dealing with multiple revenue centers, it becomes important to have adequate performance measurement yardsticks. According to Kimes (2010), the gross operating profit per available room would be the preferred metric in the future, with total revenue per available room (RevPar) and total revenue per available per square foot being measured rather than only RevPar. Hence, operational performance statistics is not enough to indicate profitability. With the growing strategic role of revenue management, performance measures need to be strategic and relevant to hotels they are measured for.

5.2 CHALLENGES

5.2.1 RISE AND THE DOMINANCE OF OTA

Internet has played a significant role in developing the distribution channels of hotels. The growth in network connectivity and internet paved way for online third-party distribution channels. Online booking channels (third party and brand websites) account for nearly 50% of the leisure traveler bookings. A large number of hotels use a plethora of distribution channels simultaneously, to achieve visibility with a greater audience. O'Connor (2003) confirmed that hotels have grown more aware of the advantages of direct online distribution through their own websites. Online travel bookings continue to gain popularity, growth, and booking volume. Freed (2013) mentioned in his article that International Hotels Group (IHG) shed some light in their 2012 annual report, on the growing dependence on online travel agents (OTAs) for business. There is no denying the huge role played by and the share of business harnessed by OTAs in getting reservations. The emergence of OTAs has made it imperative for revenue management practices to be adjusted and changed to adapt to the emerging environment. This has pushed revenue managers to have online business strategies, as a big part of their plans. OTAs dominate organic search engine results and generic keywords like hotels. Mahmoud (2015) quoted that the OTA bookings realized 15% increase from Year 2014, whereas hotel direct bookings have been decreased by 8%. Priceline and Expedia are the dominant players in the OTA field. Each hotelier should understand the relevance of each channel, examining the cost and benefit analysis to build sustainable profits with positive relationships.

5.2.2 QUALIFIED REVENUE MANAGEMENT PROFESSIONALS

Kimes (2008) identified 2 most challenging concerns out of 12 that arose, from the survey done in the study on dearth of competent revenue managers and changes in the global economy. The responsibility and competency requirements of a revenue manager have grown many folds with the growth of revenue management. Though they started with the responsibilities of the reservations department, it has become more strategic and technology driven, now including all revenue centers including rooms in the hotel. Hence, the qualification required is beyond the experience of reservation, analytical and strong communication skills becoming essential competencies for the current revenue management function. Kimes (2010), Cross et al. (2009), and Kimes (2008) in their study highlighted the four main human resource issues which impacted business. They were finding the right people, training them, retaining them, and charting out a clear future career path.

Till now the focus has been more with respect to technology, rather than concentrating on revenue management professionals. There is a need to build a proper job description for our revenue managers and train them accordingly. Otherwise, we will continue facing the challenge of finding the right revenue management professional. Wang et al. (2015) has emphasized holistic training and knowledge, being the critical factors for the strategic implementation of revenue management.

5.2.3 CHANGES IN THE GLOBAL ECONOMY

Jain and Bowman (2004) mentioned that revenue management techniques were quite successful in the 1990s and gave huge profit gains from 2% to 5% and became an integral part of strategic decision-making in hotels. The headway of revenue management practice was altered by many events, like terrorist attacks and a global weak economy. In these years, the hotels world-wide had faced major issues in terms of implementing revenue management systems. This outcome resulted due to short sightedness of managers and impulsive decisions in reaction to a weak economy, without thinking about long-term effects on its survival and growth. Butscher et al. (2009) confirmed that due to a weak global economy, monetary crisis, and falling consumer confidence in the economy, the hospitality industry has faced a steep slow down. Hence, there was an evident decline in the occupancy and revenues of all major hotel market segments catering to the likes of airline crew, corporate, and leisure. Indian hotels too faced the economic downturn due to the Mumbai terrorist attacks and swine flu. These emergencies significantly affected the inbound foreign travelers. Hotel faced a sudden fall in occupancy and revenues. But the situation has started improving especially with the growth in medical tourism as an emerging consumer segment. According to the Tourism and Hospitality report 2016, IBEF reported that the tourism and hospitality sector's direct contribution to GDP (gross domestic product) was US\$ 44.2 billion in 2015 with the number of foreign tourist arrivals having grown steadily in the last 3 years, reaching around 7.103 million during January–November 2015, recording a 4.5% growth. This discussion indicates that managers and decision makers must apply revenue management techniques strategically, even in the weak economy so as to ensure revenue optimization and higher customer satisfaction.

Published literature and studies cited earlier were largely focused on luxury hotels of the United Kingdom, United States, and Europe, and there is little research discussing the revenue management practices in India and its unique challenges. Due to the strong importance of revenue management strategies in literature and the existing practice in industry, it becomes important to study the degree of implementation in Indian luxury hotels and probe the future of revenue management from a practitioner's perspective. This research also attempts to understand the challenges faced by the Indian luxury hotels in implementing revenue management and makes recommendations that will help improve the effectiveness of such strategies applied in the hotel sector in India in general.

5.2.3.1 METHODOLOGY

Kimes and Wirtz (2003) confirmed in their study that Asian cultures and customers are less exposed to revenue management practices. Hence, they view these practices as unfair. Kimes (2008) in another study found that Asian revenue managers believe that the development of revenue management is quite slow, and technical aspects like overbooking, forecasting, etc. need improvement. The concerns and challenges were not highlighted and discussed in the study. Li (2011) has studied revenue management practices in China's overall hotel industry and confirmed that hotels in China need to manage their technical and managerial issues and should upgrade their revenue management techniques. Another study by Yousef (2007) which was based on the status of revenue management in the United Arab Emirates concluded that practice of revenue management in the country is quite high and suggested increased efforts in the area of acceptance and exposure of yield management in the UAE as whole. Taking further from here and without any evidence of in-depth research of revenue management practices in India, this research aims to understand and explore the current revenue management practices, emerging prospects and the challenges in the luxury segment from the Indian hotel operator's perspective. The study hence is exploratory and qualitative in nature. To conduct this research, in-depth semi-structured interviews have been used, based on a thorough review of literature regarding decisions with respect to revenue management strategies, the upcoming opportunities, and challenges. The general managers and revenue managers of international hotel chains in India were approached to identify and understand the revenue management practices. This study is also intended to understand the concerns and challenges of the top management, while implementing revenue management practices. This research also aims to highlight the emerging opportunities coming on the way from the hotel operator's perspective. The semi-structured interviews were divided into three phases. The first phase discussed the existing revenue management practices where questions were focused on understanding the current revenue management practices. The second phase stressed on the emerging opportunities and the future of revenue management. The final phase of the discussion was related to the challenges of revenue management with respect to the luxury segment. The analyzed data have been drawn from conversations with respective managers of luxury hotel properties, as they were the appropriate resources to discuss the strategies related to this research. The interviews were first recorded and then transcribed twice, to avoid any ambiguity of data analysis. Hotels from four prominent hotel chains, the Radisson (Carlson Rezidor), the Leela, the Lemon Tree, and the Oberoi (EIH), were approached and examined, regarding their technology policies. All four hotels have separate revenue managers at the unit level or at the central level, with general managers being responsible for the hotel's profitability. These four hotels have been designated as Hotel A, B, C, and D and their responses have been tabulated.

5.4 FINDINGS

5.4.1 *EXISTING REVENUE MANAGEMENT PRACTICES*

The practitioners were asked to identify the existing revenue management practices that they were using in their hotels, and most of the hotels agreed that they are implementing the following techniques: managing room inventory, length of stay restrictions, differential pricing according to source and segments, identifying customer value and demand control. Hotel A and D were not as positive about enforcing penalties and guarantees. Hotel A commented that "we generally impose the penalties in all case's but we also consider if there are any genuine cases of cancellation as described by the client, the top clients of our hotel sometimes do get the benefit of doubt

	A	B	C	D
Existing revenue management practices	Revenue management includes forecasting real-time customer demand at the micro-market level throughout our hotel and then optimizing the price and availability of the products on offer	Managing inventory, pricing strategy, demand supply analysis, managing Global Distribution System (GDS) and online buyers	Hot deals and promotional discounts such as early bird, last minute or applying rates close to arrival on high occupancy dates and close to departure on lower occupancy dates. Gender-specific pricing: such as Lemon Tree Diva (for single lady traveler with special inclusions in-room, complementary stay for child under 12 and airport pick up and drop included in the price). Opaque deals such as flight + hotel deals on online channels such as MakeMyTrip and train + hotel deals bundling and seasonal packaging	Managing room inventory, differential pricing according to segments, length of stay restrictions, demand control, and identifying customer value
Tactics in high and low demand	Revenue management is all about offering the best value proposition to the customers keeping in mind the revenue goals of the hotel	Implement different strategies	Closing and opening lower promotional rates, increasing and decreasing the base rate, changing the cancellation policies, restricting the arrival and departure patterns, applying length of stay restrictions to protect the shoulder periods	The focus has shifted to identifying and creating value for guests
Performance indicators	Implement revenue management through metrics like ARI (average rate index), MPI (market penetration index), RGI (revenue growth index), RPI (RevPar Index)	Along with pricing and inventory control revenue, manager's performance is monitored on the accuracy of forecasting and market intelligence. The revenue manager's performance is also measured on the involvement in GDS activities and the ranking within the competitive set of the hotel. Revenue Per Available Room (REPAR) and Revenue Market Share Index (RMSI) are popular performance metrics used	Targeted budgets and performance against last year, monitoring costs closely and competition pricing	ARR and RevPar

	A	B	C	D
Qualities of revenue managers	Responsible for inventory management, pricing and positioning of the hotel, market intelligence, yield, manage the hotel room revenue and revenue analysis and tracking Being very GDS savvy. This includes the use of daily reviews of online pricing, the study of hotel intelligence information, etc. and recommending carefully considered use of online banner advertisements and other SEO tactics	Relationship and communication skills, creative thinking, effective selling ability, property management experience, interest, and accuracy	Analytical, aware, and proactive in approach, strong market relationships with agents	Gut feeling and ability to predict future trends
Challenges in revenue management	The most challenging issues are shortage of qualified revenue managers, changes in the global economy, increased competition and pressure to reduce costs, and perhaps reduce standards of service from a variety of stakeholders	Yes indeed, it is very difficult to find a good revenue manager with the right skills	In the recent Cornell Exhibition (first time in India) held at Taj Mumbai discussed the same issue and it is true that the market is growing. However, the IHM curriculum in the hospitality schools across India is still focused on the operations and hence does not help in generating the best fit for the emerging revenue management space	None
Other comments	There is currently a proliferation of well-branded and well-managed 5-star and 5-star deluxe hotels in the area. The broad strategy has been	Accuracy of data and weak cyber laws	Expensive revenue management software, talented work force, strong learning and training processes in place to stay ahead with the new trends in the market	None

A	B	C	D
	to compete and position ourselves on the basis of gradually increasing standards of service and quality. There is also an understandable expectation that all businesses will produce more in the way of cash flow growth on a year on year basis. They have been able to grow cash flow with the help of effective and innovative revenue management and online pricing and communication techniques, but the curve is likely to level off somewhat in the future and balancing these expectations is expected to become an increasing challenge		
Emerging opportunities	Social Media sites like Facebook, Twitter, Trip advisor, YouTube, Amazon, etc. Total hotel revenue management: broadening the scope, revenue management involves the management of the entire	One of the current trends is space management for banquet spaces, restaurants, and spa	
		Indian hotels have changed from adopting revenue software to increasing visibility; reliance on online travel agents has drastically increased. As the consumer is becoming active in social media and net savvy, rate parity across all the online B2C channels has gained importance. Also, along with the traditional ways of B2B and B2C modes,	Improved forecasting models

	A	B	C	D
	revenue stream, rather than managing revenue from room inventory alone		a new trend of selling the last minute room on opaque deals has become very prominent and hotels have started selling rooms along with flights and railway bookings. On MakeMyTrip, the hotel is offering deal on room with flights and on Travelguru, the deals are clubbed with rail reservations through IRCTC. For the low demand season and to sell F&B deals, hoteliers are increasing making use of the one stop shop medium such as Snapdeals and mydala.com	Important role of revenue managers
Future of revenue management	As technology evolves, analytical pricing models and social networking and mobile technology are going to have a major impact on the future. Revenue management function is going to become more centralized and that the skills required for a successful revenue manager are going to be a combination of analytical and communication abilities. As a consequence, performance measurement will move to total revenue or gross operating profit rather than revenue per available room	The evolution of revenue management system has triggered the advent of some amazing data crunching software, which is user friendly and simpler to use. They see foresee revenue management to work in clusters rather than units	Emerging markets such as China and India have a huge growth potential. As more and more international chains are entering the market and segmenting the market into luxury, to upper upscale, upscale, mid segment and budget, the future of revenue management looks bright from the focus in the coming years moving from RevPar to REVPAG (revenue per available guest)	

keeping the long term business relation in mind." Hotel C puts it differently and says that "after realizing the daily waivers given to the early check out or the same day cancellations which lead to the loss of opportunity of revenue maximization, we enforce strict penalties on the last minute cancellations and no shows. Also the groups and MICS business has specified cut off periods." Hotel C further added that apart from these usual practices, they also have promotional discounts as early bird schemes, gender-specific pricing, opaque deals, bundling, etc. The revenue expert at the property also mentioned that it is important to do competition analysis to analyze the demand and supply in the market. This helps them in forecasting, price optimizing different mediums with deals and restrictions to maintain high yields.

All the hotels agreed on practice of group revenue management and differential pricing in case the group is going above the ceiling. Hotel C practiced group revenue management through revenue displacement, net yield of the group, competition pricing for groups, and MICS (meetings, incentives, conference, and seminar) segment contributing to almost 10% of the business. Hotel A and Hotel D are quite selective about practicing group revenue management and implement only in exceptional high demand, and sometimes shift itinerary reservations to other sister properties, that are facing lower demand as compared to other properties. Hotel A categorically comments that "Yes we do practice the group revenue management system but mostly limited to months like November, January and February when the demand is higher compared to the other months of the year. If the group is more than 25% of the inventory, the rates are taken higher and sometimes even higher than the best available rate."

Except Hotel B, other hotels do practice revenue management in banquets, spas, and restaurants, hence moving toward total revenue management.

5.4.2 REVENUE MANAGEMENT IN LOWER DEMAND AND A GLOBAL WEAKER ECONOMY

Hotel B says that "Revenue Management is all about offering the best value proposition to the customer, keeping in mind the revenue goals of the hotel." In times of a weak economy and lower demand, the hotels were quite affected as *consumer* spending was limited and travel across metro cities was reduced to the lowest levels. Therefore, the focus was shifted from being RevPar driven, to solely occupancy driven, though the revenue management process was still kept intact.

5.4.3   PERFORMANCE METRICS AND QUALITIES OF A REVENUE MANAGER

The key performance metrics highlighted by hotels were average daily rate, RevPAR, occupancy rate, revenue market share index, targeted budgets and performance against last year. Monitoring costs closely was also identified as a part of the analytical approach, toward reviewing performance.

All the hotels highlighted quite different things, when asked about measures taken to check the performance of revenue managers. Hotel B highlighted that along with pricing and inventory control, a revenue manager's performance is monitored on the accuracy of forecasting and market intelligence. The revenue manager's performance is also measured on the participation and involvement in GDS activities and the ranking within the competitive set of the hotel. Hotel B stressed on metrics like ARI (average rate index), MPI (market penetration index), RGI (revenue growth index), RPI (revenue per available room index). Hotel C had certain targets for their revenue managers and their performance was mapped accordingly. Revenue managers are also responsible and accountable for generating incremental revenue, from controlling prices and inventory. Hotel D measured the revenue manager's performance by comparing the hotel's performance as against key competitors in the city.

The important qualities that were recognized as critical for effective revenue managers were *relationship and communication skills, creative thinking, effective sales ability, property management experience, interest, and accuracy. Analytical skills, awareness of the competition's tactics, and a proactive approach, along with strong market relationships with agents too, were a part of the competency set.*

It was also clear that any individual in a revenue management role needs to be effective in *inventory management, pricing and positioning of the hotel, market intelligence, manage the hotel room revenue and revenue analysis and tracking, being very GDS savvy. This includes the use of daily reviews of online pricing, the study of hotel (competition) intelligence information, etc. and recommending carefully considered use of online banner advertisements and other SEO tactics.*

5.4.4   EMERGING OPPORTUNITIES IN REVENUE MANAGEMENT

Revenue management has evolved from yield management to inventory management to total hotel revenue management including all aspects like F&B, banquets and minor operating departments. Over the past few years, the face of revenue management in Indian hotels has changed, from adopting revenue software's to increasing online visibility, with the use of OTAs as distribution partners increasing drastically. As the consumer is increasingly active on social media and net savvy, rate parity across all the online B2C channels has gained importance. Also, along with the traditional ways of B2B and B2C modes, a new trend of selling the last minute room on opaque deals has become very prominent and hotels have started selling room along with flights and railways. The emerging opportunity lies in social media sites like Facebook, Twitter, Trip Advisor, YouTube, Amazon, etc. Hotel B also mentioned the emerging opportunities within total hotel revenue management. Stressing that broadening the scope of revenue management involves management of the entire revenue stream, rather than managing revenue from room inventory alone. Hence, one of the growing current trends is space management for banquet spaces, restaurants, and spas.

5.4.5 CHALLENGES WITH REVENUE MANAGEMENT

Hoteliers did agree that one has to be really careful in applying revenue management tactics, because customer loyalty will play a very important role in the future. The revenue manager definitely needs to be in regular communication with the entire sales team and must understand the short, medium, and long-term consequences of his or her pricing decisions on existing relationships, customer loyalty required to maximize overall revenue, and the resultant impact on medium and longer term profitability as well as cash flows. As Hotel C commented that revenue management decisions have impacts that must be viewed in a holistic manner, with strategic goals of the hotel in alignment. Therefore, in an ideal case scenario, revenue management has to be profit centric from the hotelier's perspective, but it also has to maintain the practice of the hospitality industry known for—friendly reception and offering travelers a home away from home. Therefore, one has to really careful in applying revenue management tactics, because customer loyalty again will play a very important role in the near future.

The most challenging issues that emerged are shortage of qualified managers, rapid changes in the global economy, increased competition, pressure to reduce costs, and perhaps reduce standards of service from variety of stakeholders, accuracy of data, weak cyber laws, expensive revenue software, talented workforce, strong learning, and training processes in place are all critical for any hotel to stay ahead and work with the new emergent trends in the market.

Hotel B categorically commented that currently, there is a proliferation of well-branded and well-managed 5-star and 5-star deluxe hotels in the metropolitan areas. Their broad strategy has been to compete and position themselves on the basis of gradually increasing standards of service and quality. There is also an understandable expectation that all businesses will produce more in the way of cash flow growth on a year on year basis. They have been able to grow cash flow with the help of effective and innovative revenue management, online pricing, and communication techniques; but the curve is likely to level off somewhat in the future and balancing these expectations is expected to become an increasing challenge.

IHG–Vedatya have started a collaborative program as an initiative to respond to the need and have taken a lead in terms of investing in talent development in revenue management as a strategic goal. A 1-year post graduate program in Revenue and Profit Management, is the most comprehensive program in India in this thematic space It is an exclusive industry focused program, which addresses the urgent need of highly skilled business professionals in areas of revenue management. To cope up with the new realities and changing forms of the hospitality and services industry, Vedatya's Revenue Management program focuses on developing future leaders who:

- believe in leading change rather than managing change
- are trained and developed as the best talent to meet the challenges of developing and managing revenue and profits in the services industry
- would be facilitators for awareness, understanding and implementation of revenue management strategies in hospitality and tourism Industry.

Source: Vedatya (2016)

Hotel C highlighted that in the recent Cornell Exhibition held first time in India at Taj Mumbai, business leaders discussed the same issue and it is true that though the market is growing; however, the IHM (hotel management institutes) curriculum in the hospitality schools across India is still focused on operations and hence does not help in generating the best talent for the emerging revenue management space.

Hotel A expressed a difference of opinion and stated that Revenue Management has already reached the peak of its importance and according to the product life cycle, it is going to be stagnant for some time. The evolution of the revenue management system has triggered the advent of some amazing data crunching software, which is much user friendly and simpler to use. They foresee revenue management to work in clusters rather than units.

5.5 DISCUSSION AND CONCLUSION

It is quite important and critical for hotel promoters or owners to understand and be aware of the opportunities inherent in a revenue management strategy. The concept is still evolving and the implementation impact looks bright with strong tourism trends and positive economic reforms. Implementing revenue management is also becoming more challenging with the intense competition, evolving consumer expectations, limitation in technology adoption, and generation of customized data. Therefore, it becomes critical to implement revenue management both at the operational and strategic level and devote lot of time and resources to build a strong organization wide revenue management culture. The revenue management process involves dynamic pricing, and the strategic deployment of pricing schedules with multiple sources of inventory distribution. Revenue management, marketing, sales, and operations are all functions that are truly dependent on each other, for delivering customer satisfaction and profitability growth. Strategy deals directly with customers and if not handled appropriately, it may lead to short-term revenue gains but has potential to dilute long-term profitability. Based on the above discussion, revenue management strategies should focus holistically on the following areas:

5.5.1 PRICING

Hotel pricing strategy is quite complex and lots of research has been done on effective pricing strategies to boost ARR and RevPar. The strategies at a basic level can meet three objectives: hotels wanting to achieve high ARR, hotels with the goal of filling inventory, and hotels with an objective of high RevPar. The sustainable pricing strategies for hotel profitability will be with high RevPar. Due to intelligent, well-informed customers, the pressure is on the revenue manager to effectively forecast demand, effectively implement pricing controls, and launch promotions at the right time to avoid any direct loss from competitors.

5.5.2 PROMOTION

Revenue managers do understand the advantages of working with sales professionals closely enough to manage the demand and expectations of customers. Revenue managers should communicate the demand patterns and rates for promotions to sales to be able to pitch at the right time. Similarly marketing and sales professionals can give feedback on the promotions and revenue pitches so as to adjust strategies accordingly.

5.5.3 DISTRIBUTION

There has been a tremendous shift from property website to OTAs, impacting and diluting profits through commissions. With the growing trend, revenue managers and owners will witness further degradation of revenue. Revenue managers with owners and leadership teams need to review the distribution costs and find ways to divert business to most profitable channels.

5.5.4 CONSUMER EXPECTATIONS

Effective revenue managers will analyze and align consumer expectations with pricing strategies and availability of inventory at different channels. The changing customer demands, demographics, and trends are challenging the revenue manager at a strategic level. With the advent of technology and the era of transparency, customers have been transformed. Attracting and preserving the relationship of profitable customers for lifetime is the prime strategic objective of the hotel's management and ownership alike. Understanding the preference of loyal customers to an extent whether they would like to redeem points or avail free nights, give an opportunity to personalize the package and services offered.

In the era of empowered consumers, price transparency, technology, domination of OTAs, and big data analytics, managers who are innovative and proactive will be successful.

An effective and holistic revenue management approach has a huge potential for deployment by hotels in India, as they pursue stronger bottom line profits along with growing revenues in a market, that is, growing both from demand as well as the supply end.

KEYWORDS

- **revenue management**
- **profit management**
- **average room rate**
- **RevPar**
- **strategy**

REFERENCES

Butscher, S. A.; Vidal, D.; Dimier, C. Managing Hotels in the Downturn: Smart Revenue Growth through Pricing Optimization. *J. Revenue Pricing Manage.* **2009,** *8*, 405–409.

Chiang, W. C.; Chen, J. C. H.; Xu, X. An Overview of Research on Revenue Management: Current Issues and Future Research. *J. Revenue Pricing Manage.* **2007,** *1*, 97–128.

Connolly, D. J; Olsen, M. D. An Environmental Assessment of How Technology is Reshaping the Hospitality Industry. *Tour. Hosp. Res.* **2001,** *3*, 73–93.

Cross, R. *Revenue Management: Hard Core Tactics for Market Domination.* Broadway Books: New York, 1998.

Cross, R. G.; Higbie, J. A.; Cross, D. Q. Revenue Management Renaissance: A Rebirth of Art and Science of Profitable Revenue Generation. *Cornell Hosp. Rep.* **2009,** *51*, 53–67.

Dev, C. Operating Environment and Strategy: The Profitable Connection. *Cornell Hotel Restaurant Adm. Q.* **1989,** *30*, 8–13.

Freed, J. Q. *The Evolution of Hotel Room Distribution,* 2013 (Online). Available from http://www.hotelnewsnow.com/Article/11095/The-evolution-of-hotel-room-distribution (accessed on 4 January 2016).

IBEF. *IBEF Tourism and Hospitality Industry in India,* 2016 (Online). Available from http://www.ibef.org/industry/tourism-hospitality-india.aspx (accessed on 22 September 2015).

Jain, S.; Bowman, B. Measuring the Gain Attributable to Revenue Management. *J. Revenue Pricing Manage.* **2004,** *4*, 83–94.

Kimes, S. A Strategic Approach to Yield Management. In: *Yield Management: Strategies for the Service Industries,* 2nd ed.; Ingold, A., McMahon-Beattie, U., Yeoman, I., Eds.; Continuum Press: London, 2003, pp 3–14.

Kimes, S. Hotel Revenue Management in an Economic Downturn: Results from an International study. *Cornell Hosp. Rep.* **2009,** *9*, 6–17.

Kimes, S. Hotel Revenue Management: Today and Tomorrow. *Cornell Hosp. Rep.* **2008,** *8*, 6–15.

Kimes, S. The Future of Revenue Management. *Cornell Hosp. Rep.* **2010,** *10*, 6–17.

Kimes, S. E.; Wirtz, J. Has Revenue Management Become Acceptable?: Findings from an International Study on the Perceived Fairness of Rate Fences. *J. Serv. Res.* **2003,** *6*, 125–135.

Li, W. Revenue Management in China's Hotel Industry. In: *International Conference on E-Business, Management and Economics*, Vol 3, IACSIT Press: Hong Kong, 2011.

Mahmoud, A. *Hotel ADR Rise vs. Distribution Channels Cost, What Hoteliers Need to Calculate?*, 2015 (Online). Available from http://www.hospitalitynet.org/news/4070604.html (accessed on 4 January 2016).

Marriott, Jr., J. W.; Cross, R. G. Room at the Revenue Inn. In: *Management Wisdom: Classic Writings by Legendary Managers*; Krass, P.; Wiley: New York, 2000; pp 199–208.

Noone, B. M., McGuire, K. A.; Rohlf, K. V. Social Media Meets Hotel Revenue Management: Opportunities, Issues and Unanswered Questions. *J. Revenue Pricing Manage.* **2011**, *48*, 231–245.

O'Connor, P. On-line Pricing: An Analysis of Hotel-Company Practices. *Cornell Hotel Restaurant Adm. Q.* **2003**, *44*, 88–96.

Schwartz, Z. The Confusing Side of Yield Management: Myths, Errors and Misconceptions. *J. Hosp. Tour. Res.* **1998**, *22*, 413–430.

See, B. G. C.-H.; Enz, C. A.; Lankau, M. J. Grooming Future Hospitality Leaders: A Competencies Model. *Cornell Hotel Restaurant Adm. Q.* **2003**, *44*, 17–25.

Smith, B. C.; Leimkuhler, J. F.; Darrow, R. M. Yield Management at American Airlines. *Interfaces* **1992**, *22*, 8–31.

Vedatya. *Creating Leaders for the Hospitality Industry*, 2016 (Online). Available from http://vedatya.ac.in/downloads/pgprm/PGPRM-Prospectus.pdf (accessed on 22 September 2015).

Wang, X. L.; Heo, C. Y.; Legohérel, Z. S.; Specklin, F. Revenue Management: Progress, Challenges, and Research Prospects. *J. Trav. Tour. Mark.* **2015**, *32*, 797–811.

Yousef, D. A. The Status of Yield Management in Service Organizations in the United Arab Emirates: Results of a Survey. *J. Bus. Public Aff.* **2007**, *1*, 1–9.

CHAPTER 6

SKILLING INDIA INITIATIVE: RESPONDING TO THE CRITICAL NEED FOR SKILLED, TRAINED MANPOWER FOR THE INDIAN HOSPITALITY INDUSTRY

SHWETA TIWARI*

Vedatya Institute, Gurgaon, India

E-mail: shweta.tiwari@vedatya.ac.in

CONTENTS

Abstract 106
6.1   Introduction 106
6.2   Vision for the National Skill Development Initiative in India 107
6.3   Human Resources in the Hospitality Industry 110
6.4   Human Resource in the Hospitality Industry—Supply Side 111
6.5   Human Resource in the Hospitality Industry—Demand Side 114
6.6   Issues and Constraints Related to Skilled and Trained
      Manpower in the Hospitality and Tourism Industry in India 115
6.7   Conclusion and Recommendations 119
Keywords 121
References 121
Web References 123

ABSTRACT

This chapter highlights the significance of the emerging need for skilled and trained manpower in the hospitality industry, with particular reference to hospitality businesses in the Indian setting. The purpose of this chapter is to identify and build a set of indicators that will help the hospitality industry in identifying the key factors, which have contributed to an emerging and almost critical need for skilled and trained manpower in the context of the Indian hospitality industry. The methodology involves literature review, along with aggregation and analysis of case studies from the Indian context.

The discussion includes some of the key aspects, issues, and challenges that the industry faces as it grapples with a growing demand for skilled and trained manpower and proposes a framework to address the same. The study will provide useful implications for professionals, researchers, policy makers, and academicians in the hospitality industry to address the above mentioned issue which is threatening to hold the industry back as it makes a push for growth and profitability. The "Skill India" initiative is a step in the right direction. The chapter reviews the initiative and its impact as of now, with recommendations for stronger and more effective implementation.

6.1   INTRODUCTION

Today, India is one of the youngest nations in the world with more than 62% of its population in the working age group (15–59 years), and more than 54% of its population is below 25 years of age. As per the report produced by the National Higher Education Mission, 2013, the average age of the population in India by 2020 will be 29 years as compared to 40 years in the United States, 46 years in Europe, and 47 years in Japan.

This represents both a challenge as well as an opportunity for the Indian businesses and the workforce. To capitalize on this huge demographic profit which is expected to keep going for the next 25 years, India needs to arm its workforce with employable skills and knowledge so that they can contribute substantively to the economic growth story of the country.

According to a FICCI report, India has around 5.5 million people enrolled in vocational courses, while the number stands at 90 million in China. That said the industry in general, and the hospitality industry in specific has maintained that there is a huge shortfall of well-trained, employable staff to fulfill the ever growing demand. This clearly demonstrates the gaps in availability of "readily employable" workforce. If India has to make progress in terms of becoming a manufacturing hub, and then just like China, it has to leverage the massive unskilled labor market. Lessons could be learned from Malaysia and Singapore, where through government interventions, the unskilled workforce has been skilled to match with the requirements for the nation's economic development (ETAuto.com).

Recognizing the imperative need for skill development, the National Policy for Skill Development and Entrepreneurship (2015) has been put in place with the primary objective, to meet the challenge of skilling Indian's at a scale and speed that will enable various sectors of the economy to meet its requirements for skilled employees. The "skill India initiative" is also focused to ensure that the required standards are established and skills training are imparted as per the same in a sustainable manner.

6.2 VISION FOR THE NATIONAL SKILL DEVELOPMENT INITIATIVE IN INDIA

6.2.1 SCALE OF AMBITION

At present, the capacity of skill development in India is around 3.1 million persons per year. The 11th Five Year Plan envisions an increase in that capacity to 15 million annually. India has a target of creating 500 million skilled workers by 2022. Thus, there is a need for increasing capacity and capability of skill development programs available.

6.2.2 HIGH INCLUSIVITY

The skill development initiatives will harness inclusivity and reduce divisions such as male/female, rural/urban, organized/unorganized employment, and the traditional/contemporary workplace.

6.2.3 DYNAMIC AND DEMAND-BASED SYSTEM PLANNING

The skill development initiatives support the supply of trained workers who are adjustable dynamically to the changing demands of employment and technologies. This policy will promote excellence and will meet the requirements of the knowledge economy.

6.2.4   CHOICE, COMPETITION, AND ACCOUNTABILITY

The skill development initiative does not discriminate between private or public delivery and places importance on outcomes, user's choice, and competition among training providers and their accountability.

6.2.5   POLICY COORDINATION AND COHERENCE

The skill development initiatives support employment generation, economic growth, and social development processes. The skill development policy is an integral part of comprehensive economic, labor, and social policies and programs. A framework for better coordination among various Ministries, States, industry, and other stakeholders is being established.

The following operational strategies are being adopted to achieve the vision for the National Skill Development Initiative.

6.2.6   FOLDING THE FUTURE IN

If we start from our current position, we are likely to extrapolate. Folding the future in allows us to innovate. Innovation is, therefore, an important element of the strategy.

6.2.7   THE SKILLS FRAMEWORK MUST MOVE TO A SYSTEM OF EQUIVALENCE TO DIPLOMAS AND DEGREES

The National Vocational Qualification Framework (NVQF) will be created with an open and flexible system which will permit individuals to accumulate their knowledge and skills and convert them through testing and certification into higher diplomas and degrees. NVQF will provide quality assurance across various learning pathways, through standards that are comparable with any international qualification framework. NVQF will support lifelong learning, continuous up gradation of skills and knowledge.

6.2.8   SKILLS MUST BE BANKABLE

The process of skill acquisition especially for the poor and needy persons will be made bankable. The effort would be to complement public investment with institutional bank finance.

6.2.9 CO-CREATED SOLUTIONS AND FORGING PARTNERSHIPS

We have to accept a very asymmetric India as a starting point. Partnerships will be consciously promoted between government, industry, local governments, civil society institutions, and all potential skill providers. Institutional mechanisms and standing platforms will be created to ensure sustainability (National Policy on Skill Development, 2015).

6.2.10 GAME-CHANGING DELIVERY/INNOVATION

Availability of public institutions above the high school level, after class hours for skill development by the private sector, without disturbing the normal working, will be explored. Necessary regulations would be brought in by the local management authority of the particular educational institution. According to a report of National Sample Survey Organization, 4.69% of the total workforce in India has undergone formal skill training as compared to 68% in United Kingdom, 75% in Germany, 52% in the United States, 80% in Japan, and 96% in South Korea (National Policy on Skill Development, 2015).

The skill gap study conducted by NSDC over 2010–2014 revealed that there is an additional net incremental requirement of 109.73 million skilled manpower by 2022.

Sector	Employment base in 2013 (million)	Projected employment by 2022 (million)	Incremental human resource requirement (2013–2022)
Tourism, hospitality, and travel	6.96	13.44	6.48

Skills and knowledge are the main thrusts of economic development and social advancement for any nation. Nations with higher and better levels of skills adjust more adequately to the challenges and opportunities in the world of work. The present limit of the skill advancement programs in India is 3.1 million. India has set an objective of skilling 500 million individuals by 2022. According to National Skill Development Council, the growing skills gap in India is estimated to be more than 25 crore workers estimated till 2022.

The Union Budget 2015 cleared the path for the launch of a much awaited National Skills Mission to supplement Prime Minister Narendra Modi's "skill India" and "Make in India" exhortations. The key objective of Make in

India is to advance manufacturing in 25 sectors of the economy, which will lead to job creation and consequently requirement for skilled manpower. These 25 sectors include tourism and hospitality as one of the important sectors. The current supply of skilled trained manpower is estimated to be a very dismal of 8.92%, compared to the total requirement as per study a carried out by the Ministry of Tourism.

According to a study revealed by the Institute of Applied Manpower & Research, total number of people who need to be trained by 2022 range between 249 and 290 million, across differing skill requirement scenarios in the light of the Government of India skill development initiative (Economic Times, 2013).

Subsequently, for effective delivery of services, it is quintessential for hospitality organizations to keep the customers' perspectives central, while outlining customer experiences. The need of the hour is to enhance the human resource potential and find solutions that can address the systemic and institutional bottlenecks restricting industry growth.

6.3   HUMAN RESOURCES IN THE HOSPITALITY INDUSTRY

Armstrong (2006) described the overall purpose of human resource management is to ensure that the organization is able to achieve success through people. Also, he discussed that "HRM strategies aim to support programs for improving organizational effectiveness by developing policies in such areas as knowledge management, talent management, and generally creating 'a great place to work.'" The quality of human resource is significant for the success of any industry and tourism is not an exception. The human resources approach takes a supportive and developmental route to achieve results through the cooperative efforts of employees. Workforce issues are a key challenge for the industry in India. Finding and retaining talented people, training, career planning, and leadership are areas which need to be addressed (Jauhari & Manaktola, 2009).

The hospitality industry is a human resource centric industry, where employees play a crucial and strategic role since they are an integral part of the service product and provide instrumental cues in projecting the image of the organization (Bharwani & Mathews, 2012).

With increasing global competition for skilled hospitality employees and high rates of attrition, business success in hospitality organizations is highly dependent on their ability to retain their key employees as well as recruit the right quality of new employees (Bharwani & Butt, 2012).

6.4 HUMAN RESOURCE IN THE HOSPITALITY INDUSTRY— SUPPLY SIDE

The hospitality industry in India is growing rapidly and by 2040 as per the Organization for Economic Co-operation and Development estimates, India will be the world's third largest economy. As per a recent report by KPMG, Current Hospitality and Tourism Industry, the workforce of 6.9 million is expected to increase to 13.4 million by 2022.

TRAVEL AND TOURISM INDUSTRY TO GROW 7.5% OR MORE

The industry is likely to see a spurt in growth this year on the back of new visa reforms, according to a report by the World Travel and Tourism Council. In 2014, the industry contributed Rs.7.64 trillion and 36.7 million jobs to the Indian economy. India's travel and tourism economy is poised to grow by 7.5% in 2015 over last year, exceeding the 6.9% growth that the global forum has predicted for the South-Asian region. In 2014, the industry contributed Rs7.64 trillion and 36.7 million jobs to the Indian economy. By the end of 2015, the travel and tourism sector will contribute Rs.8.22 trillion or 7% of India's gross domestic product (GDP) and 37.4 million jobs—almost 9% of total employment, the report said.

In November, India expanded the visa-on-arrival scheme to 43 nationalities from 12 countries earlier. It is in process of rolling out a similar facility for 150 countries. Investment in the sector is likely to rise by 9.3% in 2015 over 2014, when the travel and tourism investments in the country accounted for Rs.2.11 trillion, or 6.2% of total investments. "It should rise by 6.5% per annum over the next 10 years to Rs 4,337.8 billion in 2025 or 6.9% of the total," the report said, adding that the sector had the potential to contribute 46 million jobs to the India economy by 2025. Worldwide, the contribution to GDP from travel and tourism will have grown by 3.7% by the end of this year and the sector will contribute 284 million jobs, directly and indirectly, or 1 in 11 of all jobs on the planet.

India is trying to raise the share of foreign travel arrivals to 1% of total global tourists over the next couple of years, from 0.64%. In 2014, foreign exchange earnings from tourist arrivals totaled $19.657 billion, compared with $18.445 billion in 2013 (Livemint, 2015).

The report shows that the industry is changing and growing at a fast pace and the market is flooded with new opportunities. Most organizations have been forced to take a relook at their strategic initiatives and weave them with the environmental challenges for a sustainable future.

Sommerville (2007) revealed that training could be enormously demanding and should be in-depth; lack of training or poor training results in high employee turnover and the delivery of substandard products and services to the customers. The global hospitality industry faces some daunting challenges in the functional areas of marketing, operations, human resources, information technology, and finance (Jin-Zhao & Jing, 2009). Furthermore, managing the single largest operating expense—"labor cost" (typically 44.6% of total operating costs) without compromising guest satisfaction is a massive challenge, especially given the constant shortage of skilled, experienced staff (Jin-Zhao & Jing, 2009).

There are numerous HR challenges which the hospitality industry in India is confronting. This has immense implications for future development of the industry. Jauhari (2006) explained that there is mismatch of supply and demand of certain skills in the hospitality industry in India. The single largest problem in the industry which hospitality firms are trying to address today is the acute shortage of skilled and trained-employable manpower (Carlson Hotels, 2011 cited in Jauhari, 2012). Jauhari (2012) also discussed "education competencies and skill development" as one of the key workforce issues that need to be addressed for an enhanced work performance.

According to the Aspiring Minds National Employability Report, only 4–11% of the total hotel management candidates graduating from a wide range of hospitality education institutes and universities in India each year are employable; another 12–21% candidates can be employed post some internal training by the employers. According to the cited report, almost 40% of the candidates are not employable because of the gap in skills that they possess, as against the industry requirements and expectations (economic-times.indiatimes.com).

Based on the report, it is clear that employability is a big challenge for most hospitality graduates in India. Being a labor-intensive industry, tourism offers employment to skilled, semi-skilled, and unskilled workers in a roundabout way.

Soft skill is reported as one of the most vital skill set for all hospitality professionals (Chung-Herrera et al., 2003; Phelan & Mills, 2010; Tews et al., 2011; Wilson-Wünsch et al., 2015). This indicates that hospitality workers and managers need well-developed soft skills, which include communication skills, teamwork, problem solving, and flexibility, to name a few. Burns

---

ONLY 6–18% STUDENTS OF HOTEL MANAGEMENT INSTITUTES EMPLOYABLE: NATIONAL EMPLOYABILITY REPORT

The percentage of hotel management candidates who are directly employable for a hospitality job after college is quite low at 6–18%, according to the National Employability Report for Hotel Management Graduates released by employability solutions firm Aspiring Minds. The report is based on a sample of more than 3000 hotel management students from over 120 hotel management colleges across multiple Indian states that underwent a 2-h Hospitality Employability Test, India's only competency-based assessment instrument for the hospitality industry.

Candidates scored low on fundamental skills like English language skill, logical ability, and soft skills like self-management, quality orientation, managerial skills, etc.

However, there are also a good number of candidates (20–28%) who can become employable after some orientation and training by hospitality companies.According to the report, almost 19–43% of candidates are unemployable because of their lack of English language skills, the preferred language of communication in almost all luxury hotels and premium restaurants.

The report further states that females are more hirable (8–32%) as compared to males (6–16%) across all profiles. Even though females in hotel management colleges have better cognitive skills and behavioral competencies as compared to their male counterparts, the females versus males ratio in Hotel Management colleges is quite low. Employability of IHMs is significantly higher than non-IHMs and yet almost 50% of the employable pool of hotel management candidates is invisible to recruiters (economictimes.indiatimes. com).

(1997) pointed out that soft skills required inhospitality settings have no quantifiable element, and thus they often tend to be underestimated and sometimes even classified as low skills. Lundberg and Mossberg (2008) demonstrated soft skills are essential for line-level hospitality employees when dealing with critical service encounters. This fact also applies to management positions; for example, a study by Watson and McCracken (2002) identified soft skills as the key element of success for visitor attraction. While, at the same time, maintain a professional attitude and organizational control also plays a vital role in the hospitality profession (Beard et al., 2008; Wolfe et al., 2014).

It's time for the industry now to move away from the traditional reactive approach to a more proactive perspective. Baum (2007) postulated that soft skills should be bundled with traditional technical skills to delineate the skill set required in the tourism sector, as well as to identify and manage employees' talent. Besides, in light of the fact that the industry depends more on complex and changing environments, employees are required to add on some higher job-based skills. Livemint.com in its study recognizes a serious problem that currently only 52,000 trained people available to meet the hospitality industry's predicted need for 583,000 professionals until about 2017. To illustrate lack of qualified manpower is the major challenge facing India's hospitality industry today and in the future.

The availability of skilled and trained manpower is a vital component in the successful long-term development and sustainability of any tourist destination. In the ultimate analysis, skilled and trained employees will ensure the delivery of professional, high-quality service to guests, which is an immediate and evident component of a flourishing tourism industry. High standards of service are particularly important in sustaining long-term growth and competitiveness.

6.5   HUMAN RESOURCE IN THE HOSPITALITY INDUSTRY—DEMAND SIDE

According to a Livemint report, the $23 billion hotel industry plans to add at least 50,000 more rooms in the top 6 cities of India by 2016–2017. But there are concerns over whether there will be enough skilled people to meet demand in the labor-intensive sector, which is already facing a shortage of trained staff. The tourism sector on an average requires manpower about 20,000 per year and against such a requirement the actual trained output from government institutions is only 5000 per year (Subbarao, 2008).

The Indian tourism and hospitality industry has developed as one of the key drivers of development among the services sector in India. The industry is expected to generate 13.45 million jobs across sub segments such as hotels, restaurants, and travel agents/tour operators. The Ministry of Tourism plans to help the industry meet the increasing demand of skilled and trained manpower, by providing hospitality education to students as well as certifying and upgrading skills of existing service providers.

According to data released by Department of Industrial Policy and Promotion, the hotel and tourism sector attracted around US$ 8.48 billion of Foreign Direct Investment (FDI) during the period April 2000–September 2015. The tourism and hospitality sector is among the top 15 sectors in India to attract the highest FDI. The figures reflect that tourism in India has a huge growth potential. Also, according to a study conducted by SRI International, India is projected to be the fastest growing nation in the wellness tourism sector in the next 5 years, clocking over 20% growth rate annually through 2017. With the rise in the number of global tourists and realizing India's potential, many companies have invested in the tourism and hospitality sector. Thus, there is need to develop required human resource in various segments of the tourism industry. As an outcome of the fast development in tourism, there is an immediate need for innovative steps to ensure that the sector's growth story is not adversely impacted due to the human resource challenge.

6.6 ISSUES AND CONSTRAINTS RELATED TO SKILLED AND TRAINED MANPOWER IN THE HOSPITALITY AND TOURISM INDUSTRY IN INDIA

The major issues related to human resources development in the tourism sector can be summarized as follows:

- **Non standardization of the training curriculum:** It is observed that there is a variation in the quality of training imparted to students in the hospitality and tourism industry. This affects their employability for job roles and the pay on offer to trained students. While number of institutes in the space has increased, concerns over the quality of supply, as well as trainers, continue to exist in the industry.
- **Retraining cost for the employer:** Employers believe the quality of manpower coming through from the supply side, whether public or private, is not up to the mark in terms of expectations of the industry. This results in the need for re-training of the incoming manpower supply from institutions at the entry level. Thus, affecting profitability due to increase in the overall cost to company due to additional training expense as well as lost productivity and possible inefficiencies.
- **Labor shortages:** In many communities, hospitality expansion is limited not by capital, but rather by human resources. According to the International Society of Hospitality Consultants, the problem of attracting and retaining qualified workers is a major obstacle in the overall development of the tourism sector. This is quite true with respect to the Indian context.

- **The employability challenge:** As per HVS (2012), out of the total students graduating with either a degree or diploma in hospitality management every year, not all have the desired skill set and, in fact, many are not even considered employable by most hotel companies. This is an aspect that needs industry and academia to collaborate to get a fix.
- **Learning and teaching approach:** Learning and teaching approach should be revised keeping in mind a complete research-based application orientation, as learning and teaching has become a key issue in sustaining excellence in Indian education. Industry also needs to take its role more seriously by engaging with educational institutions to co-develop curriculums, training materials, and ensure continuous engagement. Interns and management trainees should be considered as a strategic resource as they essentially constitute the next generation of hospitality leaders.
- **Trainer skill gap:** Training is as good as the quality of the trainers imparting skills training to candidates for their potential employment in the hospitality industry. Industry trainers also need to upgrade their skills to match industry expectations. Here again, the industry has a role.
- **Training potential of institutes:** A vast gap exists between the training potential of the educational institutes and the real requirements of the industry. This is caused by a poor training infrastructure as well as inferior quality of training resources.
- **Lack of structured policies:** For HR planning, career enhancement and human resources development in the hospitality industry leads to further chaos.
- **Use of contemporary technology:** Complexity in keeping pace with rapid changing technological advancements and dynamic alterations in the global market place is a major challenge. Both public and private training institutions are using technology that is obsolete. There is a need to invest in technology that is currently being used by the sector to ensure updation.

Davidson et al. (2010) have noted that because of high staff turnover rates, there is increasing pressure on training requirements to maintain service levels. Frash et al. (2008) argue that training must be considered in a multi-layered approach to maximize its effectiveness.

The levels that are particularly effective are

- reactions of the trainees and their liking of the program;
- principles, facts and techniques; and
- practical application of the learned principles.

In addition to this, Altinay and Altinay (2006) proposed that service organizations need intangible knowledge-based resources to achieve a sustainable competitive advantage in an industry with changing customer expectations; and this is the reason why training can be regarded as a new competitiveness aspect and a critical success factor for the hospitality industry.

Investing in effective training for the workforce has emerged as the top initiatives toward managing costs in the hospitality industry. Davidson et al. (2011) identify that "Training and skills development have been at the forefront of the challenges facing the hospitality industry for many years, and have been the way to inculcate standards and raise customer satisfaction. It remains a critical area as there are new generations of employees coming through, but also because the industry has a very high labor turnover, and in addition now has the need to deal with expansion in the developing countries, most notably China and India."

According to the literature regarding training, there are three basic factors affecting the efficiency of training efforts:

- Individual factors (behaviors toward the job and personality, the educational level of the individuals, training expectations, and motivation levels of the individuals);
- Organizational factors (top management, support from superiors and colleagues, practicing of training with enough financial support); and
- Training programs factors (perception of training, specialties of trainers, etc.) (Aycan & Balc, 2000).

While identifying training needs, it is also important to carry out personnel need-based analysis besides job analysis. While job analysis defines the roles and responsibilities, personnel analysis gives desired information about the essential skills. Both job and personnel analysis act as a precautionary measurement for problem solving.

In addition to this, it is also imperative to investigate the training needs from the organization, the individual, and the program level outlook. For the organizational level, it is important to recognize training needs from the organizational perspective such as training cost, training output, and transferability. Also, from the individual level, it is important to consider performance evaluation as an important criterion, for the program/activity level job analysis and even performance evaluations can be useful (Yüksel, 2000).

The hospitality industry's human resource management problem, with recruitment, retention, and therefore understaffing, is well documented and well recognized by many authors and researchers (e.g., Baum, 2002; Brien, 2004; Choi et al., 2000; Gustafson, 2002; Jameson, 2000), in addition to this, Lo and Lamm (2005) concluded that although occupational stress caused staff turnover, high turnover could not be solely attributed to stress.

Hinkin and Tracey's (2000) study revealed causes of staff turnover, in which job dissatisfaction, poor employment conditions, and poor quality supervision were on the hit list. Interestingly, Lashley and Best (2002) pointed out that poor training in the hospitality industry is one of the major causes behind all these poor HRM issues.

As the hospitality industry becomes more heavily dependent on a skilled labor force, the desires, and level of quality expectations have become broader and more in-depth than in the past (Reid & Sandler, 1992). Therefore, in order to meet the higher expectations and more diverse needs of both customers and employees, a training system should be designed in a more individualized and educational format (Kim & Kizildag, 2011).

Though most hospitality organizations train their employees to behave correctly with customers, the industry has a poor reputation for training (Maxwell et al., 2004; Pratten, 2003). Researchers observe a big gap in this segment, with dearth of quality academic and training institutions, and also a lack of quality training professionals. To overcome the situation and due to acute shortage of quality training centers, many hotels are taking the initiative of opening institutes and developing new hotel management programs. ITC, EIH, IHCL are some of the prominent Indian hotel brands that have made investments in backward integration, to ensure that they have a steady flow of trained, good quality staff at various levels. These efforts have also achieved mixed level of success as the focus is on operational training rather than holistic education for employment in the sector.

The services required in the hospitality and tourism industry are highly personalized, and no amount of mechanization can replace the necessity for personal service providers. Guest contentment is the prerequisite for a smooth and successful operation in the hotel industry, requiring professionally trained and highly skilled manpower. Recognizing this as an opportunity the national skilling initiative has given tremendous impetus to organized effort for skills development with the setting up of the "Tourism and Hospitality Skills Council" (THSC).

6.6.1 SKILL INDIA INITIATIVE: THSC MANDATE

The council (THSC) has the mandate to build training programs that will allow a large number of individuals to get trained and join the hospitality workforce mainly in operational roles at the entry level and even at supervisory and management levels. The approach of developing programs in the form of "Qualification Packs" has seen the THSC develop more than 70 such qualifications, aimed at training individuals for specific qualifications or job roles.

A standardized process of training partner selection has enabled THSC to build a strong base of training partners pan India. The central government, through schemes likes the "Pradhan Mantri Kaushal Vikas Yojana" (PMKVY), is now offering onetime financial support for citizens to get trained and skilled. This support is allowing the training institutions to extend fee credit to students from poor backgrounds, allowing them to join programs, get skilled and certified, and then pay off their fee debt through an auto debit of their PMKVY remittance, post successful completion of the training program. Slowly but surely the skilling initiative is making an impact, creating a pool of well-trained employees for the hospitality sector.

There are challenges that need to be handled. The English communication skills are a big deterrent for many candidates on these usually short-term programs to find employment in the top tier of hospitality brands as English language aptitude is a prerequisite for bagging the job, especially if it is a customer facing job role. Socio cultural bottlenecks persist as many are averse to roles that are seen as servitude driven and hence seen as lowly due to largely poor work ethics. The mobilization effort is being led by NGOs and they are making an effort to bring change in mindsets. With multiple stakeholders working together, this initiative is growing and has the potential to be a game changer in terms of meeting the HR needs of the Indian hospitality sector at large.

6.7 CONCLUSION AND RECOMMENDATIONS

In light of the above studies and by considering the common workforce conditions in India, the following key issues have appeared as challenges that should be addressed:

- **Industry academia partnership:** One of the approaches to tackle the problem of lacking job readiness in the Indian hospitality sector is partnerships between the industry and academia. It is high time now for the hospitality industry to reboot the hospitality education system and joint initiatives by the industry and academia, by playing an important part in plugging the talent gap in the years to come.

- **Curriculum standardization:** Educational institutes need to transform the whole educational process including educational curriculum, learning materials, instructional practices, and education stakeholders.
- **Industry initiative:** Industry would also has a collective role to play along with academia and the government, to address the problem of attracting and retaining qualified workers for the overall development of the tourism and hospitality sector. The industry must take necessary steps in improving the working conditions for its employees, by creating a healthy work environment with a sense of belongingness and trust.
- **Technological innovation:** For qualitative delivery, technological innovation can also play an incredible role in the hospitality and tourism industry. Business processes can be managed better by using advanced technology. Organizational processes can be improved for better customer and employee experiences in the industry.
- **Trainer's skill enhancement:** Trainers also need to enhance their skills to offer better learning outcomes to the students. It is also the responsibility of the industry to support institutes in this. THSC is leading this effort in a structured manner through assessment-based certification of all trainers expected to train candidates on their programs. This is a step in the right direction.
- **Quality research:** It is the need of the hour for every institute to invest in applied research, which is essential for further growth and also to analyze the present situation. The industry should also support the research initiatives by providing timely information and data which is required for the authenticity of the research.
- **Quality training:** Given that the hospitality industry is a service-based industry, a well-skilled workforce is the key for its success and growth. Thus, there is a need of continuous quality training to all categories of employees from time to time, to upgrade their skills as well as performance in the organization. Institutes and industry should work together with each other, with THSC acting as the driving force.

There is a critical need to address the way in which the industry is dealing with its employees and industry. The academia and the government would have a collective role to play in this respect. The industry must react by making better working conditions available for its workforce. It's the responsibility of the industry to create healthy work environment at all hierarchical levels, to preserve a sense of belongingness and trust. Organizations should work toward creating a pool of talented workforce. By investing in talent, long-term gains can be realized. There is a need for constant training to all categories of employees in the organization. Technological innovation can also play an incredible role in guaranteeing quality of delivery at scale. The emerging needs of trained manpower can be solved when the government, industry, and academia work in coordination with a standard education and training system.

KEYWORDS

- **skill India**
- **THSC**
- **PMKVY**
- **human resource**
- **hospitality training**
- **manpower**

REFERENCES

Altinay, L.; Altinay, E. Determinants of Ethnic Minority Entrepreneurial Growth in the Catering Sector. *Serv. Ind. J.* **2006,** *26,* 203–221.

Armstrong, M. *A Handbook of Human Resource Management Practice,* 10th ed.; Kogan Page Limited: London, 2006.

Aycan, Z.; Balci, H. Education Is Our Company in the Event of Service You Are in Determining Factor. In: *8th National Management and Organization Congress,* Erciyes University, Nevski EHR, 2000; pp 727–729.

Baum, T. Human Resources in Tourism: Still Waiting for Change. *Tour. Manage.* **2007,** *28,* 1383–1399.

Baum, T. Skills and Training for the Hospitality Sector: A Review of Issues. *J. Vocation. Educ. Train.* **2002,** *54,* 343–364.

Beard, D.; Schwieger, D.; Surendran, K. Integrating Soft Skills Assessment Through University, College, and Programmatic Efforts at an AACSB Accredited Institution. *J. Inf. Syst. Educ.* **2008,** *19,* 229–240.

Bharwani, S.; Butt, N. Challenges for the Global Hospitality Industry: An HR Perspective. *Worldw. Hosp. Tour. Themes* **2012**, *4*, 150–162.

Bharwani, S.; Mathews, D. Risk Identification and Analysis in the Hospitality Industry. *Worldw. Hosp. Tour. Themes* **2012**, *4*, 410–427.

Brien, A. The New Zealand Hotel Industry—Vacancies Increase. *Int. J. Hosp. Tour. Adm.* **2004**, *5*, 87–104.

Burns, P. M. Hard-Skills, Soft-Skills: Undervaluing Hospitality's 'Service with a Smile.' *Progr. Tour. Hosp. Res. Program Tour. Hosp. Res.* **1997**, *3*, 239–248.

Choi, J.; Woods, R. H.; Murrmann, S. K. International Labor Markets and the Migration of Labor Forces as an Alternative Solution for Labor Shortages in the Hospitality Industry. *Int. J. Contemp. Hosp. Manage.* **2000**, *12*, 61–66.

Chung-Herrera, B.; Enz, C.; Lankau, M. Grooming Future Hospitality Leaders: A Competencies Model. *Cornell Hotel Restaurant Adm. Q.* **2003**, *44*, 17–25.

Davidson, M. C.; Mcphail, R.; Barry, S. Hospitality HRM: Past, Present and the Future. *Int. J. Contemp. Hosp. Manage.* **2011**, *23*, 498–516.

Davidson, M. C.; Timo, N.; Wang, Y. How Much Does Labour Turnover Cost?: A Case Study of Australian Four- and Five-star Hotels. *Int. J. Contemp. Hosp. Manage.* **2010**, *22*, 451–466.

Frash, R.; Kline, S.; Almanza, B.; Antun, J. Support for a Multi-Level Evaluation Framework in Hospitality Training. *J. Hum. Resour. Hosp. Tour.* **2008**, *7*, 197–218.

Gustafson, C. M. Employee Turnover: A Study of Private Clubs in the USA. *Int. J. Contemp. Hosp. Manage.* **2002**, *14*, 106–113.

Hinkin, T. R.; Tracey, J. B. The Cost of Turnover: Putting a Price on the Learning Curve. *Cornell Hotel Restaurant Adm. Q.* **2000**, *41*, 14–21.

HVS. *Forecasting Manpower Requirement by 2021*, HVS, March 2012.

Jameson, S. M. Recruitment and Training in Small Firms. *J. Eur. Ind. Train.* **2000**, *24*, 43–49.

Jauhari, V. Competencies for a Career in the Hospitality Industry: An Indian Perspective. *Int. J. Contemp. Hosp. Manage.* **2006**, *18*, 123–134.

Jauhari, V. Strategic Growth Challenges for the Indian Hotel Industry. *Worldw. Hosp. Tour. Themes* **2012**, *4*, 118–130.

Jauhari, V.; Manaktola, K. Managing Workforce Issues in the Hospitality Industry in India. *Worldw. Hosp. Tour. Themes* **2009**, *1*, 19–24.

Jin-Zhao, W.; Jing, W. Issues, Challenges and Trends Facing Hospitality Industry. *Manage. Sci. Eng.* **2009**, *3*, 53–58.

Kim, J.; Kizildag, M. M-Learning: Next Generation Hotel Training System. *J. Hosp. Tour. Technol. JHTT* **2011**, *2*, 6–33.

Lashley, C.; Best, W. Employee Induction in Licensed Retail Organisations. *Int. J. Contemp. Hosp. Manage.* **2002**, *14*(1), 6–13.

Lo, K.; Lamm, F. Occupational Stress in the Hospitality Industry. An Employment Relations Perspective. *N. Zeal. J. Employment Relat.* **2005**, *30*, 23.

Lundberg, C.; Mossberg, L. Learning by Sharing: Waiters' and Bartenders' Experiences of Service Encounters. *J. Foodserv.* **2008**, *19*, 44–52.

Maxwell, G.; Watson, S.; Quail, S. Quality Service in the International Hotel Sector: A Catalyst for Strategic Human Resource Development. *J. Eur. Ind. Train.* **2004**, *28*, 59–82.

Phelan, K. V.; Mills, J. E. An Exploratory Study of Knowledge, Skills, and Abilities (KSAs) Needed in Undergraduate Hospitality Curriculums in the Convention Industry. *J. Hum. Resour. Hosp. Tour.* **2010**, *10*, 96–116.

Pratten, J. The Training and Retention of Chefs. *Int. J. Contemp. Hosp. Manage.* **2003**, *15*, 237–242.

Reid, R. D.; Sandler, M. The Use of Technology to Improve Service Quality. *Cornell Q.* **1992**, *33*, 68–73.

Sommerville, K. L. *Hospitality Employee Management and Supervision, Concepts and Practical Applications.* John Wiley & Sons: Hoboken, NJ, 2007.

Subbarao, P. S. *Issues and Constrains in Manpower Supply in Indian Hospitality Industry.* Working Paper Series No. 2008-02-03, 2008.

Tews, M. J.; Stafford, K.; Tracey, J. B. What Matters Most? The Perceived Importance of Ability and Personality for Hiring Decisions. *Cornell Hosp. Q.* **2011**, *52*, 94–101.

Watson, S.; McCracken, M. No Attraction in Strategic Thinking: Perceptions on Current and Future Skills Needs for Visitor Attraction Managers. *Int. J. Tour. Res.* **2002**, *4*(5), 367–378.

Wilson-Wünsch, B.; Beausaert, S.; Tempelaar, D.; Gijselaers, W. The Making of Hospitality Managers: The Role of Knowledge in the Development of Expertise. *J. Hum. Resour. Hosp. Tour.* **2015**, *14*, 153–176.

Wolfe, K. L.; Phillips, W. J.; Asperin, A. Using Hotel Supervisors' Emotional Intelligence as a Benchmark for Hospitality Students. *J. Hosp. Tour. Educ.* **2014**, *26*, 2–9.

Yüksel, Ö. *Human Resources Management.* Gazi Book Store: Ankara, 2000.

WEB REFERENCES

http://www.livemint.com. *Travel and Tourism Industry to Grow 7.5% in 2015: Report,* 17 March 2016. http://www.livemint.com/politics/h3ejs6bz6nj0bow86ar1vl/travel-and-tourism-industry-to-grow-75-in-2015-report.html.

National Policy for Skill Development and Entrepreneurship, 2015, retrieved from http://skilldevelopment.gov.in/assets/images/skill India/policy booklet.v2.pdf.

www.economictimes.indiatimes.com. *Only 6–18% Students of Hotel Management Institutes Employable: National Employability Report,* 17 March 2016, retrieved from http://articles.economictimes.indiatimes.com/2012-09-06/news/33650210_1_hotel-management-aspiring-minds-employable-candidates.

www.economictimes. Indiatimes.com. *Training 500 mn People by 2022 Unrealistic: Government Think-Tank IAMR,* 17 March 2016, retrieved from http://articles.economictimes.indiatimes.com/2013-06-07/news/39815423_1_skill-development-skill-gap-ck-prahalad.

www.economictimes. Indiatimes.com. *Less than 11 Per cent of Hotel Management Graduates 'Employable': Survey. Times of India–economic times,* 17 March 2016, retrieved from http://articles.economictimes.indiatimes.com/2014-03-31/news/48735577_1_hotel-management-hospitality-industry-employability-test.

www.ETauto.com. 'Make in India' Initiative's Success Lies in Skilling India—Auto Logue by RohitSaboo|ETAuto,17March2016.ETAuto.com,retrievedfromhttp://auto.economictimes.indiatimes.com/autologue/make-in-india-initiative-s-success-lies-in-skilling-india/1041.

www.kpmg.com. *Travel and Tourism Sector: Potential, Opportunities—KPMG. Travel and Tourism Sector: Potential, Opportunities and Enabling Framework for Sustainable Growth.* KPMG, 17 March 2016, http://www.kpmg.com/in/en/issuesandinsights/articlespublications/documents/kpmg-cii-travel-tourism-sector-report.pdf.

www.labour.nic.in. Ministry of Labour and Employment, Government of India, 17 March 2016, retrieved from http://labour.nic.in/upload/uploadfiles/files/NationalSkillDevelopmentPolicyMar.pdf.

www.livemint.com. *Skill Shortage Threat to Hotel Industry Growth*, 17 March 2016, retrieved from http://www.livemint.com/companies/jbrvlcywdxqaushcxevfyl/skilled-manpower-shortage-threat-to-hotel-industry-growth.html.

www.mhrd.gov.in. National Higher Education Mission (NHEM). Government of India, Ministry of Human Resource Development, 17 March 2016, retrieved from www.mhrd.gov.in.

www.skillsdevelopment.gov.in, 17 March 2016

CHAPTER 7

LEADERSHIP DEVELOPMENT IN THE HOSPITALITY INDUSTRY: PERSPECTIVES FROM INDIA

SONIA BHARWANI*

Indian School of Management and Entrepreneurship, Mumbai, Maharashtra, India

*E-mail: sbharwaniphd@gmail.com

CONTENTS

Abstract 126

7.1   Introduction 126

7.2   Challenges Facing the Indian Hospitality Industry 127

7.3   Rationale of the Study 128

7.4   Conceptual Framework 130

7.5   Methodology 131

7.6   A Framework for Hospitality Leadership Competencies 132

7.7   Phase 1—Survey Questionnaire 136

7.8   Phase 2—In-Depth Interviews with Hospitality HR Experts 142

7.9   Conclusion 150

Keywords 152

References 152

ABSTRACT

It is relatively easy for competition to imitate the tangible aspects of the product and service offerings of a hospitality organization. With this convergence of the tangibles, the key to success lies in the intangibles, that is, the human capital of an organization. Therefore, the ability of an organization to differentiate itself on the basis of its talent pool, especially its senior management and leadership, can provide it with a consistent edge over the competition.

Effective leadership is central to organizational success. Astutely aligning leadership skills and competencies to the key requirements of the job profile is critical to capturing available growth opportunities. Thus, integrated talent management in terms of recruitment, development, and retention of senior management is one of the key challenges faced by the hospitality industry. This study aims at identifying and mapping the talent management practices adopted by hospitality organizations for leadership recruitment and development.

7.1 INTRODUCTION

India is one of the fastest growing economies in the world. It has witnessed the emergence of an open market and a dynamic operating environment, due to liberalization and globalization developments. In recent times, not only have several Indian corporations made their debut on the world stage, but India, as a market, is now indisputably an engine for growth, for many global organizations, including hospitality (Hay Group, 2007).

India has emerged out of its stereotypical image of an exotic travel destination, the land of snake charmers, elephants, and spicy curries. It is witnessing increasing footfalls from the business traveler, while remaining a destination of choice for the leisure tourist. As economic growth gathers momentum globally, companies are increasing their spending on business travel. Simultaneously, leisure travel is also experiencing a boost due to increasing levels of importance being attributed to leisure time pursuits and greater amounts of discretionary income at the disposition of the consumer. This two-pronged growth in travel has had a salubrious effect on demand levels in the tourism sector, as well as the hospitality sector, which shares a fairly symbiotic relationship with the travel and tourism industry.

As a result, hospitality and tourism have emerged as two of the most rapidly growing industries in the world, accounting for more than a third of the total global services trade (ILO, 2010). Hospitality and tourism together contributed approximately 9.8% to the worldwide GDP in 2014 and employed nearly 277 million people, creating 9.4% of the overall number of jobs worldwide, both directly and indirectly (WTTC, 2015). The Indian hospitality and tourism industry, too, is one of the key drivers of growth amongst the services sectors in India. It is a sunrise industry, an employment generator, a significant source of foreign exchange—a potential game changer (KPMG, 2013). It contributed 6.7% to the country's GDP and accounted for 8.7% of the overall employment in India in 2014, including jobs supported indirectly (WTTC, 2015). The immense employment potential of this sector is evident in that it supported the creation of almost 25 million direct and 40 million total jobs in India in 2014 (KPMG, 2014).

7.2   CHALLENGES FACING THE INDIAN HOSPITALITY INDUSTRY

Rapid globalization and economic development have dramatically altered the competitive landscape of the Indian hospitality industry. Competition has intensified. Several global hospitality chains have taken cognizance of the growth potential of the hotel segment and seized the opportunity to enter the market, by ramping up their presence in India. From about 8 to 9 branded hotel chains at the turn of the millennium, by 2011, India had approximately 40 hotel brands (Vivek et al., 2009).

Hotel guests have become more demanding, discerning, and hypersensitive to value. Steep discounting of room rates has become widespread, resulting in a fall in revenues and much thinner operating margin. This has led to profitability pressures on hotel properties, making it imperative to use revenue management strategies. It has also become increasingly important to understand customer behavior, at both the macro- and micro-levels, in order to attract guests as well as maximize their in-house spending to increase hotel revenues (Burns, 2010).

There has been an increased usage of new technologies to aid performance agility and add speed to the market. Online reservations through the global distribution systems and websites, and the usage of social media networking sites, like Trip Advisor, as a marketing and guest feedback tool have become common. The industry is also building its analytic capabilities for delivering tailored and personalized customer experiences and optimizing operational efficiency (Accenture, 2012).

Talent management is another key challenge faced by the hospitality industry. "Successfully aligning job demand and employee skill is critical to capturing available growth opportunities" (Travel Rave, 2013, p. 24). However, limited availability of skilled personnel especially at the senior levels and in the management cadres and high levels of employee attrition are common problems, bringing in the need for employee training, engagement, and commitment initiatives (Deloitte, 2010).

As is evident from the foregoing discussion, the hospitality industry is going through "a period of unprecedented change. Customers are changing, technology is changing and markets are changing" (Amadeus, 2008, p. 18). In this atmosphere of volatility and rapid change, hospitality service leaders and executives, especially the senior managers and General Managers, are faced with a host of challenges, which are significantly enhanced and somewhat different to those in the past. This has thrown up a new set of role demands and professional challenges for senior managers and leaders in Indian hospitality organizations. Hospitality organizations, therefore, must develop leaders with competencies that correspond with and are specific to their distinct business challenges and goals.

7.3   RATIONALE OF THE STUDY

Major hotels of today are diverse, multifaceted and fast paced businesses, engaged in a wide variety of activities (Nebel & Ghei, 1993). Being in the service industry, a hotel has unique characteristics which can place stringent demands on its employees and, of course, the managerial cadre. Senior managers and particularly General Managers play a pivotal role in hospitality operations. As the operations leader of the hospitality unit, the General Manager of a hotel is ultimately responsible for the entire property under his charge including supervision of all its employees. Further, he or she is "held directly accountable by the corporation or owners for the operation's level of profitability, too" (Walker, 2004, p. 747).

To start with, hotels require heavy capital expenditure, especially in view of the escalating prices of real estate. The typical developmental cost per room (excluding land) for an upscale hotel in India is in the range of Rs. 85 lakhs to Rs. 1.25 crores (Khanna & Thadani, 2010), while in the case of luxury hotels, this could range even upward of Rs. 1.25 crores going up to Rs. 2.70 crores (HVS, 2012). The General Manager is entrusted with a very valuable asset in terms of the hotel property and is accountable for ensuring that an appropriate return on investment is generated for that asset.

Further, as entities that function around-the-clock, hotels are highly labor intensive and contain a diverse range of employees (Blayney, 2009). "As other sources of competitive success become less important, what remains as a crucial differentiating factor is the organization, its employees and how they work" (Pfeffer, 1994, p. 96). This includes elements of both human capital (employee knowledge, experience, skills, and commitment) and social capital (relationships among employees and employees' relationships with others outside the firm). The General Manager is the unit head of a multi-crore property and shoulders the responsibility for the entire management team. Therefore, the competencies required of him to carry out this role effectively assume great significance in context of the above observations.

The General Manager's role demands sophisticated talent, with global acumen, a multicultural perspective, people-handling skills, technological proficiency, strategic and entrepreneurial skills, and the ability to manage an increasingly de-layered organization. Despite the significance of the General Manager's role, not much initiative has been taken to understand the essential competencies and capabilities required for management success, in the context of the Indian hospitality sector.

Managers in the industry generally rise through the ranks (Jones & Pizam, 1993) and though they may have sound operational skills, the development of their leadership and managerial skills is usually not given due attention. In India, majority of the hospitality education institutions in the private and public sector are operations oriented rather than management orientated (Jauhari, 2006). This lack of leadership and management focused training in the Indian hospitality sector leads to a myopic view of the industry, as "the focus is just on cooking and delivering food with little concern for building management competence, cost management, building brand equity, developing a national or international brand" (Jauhari, 2006, p. 127).

Effective leadership is central to organizational success. Therefore, it is imperative to understand, develop and establish a sustainable leadership model. On the basis of this potential model, highly focused talent management and leadership development initiatives should be operationalized for the senior managerial cadre of the hospitality industry. In an attempt to address this important research area, this study examines the essential competencies and skills required by a General Manager in luxury and upscale hotels in India and highlights the lacunae and challenges in leadership development programs currently adopted by hospitality organizations.

7.4   CONCEPTUAL FRAMEWORK

"The ability to identify the skills and competencies required for tomorrow's hospitality industry leaders is essential for companies that hope to remain competitive in the business" (Chung-Herrera et al., 2003, p. 17). Due emphasis needs to be given not only toward identifying competencies but also implementing training initiatives for developing identified leadership competencies that correspond with and are specific to distinct business challenges and goals of hospitality organizations.

In the hospitality industry, it is relatively easy for competition to imitate the tangible aspects of the product and service offerings of an organization. With this convergence of the tangibles, the key to success is likely to be dependent on the competitive advantage created through the intangibles, that is, the human capital of an organization. The ability of an organization to differentiate on the basis of its talent pool, especially its senior management and leadership, can provide it with a sustainable edge over the competition (Bharwani, 2014). Further, the issue of talent attraction and retention is indeed one of the most ubiquitous and pressing human resource challenges faced by the hospitality industry across the world (Bharwani & Butt, 2012).

This calls for integrated talent management practices to serve as a blueprint for strategic human resource management in hospitality organizations. Talent management is a multifaceted concept, fueled by the war for talent, which involves strategically cultivating an organizational culture in which employees are truly valued as a source of competitive advantage and designing of effectively integrated HR policies and practices (Hughes & Rog, 2008). Any coordinated or strategic effort for talent management requires a *lingua franca*, a common language. Competency models can serve as the *lingua franca* for strategic human resource management. Competencies can become the link that integrates a range of talent management practices from interviewing, selection, performance assessment, leadership training and development, succession management to deployment (Orr et al., 2010).

When different talent management practices are designed and implemented using the same model, it creates a holistic, self-reinforcing system as depicted in Figure 7.1. For example, when an organization recruits, trains, develops, rewards, and promotes employees based on the same repertoire of competencies, the consistency clearly communicates the strategic importance of these competencies to its employees. This creates a robust organizational climate that is conducive to the creation of high performance work systems (Bowen & Ostroff, 2004).

FIGURE 7.1   Integrated talent management—a competency-based approach.

Source: Researcher's distillation.

"A competency-based approach has as its frame of reference the performance of the very best people in the job" (Hay Group, 2003, p. 4). By recruiting and selecting candidates with these competencies, organizations can improve their overall performance. They can also devise highly focused talent management initiatives to develop the essential competencies that may help the average performers in the organization move up to the next level.

7.5   METHODOLOGY

The aim of this study is to identify and map talent management practices adopted by hospitality organizations to highlight the lacunae and challenges in the leadership development programs currently adopted by hospitality organizations in India. The study begins with the identification of a relevant competency framework for General Managers in the Indian hospitality industry through an extensive review of literature. This competency framework then formed the basis for carrying segmental primary research in Phase

1 of the study. A survey questionnaire was used to gather data from General Managers of luxury and upscale hotels in India, regarding training interventions for leadership competencies development adopted in the industry. In Phase 2 of the study, these data were supplemented by conducting in-depth interviews with select human resource experts from the hospitality industry. Thus, the perspectives of both the organizers and the beneficiaries of the training interventions are included.

7.6   A FRAMEWORK FOR HOSPITALITY LEADERSHIP COMPETENCIES

Competency models gained popularity in the 1980s and are being increasingly used since then as a key tool in human resource management and development, to improve both individual job performance and overall organizational effectiveness. Competency research is generally initiated for certain pivotal job positions that have high salience in context of an organization's strategic plans. Such job roles are strategic in nature and contribute to the overall success and the bottom-line of the organization. As a senior manager and the leader of operations of a hotel, the General Manager's role is of strategic importance. He has moved beyond his traditional role of just maintaining and improving the operational efficiency and work processes in the hospitality unit. He is now expected to wear hats of an operation expert, a business strategist, a people's champion, and a change catalyst. The industry, thus, needs competent hospitality General Managers who can effectively lead this highly people-centered business.

The competency approach advocates observing and studying individuals who are successful and effective job performers so as to ascertain what sets them apart from less successful performers (Delamare Le Deist & Winterton, 2005). Thus, human resource management consultants and practitioners have been increasingly using the terms *competence* and *competency* in the context of managerial performance assessment and managerial development.

Competencies refer to behavioral dimensions that an individual brings to a position to enable him to perform the job competently. It is frequently used as an overarching term to include almost anything that might directly or indirectly have a bearing on job performance (Woodruffe, 1993). Competencies could thus include motives, traits, self-concepts, attitudes or values, knowledge of specific content areas as well as cognitive, behavioral, or physical skills (Boyatzis, 1982; Spencer & Spencer, 1993). It refers to the willingness and capability (motive and traits) to behave in a competent manner and incorporates knowledge, skills, behaviors, and attitudes into a single core unit.

Competencies can be classified into broad categories based on whether they are related to the *functional aspects* of a particular job or to an *individual's personality*. Competencies can also be categorized on the basis of whether they are associated with *mental aptitude* or with *operational abilities* to perform in a given job role. Thus, individual competencies can be broadly categorized as depicted in the typology given in Figure 7.2.

	Occupational	Personal
Conceptual	**Cognitive Competencies** *Knowledge*	**Meta Competencies** *Motives and Traits*
Operational	**Functional Competencies** *Skills*	**Social Competencies** *Attitudes and Behaviours*

FIGURE 7.2 Typology of dimensions of competencies.

Source: Adapted from Delamare Le Deist and Winterton (2005).

- *Cognitive competencies (knowledge)* are related to the conceptual knowledge of an individual.
- *Functional competencies (skills)* are related to the job-specific technical skills of an individual.
- *Social competencies (attitudes and behaviors)* are related to the interpersonal attitudes and behavior of an individual and their ability to effectively interact with others.
- *Meta competencies (motives and traits)* are higher order personal competencies concerned with the ability to understand the situation on hand, adapt, and apply existing competencies or acquire new competencies as and when required.

In order to develop a comprehensive competency framework that would be useful in recruiting and selecting hotel General Managers as well as in their leadership and managerial development, all the four aforementioned dimensions of competencies were included in the framework. Knowledge-related competencies were categorized as *cognitive competencies*, skills were categorized as *functional competencies*, and behavior and attitudes as *social competencies*. To make the framework more holistic, the fourth higher order dimension of *meta competencies*, which are overarching personal competencies concerned with an individual's ability to apply and acquire other competencies, was also included. The concept of *meta competency* was initially proposed by Briscoe and Hall (1999), as a competency that is so powerful that it influences an individual's ability to apply and acquire other competencies. **Meta competencies** are *overarching personal competencies* addressing the ability to understand the situation on hand, adapt, and apply existing competencies or acquire new competencies as and when required (Delamare Le Deist & Winterton, 2005).

The knowledge, skills, attitudes, behaviors, motives, and traits required by a General Manager of a hotel which contribute to a superior level of performance at the workplace can be identified and categorized into the four broad dimensions discussed. Based on an extensive review of literature and empirical research, Bharwani (2015) has proposed a 43-item competency framework for General Managers in the context of luxury and upscale hotels in the Indian hospitality industry, using the above 4-dimensional typology detailed in Table 7.1.

Cognitive or conceptual competencies help in understanding and responding to complexities and challenges that are an inbuilt part of the operating environment. They are gathered through systematic knowledge acquisition and include competencies like critical thinking, analytical skills, creativity, strategic thinking, and decision-making. **Functional or technical competencies** help in performing concrete activities for running the day-to-day business operations and for hotel General Managers include job-specific skills such as guest handling through service orientation, revenue management skills, employee performance appraisal skills, and IT skills. **Social or interpersonal competencies** are useful in establishing and maintaining relationships with others and include people skills like effective communication, empathy, teamwork orientation, fostering motivation, developing, and coaching others. Lastly, **meta competencies** are overarching personal competencies such as self-awareness, self-management, achievement orientation which enable an individual to understand, monitor, and manage their own performance. They refer to abilities that underpin the development of other competencies such as initiative, openness, and willingness to learn as well as intrinsic personality traits like emotional resilience, optimism, and diplomacy. Meta competencies along with key cognitive abilities, technical skills, and interpersonal skills help an individual to deliver superior performance.

TABLE 7.1   Competency Framework for General Managers in the India Hospitality Industry.

Cognitive competencies	Social competencies
Strategic thinking	Empathy
Decision-making skills	Effective communication skills
Creativity and innovation	Networking skills
Systems thinking	Conflict management and resolution
Information gathering skills	Teamwork orientation
Planning prowess	Diversity management skills
Critical thinking and analytical skills	Fostering motivation
Risk taking	Active listening skills
Change management	Developing others
Functional competencies	**Meta competencies**
Service orientation guest	Emotional resilience and composure
Business and industry expertise	Optimism
Revenue management skills	Achievement orientation
Interviewing and selection skills	Self-awareness
Quality control	Self-confidence
Resource allocation skills	Self-management
Crisis management skills	Initiative
Employee performance appraisal skills	Diplomacy
Ability to manage stakeholders	Time management
IT (computer) skills	Ethics and Integrity
Financial analysis and cost control	Adaptability and flexibility
Knowledge of statutory compliances	Tenacity and perseverance
	Openness and willingness to learn

Source: Bharwani (2015).

7.7   PHASE 1—SURVEY QUESTIONNAIRE

A survey questionnaire, designed using Bharwani's (2015) four dimensional competency framework detailed earlier, was used for data collection. Within the Indian hospitality sector, the study focused on the product segment of the luxury and upscale hotels. This segment, comprising 5-star deluxe, 5-Star, and 4-star hotels, offers a full range of first class amenities and customized services including premium guest room amenities and facilities, elegant and distinctive quality décor, upscale restaurants, and high staff-to-guest ratio. Full-service hotels provide their managers with a larger canvas, to display the entire range of their competencies and skills and also have more structured training and development programs in place (Dubé-Rioux, 1999). Hence, this study drew its sample from among senior managers of only 5-star deluxe, 5-star, and 4-star hotels in India.

The Federation of Hotels & Restaurant Associations of India (FHRAI) is the apex body of the four regional associations representing the hospitality industry in India with 2484 hotel members under their wing (www.fhrai.com). The Hotel Association of India (HAI) is another apex body of the Indian hotel industry with approximately 300 member hotels and resorts (www.hai.com). In the researcher's opinion, the FHRAI and HAI constitute the best representation of the population of registered hotels in India; with their membership extending from major hotel groups, boutique hotels, and heritage hotels to mid-size and small hotels. The membership of the two associations represents almost the entire spectrum of the hospitality industry in India and was considered to be suitable representative of the population of hotels in India, from which the sampling frame of luxury and upscale hotels could be drawn.

The directories of members 2014 issued by both the FHRAI and the HAI comprised the most practically available sampling frame for drawing the sample of General managers and Deputy General Managers (also known as Hotel Managers, Resident Managers, Executive Assistant Managers) of 5-star deluxe, 5-star, and 4-star hotels to whom the questionnaires were sent. A total of 323 luxury hotels were identified from the directories to comprise the target population, the star category-wise break up of which is presented in Table 7.2.

A non-probability convenience sampling technique based on the judgment of the researcher was used to draw an appropriate sample of luxury hotels from the target population using the sampling frame suggested above. Respondents were guaranteed anonymity and were assured that neither the submission of financial data nor other privileged information was necessary to participate in the survey. On the basis of the accessibility of the target population, a final list of 255 eligible prospective respondents, that is, General Managers and Deputy General Managers, was prepared and the questionnaire was sent out to them. Out of the 255 questionnaires sent out, a total of 157 questionnaires were returned, yielding a response rate of 61.57%. Of the returned questionnaire responses, 100% of the data was usable.

TABLE 7.2 Sampling Frame of Luxury Hotels in India.

Category of hotel	Number of hotels in the sampling frame
5-Star deluxe	118
5-Star	101
4-Star	104

7.7.1 RESEARCH INSTRUMENT

To address the research question regarding the type of HR programs and initiatives that are prevalent in hospitality organizations in India to develop the competencies of General Managers, primary data relevant to competency development initiatives were collected through the survey questionnaire. The research instrument was in the form of a self-administered questionnaire and comprised two sections:

Section 1: A list of 43 competencies necessary for success as a General Manager of a hotel in India (Bharwani, 2015) was included in Section 1. These competencies were grouped under four broad dimensions: *cognitive competencies*, *functional competencies*, *social competencies*, and *meta competencies*. For each of the four dimensions of competencies, respondents were asked two questions related to training for senior managers. The questions were did the organization in which they were employed conduct training interventions related to the given competencies and whether they had attended any training programs to develop the given competencies.

Section 2: Demographic characteristic information of the respondent and information of the property they were currently managing was gathered in Section 2. Demographic data such as designation, nationality, and years of experience in the industry were collected for all participants. They were also asked to provide information regarding the category or star-rating (5-star deluxe, 5-star, and 4-star) and their affiliation (to a foreign hotel chain, to an Indian hotel chain, or no affiliation).

7.7.2   PROFILE OF RESPONDENTS

A total of 157 respondents participated in the survey. Almost 90% of the respondents were General Managers while the remaining 10% were Deputy General Managers. In terms of nationality, 80% of the respondents were Indian and 20% were expatriates making the ratio of Indian managers to foreign managers 4:1. With regards to the professional background, the survey results showed that almost 50% of the respondents had more than 20 years of experience in the industry, 37% of the respondents had between 15 and 19 years of experience, and 13.5% of the respondents had between 10 and 14 years of experience. No respondent had less than 10 years of experience. Table 7.3 summarizes the demographic profile of the respondents.

TABLE 7.3   Demographic Profile of Respondents.

Demographics	Frequency	Percent
Designation (n = 157)		
General Manager	141	89.8
Deputy General Manager	16	10.2
Nationality (n = 157)		
Foreign national	31	19.7
Indian	126	80.3
Years of industry experience (n = 157)		
Less than 10 years	0	0
10–14 years	21	13.4
15–19 years	58	36.9
20 years or more	78	49.7

In terms of the star rating of the hotels, a large majority of the respondents, that is, 65% managed 5-star deluxe properties, while 26.8% of the respondents led 5-star hotels and only 8.2% of the respondents took care of 4-star hotels. With regards to the affiliation enjoyed by the hotels, almost 40% of the respondents worked for hotels affiliated to an Indian hotel chain, 56% were employed by hotels with an international affiliation while only 4.5% managed independent hotels with no affiliation. This clearly mirrors the trend of the increasing number of international hospitality organizations which have made a foray into the lucrative and growing Indian hospitality sector in the recent past. Table 7.4 presents the organizational profile of the respondents.

TABLE 7.4 Organizational Profile of Respondents.

Organizational profile	Frequency	Percent
Star rating of hotel ($n = 157$)		
5-Star deluxe	102	65.0
5-Star	42	26.8
4-Star	13	8.2
Affiliation of hotel ($n = 157$)		
Affiliated to Indian hotel chain	62	39.5
Affiliated to international hotel chain	88	56.0
Independent	7	4.5

7.7.3 DATA ANALYSIS

For each of the four dimensions of competencies, respondents were asked two questions related to training:

Q1. Does the organization you currently work for organize training programs for developing any of the competencies under the given competency dimension?

Q2. Have you attended any training programs for developing any of the competencies under the given competency dimension?

The questions were designed to elicit binary responses in the form of Yes/No. The responses to questions 1 and 2 for each of the four dimensions of the competencies are tabulated in Tables 7.5 and 7.7, respectively.

TABLE 7.5 Hospitality Organizations undertaking Competency Development Initiatives.

Does the organization you currently work for, organize training programs for developing any of the competencies under the given competency dimension?

Competencies dimension	Percentage of responses	
	Affirmative (%)	Negative (%)
Cognitive	84.1	15.9
Functional	87.9	12.1
Social	76.4	23.6
Meta	62.4	37.6

Analysis of the response data showed that of the four competency dimension, a larger percentage of hospitality organizations have training programs for developing functional competencies (skills) and cognitive competencies (knowledge). Almost 88% of the hospitality organizations have HR initiatives for developing functional competencies for their senior managerial cadre while 84% have cognitive competencies training programs. This could be attributed to the fact that both these categories of competencies, that is, skills and knowledge, are relatively surface characteristics and hence are easier to observe and also have a trainability dimension. Social competencies' development programs were implemented by more than three quarters of the organizations (76%) for which the respondents worked. Social competencies include individual attitudes and their manifested behaviors which are very important for the senior managerial cadre in the hospitality industry which is highly people centric. These can also be modified or molded to some extent and are more susceptible to learning. Thus, the knowledge, skills, and attitudes aspects of competencies are useful in managerial development and majority of the surveyed organizations had HR initiatives in place for developing these three types of competencies in their senior managers.

However, the underlying characteristics, self-concept traits, and motives, that is, meta competencies of an individual are more covert and intrinsic to an individual's personality and hence enduring and more stable. These competencies are related to the personality, core traits, and motives of an individual. They are more difficult to assess and develop but are useful during the recruitment and hiring process, while determining a fit between a job profile and an individual (Spencer & Spencer, 1993). Thus, only 62.4% of the hospitality organizations had training programs for developing meta competencies.

The study analyzed negative responses to both the questions in an attempt to home in on the gaps and lacunae in the competency training initiatives in the Indian hospitality organizations. On further analysis of the negative responses to question 1 in context of the organizational profile of the respondents, some important observations were noted. With regard to affiliation of hotel, in the original sample of 157, 39.5% of the respondents worked for Indian hotel chains, while 56% were employed with international chains. However, the negative responses were skewed in the opposite direction for especially cognitive and social competencies dimensions. This indicated that of the hotels which did not conduct cognitive and social competency training programs, a greater percentage of hotels were affiliated to Indian hotel chains rather than to international chains. Table 7.6 gives the detailed breakup of the negative responses based on the affiliation of hotel criteria.

TABLE 7.6 Distribution of Responses to Question 1 Based on the Organizational Profile of Respondents.

Competencies dimension	No. of negative responses (total $n = 157$)	Negative responses distributed by affiliation of hotel		
		Indian chain (%)	International chain (%)	Independent (%)
Cognitive	25	60	36	4
Functional	19	47.5	47.5	5
Social	37	57	38	5
Meta	59	44	53	3

However, no significant difference was observed in the negative responses to question 1 based on star-rating of the hotels in which the respondents worked. Thus, it emerged that international hotel chains were more inclined to conduct competency training as compared to their Indian counterparts, while the proclivity of hotels to conduct competency training initiatives was not impacted by their star-category.

TABLE 7.7 Respondents Have Attended Competency Development Programs.

Have you attended any training programs for developing any of the competencies under the given competency dimension?		
Competencies dimension	Percentage of responses	
	Affirmative (%)	Negative (%)
Cognitive	89.8	10.2
Functional	89.2	10.8
Social	79.0	21.0
Meta	61.1	38.9

Almost 90% of the respondents claimed that they had attended training programs to develop cognitive and functional competencies. Only 79% had attended programs which developed their social competencies, while the proportion of respondents who had attended programs to develop meta competencies was even lower at only 61%. The lower emphasis given to training initiatives to develop meta competencies could be attributed to the fact, that meta competencies are of a higher order, intrinsic personality traits which have a lower trainability dimension as compared to other categories of competencies (Briscoe & Hall, 1999).

Further analysis of the responses to question 2 in context of the demographic profile of the respondents threw up valuable insights. With regard to the nationality of the respondents, in the original sample of 157, 80% of the respondents were Indian nationals, while 20% were foreign nationals. However, it emerged that among the respondents who answered in the negative regarding attending competency training programs, the ratio of Indian managers to foreign managers was 9:1. This was significantly higher than the proportion of Indians to foreign nationals (8:2) in the original sample, indicating that a larger number of Indians as compared to foreign nationals had not an opportunity to attended training programs for leadership development. Table 7.8 gives the detailed breakup of the negative responses on the basis of nationality.

TABLE 7.8 Distribution of Responses to Question 2 Based on Demographic Profile of Respondents.

Competencies dimension	No. of negative responses (total n = 157)	Negative responses distributed by nationality	
		Indian nationals (%)	Foreign nationals (%)
Cognitive	16	88	12
Functional	17	94	6
Social	33	91	9
Meta	61	87	13

However, other demographic factors like the designation of the respondents and the number of years of work experience did not significantly impact their attendance of competency training programs.

7.8 PHASE 2—IN-DEPTH INTERVIEWS WITH HOSPITALITY HR EXPERTS

The final stage of the study involved triangulation of research data by carrying out in-depth interviews with select human resource experts from the hospitality industry. Researchers have often done triangulation by using qualitative tools, such as in-depth interviews for validating quantitative research instruments. *Methodological triangulation* is defined as the use of multiple methods, mainly quantitative and qualitative in studying the same phenomenon for the purpose of increasing credibility of the study

(Flick et al., 2004). Both quantitative and qualitative methods have their own strengths and weaknesses. By using both the methods in conjunction with each other, there is a high likelihood of neutralizing the flaws of one method and strengthening the benefits of the other for better research results (Hussein, 2009). Hinds (1989) has pointed out that by combining both qualitative and quantitative methods, researchers can rule out rival explanations of observations and reduce the skepticism in the findings of a study.

Select HR experts from the hospitality industry were interviewed to triangulate the study. This was done to give a practical context to the findings of the study and to provide a more complete picture of training initiatives adopted by Indian hospitality organizations, for developing their senior managers. In-depth interviewing is a qualitative research technique that involves conducting intensive individual interviews with a small number of respondents, to explore their perspectives on a particular issue or situation (Boyce & Neale, 2006). It usually involves asking open-ended questions that elicit depth of information from relatively few people. An in-depth interview should ideally be discursive enough to allow the researcher and respondent latitude, to explore an issue within the focused framework of guided conversation (Prairie Research Associates, 2001).

7.8.1 PROFILE OF INTERVIEWEES

A total of 10 prospective interviewees were shortlisted for the in-depth interviews. A cross section of expertise was sought while choosing the HR experts, to ensure the inclusion of a range of perspectives. Endeavors were made to enlist corporate human resource directors from Indian and international hospitality chains, operating in the luxury and upscale segment in India as well as senior directors from prominent hospitality consulting companies, who were involved in recruitment and training of senior hospitality talent. Personal contacts of the researcher were used as the initial contact points. Thereafter, the snowball sampling technique was used by asking the initial contacts to provide recommendations for other experts who could be potential interview participants.

With respect to sample size, "the general rule on sample size for interviews is that when the same stories, themes, issues, and topics are emerging from the interviewees, then a sufficient sample size has been reached" (Boyce & Neale, 2006, p. 4). Thus, for the purpose of triangulation, initially five HR experts were shortlisted and interviewed. As common themes, issues, and topics were seen to emerge from the five interviews, it was concluded that a sufficient sample size had been reached and interviewing more respondents would not yield materially content enriching data. It was, therefore, decided to restrict the sample size for in-depth interviews to five interviewees. Table 7.9 gives a summary of the profile of the five interviewees who participated in Phase 2 of the study.

TABLE 7.9   Profile of the Interviewees.

No.	Designation	Area	Current organization	Years of experience[a]
1	Regional Director	Corporate HR	International Hospitality Chain	7
2	Director	Skills development	Hospitality Consultancy	6
3	Regional Director	Corporate HR	International Hospitality Chain	14
4	Vice President	Corporate HR	Indian Hospitality Chain Hospitality Chain	9.5
5	Regional Director	Corporate HR	International Hospitality Chain	5

[a]In senior corporate roles.

Three of the participants were Regional Directors for the South Asian region and headed the human resources function for three well-known international hospitality chains, which operate in the luxury and upscale segment in India. One of the participants was the Vice-President of Corporate HR for a leading Indian hospitality chain, again operating in the premium segment of hotels. The fifth participant was the director of the training vertical of a leading international hospitality consulting, company which is actively involved in recruitment and development of senior hospitality leadership. All the prospective interviewees had a minimum 10 years experience in the field of hospitality human resource management; of which at least 5 years was in a senior corporate level position in the area of human resource and talent management.

7.8.2   RESEARCH INSTRUMENT

An initial telephonic contact was made with the prospective interviewee to seek an appointment for conducting an in-depth interview. Face-to-face interviews were conducted in the respective offices of the interviewees and spanned between 45 and 60 min. A semi-structured interview format was used with the aid of an interview guide, which comprised nine specific questions related to competency-based HR practices for leadership development as presented in Table 7.10. However, the interview was kept conversational with questions flowing from previous responses whenever possible. The researcher endeavored to use effective interviewing techniques such as avoiding yes/no and leading questions and used appropriate body language to express interest and show active listening. Efforts were made to keep personal opinion in check and to limit personal bias from creeping in while recording the data.

TABLE 7.10 Interview Guide.

Questions
1 In your opinion, are there any competencies that contribute to the successful performance of a General Manager that have not been already included in the 43 competencies framework?
2 According to you, which are the top five competencies that contribute to the successful performance of a General Manager?
3 Do you use a competencies framework as a template while recruiting and selecting General Managers in your organization?
4 Which are the top five competencies that you evaluate while selecting and recruiting an individual for a General Managerial position in your organization?
5 What kind of leadership development programs does your organization have for General Managers?
6 Name any three competencies which have been the focus of recent training programs for General Managers in your organization.
7 On what basis do you decide on the General Managers participants who attend these programs?
8 Do you use a competency-based approach for performance appraisal of General Managers?
9 Do you think a competencies framework for General Managers would have any utility for talent management in the Indian hospitality industry?

Before beginning the interview, the informed consent of the interviewee was sought and the purpose of the interview was re-explained. Thereafter, the reason for choosing the respondent for the interview and the expected time duration was stated. The interviewee was assured that the data collected would be used for academic purposes only. The researcher took notes throughout the interview, in order to validate the findings from Phase 1.

7.8.3 DATA ANALYSIS

Hard-copy printouts of the 43-competencies framework model (Bharwani, 2015) were shared with the interviewees to provide a context to the study. The nine main questions listed in the interview guide were used as a template for conducting the in-depth interviews. Data were analyzed by reviewing and looking for patterns or themes among the participants' responses.

In response to the opening question about the comprehensiveness of the 43-competencies framework which was shared with them, 4 out of the 5 interviewees were of the opinion that the competencies framework which included 43 competencies was a panoptic one and included almost all the competencies that contributed to the successful performance of a hospitality General Manager. According to one HR expert, *customer relationship management* and *maintaining industrial relations* were important competencies which seemed to be missing from the list. On probing further, it emerged that by *customer relationship management* the respondent meant a General Manager's *guest handling skills*. The competencies framework presented by the researcher had clubbed *guest handling skills* with *service orientation*; therefore, though it was included in the framework, it did not appear as a separate competency.

With respect to *maintaining industrial relations* with employee associations and trade unions, the union density is extremely low in the Indian hotel industry. The high fragmentation of the workforce on account of diverse ethnicity and large proportion of contract workers employed in hotels as compared to regular workers (Ferus-Comelo, 2015) is a prominent feature. Thus, this competency was not included as a separate item but was covered under *ability to manage stakeholders*, where one group of stakeholders is the employees.

While each of the five experts had different "top 5 competencies" lists, the three competencies that appeared in all the lists were *service orientation*, *teamwork*, and *strategic thinking*. *Ability to manage stakeholders* also was rated as a very important competency by three of the experts, especially in the context of the new reality of the increasing number of managed and franchised hotels in the Indian hospitality industry characterized by a plurality of stakeholders.

Strategic thinking was considered to be a very important competency for General Managers given the globalized context in which the hospitality industry operates today, where the hotels have to grapple with the rapidity of change and the challenges of functioning in an information-based, knowledge-intensive, service-driven economy.

> It is the responsibility of the General Manager to chart out the broad strategic direction for the hotel and proactively analyse and assess the internal operations of the hotel as well the external competitive environment.

They need to have good *business and industry knowledge* to enable them to devise and implement appropriate strategies, and to create a sustainable competitive advantage is crucial, while judiciously balancing the needs of the key stakeholders in the hotel. The importance of tact and *diplomacy* as well as *networking skills* in achieving the strategic objectives of the business was also highlighted.

Out of the four dimensions in the proposed competency framework, the experts considered social competencies to be the most important dimension given the people-centric nature of the hospitality industry.

> The people-handling skills, that is dealing guests and employees, are all the more accentuated for GMs of luxury hotels

In the opinion of the experts, interpersonal competencies are critical for General Managers of hotels in the premium segment due the emphasis laid on the delivery of excellence in service quality. A General Manager is dependent on his staff for service delivery and, therefore, has to have the competency to build a talented, committed and self-motivated team.

According to HR experts, despite the importance accorded to social competencies, hospitality organizations had more training programs and initiatives for developing cognitive and functional competencies. The least emphasis was given to training initiatives for developing meta competencies, although these are really the key competencies needed for senior leaders like General Managers. This could be attributed to the fact that meta competencies are of a higher order intrinsic personality traits, which have a lower trainability dimension as compared to other categories of competencies. This view of the experts validated the survey findings from Phase 1 and helped in triangulation of the research data.

There were mixed responses on the query about using a competencies framework as a template, while recruiting and selecting General Managers. The HR experts who worked for international hospitality chains answered in the affirmative, while the expert from the Indian chain stated that there was no formalized template used since promotions to General Managerial positions were usually made organically from within the organization and based on the performance of the individual and recommendations of the senior executives, who had interacted or worked with the prospective candidate in the past. However, while hiring an external candidate, more emphasis was laid on their ability to fit in with the organizational culture in terms of service and teamwork orientation.

The expert from the consulting company put this difference in recruiting practices in perspective by pointing out that most of the international chains had made a recent debut in the Indian market. Therefore, they hired leadership talent from the open market as and when they opened new properties. They adopted adaptations of the competencies frameworks used in their international hotels as templates while recruiting. On the other hand, most of the Indian hospitality chains are veterans in the field and usually have their own in-house hospitality management development institutes to home-grow talent. Thus, they probably inculcate the required competencies in an individual at the management trainee stage itself and promote on the basis of performance and recommendations.

People m*anagement skills, service orientation, decision-making skills, critical thinking and analytical skills,* and *effective communication skills* were rated as the top five competencies which were evaluated while recruiting and selecting individuals for General Managerial positions. The experts agreed that *people management skills* and *service orientation* were sine qua non competencies that every manager working in a people centric, service industry like the hospitality industry, must necessarily possesses. Competencies like *effective communication skills, diversity management, achievement orientation, active listening skills,* and *time management* were considered by experts to be important for managers in the hospitality industry, irrespective of their hierarchical position. The utility of *decision-making skills, critical thinking,* and *analytical skills* increased as the managers moved up in hierarchy and therefore were rated as a very important for General Managers.

According to experts, leadership development programs for General Managers in the hospitality industry are usually held on an ad-hoc basis. Some hospitality chains conduct coaching/mentoring programs that are customized for each individual General Manager on the basis of 360 degree feedback and psychometric testing. An external training coach who has face-to-face sessions at regular intervals, is usually assigned to the General Manager. An important aspect of such a coaching program is obtaining a buy-in from the General Manager, where he recognizes the need and the utility of such an initiative and is a willing participant.

One international hospitality chain has partnered with a leading hospitality management school to conduct online leadership courses for its General Managers. They also have an e-learning platform which provides access to self-paced courses in leadership and hotel operations. Along with this, monthly webinars of 1-h duration are held which address emerging challenges and new developments. Other hospitality organizations conduct face-to-face leadership development programs on a range of topics like *strategic thinking, change management, creativity and innovation, conflict management*, and so on. However, the choice of program depends more on the availability of a suitable training resource who can deliver the program rather than being guided by training need analysis. Further, usually all the General Managers of hotels belonging to a particular brand or a segment within the group, and are invited to participate in these programs.

According to experts, the competencies which were commonly the focus of leadership development programs for General Managers include *strategic thinking, change management, teamwork orientation*, and *service orientation*. Among functional competencies training programs are largely held for developing *revenue management skills* and *financial analysis skills*.

While some hotel chains used competency-based performance appraisal systems, others used balanced scorecards for evaluating the performance of its General Managers. The competencies which were commonly used for evaluating a General Manager's performance included *people development skills, team building, business ethics, change management*, and *achievement orientation*.

One of the experts commented that though hospitality organizations in India did use competencies in certain aspects of talent management, there was a lack of an integrated approach. All the experts concurred that there was lack of an industry-specific leadership competency model for the Indian hospitality sector; which could be used as a blueprint for developing competency frameworks tailored to the needs of individual organizations that is aligned with their unique vision, strategies, and culture. A robust leadership competency model would facilitate competency identification and measurement and keep the leaders focused on areas which are crucial for success and development.

> There is a direct correlation between competency proficiency and successful performance.

Competency models are thus useful, in identifying developmental needs and measuring quality of performance. They provide a systematic means of developing hospitality managers along the leadership pipeline to take on the mantle of a General Managerial role and help build long-term leadership success.

7.9 CONCLUSION

Leadership competency requirements for General Managers in service environments like the hospitality industry are distinct from those required in other industries. Building leadership competencies is a long-term, career-spanning activity for managers irrespective of whether they want to maintain a competitive edge in their current positions, or they want to move up the corporate ladder into bigger, more challenging job roles.

Managers face a critical transition when they move up the hierarchy from being functional experts to becoming General Managers. As a young hospitality manager, success is achieved by specializing and becoming a functional expert in a particular hotel department. However, transitioning to senior management role, like that of a General Manager, has its unique challenges. The first major challenge for General Managers is developing the ability to see linkages and interconnections across the organization. Transitioning from driving excellence in a single functional area to integrating consistency, cohesion, and alignment across, many departments in the hospitality unit requires an enhanced set of competencies. The next big challenge is switching from being a hands-on doer to achieving leverage by building an effective team and delegating (Lagace, 2007).

Embracing the role and responsibilities of a General Manager requires a fundamental shift in the mind set and perspectives of an individual from specialist to generalist, from analyst to integrator, from tactician to strategist, from warrior to diplomat, from bricklayer to architect, and from role holder to role model (Watkins, 2012). Further, in recent times, the role of a General Manager has transitioned from operational to strategic leadership. In addition to the traditional responsibility of managing day-to-day hospitality operations, he is also responsible for achieving longer term strategic business results. And, these transitions necessarily warrant a clear understanding of the repertoire of competencies required by the incumbent, as well as updating the relevant skill sets and competencies too.

In the context of the industry-wide war for talent, especially for the senior management cadre, hospitality organizations have long struggled with high turnover rates and the challenge of talent retention. Competency-based talent management presents a particularly intriguing opportunity, for attracting and recruiting employees with the requisite skills set and experience. A recruitment process based on competency assessment, behavioral profiling, and psychometric testing would go a long way in ensuring a suitable fit and longevity of tenure. From a diagnostic perspective, a robust competency model can provide an excellent framework for identifying core strengths while recruiting, assessing managerial performance as well as charting the development needs related to career path planning and promotion decisions. Highly focused training initiatives can be devised to develop the essential competencies that may enable average performers in the organization to move up to the next level along the talent pipeline. Hospitality employees, too, can gain a clear understanding of the competencies required for professional advancement and chart their career paths accordingly. Thus, a competency-based integrated approach to talent management would foster *employee engagement* by ensuring the right fit for the job, *employee enablement* by addressing their developmental needs, and *employee commitment* and retention by taking care of their career progression.

The findings of the study revealed that while hospitality organizations in India recognize the importance of a holistic competency-based approach in leadership development, there was a lack of a structured, competency-based training need analysis to assess the developmental needs of General Managers. Further, competency development initiatives for General Managers were usually conducted on an ad-hoc basis depending on the availability of suitable external training resources. There was a higher degree of focus on *functional* and *cognitive competencies*, while designing training initiatives as these competencies are readily identifiable and measurable. However, there are several other *social* and *meta competencies* that are covert, below the surface, and are more difficult to detect and yet are highly significant. For complex and senior level job roles like General Managers, it is more likely that the superior performance is driven by the underlying personal characteristics, self-concept, core traits, and the motives of an individual which are covert and intrinsic to an individual's personality and hence enduring and more stable. These are more difficult to assess and develop as compared to task-related skills and knowledge. However, it is imperative to identify these deeply rooted competencies to make an apt selection of high-potential candidates, who present the best fit for senior level job roles. Developmental programs related to *social* and *meta competencies* also need to be increasingly conducted, to help senior managers to become better self-aware of and polish these intrinsic traits and core competencies.

To conclude, a General Manager must possess *functional competencies* which are important for the smooth operation of the hotel. *Cognitive competencies* like strategic thinking and the ability to handle multiple stakeholders play a critical role in building strategic and tactical partnerships with customers, suppliers, competitors, and other external influencers of business to enhance operational effectiveness. Further, as teams are an integral part of hospitality organizations, General Managers must also acquire *social competencies* to handle the unique challenges of leading teams. Finally, a General Manager must also possess *meta competencies* which are overarching personal competencies and intrinsic personality traits which enable an individual to understand, monitor, and manage their own performance. They enable General Managers to develop just-in-time competencies allowing them to dynamically adapt to ongoing business challenges. Thus, as a strategic leader, the General Manager needs to have functional expertise as well as the ability to anticipate change, maintain flexibility, think strategically, and work with and through his team to create memorable experiences for the hotel guests and a viable future for the organization.

KEYWORDS

- **leadership development**
- **competencies**
- **hospitality general managers**
- **strategic leader**
- **talent development**

REFERENCES

Accenture. *Getting Personal: Mastering the Digital Revolution in the Lodging Industry.* Accenture: New York, NY, 2012.

Amadeus. *The Future of the Hotel Industry: Closing the Gap between Dreams and Reality*, 2008.

Bharwani, S. Hospitality Innovations in the Emerging Experience Economy: A Case Study of the Oberoi Resorts. In: *Innovations in Services Marketing and Management: Strategies for Emerging Economies*; Goyal, A., Eds.; IGI Global: Hershey, PA, 2014; pp 307–328.

Bharwani, S. Essential Competencies for Senior Managers in the Indian Hospitality Industry, Unpublished Doctoral Thesis, Aligarh Muslim University: Aligarh, 2015.

Bharwani, S.; Butt, N. Challenges for the Global Hospitality Industry: An HR Perspective. *Worldw. Hosp. Tour. Themes* **2012**, *4*(2), 150–162.

Blayney, C. Management Competencies: Are They Related to Hotel Performance? *Int. J. Manage. Mark. Res.* **2009**, *2*(1), 59–71.

Bowen, D. E.; Ostroff, C. Understanding HRM-Firm Performance Linkages: The Role of the "Strength" of the HRM System. *Acad. Manage. Rev.* **2004**, *29*(2), 203–221.

Boyatzis, R. *The Competent Manager: A Model for Effective Performance.* John Wiley & Sons: New York, NY, 1982.

Boyce, C.; Neale, P. *Conducting In-depth Interviews: A Guide for Designing and Conducting In-depth Interviews for Evaluation Inputs.* Pathfinder International: Watertown, MA, 2006.

Briscoe, J. P.; Hall, D. T. Grooming and Picking Leaders Using Competency Frameworks: Do They Work? An Alternative Approach and New Guidelines for Practice. *Organ. Dyn.* **1999**, *28*(2), 37–52.

Burns, J. *Invent the Future: The New Normal for Hotels in 2010 and Beyond.* Amadeus: Madrid, 2010.

Chung-Herrera, B. G.; Enz, C. A.; Lankau, M. J. Grooming Future Hospitality Leaders: A Competencies Model. *Cornell Hotel Restaurant Adm. Q.* **2003**, *44*(3), 17–25.

Delamare Le Deist, F.; Winterton, J. What is Competence? *Hum. Resour. Dev. Int.* **2005**, *8*(1), 27–46.

Deloitte. *Hospitality 2015: Game Changers or Spectators.* Deloitte: London, 2010.

Dubé-Rioux, L. *American Lodging Excellence: The Key to Best Practices in the U.S. Lodging Industry.* American Hotel Foundation: Washington, DC, 1999.

Ferus-Comelo, A. Labour Geographies in India's Hotel Industry. In: *A Hospitable World?: Organising Work and Workers in Hotels and Tourist Resorts*; Jordhus-Lier, D.; Underthun, A., Eds.; Routledge: Abingdon, 2015.

Flick, U.; Kardoff, E.; Steinske, I. *A Companion to Qualitative Research.* Sage Publications: Los Angeles, CA, 2004.

Hay Group. *Using Competencies to Identify High Performers: An Overview of the Basics.* Hay Group: Philadelphia, PA, 2003.

Hay Group. *The Indian CEO: A Portrait of Excellence.* Hay Group: London, 2007.

Hinds, P. S. Method Triangulation to Index Change in Clinical Phenomena. *West. J. Nurs. Res.* **1989**, *11*(4), 440–447.

Hussein, A. The Use of Triangulation in Social Services Research: Can Qualitative and Quantitative Methods Be Combined? *J. Comp. Soc. Work* **2009**, *2009*, 1–12.

Hughes, C. J.; Rog, E. Talent Management: A Strategy for Improving Employee Recruitment, Retention and Engagement within Hospitality Organizations. *Int. J. Contemporary Hosp. Manage.* **2008**, *20*(7), 743–757.

HVS. *Hotel Room Supply, Capital Investment and Manpower Requirement by 2021.* HVS Consulting: Gurgaon, 2012.

ILO. *Developments and Challenges in the Hospitality and Tourism Sector.* International Labour Organization: Geneva, 2010.

Jauhari, V. Competencies for a Career in the Hospitality Industry: An Indian Perspective. *Int. J. Contemporary Hosp. Manage.* **2006**, *18*(2), 123–134.

Jones, P.; Pizam, A. *International Hospitality Management—Organizational and Operational Issues.* Pitman: London, 1993.

Khanna, A.; Thadani, M. *Ten Trends Influencing Hospitality in India: How the Game is Changing.* HVS International: New Delhi, 2010.

KPMG. *Travel and Tourism Sector: Potential, Opportunities and Enabling Framework for Sustainable Growth.* KPMG-CII: Chandigarh, 2013.

KPMG. *Tourism: Post-Budget Sectoral Point of View—India Union Budget 2014.* KPMG: Delhi, 2014.

Lagace, M. Making the Move to General Manager. *HBS Working Knowledge*, 2007, Retrieved 15 November 2015, from http://hbswk.hbs.edu/item/5608.html.

Nebel, E.; Ghei, A. A Conceptual Framework of a Hotel Manager's Job. *J. Hosp. Tour. Res.* **1993**, *16*, 27–38.

Orr, J. E.; Sneltjes, C.; Guangrong, D. *Best Practices in Developing and Implementing Competency Models.* The Korn/Ferry Institute: New York, NY, 2010.

Pfeffer, J. *Competitive Advantage through People: Unleashing the Power of the Work Force.* Harvard Business School Press: Boston, MA, 1994.

Prairie Research Associates. *The In-depth Interview.* Prairie Research Associates, Inc.: Winnipeg, 2001.

Spencer, L. M.; Spencer, S. M. *Competence at Work: Models for Superior Performance.* John Wiley & Sons: New York, 1993.

Travel Rave. *Navigating the Next Phase of Asia's Tourism: Insights on the Future of Tourism in the World's Fastest Growing Travel Market.* Singapore Tourism Board: Singapore, 2013.

Vivek, S.; Das, D.; Vaid, K. *India Report, The Voyage: An Exploration of the Key Hospitality Markets in India.* Cushman & Wakefield: Mumbai, 2009.

Walker, J. R. *Introduction to Hospitality Management.* Pearson Prentice-Hall: Upper Saddle River, NJ, 2004.

Watkins, M. How Managers become Leaders. *Harv. Bus. Rev.* **2012,** *90*(6), 64–72.

Woodruffe, C. What is Meant by a Competency? *Leadersh. Organ. Dev. J.* **1993,** *14*(1), 29–36.

WTTC. *Travel & Tourism—Economic Impact 2015 India.* World Travel & Tourism Council: London, 2015.

CHAPTER 8

ARTS-INFORMED LEADERSHIP IN FAMILY-RUN BUSINESS: ARTS IN PLAY

VIMAL BABU[1]* and AMIRUL HASAN ANSARI[2]

[1]*School of Business, Auro University, Hazira Road, Opp. ONGC, Surat, Gujarat, India*

[2]*Centre for Management Studies, Jamia Millia Islamia Central University, New Delhi, India*

Corresponding author. E-mail: vimalsairam@gmail.com

CONTENTS

Abstract 156
8.1 The Indian Hospitality Industry's Current Performance 156
8.2 Connecting Arts and Business 158
8.3 Leadership and Art Forms 160
8.4 Family-Run Business: Leadership and Decision-Making 165
8.5 Methodology 166
8.6 Results and Discussions 169
8.7 Managerial Perspective of Art Forms in Family Business 173
8.8 Implications of the Present Study 174
8.9 Conceptual Model of Engaging Employees
     through Learning—Applying Art Forms 175
8.10 Conclusion 177
8.11 Further Scope of Research 178
Keywords 178
References 179
Appendixes A8.1 to A8.7 180

ABSTRACT

Due to macroeconomic factors and industry-prone changes, umpteen family-run businesses are mirroring the deteriorating conditions affecting their business. Essentially, they are sensing an immediate necessity to scale up their business in the given competitive environment.

Against the backdrop of such erratic consequences of family-run businesses, this chapter attempts to explore the concept and application of leadership affecting the various aspects of decision-making in family-run fast-food businesses in the city of in Gujarat, India. Researchers have taken art forms and its intersecting impact on family businesses under parameters such as imagination, inspiration, concentration, innovation, learning, and role identification as an artistic process. This has paved the way to understand the intersecting space between arts and business. This study attempts to establish arts as an artistic process and considers leadership as an arts-informed approach. The larger ambit of inquiry is to understand, how arts as a process facilitates in taking decisions in selected family businesses in Surat city. The methodology of conducting research has been stimulating and thought provoking as well. Focus group discussions and in-depth interviews were organized. Qualitative data were collected from consumers, family-run business owners, and local civic agencies, etc. to deduce appropriate learning and develop a complete view in the present study. The study proves that family-business owners can scale up their business by adopting an arts-informed leadership. Based on the study, researchers propose a conceptual model of arts driven learning process to engage employees in family businesses. To facilitate such an arts-informed leadership; an arts driven learning process must be incorporated to engage employees and make them feel connected to the vision of the business as a whole.

8.1 THE INDIAN HOSPITALITY INDUSTRY'S CURRENT PERFORMANCE

The 21st century has witnessed some incredible growth prospects of businesses around the world. In the Indian context, the tourism and hospitality industry has been showing promising economic growth over the last two decades. According to India Brand Equity Foundation (2015), tourism has increased its contribution to 6.8% of the gross domestic product (GDP) of India and it has also become the 3rd largest foreign exchange earner. The direct contribution to GDP by the industry had added up to US $44.2 billion

in 2015. Topping it up, the Indian Tourism and Hospitality industry is anticipated to rise up to 7.2% per year by 2025. The net worth of the industry is
expected to be approx. US $88.6 billion (Fig. 8.1).

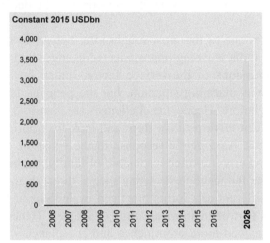

FIGURE 8.1   Direct contribution of tourism and hospitality to GDP (US$ billion).

(Reprinted from World Travel & Tourism Council, Travel & Tourism Economic Impact
2016 World. https://www.wttc.org/-/media/files/reports/economic%20impact%20research/
regions%202016/world2016.pdf. With permission.)

Within the ambit of the hospitality industry, the food industry in India is
also growing at a faster pace over the last few years.

The Indian hospitality industry represents a business space that is poised
for strong growth in terms of top-line revenues. This growth is currently
riding largely on the capacity addition that is organic in nature. Nearly all
segments that constitute the hospitality industry including hotels, restaurants,
catering, and events have experienced revenue growth supported by capacity
expansion. It is interesting to further analyze where this growth has come
from, in terms of geographic, demographic, and the sociocultural contexts.

The above-discussed top-line growth however needs to be viewed from
the lens of profitability. Both domestic as well as international hospitality
businesses have reported pressure on their bottom lines. While some like
IHCL have witnessed steep losses quarter on quarter, others too have struggled to achieve healthy profitability. Reasons for this rather indifferent
performance need to be investigated. Is this a result of ill thought investments toward capacity building or is it about efficiency-related issues in
the operational context? The "owners" as well as "operators" of hospitality
businesses are struggling to return to healthy profitability. This chapter will
evaluate this dilemma and offer a perspective.

The peoples challenge, especially on the leadership front continues to be an issue; this critical success factor would be given due space in this chapter in order to offer a comprehensive response and recommendation based on the needs of the hospitality industry to take decisive steps to fix this problem.

Leadership is one of the most sought after behaviors in the hospitality industry today. India is facing unprecedented changes both at the economic and social dimensions of the service sector. Indian business leaders are responding to this alarming situation, but the people's issues are surging more than ever before. Hence, the challenges are manifold and it is through leadership one can drive positive steps and look for solutions in these hard times in business. As a gentle response to the situation, the focus of the chapter is around arts-informed leadership of family-run businesses in food restaurants in the Indian context, with a special thrust on the artistic process derived from different arts forms practiced by individual family-run business owners as part of their leisure time or interest. Hence, such a leadership approach gained more prominence and acceptance with the changing demands, tastes and preferences of food, and surrounding ambience of the Surat region and its ethnicity.

8.2   CONNECTING ARTS AND BUSINESS

The way we all think is a process we do continuously without halting for a moment. Similarly, creativity is something which must become a part of our daily life and routine. And, the way we think is the way we all are creative, which can be enhanced by immersing in a culture supporting innovation all around. Such a culture is possible to be built if we embrace arts as a medium. Arts possess the potential to build a congenial culture filled with creativity and imagination in modern organizations of the 21st century. Because we are all in a so-called new business landscape, we need new competencies, models, frameworks, cutting-edge technologies, and innovation to address new and unprecedented decision-based challenges. Hence, arts are an answer to a lot many issues confronted by today's business organizations. In fact, these organizations are looking forward to unconventional thinking, assuring a dynamic change in the whole system and practices.

To study the effectiveness of arts in finding solutions to business issues, there have been many research projects planned and completed successfully in most of the European countries over the last decade. Some of the prominent studies were (a) the AIRIS (Artists in Residence) Program, conducted in Sweden, (b) the NyX Innovation Alliances Program, in Denmark, and (c) the Unilever's Catalyst Program.

(a) *The AIRIS Program* in Sweden was conducted to understand the possible impact of artists coming in contact with business managers and business-related issues. The purpose was to attend to issues from a different and novel perspective of artists. Artists are the ones who carry the artistic blend of mind to "think" beyond limitations. AIRIS program was supported by intermediary organization, TILLT. Artists carrying different background in arts were paired together with diverse business organizations: private firms, public firms, municipal authorities, etc. The duration of time assigned to artists was for 10 months, to act as creative consultants in tandem with the business firms. The experience identified many gaps and brought many new observations in the whole process of aligning arts and business. The experience enabled researchers to pursue further studies in this direction. Katja Lindqvist studied projects pertaining to this from the years 2002 to 2004, and then Alexander Styhre and Michael Eriksson studied projects from 2005 to 2008 (Eriksson, 2009; Lindqvist, 2005; Styhre & Eriksson, 2008).

(b) *NyX Innovation Alliances Program* was also on the same agenda to understand how artists can make a significant difference in a business unit. Twenty artists were chosen to pair up with 20 different organizations from different industries. The duration of time was 20 days. Two researchers, David Barry and Stefan Meisiek, have been interested to carry out this project with the purpose to shed some light on, how these artists and business issues can be related in a manner that it could produce some results in terms of understanding how and when they jointly work or do not work (Barry & Meisiek, 2004).

(c) *Unilever's Catalyst Program*: This initiative of Unilever was commendable in this direction. The program stood out amongst some of the major studies carried out in arts and business in Europe, so far (e.g., Arts & Business, 2004; Buswick et al., 2004; Darsø, 2004; Schiuma, 2009). The program stretched from the year 2000 through 2007. Because of its extensive duration, a lot of arts-based initiatives were explored. It was one of its kind and the largest corporate arts event in the United Kingdom (Arts & Business, 2004:23). The idea of having such an art intervention was proposed to Unilever by Alaistair Creamer, an external arts consultant. There were many varied arts-based activities introduced along with artists-in-residence projects as well. The Catalyst program was conducted in two companies of Unilever, Lever Fabergé, and Unilever & Frozen Food. Employee participation was quite satisfactory comprising of nearly 70% of staff. The staff participated in at least one of the activities conducted; 23% employees were serial participants for the initial four consecutive years of the program.

Based on these studies, it was clear that arts and business, although appearing to have no real connection, have an underlying strong interrelationship.

Drawing inputs from such studies, researchers were motivated to explore further about art forms. The purpose was to see whether there exists any work of arts evolving out of different art forms being practiced by family-business owners. Also, efforts were made to see if a novel leadership style can be thought of or proposed by incorporating an artistic process of a particular art form like music, dance, drama, painting, etc. In addition, efforts were also directed toward proposing a conceptual model of an arts-driven learning process to engage employees. Researchers believe in leadership which possesses the ability to visualize, imagine, and concentrate better while taking decisions. In order to take better decisions for the business, the owner is supposed to cultivate a learning environment for its employees, in turn, making them more engaged with their jobs and the organization as well. Hence, the purpose is to encourage leadership which can engage employees through effective learning processes. As a result, such an ambience of learning would surely impact decision-making instances among family-business owners.

8.3   LEADERSHIP AND ART FORMS

Referring to arts informed research, researchers believe that leadership is grounded in the arts in several ways. Such an existence must be presented explicitly to diverse audience through means that rely on arts. Hence, arts-informed leadership becomes relevant due to its deep-rooted presence in arts and its applicability in different and varied disciplines of interest. According to Adler (2006), the new ways of managing business must come from innovative practices. She states,

Given the dramatic changes taking place in society, the economy, and technology, 21st-century organizations need to engage in new, more spontaneous, and more innovative ways of managing. I investigate why an increasing number of companies are including artists and artistic processes in their approaches to strategic and day-to-day management and leadership. (p. 486)

Similarly, Pink (2004) in Harvard Business Review quoted, "The MFA is the New MBA ... An arts degree is now perhaps the hottest credential in the world of business". (21)

Adler (2006) in her chapter titled, *The Arts and Leadership: Now That We Can Do Anything, What Will We Do?* mentioned an email from Rob Auston, Professor of Technology and Management at Harvard Business School who stated, "The economy of the future will be about creating value and appropriate forms, and no one knows more about the processes for doing that than artists."

8.3.1 INSTRUMENTAL ROLE OF ARTS IN CULTIVATION OF ARTS-INFORMED LEADERSHIP

The manager will be in a better position to run the business if the system is organized, programs are well-defined, objectives are clear, targets are achieved regularly, structure is yielding results, technology is friendly to use, communication channels are effective to transfer the intent of management to all stakeholders, market is stable, customers are responding to products/services offered, and most importantly, subsystems and projects are standardized and uniform. The manager is able to do so due to the recurrent and conventional nature of his job. Hence, the manager will have sufficient time to plan, gather resources, and implement in terms of responding and handling to any challenge coming his way.

Contrarily, in wake of the erratic behavior of business on account of industry prone factors or macroeconomic instability with high market volatility; the manager will have to change the managerial mode to leadership mode. The entire organizational system would call for an overhauling in terms of revisiting the vision, mission, and objectives of the company. This happens due to factors such as changing market, underneath chaos in the system, undefined programs, unclear objectives, difficulty in achieving targets, incapable structure yielding poor results, sophisticated and nonuser friendly technology, improper and complex communication channels, indifferent customers, imitation of products, and services by competitors. Moreover the subsystems, processes, operations, communication channels, etc. must be revitalized and reinvented. It must be done in such a manner that the consistent usage of different structural components of the system must not crumble. In case such a crumbling occurs, it will lead to unbearable shockwaves jolting the entire organizational system. Such shockwaves may be either originating from the internal system or emanating through external disruptions.

Correction in the organizational system may be successfully carried out by an effective leader. However, a lot has been researched on leadership. Different leadership models and approaches have been studied and implemented all this while. But so far, business has failed to identify a leadership model or approach which can be equally effective in terms of attaining defined business objectives, and balancing with employee engagement, well-being, and happiness engrossing the long-term business sustainability. The chapter suggests an alternate mode of leadership approach fueled by a separate field of study altogether, that is, arts-informed leadership. Broadly, the chapter is based on its current focus of research in arts-informed leadership that strives to address the issue of decision-making processes among family-business owners.

Today, leadership lacks facets such as creativity, sensitivity, hope, emotional stability, perseverance, imagination, intuitive mindset, concentration, identification of characters in the larger environment of business. These features have been focused upon due to their rejuvenating capacity to initiate change in the chaotic and undemocratic system in business. No more, business can be run with stiffness, a standardized approach and conventional thoughts of mass production and consumption; wherein revenue generation, profit maximization, and shareholders' dividends are kept at the center of all business-related objectives. Management issues which do not fall into the existing category are considered to be mediocre, less viable, and inflexible. Going forward, these are considered to be extremely challenging situations for discussion and inclusion by management practitioners of the industry. But the question is how do we do it? The answer lies somewhere in the interdisciplinary approach of finding solutions. A discipline which is considered to be different from business and management is the world of arts. Quite often business lacks a "thinking" approach or the creative sense. This leads management to continue to run on a mechanistic approach while tackling business situations in the industry. But researchers are now taking keen interest in the belief, that creativity and innovation in work settings are "must" factors for a congenial and learning environment. Darso and Dawids (2002) have acknowledged the role of arts-based learning in relation to some of the identified behaviors and competencies which have shown improved performance benefits. For a new leadership to emerge, arts and artists can be a source of immense inspiration. Arts hold the vision, intuition, concentration, imagination, ideas, feelings, creativity, etc. However, these attributes are lacking in today's 21st century of business organizations. Thus, researchers strive to establish the relationship between how arts can impact the results of business when integrated. Arts can be instrumental in enriching the new leadership order in business by offering imagination, intuition, envisioning ability, self-expression, etc. As a leader, it would enable him to view the larger picture without losing attention of the core aspects of business.

8.3.2 ART FORMS: FACILITATOR OF INNER TRANSFORMATION AND AWAKENING OF CONSCIOUSNESS

Arts are all about the outlet or a channel of expressions. Art is more of a creative impulse evolving from deep within. It gets expressed through physical manifestation. These expressions are deeply influenced by culture. With the passage of time, arts even help in changing the culture. Different art forms such as *visual arts* (painting, drawing, ceramics, and sculpting); *performing arts* (music, dance, theater); *culinary arts* (baking, chocolate making, and winemaking) have been instrumental in transforming cultures through the ages. These different art forms carry an innate sense of traits, which can be identified and replicated into other disciplines such as diverse business functions and domains. These functions and domains cater to the needs of millions of customers offering products and services. An art form is centered around creativity, and it involves predominantly the element of creativity and innovation. The creativity itself is a big transforming element, from commencement through culmination of art forms such as drawing, painting, dance, music, drama, storytelling, inter-alia.

Hence, dwelling into arts and its distinctive features, must be studied in the light of business and management. Precisely, conventional business processes and practices are being carved and planned with calculated success rates in the absence of artistic processes. But these calculated success rates have never been successful for long, and they have diminished over shorter periods of time. On the contrary, by zeroing in on the artistic process through arts, the success rates of business solutions would multiply and in turn, it would enable a more sustained and holistic result for the business community of the 21st century. Since the field of study is relatively new, a lot of research inputs in this direction are to be generated in order to justify this assumption. However, according to Paintner (2007), since art forms are expressive arts and it is found to be very liberating; the focus of such expressive arts is on the process of art making, not on the art product or end product itself. Further, the focus of expressive arts is on the power and process of symbolic expression in any of the arts. When expressive arts emphasizes on process as the goal instead of product, the arts create a room for experimentation and possibilities of new frontiers of gains. Art making enables the individual to notice stimulations within, such as joy, insight, happiness, resistance, queries, etc. in turn, leading to self-introspection, forging connections, and affiliating with others effectively.

Traditionally, business sees arts for decoration. Gradually, business started using arts for entertainment. It was seen as a leisure generating experience for the employees. A little more seriousness was observed, when business started recognizing arts as an instrument to tackle issues of working teams, improving communication channels, instilling leadership qualities amongst managers, introducing innovation as a practice, etc. But the impact has been ephemeral. Hence, the business fraternity is really not in a position to accept the fact that arts or art forms possess the potential to offer sustainable results in terms of generating the creative element amongst staff and managers. Business communities are divided into silos. They are at loggerheads to consider arts as an effective medium toward changing the leadership approach. It could be by bringing change in various subsystems of modern organizations. Giving due consideration to the way arts is being seen as an instrument, the present chapter proposes that managers and practitioners in business organizations experience arts a strategic process of transformation through personal development and leadership, culture and identity, creativity, and innovation.

According to Darso (2004), artful creation is all about art experiences that initiate an inner transformation, which opens up a special kind of consciousness developed through direct experiences. It involves feelings that touch the person profoundly. Such an unprecedented view on arts will change the whole approach toward attempting the business issues. Moreover, the solutions would become a part of the process itself. Unlike the ephemeral end results are visible only when the programs, trainings, and conventional interventions get over. As a result, such ephemeral end results offer very little room for improvement and corrections in between.

8.4   FAMILY-RUN BUSINESS: LEADERSHIP AND DECISION-MAKING

In order to establish a sound connect between arts, leadership, decision-making, and learning in family-run businesses, it is important to keep abreast with the dynamic changes happening in the arena of family businesses over the last few years globally. Today, the world economy is strongly supported by family businesses operating in developed and developing economies. The contribution is more than 75% in terms of GDP in most countries. Also, the family businesses have its contribution in terms of generating employment for more than 85% of the working population around the globe (Poza, 2007).

It is astonishing to know that 80% of the world's business organizations are considered to be family businesses as per the World Competitive Report released in the year 2000 (Lee & Li, 2009). In European countries like Germany and Britain; family-business organizations generate a total national employment of up to 75% and 50%, respectively. Moreover, Germany's family businesses contribute about 66% of GDP. On the other hand, it is also seen that family businesses are equally strong in their presence and contribution in Asian and South-east Asian countries as well. Family businesses in countries like Taiwan, Malaysia, and Korea have GDP contributions of 61.6%, 67.2%, and 48.2%, respectively.

Family businesses have not been well researched at the global and local level, particularly in the light of today's economic order. The intricacies of family business remain unwatched on account of limited research, with less collaborative efforts amongst different countries. It is necessary to carry out joint research in the interdisciplinary areas of arts and business. As a result, it created gaps in developing an integrated theory of family firms (Brice, 2007). According to Dyer (2003), family-business research did not receive its due attention due to the overlooking tendency of business researchers. They failed to sharply focus at relevant family-business issues primarily leadership, governance, strategy, structure, people, processes, culture, succession planning, conflict resolution, change, etc.

Researchers like Astrachan (2010) emphasized on expediting attention toward extensive research and theory building in family businesses. However, he acknowledged and stated that family businesses have been proportionally superior to other businesses. Employment and growth have been quite significant (IFERA, 2003), due to the contribution of family business to the gross world product.

Therefore, taking cognizance of the situation, this inadequate research work calls for a focused approach and comprehensive study on the decision-making of family-business leaders. Here, decision-making is to be seen within self as, an outcome of the deliberations by the family-business leader. The factors responsible in the building up of a mindset of decision-making must be studied extensively. Such an envisioned study will pave way for strengthening the knowledge of mechanisms, in turn leading organizations to contribute in socioeconomic and -cultural growth and development of nations as a whole. Past limited research suggests that family-run businesses do not always succeed generation after generation. Reasons have been unearthed in many research studies, but the key factor that emerges out of all is still being studied and researched in various conditions, contexts, and cultures. By and large, the key factor remains the family member's ability to make sound and judicious decisions together (Tisue, 1996).

8.5 METHODOLOGY

Design of the study

This is a qualitative study using grounded theory.

The methodology of conducting research has been stimulating and thought provoking as well. Focus group (FG) discussions and in-depth interviews (IDIs) were organized as part of data collection. Qualitative data were collected from consumers and family-run business owners in the city of Surat located in the state of Gujarat, India. In addition, feedback was collected from local civic agencies as well, to deduce appropriate learning so as to develop a complete understanding about the prevailing conditions.

Out of the 107 fast-food restaurants in Surat, 84 fast-food restaurants were owned and run by family members. In order to move from the present contextual data to theoretical underpinnings, the grounded theory was, therefore found suitable for the development of contextualized theories. Based on the literature review, researchers were intrigued by the research question as:

"How do family-business owners with genuine interest and practice in arts forms experience ease in decision-making process and, in turn, evolve and manifest sound leadership?"

The phenomenon identified in the stated research question by researchers was the commencement of work in the direction of grounded theory.

8.5.1 OBJECTIVES OF THE STUDY

- To study the interest of family-owned business owners in different art forms.
- To explore reasons of such engagement in art forms by family-run business owners.
- To explore the relationship between art forms and decision-making of family-owned business owners in food restaurants in Surat.
- To familiarize with the leadership styles of family-run business owners taking interest in art forms.
- To understand the role of learning in engaging employees through art forms as practiced by family-run business owners in the food restaurants in Surat.

Research was conducted through initial interactions with 84 family-business owners to know their interest toward art forms. The purpose was to shortlist only those family-run business owners, who were engaged with one or the other art forms so that extensive FG discussions and IDIs may be conducted. Having had such personal interactions, eventually researchers arrived at 58 family-business owners who demonstrated their hobbies and interest toward art forms. Thus, focus-group discussions and IDIs with 58 family-run business owners in Surat were organized to specifically understand, how they were engaged with one or the other art forms as part of their hobbies or interests related to music, painting, drama, drawing, storytelling, dancing, etc. Further, it was also done to understand as how these art forms affected their leadership style, ability to take decisions, attitude, personality, creative thinking, visualization, imagination, pro-activeness, and spontaneity to situations.

FGs followed by IDIs were used to conduct qualitative research for the sample size of 58 family-run business owners of fast-food restaurants in Surat city, in the state of Gujarat in India. The purpose of using these types of qualitative methods was to obtain detailed information about personal and group feelings, perceptions, and opinions. Since we were in the initial stages of research, the usage of both methods was helpful in dealing with a small number of exploratory groups. Also, the population has not been studied extensively before. In addition, the field of study is relatively unexplored. FGs followed by IDIs, both have been compatible in terms of results among different groups of participants.

For the analysis of FG data, qualitative or ethnographic summary was used. As part of categorization of participants, researchers have categorized them using demographic factors, such as geographical locations, age groups, gender, size of the family, profit margin of business, participant's interest in a particular art form. In order to refer to individual categorization of these factors, the details are available in figures from Appendices A8.1–6.

FG discussions were conducted with each of the seven groups of family-business owners. These family-business owners were initially divided among seven groups based on different locations in Surat city. Also, classification was done based on gender male and female. Besides, size of the family, profit margin of the business (approx.), and participant's interest in a particular art form was also tabulated.

FG discussions were planned to be conducted keeping in view the participants availability and convenience to reach the venue. Family-business owners in different locations like Adajan, Bhatar Road, Dumas Road, Piplod, City Light Road, Vesu, and Ghod Dod Road in Surat city were personally contacted and objectives of the present research were shared. Their permission was sought to conduct FG discussions followed by IDIs at an individual level as per the given venues in Table 8.1. The venues ($N = 07$) were selected as per the seven locations of these fast-food restaurants run by family-business owners.

TABLE 8.1 Venue and Date of Focus Groups and Interviews.

S. No.	Venue/Location in Surat	Date of focus groups and in-depth interviews
1	Adajan	03:00–06:00 pm, 4 October 2015
2	Bhatar Road	10:00 am–01:00 pm, 11 October 2015
3	Dumas Road	10:00 am–01:00 pm, 18 October 2015
4	Piplod	10:00 am–01:00 pm, 25 October 2015
5	City Light Road	03:00–06:00 pm, 1 November 2015
6	Vesu	10:00 am–01:00 pm, 8 November 2015
7	Ghod Dod Road	03:00–06:00 pm, 15 November 2015

Researchers collected the data through initial open coding followed by axial coding. The IDIs, led to the process of theoretical sampling in the light of categories. Essentially, it was to check emerging theory keeping in view the reality through sampling incidents. The purpose was to arrive at theoretical saturation, eventually. Tentative linkages between categories were established, resulting into multiple returns to the field to collect further data. Memo-writing was maintained throughout the process of data collection and analysis to keep written record of theory development.

In the analysis, the researchers have given special attention to the words and their meaning and the context in which the comments were made during the conduction of FGs and IDIs. Also, internal consistency, frequency, the specificity of answers, extent of comments, etc. have also been given due consideration.

In addition, separate interviews were conducted with consumers who were regular customers of these fast-food restaurants. They have shared their overall experiences of having food and services provided by these restaurants. Besides, the civic agency of Surat has also been contacted to receive inputs on the directives and actions taken to ensure hygienic conditions, food, and safety measures offered by family-run food Restaurants in Surat. The details are mentioned in Section 8.5.

8.6   RESULTS AND DISCUSSIONS

Initially, the work appeared to be unending due to the abundance of data and information. A big portion of data and information was to be analyzed in a stipulated period of time. Hence, the work has been challenging and time-consuming. Interactions within family-business owners were to be analyzed and that they needed to be structured as part of discussion. Besides, the views and responses from customers and feedback from civic agency of Surat were to be incorporated as part of analysis of data collected for the present study. In the present section, researchers have done the study in three-fold: (a) focus groups; (b) IDIs; and (c) customer response and feedback from the civic agency of Surat.

8.6.1   FOCUS GROUPS

People like to share their experiences, interests and ideas, either in a manner of open-ended discussions or in a shared environment. The primary focus was with respect to each person's reality at an individual level. Going forward, it addresses the people as a whole. They like to seek appreciations or suggestions from others in order to get better understanding of what they have been thinking and experiencing. Such sought appreciations or suggestions from others have to be met through application of certain methods or techniques. In the present study, researchers decided to apply FG discussion as one of the qualitative research methods available in order to analyze the interaction inside the group, along with the presence of moderator stimulating the subject or comments. Finally, based on the data collected, transcripts of the group discussions have been produced along with the moderator's observations, reflections, and annotations as well.

Participants were invited on mutually agreed dates. The seven venues were selected based on the participant's convenience. The venues were Adajan, Bhatar Road, Dumas Road, Piplod, City Light Road, Vesu, Ghod Dod as mentioned in Table 8.1. FG discussion was carried out with each group on specified date within the period of 40 days, commencing from the October 4 through November 15, 2015. Each group had 8–10 participants for the FG. The total numbers of participants were 58. All FG discussions went on for 90 min each.

Participants were asked questions in relation to their background, family members, size of the family; reasons of joining the family business; profit margin of their business; their hobbies and interests; past experiences relating to their interests in art forms; how they would spend quality time performing these art forms; about their views on engaging in art forms resulting into positive outcomes in running family-owned restaurant business; narrated instances in family-run business wherein they experienced the presence of art form; their views on benefits of engaging in art forms leading to better decision-making abilities in their business; the possible drawbacks of not engaging in any of the art forms in one's life; their success in retaining customers and increasing the customer base and the role of art forms facilitating the goal of customer retention; contribution of engagement in art forms in improving their decision-making abilities; contribution of engagement in art forms in building an effective leadership style.

For this part of the study, apart from background and family-related information, researchers paid more attention to the above queries and questions related to participants' art forms and its connection with family-run food restaurant business. It focused on leadership style, decision-making ability, attitude, personality, creative thinking, pro-activeness and spontaneity as shared in the FG discussions followed by IDIs.

8.6.1.1 FOCUS GROUP DISCUSSION: GROUP/LOCATION A-ADAJAN

Group A, of FG included 10 family-run business owners of fast-food restaurants from Adajan location in Surat. All family-run business owners reached on time and we could start at 03:00 pm, October 4, 2015 (Sunday). The entire FG discussion went on for 90 min giving ample time to speak, share, differ and agree upon views by one and all participants. In fact, this ample duration gave enough inputs to researchers in collecting research data. Moderator initiated the talk and briefly explained the purpose and the structure of the FG. It was clearly stated that each participant must speak his own mind and that he/she should not get carried away by others opinion or viewpoints. Moderator started with the first question by asking each one to share their background in brief. They were asked to share the reasons for joining their business as well. The summarized version of the key findings is available in Appendix A8.7.

Having done the introduction of each participant along with individual reasons of joining their family-owned restaurant business, researchers asked other relevant questions. These questions were answered by participants on one-on-one basis. Some of the relevant questions were: How do you generally spend your free time apart from working in your restaurant? Do you engage in any sort of art form? How do you think art form helps in one's grooming? What are some of the art forms you generally perform in your leisure time? How do you see engaging in art form helps you in your business? Narrate some of the instances in your family business, where you experienced the presence of art form? How do you think the benefits of engaging in art forms have enabled you to become a good and effective leader in your business? How do you think the benefits of engaging in art form have enabled you to have better decision-making abilities in your business? How important is learning for employees working in your family-run business? What are the possible drawbacks if someone from your family-run business does not engage in any of the art forms?

Researchers conducted FGs discussions with group 1, Location-A, as per the above inferences. Similarly, researchers carried out six FG discussions with the remaining categories of FGs in other locations as well. Out of all the FG discussions conducted by researchers, it became feasible for them to understand and relate better as how effective it is to have benefits of art forms such as painting, dancing, drama, acting, singing, drawing, calligraphy, etc. in family businesses. Following elements have been identified as key attributes based on the performance and practice of art forms by these family-business owners running family restaurants in Surat. Accordingly, engaging or participating in arts forms improves concentration; invokes inspiration from within; enables creative thinking; helps in visualizing and imagining better; builds up confidence and courage; enables calmness and warmth; enables pro-activeness and spontaneity; cultivates prudence in decisions and most importantly, it connects one to spirituality.

8.6.2   IN-DEPTH INTERVIEWS

IDIs were conducted after the completion of each FG discussion as per the scheduled dates in Table 8.1. IDIs were extensive in comparison to FGs. Here, each individual family-run business owner was interviewed at length. Some of the broad areas of IDIs were related to participants' personal time and interest specially when they are not engaged with customers at their restaurants; their personal preference to spend free time; their gains or outcomes based on their interest in art forms such as singing, dancing, drama, painting; their association and duration of practice of art forms; their involvement in art forms through practice and preparation and the time devoted for the same; and the ways the art forms helped them in deriving benefits in other facets of their life as well.

8.6.3   CUSTOMER FEEDBACK

In addition, consumers were also contacted. These consumers were regular visitors of selected fast-food restaurants run by family-business owners in Surat city. Some of these loyal customers were so regular that they have been coming to these food restaurants for more than two or three decades with their entire family members. These customers shared their views on the quality of food. They gave excellent feedback and also appreciated the hospitality rendered by these restaurants. When asked about the family-business owners of these restaurants and their behavior toward regular customers, they gave very positive responses saying that the owners have been very cordial and supportive. Cited instances where these family-business owners had gone out of their ways to render support to these customers in need. Their approach toward customers has been friendly with warmth in their talk. According to these customers, these family-run business owners also take good care of their staff who are employed on monthly salaries.

Feedbacks received from the civic agency of Surat with regard to these family-run restaurants have been extremely positive. According to them, by and large, these family-run food restaurants have been complying with the health measures and guidelines issued by the Corporation on a regular basis. Some of these family-run restaurants have earned award as well.

8.7 MANAGERIAL PERSPECTIVE OF ART FORMS IN FAMILY BUSINESS

Across the globe, companies have been striving for better performance and profitability. These companies have been worrying about finding new and innovative ways to solve managerial and business problems, keeping in view limited resources and the cost factor. However, due to constant change dynamics, businesses have no other option but to respond to changes. Such an approach calls for unconventional practices and path-breaking solutions in their market. These MNCs and smaller companies across the globe have been run either by family businessmen or professionals or both. The flip side relates to the employees working in these organizations. Since these employees are associated with these big, medium, or smaller firms, they are on the verge of extreme pressure to deliver so as to meet high targets and raise the productivity as well. Such a pressurized culture invites an unwanted stressful life affecting severely individuals' mind and their personal life. On the other hand, due to this stressful life, employees find themselves in a confused state of mind as they do not know much about the situation. Also, they are not aware of effective ways of dealing with such complex environment as well.

Regarding the present study, family-business owners have admitted the fact that they have been taking keen interest in art forms leading to a lot of benefits at a personal front. They also acknowledged the fact that these benefits have brought in a lot of changes in the ways they pursued their overall family business. Respondents have mentioned about their interest toward music, singing, drawing, painting, dancing, acting, drama, calligraphy, etc. These art forms have been highly effective for them in terms of helping them exceptionally, rather than resulting into whiling away their time. The art forms helped them in observing things minutely. It enabled them to understand every aspect of an issue before arriving at a conclusion. Art forms enabled them to remain calm and composed particularly during the moments of tension and stress. They acknowledged the role of their individual art forms in establishing clarity of thoughts while dealing with customers, suppliers and distributors. Also, they witnessed the impact of art forms in their overall personality. They have become well-rounded personality specially dealing with different types of people. Such a change was visible when customers would interact with them with more affinity and trust than ever before. Engaging with art forms generated a lot if ideas and concepts for their businesses in terms of reducing cost and improving customer experience. This has positively influenced their creativity. Respondents have shared instances of creative sense in their communication and complex situations as well. Associating with art forms for longer period of time has helped them in nurturing their own leadership styles. Be it painting, dance, or music, one has to take lead if one is driven by passion to do something great. Such a motto in mind drives individual to take lead and take charge as well. Identification of right leadership is again a process of observation in oneself. Such a right leadership is recognized based on one's own individual experience with people. Here, the family-business owners have been experiencing their own individual leadership styles. These leadership styles got validated when they started practicing them with customers and other stakeholders while doing business. Similarly, respondents have acknowledged the role of visualization of their business. Such a visualization capability got gradually nurtured as part of their association with concerned art forms such as music, dance, painting, etc. In the context of business, visualization has been considered to be a great quality when the business is waiting to scale up. If the family-business owners have no such visualizing capability, chances of taking the business to the next level gets blurred. Critics may like to defend by saying that these qualities are unevenly present in individuals and they are far away from embracing art forms in their personal life. It might be true. However, associating with art forms naturally yield such benefits in terms of abilities of visualizing the larger picture and benefitting other aspects of one's own life. In the present study, family-business owners have been part of such association with different art forms and that they evidenced that such art forms have immensely contributed in their personal and business life.

8.8 IMPLICATIONS OF THE PRESENT STUDY

Based on the present study, certain gaps have been identified as why in most cases, employees in business do not like to perform in the given job or task. In business, employees are hired for a specific job. It means job is first created followed by the selection of candidate in order to fit the job requirements. An employee has to perform the way the superior sets goals for him with/without one's consent. Hence, it is necessary for the organizational system to generate an approach, which can cater to the needs and interests of employees. While designing jobs, the organizational system will take employees' interest into account. The focus will be given in terms of different components of expected work. Such an effort would possibly arrest the problem of disengagement of employees. According to the latest report by AON Hewitt (2015): *Trends in Global Employee Engagement*, the top employee engagement drivers that been identified were career opportunities, managing performance, communication, valuing people, HR practices, recognition, work processes, senior leadership. All these drivers have been seen as significant for an employee to be well engaged with his job in the organization. These drivers are clear indicators that organizations have not been putting due attention to take corrective measures on these aspects. Hence, it calls for a new framework or approach to bridge the gaps and the expected change in the system. However, there exist different models, approaches, and methodologies to bring such progressive change. Quite often, effectiveness of them in yielding results has been challenged. The present study becomes meaningful and adds value to address such progressive change. It points at an interdisciplinary approach of arts and its artistic process, so as to emulate the same for different challenges of organizational systems in business.

8.9   CONCEPTUAL MODEL OF ENGAGING EMPLOYEES THROUGH LEARNING—APPLYING ART FORMS

8.9.1   ABOUT LEARNING AND ITS RELEVANCE IN BUSINESS

Researchers have found that the family-business owners have a strong interest toward art forms. The inclinations toward art forms have shown ample evidence in terms of positive effects to their family-run business. For a business to flourish, organizations have to have a culture of absorbing new ideas and implementing them in a systematic and planned way. But to have such a well-nourished culture, organization needs to cultivate a learning environment. Learning organizations are those companies that facilitate learning of all its employees. It ensures to utilize learning in the smooth transformation of the organization. Learning environment helps the employees to keep abreast with the changes taking place and how those changes would affect their own existence and growth in the company. Hence, managers at all levels shoulder the responsibility to find, explore, and launch various ways and methods to facilitate organizational learning. More importantly, learning has been now correlated with fun as well. Fun element actually increases the attainment of knowledge through effective learning processes. However, organizations have adopted different training methods and processes to ensure better imparting of such learning. But the effectiveness of such learning processes has been challenged by authority for quite some time now. Hence, based on present research and various other studies conducted, researchers have proposed a model of arts driven learning process to engage employees.

Proposed Model of Arts Driven Learning Process to Engage Employees

The following conceptual model of an arts-driven learning process has been proposed by the researchers. The purpose of the model is to engage employees by merging the two different disciplines of study. The objective is to understand and explore different possibilities out of such merging efforts. This could be in the form of finding best solutions of the current problems in family-run businesses of the 21st century. However, futuristic challenges may also be covered while attending to prevailing problems and executing solutions as well. By and large, these issues are common in business across the globe and that the solutions too can be replicated in different scenarios with slight modifications and changes in the managerial approach or style (Fig. 8.2).

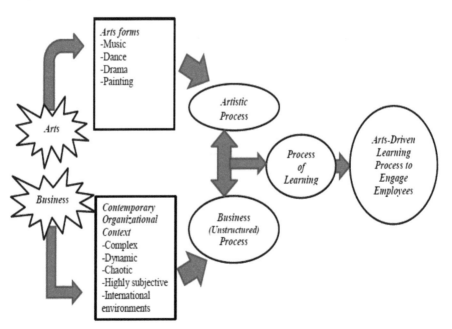

FIGURE 8.2 Conceptual model of arts-driven learning process to engage employees in transformational organization.

8.10   CONCLUSION

Researchers made recommendations in light of the present study that has been completed. The family-business owners running food restaurants were found to be running their business with much higher satisfaction and engagement particularly after engaging with art forms. Qualitative research data revealed that they have been highly influenced by art forms. Since the family-business owners selected for the study were in one or the other way, associated with painting, dance, music, calligraphy, drama, etc., their individual behavior toward others have changed and influenced their own business as well. Dealings with the customers improved and the difference in their approach affected their profit margin, positively.

Family-business owners were able to concentrate better in their businesses. Such concentration is attributed to art forms. Their focus toward business has improved like never before. They acknowledged that art forms have enabled them to visualize various aspects of their business and life at large. Their abilities to take decisions improved, significantly due to the enhanced power of intuition. Intuitive skills improved, significantly due to their continuity with concerned art forms, as art forms enable a person to be intuitive by nature and prepare to act on things which come subsequently. Also, imagination saw the difference. They affirmed that their ability to think unconventionally is something they noticed as an improvement in the long run. Innovation with respect to running the restaurant in a more attractive and sensitive manner has facilitated these family-business owners to prosper, in comparison to other non-family-business owners in the restaurant business in Surat city. Thus, these family-business owners share and practice these attributes in running their business effectively with better results. Collectively, these attributes are put together to form an arts-informed leadership.

An arts-informed leadership is what the present research work endeavors to capture. As mentioned, family-business owners have been deriving the benefit of arts not only in their personal life, but it also impacted in several ways in building and growing their family businesses. Given the kind of results and benefits, researchers have been successful in emphasizing on, arts-informed leadership holds the potential to bring innovation, efficiency, and eventually profitability in the long run.

A lot of research work in the field of arts and business is being undertaken in different parts of the world. Researchers are interested to understand the effective processes in arts, by which the learning outcomes may be achieved, in turn resolving business issues.

Essentially, the question of how to drive, retain, and sustain the desired impact through applied arts-based processes is also being considered. Future scope of research could be in the direction of arts as a process focusing toward training, organizational change, organizational structure, managerial processes, organizational culture, innovation and creativity, performance management, effective communication, better coordination among teams, and cultivating first- and second-level leadership. Such an approach will be worthwhile in terms of organizational effectiveness and sustainable practices.

To conclude, the research phase is in its embryonic stage. A lot of studies in different contexts with effective methodologies are to be adopted in order to validate the present findings. Moreover, these results are observed with the present category of sample. Hence, the results must be tested and validated in different cultural context as well. However, the present study was successful in introducing such an ethnographic phenomenon of an arts-informed leadership and engagement practices through learning by family-business owners in food restaurants in Surat city.

8.11   FURTHER SCOPE OF RESEARCH

Further scope of research exists in terms of studying how and in what manners artistic processes contribute or impact business organizations, widely. Research should also focus on the measurement of these artistic processes to prove their connections moving parallel or in sync with existing business processes of organizations operating in varied, modern, complex, dynamic, chaotic, and a highly subjective international environment.

KEYWORDS

- **arts**
- **family-run business**
- **leadership skills**
- **entrepreneurship**
- **restaurants**

REFERENCES

Adler, N. The Arts and Leadership: Now That We Can Do Anything, What Will We Do? *Acad. Manage. Learn. Learn.* **2006,** *5*(4), 486–499.

AON Hewitt. 2015 *Trends in Global Employee Engagement,* 2015. AON Hewitt. Retrieved from http://www.aon.com/germany/downloads/aonhewitt/aon_2015_trends_in_global_employee_engagement_report.pdf.

Arts & Business. *Art Works. Why Business Needs the Arts, Report.* Arts & Business: London, 2004.

Arts & Business, London. Retrieved from http://www.artsandbusiness.org.uk/Media%20library/Files/Research/Mapping%20ABIs%20%20Prof%20SchiumaFINAL.pdf.

Astrachan, J. Strategy in Family Business: Toward a Multidimensional Research Agenda. *J. Fam. Bus. Strat.* **2010,** *2010,* 6–14.

Barry, D.; S. Meisiek. *NyX Innovation Alliances Evaluation Report,* 15 September 2004, retrieved from http://www.dpb.dpu.dk/dokumentarkiv/Publications/20051215151928/CurrentVersion/rapport.pdf.

Brice, W. D. *The Cultural Basis of Management Strategy—Professional vs. Family Business Management in Three Countries,* Ph.D. diss., University of Hawaii, 2005.

Buswick, T.; Creamer, A.; Pinard, M. *(Re)Educating for Leadership. How the Arts Can Improve Business,* 2004.

Darso, L.; Dawids, M. It's Time for the Artists to Help the Poor Business People. *Learn. Lab Denmark Q.* **2002,** *October,* 6–7.

Darsø, L. Artful Creation: Learning-Tales of Arts-in-Business. Samfundslitteratur, Denmark, 2004.

Dyer, W. G. The Family: The Missing Variable in Organizational Research. *Entrepreneurship Theory Pract.* **2003,** *27*(4), 401–416.

Eriksson, M. *Expanding Your Comfort Zone—The Effects of Artistic and Cultural Intervention on the Workplace. A Study of AIRIS 2005–2008 (Including GenklangVara 2006–2008).* Institute for Management of Innovation and Technology: Göteborg, 2009.

India Brand Equity Foundation. *Tourism and Hospitality Industry in India,* September 2015. Retrieved from http://www.ibef.org/industry/tourism-hospitality-india.aspx (last accessed 8 December 2015).

International Family Enterprise Research Academy (IFERA). Family Businesses Dominate. *Fam. Bus. Rev.* **2003,** *16*(4), 235–240.

Lee, J.; Li, H. Wealth Doesn't Last 3 Generations—How Family Businesses Can Maintain Prosperity. *World Sci.* **2009,** *2009.*

Lindqvist, K. *Attgöradetfrämmande till sitt. Konstärerocharbetsplasterisamarbetsprojekt (Accommodating the Unfamiliar. Artists and Workplaces Collaborating).* Stockholm University: Stockholm, 2005.

Paintner, C. V. The Relationship between Spirituality and Artistic Expression: Cultivating the Capacity to Imagining. *Spiritual. High. Educ.* **2007,** *03*(02).

Pink, D. H. Breakthrough Ideas for 2004. *Harv. Bus. Rev.* **2004,** *February,* 21–22.

Poza, E. J. *Family Business,* 2nd ed. Thomson South-Western, 2007.

Schiuma, G. *The Value of Arts-Based Initiatives. Mapping Arts-Based Initiatives,* 2009.

Styhre, A.; Eriksson, M. Bring in the Arts and Get the Creativity for Free. A Study of the Artists in Residence Project. *Creat. Innov. Manage.* **2008,** *17*(1), 47–57.

Tisue, L. *Facilitating Dialogue and Decision-making in a Family Business.* Ph.D. Diss., The University of Tennessee: Knoxville, 1999.

APPENDIX A8.1

LIST OF FAMILY BUSINESS FOOD RESTAURANTS IN SURAT CITY, GUJARAT (LOCATION-WISE)

FIGURE A8.1.1   Group/Location-A.

S. No.	Restaurant	Location
1	Humpty Dumpty	Adajan
2	Green Apple—The Restaurant	
3	Exotic Island	
4	Real Madrid Restaurant	
5	The Glorious Restaurant	
6	Krishna	
7	Neapolitan Pizza	
8	Dawat Restaurant	
9	Navjivan Restaurant	
10	South India Restaurant	

FIGURE A8.1.2   Group/Location-B.

S. No.	Restaurant	Location
1	Panino—The Sandwich World	Bhatar Road
2	Hot-N-Cool	
3	Hotel Shyam	
4	Mealons-N-Chillons	
5	Flow Cafe—The Gateway Hotel	
6	Golden Gate Restaurant	
7	Spice and Chilly Restaurant	
8	Spice of India	

FIGURE A8.1.3   Group/Location-C.

S. No.	Restaurant	Location
1	TGB Restaurant	Dumas Road
2	Deepkala	
3	Gini & Jony	
4	Cafe Drums—The Grand Bhagwati	
5	Cilantro Restaurant	
6	Sugar N' Spice	
7	Deewan-E-Khaas	
8	Mosum—Best Western Yuvraj	
9	Indian Route Restaurant	

FIGURE A8.1.4   Group/Location-D.

S. No.	Restaurant	Location
1	Tempting Barbeque	Piplod
2	Smaaash Bazinga—The Sports Cafe	
3	Pearl Restaurant—Hotel Oyester	
4	Sqoopings'	
5	JD Restaurant	
6	Majhdhar Restaurant	
7	Swaad Restaurant	
8	Khushiyaan Restaurant	

FIGURE A8.1.5   Group/Location-E.

S. No.	Restaurant	Location
1	Basant Vihar Restaurant	City Light Road
2	Gluttony	
3	Kailash Fast Food & Restaurant	
4	Mamta Restaurant	
5	City Light Restaurant	
6	New Chhappan Bhog	
7	Kailash	
8	Hotel Girnar	

FIGURE A8.1.6   Group/Location-F.

S. No.	Restaurant	Location
1	The Hide Out Restro	Vesu
2	Blue Pearl—The Restaurant Lounge	
3	Shrinathji's Multi-Cuisine Fine Dine Restaurant	
4	Knockout Resto Lounge	
5	Sri Ram Snacks & Juice	
6	Hamdam Fast Food Corner	
7	Hotel Swagat Inn & Guest House	
8	Tipsy Topsy	

FIGURE A8.1.7   Group/Location-G.

S. No.	Restaurant	Location
1	Smokin' Joe's	Ghod Dod Road
2	Royal Treat—The Multi-Cuisine Restaurant	
3	Saffron Trade	
4	Mainland China	
5	Woodland's Fast Food & Caterers	
6	Flavours—The Multi-Cuisine Restaurant	
7	Sizzling Times	
8	Delight Restaurant	

APPENDIX A8.2

AGE GROUPS OF FAMILY-RUN BUSINESS OWNERS OF FAST-FOOD RESTAURANTS IN SURAT CITY

Age group	No. of participants
21–30	12
31–40	14
41–50	15
51–60	10
61–70	07
Total	58

APPENDIX A8.3

GENDER

Male	Female
47	11

APPENDIX A8.4

SIZE OF THE FAMILY OF FAMILY-RUN BUSINESS OWNERS IN SURAT CITY

FIGURE A8.4.1   Group/Location-A.

S. No.	Restaurant	Members in the family
1	Humpty Dumpty	12
2	Green Apple—The Restaurant	11
3	Exotic Island	9
4	Real Madrid Restaurant	8
5	The Glorious Restaurant	6
6	Krishna	9
7	Neopolitan Pizza	10
8	Dawat Restaurant	11
9	Navjivan Restaurant	14
10	South India Restaurant	12

FIGURE A8.4.2   Group/Location-B.

S. No.	Restaurant	Members in the family
1	Panino—The Sandwich World	13
2	Hot-N-Cool	11
3	Hotel Shyam	13
4	Mealons-N-Chillons	14
5	Flow Cafe—The Gateway Hotel	12
6	Golden Gate Restaurant	11
7	Spice and Chilly Restaurant	13
8	Spice of India	14

FIGURE A8.4.3   Group/Location-C.

S. No.	Restaurant	Members in the family
1	TGB Restaurant	10
2	Deepkala	11
3	Gini & Jony	12
4	Cafe Drums—The Grand Bhagwati	11
5	Cilantro Restaurant	13
6	Sugar N' Spice	14
7	Deewan-E-Khaas	12
8	Mosum—Best Western Yuvraj	15
9	Indian Route Restaurant	13

FIGURE A8.4.4   Group/Location-D.

S. No.	Restaurant	Members in the family
1	Tempting Barbeque	9
2	SmaaashBazinga—The Sports Cafe	7
3	Pearl Restaurant—Hotel Oyster	12
4	Sqoopings'	14
5	JD Restaurant	11
6	Majhdhar Restaurant	11
7	Swaad Restaurant	8
8	Khushiyaan Restaurant	14

FIGURE A8.4.5   Group/Location-E.

S. No.	Restaurant	Members in the family
1	Basant Vihar Restaurant	8
2	Gluttony	9
3	Kailash Fast Food & Restaurant	12
4	Mamta Restaurant	11
5	City Light Restaurant	13
6	New Chhappan Bhog	14
7	Kailash	12
8	Hotel Girnar	11

FIGURE A8.4.6   Group/Location-F.

S. No.	Restaurant	Members in the family
1	The Hide Out Restro	16
2	Blue Pearl—The Restaurant Lounge	13
3	Shrinathji's Multi-Cuisine Fine Dine Restaurant	8
4	Knockout Resto Lounge	7
5	Sri Ram Snacks & Juice	12
6	Hamdam Fast Food Corner	11
7	Hotel Swagat Inn & Guest House	13
8	Tipsy Topsy	9

FIGURE A8.4.7   Group/Location-G.

S. No.	Restaurant	Members in the family
1	Smokin' Joe's	8
2	Royal Treat—The Multi-Cuisine Restaurant	12
3	Saffron Trade	11
4	Mainland China	11
5	Woodland's Fast Food & Caterers	9
6	Flavours—The Multi-Cuisine Restaurant	11
7	Sizzling Times	10
8	Delight Restaurant	15

APPENDIX A8.5

PROFIT MARGIN (ANNUALLY) OF FAMILY-RUN BUSINESS OWNERS OF FAST-FOOD RESTAURANTS IN SURAT CITY

FIGURE A8.5.1   Group/Location-A.

S. No.	Restaurant	Approx. profit margin (%)—annually
1	Humpty Dumpty	4
2	Green Apple—The Restaurant	5
3	Exotic Island	5
4	Real Madrid Restaurant	3
5	The Glorious Restaurant	4
6	Krishna	4
7	Neopolitan Pizza	3
8	Dawat Restaurant	4
9	Navjivan Restaurant	5
10	South India Restaurant	7

FIGURE A8.5.2   Group/Location-B.

S. No.	Restaurant	Approx. profit margin (%)—annually
1	Panino—The Sandwich World	6
2	Hot-N-Cool	5
3	Hotel Shyam	6
4	Mealons-N-Chillons	5
5	Flow Cafe—The Gateway Hotel	5
6	Golden Gate Restaurant	4
7	Spice and Chilly Restaurant	4
8	Spice of India	5

FIGURE A8.5.3   Group/Location-C.

S. No.	Restaurant	Approx. profit margin (%)—annually
1	TGB Restaurant	4
2	Deepkala	3
3	Gini & Jony	4
4	Cafe Drums—The Grand Bhagwati	4
5	Cilantro Restaurant	5
6	Sugar N' Spice	5
7	Deewan-E-Khaas	3
8	Mosum—Best Western Yuvraj	5
9	Indian Route Restaurant	4

FIGURE A8.5.4   Group/Location-D.

S. No.	Restaurant	Approx. profit margin (%)—annually
1	Tempting Barbeque	4
2	SmaaashBazinga—The Sports Cafe	4
3	Pearl Restaurant—Hotel Oyester	5
4	Sqoopings'	6
5	JD Restaurant	5
6	Majhdhar Restaurant	6
7	Swaad Restaurant	4
8	Khushiyaan Restaurant	4

FIGURE A8.5.5   Group/Location-E.

S. No.	Restaurant	Approx. profit margin (%)—annually
1	BasantVihar Restaurant	3
2	Gluttony	4
3	Kailash Fast Food & Restaurant	4
4	Mamta Restaurant	3
5	City Light Restaurant	4
6	New Chhappan Bhog	5
7	Kailash	4
8	Hotel Girnar	4

FIGURE A8.5.6   Group/Location-F.

S. No.	Restaurant	Approx. profit margin (%)—annually
1	The Hide Out Restro	4
2	Blue Pearl—The Restaurant Lounge	4
3	Shrinathji's Multi-Cuisine Fine Dine Restaurant	3
4	Knockout Resto Lounge	4
5	Sri Ram Snacks & Juice	4
6	Hamdam Fast Food Corner	5
7	Hotel Swagat Inn & Guest House	5
8	Tipsy Topsy	6

FIGURE A8.5.7   Group/Location-G.

S. No.	Restaurant	Approx. profit margin (%)—annually
1	Smokin' Joe's	6
2	Royal Treat—The Multi-Cuisine Restaurant	6
3	Saffron Trade	6
4	Mainland China	4
5	Woodland's Fast Food & Caterers	5
6	Flavours—The Multi-Cuisine Restaurant	5
7	Sizzling Times	4
8	Delight Restaurant	4

APPENDIX A8.6

PARTICIPANT'S (FAMILY-RUN BUSINESS OWNERS) INTEREST IN AN ARTS FORM

FIGURE A8.6.1   Group/Location-A.

S. No.	Restaurant	Interest in arts forms
1	Rani Mehta, Humpty Dumpty	Music and singing
2	Sachin Patel, Green Apple—The Restaurant	Music and singing
3	Rosy Khemka, Exotic Island	Dancing
4	Ashish Kukreja, Real Madrid Restaurant	Music/Singing
5	Kishan Patel, The Glorious Restaurant	Dancing
6	Neha Kedia, Krishna	Drama and theater
7	Raj Chaliawala, Neopolitan Pizza	Painting and drawing
8	Ninad Parekh, Dawat Restaurant	Dancing—contemporary style
9	Jash Patel, Navjivan Restaurant	Dramatics/Theater
10	Raj Kanwar, South India Restaurant	Painting and drawing

FIGURE A8.6.2   Group/Location-B.

S. No.	Restaurant	Interest in arts forms
1	Aditya Bagla, Panino—The Sandwich World	Drawing
2	Divyam Mehta, Hot-N-Cool	Drama
3	Nisarg Jain, Hotel Shyam	Drawing
4	Dhrashti Patel, Mealons-N-Chillons	Music
5	Raj Vankawala, Flow Cafe—The Gateway Hotel	Calligraphy
6	Manan Jain, Golden Gate Restaurant	Dancing
7	Deepak Kanojia, Spice and Chilly Restaurant	Painting
8	Diya Patel, Spice of India	Drama

FIGURE A8.6.3   Group/Location-C.

S. No.	Restaurant	Interest in arts forms
1	Vimal Jain, TGB Restaurant	Music
2	Sagar Patel, Deepkala	Dancing
3	Sachin Patel, Gini & Jony	Drama
4	Rajesh Daruwala, Cafe Drums	Music
5	Raj Mehta, Cilantro Restaurant	Dancing
6	Rakhi Patel, Sugar N' Spice	Dancing
7	Kishan Jain, Deewan-E-Khaas	Music
8	Anshul Adhiya, Mosum—Best Western Yuvraj	Calligraphy
9	Prasoon Jain, Indian Route Restaurant	Drama

FIGURE A8.6.4   Group/Location-D.

S. No.	Restaurant	Interest in arts forms
1	Jigar Malik, Tempting Barbeque	Dancing
2	Sameer Daruwala, SmaaashBazinga	Drama
3	Nirmal Shah, Pearl Restaurant—Hotel Oyester	Music
4	Anjana Jain, Sqoopings'	Drama
5	Sanjeev Vankawala, JD Restaurant	Dancing
6	Shahbaaz Ali, Majhdhar Restaurant	Music
7	Suresh Dhbiwala, Swaad Restaurant	Painting
8	Vidhi Batliwala, Khushiyaan Restaurant	Painting

FIGURE A8.6.5   Group/Location-E.

S. No.	Restaurant	Interest in arts forms
1	Keshav Patel, Basant Vihar Restaurant	Drama
2	Rohit Shah, Gluttony	Dancing
3	Aditya Jain, Kailash Fast Food & Restaurant	Music
4	Shubhangi Shah, Mamta Restaurant	Drawing
5	Ravi Jham, City Light Restaurant	Painting
6	Anmol Mehta, New Chhappan Bhog	Calligraphy
7	Sachin Shah, Kailash Hotel	Music
8	Hitesh Jain, Hotel Girnar	Dancing

FIGURE A8.6.6   Group/Location-F.

S. No.	Restaurant	Interest in arts forms
1	Kishan Mehta, The Hide Out Restro	Dancing
2	Raveesh Nath, Blue Pearl Restaurant Lounge	Drama
3	Vihit Pancholi, Moonlight Restaurant	Music
4	Jay Narola, Knockout Resto Lounge	Drawing
5	Chiranjeev Jain, Sri Ram Snacks & Juice	Calligraphy
6	Simran Naaz, Hamdam Fast Food Corner	Painting
7	Mohit Jain, Hotel Swagat Inn & Guest House	Drama
8	Dhirendra Singh, Tipsy Topsy	Music

FIGURE A8.6.6   Group/Location-G.

S. No.	Restaurant	Interest in arts forms
1	Rishi Shah, Smokin' Joe's	Music
2	Sanjay Sanghvi, Royal Treat Restaurant	Drama
3	Safhan Zariwala, Saffron Trade	Painting
4	Atraya Patel, Mainland China	Music
5	Rashmi Jain, Woodland's Fast Food & Caterers	Drama
6	Ravi Thakkar, Flavours of India	Drama
7	Vishal Thakur, Sizzling Times	Dancing
8	Md. Younus, Delight Restaurant	Calligraphy

APPENDIX A8.7: MAJOR FINDINGS OF FOCUS GROUP DISCUSSIONS—GROUP/LOCATION A—ADAJAN

RESPONDENTS' CONNECTION WITH ARTS FORMS AND BENEFITS IN FAMILY BUSINESS

	Background and reasons of joining family business	Role of arts forms in personal life	Interest in specific arts form	Benefits of arts forms in family business	Ways of arts forms enabling leadership formation in family business	Ways of arts forms enabling better decision-makings abilities
Respondent 01: Rani Mehta, Humpty Dumpty	150 years old FB; four brothers; prefers autonomy	Loves music; a passionate singer; the best way to relieve stress; brings peace to heart and soul	Music/Singing	Stress-reliever; enables creativity; generates visualization; increases persistence to deal with situations; cultivates proactive behavior; builds up rounded personality	Singing calls for a lot of initiatives; facilitates in taking charge of situations; cultivates clarity of thoughts being a leader; helps in taking unconventional steps in business	Enables better observational skills to understand situations; helps in searching for alternatives; facilitates to go deeper into the subject
Respondent 02: Sachin Patel, Green Apple-The Restaurant	50 years old food business; run by two brothers Joined family business to support the family	Passionate singer; loves Sufi music; performed in music events; brings happiness	Music and Singing	Builds concentration; enables creativity; facilitates new ideas; helps in connecting with others; cultivates proactive behavior; builds up rounded personality	Leadership helps in analyzing the situation well; it enables the ways of motivating others; leadership facilitates in connecting with others at an emotional level	Increases spontaneity; helps in having more choices; empathetic approach ensures balanced decision; facilitates better channels of communication
Respondent 03: Rosy Khemka, Exotic Island	22 years old FB; crowd pullers are young generation; designs, artistic decorations, and customized services are the USP	Dancing helps in relieving stress; helps in progressing for perfection; medium of effective communication	Dancing	Enhances visual–spatial skills; facilitates imagination for business; enables formation of connected thoughts to improve family business; increases self-satisfaction	Leadership encourages ideas and contribution from others; builds balance between individual vs. group interactions; leadership prioritizes vision and the clear communication of that vision; cultivates positive attitude and empathy to strengthen leadership practice	Increases agility and focus in decision-making; ensures larger view of scenario; others view and opinion is taken into account; increases transparency in communication

APPENDIX A8.7 *(Continued)*

	Background and reasons of joining family business	Role of arts forms in personal life	Interest in specific arts form	Benefits of arts forms in family business	Ways of arts forms enabling leadership formation in family business	Ways of arts forms enabling better decision-makings abilities
Respondent 04: Ashish Kukreja, Real Madrid Restaurant	Migrated from Multan during partition of India-Pak; 67 years old FB; middle-aged and senior citizens are primary customers; joined FB to support family; prefers autonomy	Listening to music during free time; enjoys old melodies; likes to meet accomplished singers and musicians Singing brings satisfaction	Music/Singing	Helps in thinking innovatively; generates inner peace; generates sincerity toward employees; builds humility with customers; builds up rounded personality	Leadership challenges the status quo; helps in streamlining thinking process; generates a clear notion and reduces ambiguity; builds cordial relationships	Helps in searching for alternatives; facilitates to go deeper into the subject; increases agility and focus in decision-making; ensures larger view of scenario
Respondent 05: Kishan Patel, The Glorious Restaurant	45 years old food business; did MBA; prefers innovative ways of attracting customers; want to implement the learning of MBA in FB	Dancing brings novelty in terms of ideas; helps in seeing others better; learn to stay calm and composed	Dancing	Induces inspiration in oneself to tackle challenges in business; builds concentration toward various family business issues; helps in identifying with different roles and characters I play in family business; builds up rounded personality	Leadership builds trust; enhances commitment in employees; instills confidence and courage in taking initiatives; facilitates "thinking" environment in business; cultivates positive attitude and empathy to strengthen leadership practice	Facilitates clarity of thoughts; increases patience in listening to all parties; cultivates better negotiation skills; helps in identifying better channels of communication; helps in gathering and sorting out information
Respondent 06: Neha Kedia, Krishna	48 years old FB; specializes in Gujarati food; autonomy is essential	Dramatics and theater; acting is passion; understands emotions well; likes interacting with expressions	Drama and theater	Enhances imagination helping to see the right direction of business; builds up strong communication channels for different layers of people in business; helps in building courage and confidence; facilitates interpersonal skills	Helps in inculcating a different mindset to take new routes; facilitates individual to dive deep into the problem and explore solutions; generates expertise in playing different roles in business	Empathetic approach ensure balanced decision; cultivates better negotiation skills; increases agility and focus in decision-making; helps in identifying better channels of communication

APPENDIX A8.7 (Continued)

	Background and reasons of joining family business	Role of arts forms in personal life	Interest in specific arts form	Benefits of arts forms in family business	Ways of arts forms enabling leadership formation in family business	Ways of arts forms enabling better decision-makings abilities
Respondent 07: Raj Chaliawala, Neopolitan Pizza	68 years old FB; father and daughter duo; introduced major changes over 5 years; aspires to be an reputed entrepreneur	Painting is most focused work; painting enables deep thoughts to evolve; helps in understanding combinations of colors	Painting and drawing	Enables intellectual and emotional involvement together; helps in self-awareness; generates a lot of ideas; enables visualization; helps in becoming systematic in doing things	Develops ability to pursue things keeping the larger picture in view; helps in increasing deeper insights on issues in business; pays importance to all stakeholders in business	Increases spontaneity; helps in having more choices; increases patience in listening to all parties; increases agility and focus in decision-making
Respondent 08: Ninad Parekh, Dawat Restaurant	3 generational FB; strong role of elders; take care of customer interface role	Dancing is about connecting body and soul; it is fulfillment of desires; brings a lot courage and satisfaction	Dancing-contemporary style	Helps in understanding self; increases concentration; builds strong communication with employees; increases visualization in seeing the future of family business	Cultivates positive attitude and empathy to strengthen leadership practice; leadership demands vision and the clear communication of that vision	Enables better observational skills to understand situations; ensures larger view of scenario; others view and opinion is taken into account
Respondent 09: Jash Patel, Navjivan Restaurant	30 years old FB; father retired due to old age; taken leadership role; wanting to expand FB	Drama engages mind to learn changes; it helps to understand relationships; tells how to balance differences; offers clarity of thoughts	Dramatics/ Theater	Helps in identification of characters people play in family business; improves presentation skills; helps in working in team; explores notion of trust and rapport; helps in giving and receiving feedback for improvement	It enables different ways of motivating others; leadership facilitates in connecting with others at an emotional level; cultivates positive attitude and empathy to strengthen leadership practice	Increases transparency in communication; facilitates to go deeper into the subject; facilitates clarity of thoughts; ensures larger view of scenario; helps in searching for alternatives
Respondent 10: Raj Kanwar, South India Restaurant	Operational for 66 years; receives support from elders; single-handedly run FB; parents retired	Painting enables expressions; enrich with ideas; visualization becomes sound	Painting/ Drawing	Cultivates proactive behavior, enables visualization, enhances imagination helping to see the right direction of business	Leadership challenges the status quo; helps in taking unconventional steps in business; generates expertise in playing different roles in business	Helps in having more choices; increases spontaneity; cultivates better negotiation skills; helps in identifying better channels of communication

CHAPTER 9

SERVICE QUALITY AND CUSTOMER EXPERIENCE: THE KEY TO BUILDING SUSTAINABLE COMPETITIVE ADVANTAGE IN FINE DINE RESTAURANTS

GAURAV TRIPATHI[1]* and KARTIK DAVE[2]

[1]*Assistant Professor, Marketing Area, Birla Institute of Management Technology, Greater Noida, Uttar Pradesh, India*

[2]*Associate Professor, Marketing School of Business, Public Policy and Social Entrepreneurship, Ambedkar University, Delhi, India*

*Corresponding author. E-mail: tripathi_gaurav@hotmail.com; gaurav.tripathi@bimtech.ac.in

CONTENTS

Abstract 196
9.1   Introduction 197
9.2   Review of Literature 200
9.3   Hypotheses 206
9.4   Methods 207
9.5   Analysis 208
9.6   Discussion 210
9.7   Conclusions, Limitations, and Scope for Further Research 214
9.8   Managerial Implications 216
Keywords 218
References 218
Appendix 223

ABSTRACT

Delivering excellence in every facet of restaurant services is achieved by providing high levels of sustained service quality (SQ). It is all about understanding and delivering what the customers want at the service outlet. SQ is a measure of the customer's perception that influences customer satisfaction that in turn influences their behavioral intentions. It is worth mentioning that higher levels of SQ results in increased number of customers patronizing the restaurant. Customers who encounter superior SQ levels are satisfied, and they show their appreciation by spreading a positive word of mouth reference and frequent visits to the restaurant.

In the present era, the restaurant business has a lot to do with customer experience due to its intangible characteristic. Sometimes, a memorable experience takes precedence over the tangible aspects of the services offered. It is also a key to retaining and bringing back customers frequently to the restaurant. The restaurant theme, cuisine, or food taste may not be the only reasons for these phenomena, as these are observable and imitable. However, SQ aspects are generally difficult to copy. SQ encompasses factors such as, providing an ambient environment, decor, staff responsiveness, empathy, etc. SQ is what the restaurant can provide to its customers based on their own understanding of customer needs. However, the quality of customer experience is the judgment of the restaurant patrons, which is based on their measurement of SQ. In other words, it is about building exceptionally positive perceptions in the minds of the customers, based on both tangible and intangibles service perceptions.

Competitive advantage is achieved by offering superior quality of services in comparison to the competitors. If a restaurant can retain its customers and their customers share a positive review, then it translates into a competitive advantage. However, sustaining the competitive advantage is a humongous task, because the competitors are always making an attempt to create a dent in the share of other players in the market. Imitating what others are doing is one of the ways to eat into the market share of competitors. If the restaurant management can prevent any erosion in profits or imitation of service offerings by the competitors, then sustainable competitive advantage is achieved. This differentiation or uniqueness can be achieved phenomenally, by providing an exclusive and memorable customer experience during the service consumption process.

This chapter is an amalgamation of empirical and qualitative research. The relationship between SQ, customer experience, customer satisfaction, and behavioral intentions is established, using extant literature and then tested using a customer survey. The empirical results are then validated and linked with, what the restaurants are expected to do for providing superior SQ levels and memorable experiences. Further, a discussion on how efforts made by the restaurant management could result in a competitive advantage and how they can sustain them is provided. This chapter will help the restaurant business owners and managers to understand the importance of SQ and customer experience in attaining sustainable competitive advantage.

9.1   INTRODUCTION

A fine-dining restaurant is a service facility, where the patrons experience high-quality food service on the table itself. The focus is on the visual appeal of the food, which is based on the talent of the highly qualified and experienced chefs. The table settings are impressive and include use of high-quality cutlery set in a specific manner, which is often correlated to the type of cuisine being served. Such restaurants emphasize on a high quality of ambient environment, décor, and well-dressed employees (Harr, 2008) to create a superior customer experience. The bill is presented after the dining process is completed on the table. The role of service personnel is critical from the point of view of service creation (Verma, 2012), and building memorable experiences.

In 2014, fine-dining restaurants had registered a growth of 13% in value terms, which amounts to Rs. 3.6 trillion (Euromonitor, 2015). The fine-dining restaurants in India are mainly stand-alone outlets or located in up market hotels. However in recent times, restaurant chains have been expanding from metropolitan cities to smaller cities. Chain restaurants are showing higher growth rates due to a smaller base. However, it is worth noting that the industry is very fragmented in terms of market share, with the absence of a single brand (or few) dominating the market. Barbeque Nation has been among the top players in the chain restaurant segment and exhibits uniqueness by deploying a live grill concept. Independent and stand-alone outlets comprise 96% of the restaurants. However, the trend is shifting toward chain outlets as the patrons can identify with the cuisines served. The independent category is preferred by customers, as they are more interested in authentic food (Euromonitor, 2015). There is a growing competition between Indian and European fine-dining restaurants. The fine-dining restaurants are expected to grow at a CAGR of 4% from 2014 to 2019, to reach Rs. 4.3 trillion. However, certain challenges are becoming apparent, such as growing rentals of the outlet property, high attrition, and increased competition from quick service restaurants (QSRs), kiosks, cafes, and take-away outlets.

Indian fine-dining restaurants have been focusing on typically North Indian and South Indian cuisines along with Italian, Chinese, and Thai food fare. More recently, cuisines from the Middle-East, Mexico, etc. have become popular. Some of the popular fine-dining restaurants chains include Barbeque Nation, Punjabi by Nature, Moti Mahal, The Kebab Factory, etc. The food service industry has witnessed 2015 as the year of food invest-ments, with over 100 companies receiving huge funding. Many upcoming restaurants are expanding across pan India. Italiano, a Gurgaon-based chain is looking forward to opening 20 new outlets in the next 5 years (Nusra, 2016a). On the other hand, Moets which had 10 sub-brands operating under it plans to open only one or two outlets in a city (Nusra, 2016b). In addi-tion, Jiggs Kalra, the celebrity chef, has collaborated with the Mirah Group for a new venture called Massive Restaurants Pvt. Ltd., which will focus on fine-dining outlets with a capacity of 90–100 patrons, spreading across 3500–4000 sq. ft. (Tiwari, 2012). Some companies have used private equity investments to finance casual dining and quick service categories in the chain restaurant segment. The names include Everstone Capital, Goldman Sachs, India Value Fund Advisors, and Samara Capital. In addition, the venture capital players are also foraying into this business. There are investments into the fine-dining segment from private equity players and venture capital-ists. However, the interest of the investors is tilted toward categories which are currently attractive and emerging, and this is posing a major challenge for the fine-dining categories (Sathyanarayanan & Babar, 2015).

The growth in fine-dining restaurants is attributed to infrastructure facili-ties, increase in travel business, international cuisines moving to smaller cities, rising disposable incomes in the urban areas, and more people preferring to dine out for their parties and events. However, challenges are apparent, which are pertaining to standardization and availability of fresh food supply. Food service companies are looking at innovative methods to cater to customer needs, by using alternate channels of delivery and ordering, also focusing on acquisitions (Nusra, 2016c). Recently, the Delhi govern-ment is looking forward to allow restaurants and bars to open round the clock (Economic Times, 2016a). This would certainly add to the patronage by customers and the revenues earned by the establishments. In addition, Paylo.in has acquired Ruplee which is an in-restaurant payment app, which would boost a cashless experience for the customers (Economic Times, 2016b). These events strongly indicate a growing future, which is focused toward making the restaurant business more sustainable.

Sustainable competitive advantage has a strong linkage with customer's expectations from the service provider. Customers whose expectations are met are the satisfied customers. Satisfied customers have a tendency to consume services again and again, which at times is sustained over months and even years. These customers later on become apostles and express positive opinions on the restaurants' services to their peers, hence contributing to an increase in their customer base. Therefore, the key questions for the restaurant service providers are what are those customer's expectations and which of those expectations significantly contribute to their satisfaction. The omni-channel phenomenon is impacting all kinds of service industries in a big way. However, from the marketing viewpoint, it is essential to concentrate on core offerings as these are the supporting activities or business enablers. Hence, focusing on acquiring new customers and maintaining the existing ones should be the focal points for restaurants in order to sustain revenue growth and profitability.

According to Bharadwaj et al. (1993), quality, customer service-related skills, and functional skills lead to competitive positional advantage, which if sustained can lead to long-term superior performance. Competitive positional advantage includes differentiation and cost advantage. According to Rust et al. (1995), service quality (SQ) is strongly linked with financial returns. The authors provided several managerial inputs for measuring return on quality. Specifically, customer retention and customer satisfaction have been identified as the key performance indicators. It is pointed out that customer retention should be matched with customer satisfaction surveys. This is because customer database management is not so strong for many of the restaurants (especially in the stand-alone category). Hence, revisit intentions should be a part of customer satisfaction surveys. In addition, SQ improvements are related to expenditure on such processes rather than cost reduction. A wide scale problem for the management is to decide, which aspects have to be focused upon while making investments in improvements (Rust et al., 1995). Further, SQ factors which are critical should be considered in a way that they should reflect a memorable customer experience, which will impact customer satisfaction and behavioral intentions in the long run.

Customers visit restaurants for experiencing the pleasure of dining out. They may love to eat high-quality food with exotic ingredients. However, such ingredients and recipes are widely available in the markets of urban metros; hence, the high-quality food is not the only thing which the restaurants focus upon. In the present scenario, restaurant patronage is strongly linked to various elusive aspects. This can be the ambient environment, personalized services, and happiness. The desire to visit and revisit a restaurant is largely subjective rather than objective. It is based on the feelings evoked.

This chapter is further structured in the form similar to a research paper. The next section presents a review of literature. It encompasses a discussion on SQ pertaining to restaurants. Furthermore, the discussion focuses on the consequences of SQ, customer experience, customer satisfaction, and behavioral intentions. Research methods are then discussed which mainly encompass the description of the survey instrument used and the method of data collection. The next section describes the data analysis techniques employed and focuses on the model fit and the testing of the hypothesis. Thereafter, a discussion is presented along with conclusions and limitations, based on the data analysis carried out in the earlier section. Managerial implications are presented at the end to conclude the analysis outlined.

9.2   REVIEW OF LITERATURE

9.2.1   SERVICE QUALITY

Sulek and Hensley (2004) pointed out that the restaurant managers have the onus of finding out whether the customers are happy with the food, service, and the restaurant settings, as these aspects are related to customer satisfaction and the customers' dining experience. If the customers are satisfied, they would return. On the other hand, most of the discontented customers never tend to come back and also discuss the poor quality of restaurant services with other customers (Stevens et al., 1995), spoiling the loyal customer base. Although restaurants are known for selling food only, but in reality, they are the retailers of food service experience (Yüksel & Yüksel, 2002). Food is an important aspect of restaurant service, but it is perhaps not the most important part (Muller, 1999; Robson, 1999). Restaurant services are blended with many intangible and tangible aspects. During the interaction with the customers, the restaurant demonstrates its quality of services. This process is critical as it is significantly related to the customer's evaluation of restaurants services. SQ has two important components, technical and functional. The former is related to what the consumer receives and the later is about how the services are delivered to the customer (Grönroos, 1984). If the technical quality meets the expected standards, the functional quality holds greater importance as a measure for customer satisfaction (Bitner, 1990; Grönroos, 1984). Therefore, it is quite understood that if a restaurant delivers high levels of SQ on a regular basis, than it can gain competitive advantage in the long run.

9.2.2 EFFECT OF AN AMBIENT ENVIRONMENT ON THE PERCEPTIONS OF SERVICE QUALITY DELIVERED

Olson and Jacoby (1972) stated that services comprise intrinsic and extrinsic cues, which function as a substitute for indicating quality. Intrinsic cues are core aspects while extrinsic cues are related to the peripheral or related aspects of the service (Zeithaml, 1988). The intrinsic cues that infer quality of services are limited in comparison to the products (Ha & Jang, 2012). Hence, consumers look for peripheral cues to make an opinion about the quality of the service. According to Zeithaml (1981), physical surroundings can be used to make inference about the quality of services. The service environment comprises elusive aspects which can be experienced during service consumption and experience. It has a significant influence on how consumers make perceptions about the quality of service. This was concluded in retail settings by Baker et al. (1994) and Reimer and Kuehn (2005); while Reimer and Kuehn (2005) and Wall and Berry (2007) discussed this aspect in the context of restaurants. Ha and Jang (2012) concluded, based on the extant literature, that ambient environment influences SQ perceptions immensely.

9.2.3 CONSEQUENCES OF SERVICE QUALITY ON CUSTOMER PERCEPTIONS

SQ predominantly focuses on customer satisfaction. It includes behavioral intentions of customers, comprising loyalty and WOM (word of mouth) interactions. It also impacts customer experience during service consumption.

9.2.4 CUSTOMER EXPERIENCE

Customer experience is a quality assessment which indicates how exceptionally are the restaurant services perceived or judged by the patrons, which is based on the measurement of SQ (Lai & Chang, 2013; Lemke et al., 2010). SQ planning is based on the management philosophy of the organization, focused on how they perceive certain service aspects as critical to their patrons. However, the quality of customer experience is the opinion of the patrons, pertaining to their perception of SQ (Lai & Chang, 2013).

Meyer and Schwager (2007) mention that customer experience encompasses every aspect of consumer offering including service attribute. Only few service companies have been focusing on customer experience, while plenty of them have been considering the measurement of customer satisfaction with lot of analysis. However, it is worth noting that measurement of customer satisfaction is not an indicator of how it is achieved. Numerous customer experiences end up in customer satisfaction. These experiences can be positive or negative. The result is customer satisfaction. If positive experiences are greater than the negatives ones, then customer satisfaction is positive while it is negative when positive experiences are less than the negative ones. Therefore, customer satisfaction can be better understood and evaluated based on observing customer experiences across a certain timeframe.

In addition, Meyer and Schwager (2007) stated that customer experience is the subjective response to any kind of contact with the company. In case of services SQ, it is linked with customer experience. This is particularly the case with product offerings which have service as their core aspect. This case is befitting for the restaurant business, where the intangible aspects of services have taken precedence over food quality. These intangible aspects are the reason why people look forward to eating out rather than eating at home. It is also useful to know that the restaurant patrons set their expectations based on their latest experience. Hence, the service provider needs to consistently deliver on spot immaculate service, to continue being the preferred choice in the highly competitive marketplace.

Competitive advantage build through consumer experience is not only difficult to imitate but it also cannot be properly substituted (Pine & Gilmore, 1998). The restaurant industry encompasses a rich meal experience which is based on several factors (Campbell-Smith, 1967; Johns & Pine, 2002). The SERVQUAL model discusses service attributes based on the quality of service; however, it doesn't discuss its role in building customer experience (Johns & Pine, 2002). Bujisic (2014) used Rust and Oliver's (1994) model to discuss the antecedents of customer experience. These were categorized under three main headings, convenience, price fairness (perceived), and quality attributes including the physical and social environment. These three broad set of attributes have a profound effect on customer experience.

The social environment can be understood as part of the atmosphere (Heide & Grønhaug, 2006), which can be related to the presence of other customers (Tombs & McColl-Kennedy, 2003). This can be connected with privacy and the noise factor present in restaurant settings (Tripathi & Dave, 2014). Various aspects of convenience have been described in literature in the context of hospitality, which includes operating hours, location (Crim,

2008), parking (Kivela et al., 1999), etc. These aspects apart from the popular aspects of restaurant SQ model, like reliability, responsiveness, empathy, tangibles, and assurance, can be combined under the purview of SQ, which can be witnessed in the extended model of SQ (Tripathi & Dave, 2014).

Although various research citations discuss the impact of SQ on customer satisfaction, the inclusion of customer experience has been limited. However, it is worth noting and establishing how and why customer experience is important in the context of the hospitality industry. Hemmington (2007) presents a clear distinction between service and experience. To a quote a few hospitality industry players, they consider customers as guests (Lashley, 2000), and the manger as the host (Jayawardena, 2000). The delivery goal moves from customer service to performance (Kivela et al., 2000; Winsted, 2000), the customer needs move from functional to experiential (Hansen et al., 2004), the demand factor moves from benefits to sensation (Braithwaite, 2003), and the nature of offering upgrades from intangibles to memorable experiences (Pine & Gilmore, 1999).

Cole and Scott (2004) in the context of tourists' experience suggested that experience is cumulative in a way that performance quality influences experience quality and experience quality leads to customer satisfaction. Cole and Chancellor (2009), in the context of festivals, found that entertainment quality has a major impact on the overall experience. Oh et al. (2007) in the context of bed-and-breakfast setting also found similar results with aesthetics being the major determinant leading to experience based outcomes. In the context of heritage tourism, Prayag et al. (2013) also tested the influence of customer experience on satisfaction which ultimately influences behavioral intentions. In this case, experiences were indicated by using emotional aspects, such as joy, love, surprise, and unpleasantness.

Based on the above discussions, it is well understood that there is enough support in literature to establish the influence of SQ factors on customer experience and the influence of customer experience on customer satisfaction. Research on these relationships which involves customer experience is significant, in the larger set of the hospitality industry, as limited research exists specifically applicable to the restaurant industry.

9.2.5 CUSTOMER SATISFACTION

Satisfaction is basically a judgment of the customer in which he or she makes comparisons between the expected and actual performances from any service (Cardozo, 1965). This phenomenon can also be connected with the expectancy–disconfirmation theory, in which customer satisfaction is understood as a subjective phenomenon.

The service businesses expect customers to show a positive disconfirmation which is an indicator of customer satisfaction. Other definitions of customer satisfaction discuss similar aspects. Expectation related to performance-specific aspects and expectancy disconfirmations are important dimensions related to customer satisfaction. According to Engel and Blackwell (1982), satisfaction is an evaluation of the selection made in line with past beliefs gained about that particular option. According to Yi (1990), it should be considered from the point of view of evaluation of the performance. It is worth noting that since the concept of marketing aims at delivering customer satisfaction, hence, it is strongly related to meeting the consumer needs. It is a main criterion for determining SQ, which is in fact delivered by the service providers to their customers (Vavra, 1997). Various studies have suggested that it is five times more costly in terms of money, time, and other resources to gain new customers in comparison to maintaining existing one (Naumann & Giel, 1995).

Under customer satisfaction research, modeling is highly important for which two main approaches are considered. One is the transaction specific and other is cumulative (Anderson et al., 1994; Boulding et al., 1993). The former approach is transient which focuses at a given point in time while the later approach is about the total consumption experience (Cronin Jr. & Taylor, 1992). It directly affects the post-purchase behavior, which includes change in attitude and behavioral intentions (Johnson & Fornell, 1991).

Newer research on customer satisfaction has similar viewpoints. According to Yüksel and Yüksel (2002), increase in repeat visits is contingent to higher levels of customer satisfaction, which in itself is a concept that works on relative phenomenon based on a certain standard or benchmark. Customer satisfaction is also based on the cognitive and affective behavior of the consumers. The former is based on objective knowledge while the latter is based on the feelings and emotions related to the service experiences (Edvardson, 2005). If the performance of product and service is as per the expectations of the customers, they are satisfied else they are dissatisfied (Bowden & Dagger, 2011).

9.2.6 BEHAVIORAL INTENTIONS

Behavioral intentions are important in the context of services as it caters to the sustainability of the service business in the long run. It is the surrogate indicator of the actual behavior of the consumer (Fishbein & Ajzen, 1975). In addition, behavioral intentions encompass the belief of the people which they express in particular situations (Ajzen & Fishbein, 1980). It is worth noting that the result of customer satisfaction is related to what the consumer will decide, about using a particular brand of service in a specific situation (Cronin Jr. & Taylor, 1992).

The service provider always looks forward to the customers saying positive things about their service to others (Zeithaml et al., 1996). It includes customers recommending their services to others, remain loyal to the company, devote more time to their services, and spend more money in procuring them (Zeithaml et al., 1996). Loyalty is basically all about showing preference for a particular service brand in comparison to others. This helps in increasing their business and hence accounts for sustainability.

One of the main components of behavioral intentions is customer loyalty. It is all about the strength of the relationship between the relative attitude of the customers, with respect to the competitor and repeat visits (Dick & Basu, 1994). Similarly, Bennett and Bove (2002) have provided a similar viewpoint about customer loyalty which can be understood from the term "attitudinal predisposition." It is linked to repeat consumption of service. It is a particular type of attitude encompassing frequent exchange in their relationship, based on previous experiences (Czepiel & Gilmore, 1987).

WOM is another key aspect of behavioral intentions, which customer's exhibit based on their service experiences. It is a key form of communication (Swanson & Davis, 2003) which is disseminated by them to their peer groups. WOM communication helps customers in spreading their opinion about the services they consume (Fong & Burton, 2006). It is useful in bringing down the perception on the risk levels and related ambiguities in connection with the subscription of services (Mangold et al., 1999). WOM is a source of information which also acts as an influence in the decision-making process of prospective consumers (Ng et al., 2011). WOM is related to customer satisfaction in a significant way as it is a basis for restaurant services to make recommendation to their peers (Ladhari et al., 2008).

9.2.7 RELATIONSHIP BETWEEN SERVICE QUALITY, CUSTOMER SATISFACTION, AND BEHAVIORAL INTENTIONS

SQ and related models including its variants are the most referred models in the context of services marketing. The importance is relevant due to factors which possess the ability to influence customer satisfaction. Customer satisfaction in turn has the ability to influence behavioral intentions (Bujisic et al., 2014; Ha & Jang, 2012). According to Bowden-Everson et al. (2013), customer satisfaction has been understood as a predictor of customer loyalty, repurchasing, and long-term relationships. Behavioral intentions encompass the customers' desire to revisit the restaurant for experiencing its services. It also includes the intention of its patrons to spread a positive WOM reference about the service and the experience they go through in their previous visits to the restaurant. However, this may have negative connotations. Discontentment can lead to a negative WOM on the service of the restaurant. Hence, delivering high levels of SQ is not just important for the survival of restaurant, but it is also critical as the restaurant may incur losses due to poor SQ. Restaurant should endeavor to reduce the gap between the expected SQ levels demanded by its patrons and what they actually perform (Grönroos, 1984).

9.3 HYPOTHESES

Based on review of literature, the following hypotheses are envisaged. The ambient setting influence the five SQ factors which further influence other factors in the model consequently. It includes the following SQ factors influencing customer experience:

H_a: *Ambient settings directly and positively influence impressions*

H_b: *Ambient settings directly and positively influence aesthetics*

H_c: *Ambient settings directly and positively influence reliability and responsiveness*

H_d: *Ambient settings directly and positively influence empathy*

H_e: *Ambient settings directly and positively influence privacy and entertainment*

H_f: *Impression directly and positively influence customer experience*

H_g: *Aesthetics directly and positively influence customer experience*

H_h: *Reliability and responsiveness directly and positively influences customer experience*

H_i: *Empathy directly and positively influences customer experience*

H_j: *Privacy and entertainment directly and positively influences customer experience*

H_k: *Customer experience directly and positively influences customer satisfaction*

H_l: *Customer satisfaction directly and positively influences loyalty*

H_m: *Customer satisfaction directly and positively influences WOM intentions*

These hypotheses represent the paths in the structural model.

9.4   METHODS

This study is empirical in nature and involves use of quantitative data. A questionnaire-based survey is used to collect data from the respondents, who have patronized a fine-dining restaurant in last one month. The questionnaire was developed using a collection of variables from existing literature on restaurant SQ. The variables for SQ were largely referred from Stevens et al. (1995), who delivered the DINESERV model specifically for SQ in restaurants. However, to fit into the Indian context, the recent work of Tripathi and Dave (2014) was referred to for adaptability into the Indian context. This also includes variables related to the ambient environment in restaurants. Behavioral intentions were divided into two separate factors, loyalty and WOM intentions. Loyalty variables were taken up from studies by Kim et al. (2006) and Liang and Zhang (2012). WOM intentions were considered from studies conducted by Kim et al. (2006) and Ng et al. (2011). In addition, variables comprising the satisfaction factor were referred from Kim et al. (2006) and Meng and Elliott (2008). Scale items for customer experience were extracted from the research work of Kim (2009).

These variables are setup in the questionnaire using a 7-point Likert scale. These scale items comprise the first section of the questionnaire. In this, the following conventions were followed with the 7 rating points "1—strongly disagree," "2—disagree," "3—partly disagree," "4—indifferent or neutral," "5—partly agree," "6—agree," "7—strongly agree." The second section of the questionnaire includes the categorical variables pertaining to the respondent profile. These include gender, age, and income. Income was the annual family income of the respondent's family. Data were collected using the mall intercept method. It can also be understood as market place intercept method. The method finds its applicability in various studies based on consumer surveys. This method is effective in situations which involve time and financial constraints. The targeting of desired respondents for the survey purpose can be used if convenient based on this method (O'Cass & Grace, 2008; Prasad & Aryasri, 2011).

The survey was conducted in the National Capital Region (India) and included the three main cities of New Delhi, Noida, and Gurgaon. The target areas were the urban localities, popular malls, and market places. About 400 questionnaires were circulated amongst the respondents in the markets. However, out of these, only 268 were considered functional for the present research work. The criteria for dropping out certain responses were based on incompleteness of the questionnaires. Some questionnaires were responded in surprising manner, where all scale items were rated with the same score. According to Anderson and Gerbing (1988), a sample of 100–150 subjects was befitting enough for studies involving use of structural equation modeling. Schumacker and Lomax (2004) reviewed several articles and concluded that most research works use a sample size varying between 250 and 500 responses. According to Bentler and Chou (1987), a minimum of five samples per observed variable is suitable, and in case the latent constructs are having several variables as their indicators, the ratio shall go up to 10. However, in the later case, the minimum number for considering multiple indicators is not well specified. In the present research work, the number of observed variables for SQ is only 15, while the total number of observed variables including SQ, its antecedents, and consequences are 29. If we consider the minimum benchmark of five observations per variables, then the sample size of 145 is required. If we consider the minimum of 10 observations per variable, then the required sample size is 290. However, as mentioned earlier, the concept of multiple indicators is not well specified; therefore, the sample size of 268 observations is befitting to the requirements of this study.

9.5 ANALYSIS

The confirmatory factor analysis (CFA) was run twice. The first CFA was run involving the five SQ factors only. These include *impressions, aesthetics, reliability and responsiveness, empathy, privacy*, and *entertainment.*

The CFA results were as follows $\chi^2 = 254.00$, df = 80, $\chi^2/df = 3.18$, GFI = 0.94, NFI = 0.93, IFI = 0.95, TLI = 0.94, CFI = 0.95, RMSEA = 0.07, SRMR = 0.0413. This shows a good fit of the measurement model. Also, all the observed variables taken up from the questionnaire represented their associated factors. This was based on their individual loading (or regression weights). All of these variables show significant loading with their corresponding factors, hence validating the measurement model of involving five SQ factors in the context of fine-dining restaurants. This conformed to the recommendations of Byrne (2001) stated earlier. The five factor model confirmed in this case is different from the DINESERV model of Stevens et al. (1995).

The measurement model was also tested for construct validity (see Table A9.1). The whole idea is to test how well the associated factors are well represented by the SQ factors (Hair et al., 2006). Face validity of the model is pre-established as the observed variables are referred from the extant literature. The convergent validity is established as all the factor loadings for each scale-item were significant (p-value < 0.001). In addition, the average variance extracted was above the minimum requirement of 0.50. This was confirmed for each of the five SQ dimensions. This conformed to the recommendations by Fornell and Larcker (1981). Discriminant validity was also established. This was done by inspecting the inter-construct correlations with the average variance extracted. In this case, average variance extracted was greater than the square of inter-construct correlations. Hence, the discriminant validity was established which was based on the recommendations of Fornell and Larcker (1981).

After this stage, the second CFA was run which involved all other factors apart from the restaurant SQ factors. These include ambient settings, customer experience, customer satisfaction, loyalty, and WOM intentions. In this case, the model fit of this measurement model was found good. The key indicators are $\chi^2 = 756.78$, df = 332, χ^2/df = 2.28, GFI = 0.91, NFI = 0.91, IFI = 0.95, TLI = 0.93, CFI = 0.95, RMSEA = 0.05, SRMR = 0.0399. In addition, the regression weights were all significant.

This measurement model also conformed to the construct validity requirements (see Table A9.2). There was no issue with respect to face validity, as the scale items were derived from the extensive review of literature. The convergent validity was also confirmed as the AVE for each factors were greater than 0.50 and all factor loadings were significant with p-value less than 0.001 (Fornell & Larcker, 1981). Discriminant validity was established by comparing the inter-construct correlations, with the average variance extracted. Since the AVE was greater than the square of inter-construct correlations, the discriminant validity was confirmed (Fornell & Larcker, 1981).

After the measurement models are confirmed with the display of good fit, the structural model is tested for the fit and also examining the relationships involving latent constructs. The structural model fit was examined at the beginning. The indices are $\chi^2 = 1067.40$, df = 364, χ^2/df = 2.93, GFI =

0.90, NFI = 0.90, IFI = 0.94, TLI = 0.93, CFI = 0.94, and RMSEA = 0.05, SRMR = 0.0476).

The hypothesis results are provided under Table A9.3. The ambient factor had significant and a positive influence on the five restaurant SQ factors. However, all the paths leading from these five SQ factors did not significantly differ. The three factors, reliability and responsiveness, empathy, and aesthetics, also extend significant and positive influence on customer experience. Although aesthetics was significant, however, it was having a p-value of 0.04 which indicates that the aesthetics influence on customer experience is not as significant as is the case of empathy, reliability, and responsiveness. Furthermore, customer experience had a significant and positive influence on customer satisfaction. Customer satisfaction was seen to significantly and positively influence customer loyalty and customer's WOM intentions.

9.6   DISCUSSION

Based on the structural model, the path analysis was carried out. The path analysis is able to outline the relationships which are significant in the structural model. At first, the ambient settings are tested for their influence on the restaurant SQ factors. In this study, the ambient settings comprise color settings, temperature, and lighting arrangements. These aspects form the ambient environment in the restaurant, which helps in a positive evaluation of the restaurant's services. This means that the perception of services quality in restaurant improves if the ambient environment is befitting to the consumers' expectations.

The impression comprises parking areas, building exteriors, and attractive dining areas. Importantly, the first two aspects are not under the control of the restaurant management. This is because most of the modern restaurants in the urban areas are located in popular malls and markets places. Some part of the restaurant exterior can be managed by the restaurants, but largely not the building exteriors. The dining area is however managed by the restaurant itself. In case, the restaurant patrons are displeased with the parking arrangements or the building exterior, the high quality of the restaurant's ambience can bring down the discomfort. For example, the soothing colors on the walls inside the restaurant could please the customers and make them stay longer.

Aesthetics are a key aspect of restaurant SQ. It includes comfortable seating, visually attractive interiors, and table settings. These aspects are the tangible components. Hence, they go through regular wear and tear over a period of time. Maintenance is difficult and small wear and tear is usually ignored or is not taken care of frequently. In this case, appropriate ambient settings would help in reducing such small wear and tear which is not frequently taken care of by the restaurant management. Temperature, lighting, and color setting would help in more positive evaluations of the aesthetics of the restaurant by its patrons.

The next restaurant SQ factor which is influenced by an ambient setting is reliability and responsiveness. It is related to the service deliveries by the restaurant which can be based on the time they promise to their patrons, no discrepancy between the order taken and delivered and also quick and prompt services. The biggest problem which the customers face in a restaurant is the waiting time between the order taken and the order delivered. This time is difficult to pass for the consumers. At this point the role of ambient setting is crucial in bringing down the boredom levels of the consumers. The consumers who are hungry many find a short waiting time too long. Good soothing music would be the best remedy in such situations. This will help in a more positive evolution about the reliability and responsiveness of the consumers.

Empathy is one of the most elusive aspects of restaurant SQ. It is all about how sensitive the restaurant employees are toward the needs and expectations of their customers. Many of these needs and expectations are unsaid or never specifically mentioned by the patrons and hence the employees need to remain vigilant to such needs. In other words, these needs are to be anticipated. The restaurant should train its employees in such a way that they should treat every customer as their special customer. Since empathy is elusive in nature, hence its evaluation is highly subjective in nature and can go either way based on the consumer's mood. A nicely crafted ambient setting would help in moving the balance in favor of the restaurant, where the customer would be able to make more positive meaning of the empathy levels delivered by the restaurant employees. This would involve appropriate setting of lights based on the theme of the restaurant. A comfortable temperature setting would bring down the anxiety levels among the restaurant consumers. A soothing or warm color scheme would make the patrons comfortable and relaxed and would make them stay longer.

Privacy and entertainment are strongly related to ambient settings and are very significantly affected by them. In a fine-dining restaurant, consumers expect that the privacy level should be well maintained, there should not be much noise which may act as a deterrent to their experience, and music should complement the dining atmosphere. In fact, both the factors in this case are strongly related. It is all about how the lighting and color planned and temperature settings are managed so that it builds up the privacy and entertainment.

Furthermore, these services quality factors pertaining to a restaurant were tested for their influence on customer experience. Customer experience is all about how engrossed the customer is while consuming the services of the restaurant. It also includes the enjoyment which the consumer goes through at the restaurant customer experience is positively and significantly influenced by three of the five SQ factors. Impression, privacy, and entertainment are significant predictors of customer experience.

The customers can cook and eat at home but what they don't get at home is the service experience. The experience is largely dependent upon the SQ factors. This was established through hypotheses testing. Aesthetics is the first factor which was found significant in influencing the customer experience. High-quality table setting is extremely important. Table setting should reflect the high levels of SQ exhibited by the restaurant. Mostly, the table setting is specific to the type of cuisine offered by the restaurant, which cannot be subsided in high-quality fine-dining settings. The seating has to be comfortable as customers intend to stay in fine-dining settings for longer durations. Here, the comfort factor is evoked in building a high-quality experience for the patrons. Visually attractive interiors are the key differentiators at times, especially in theme based fine-dining restaurants. It is done to provide differentiation from the competitors and hence attempts to add to the unique service experience of the restaurant customers.

Reliability and responsiveness has shown strong positive significance toward building customer experience. The patrons remember such experiences wherein they found timely delivery of servings as per their customized orders. Promptness from the service providers' end adds to the positive experience. Again, it is important to note that the waiting time could lead to negative experiences, especially if customers love the restaurant cuisine. Also, fine-dining customers look for specific tastes, as the food is not prepared with an objective of economies for scale which is the case with the fast food restaurants. Hence, customization is highly expected by the patrons and it obviously builds positively toward their experience.

Empathy is another key restaurant SQ factor which adds positively to the customer experience. This aspect of restaurant SQ is highly elusive and effective in nature. The customers are sensitive to minute aspects of service. The restaurant employees should be trained in a way that their employees are vigilant toward such unspecified needs of the customers. However, at times, it is difficult for the employees to help out customers in certain situations, for which the restaurant management must allow some flexibility to their employees in overriding the policy and procedures to a small extent. This way, the customers would feel special when they are well empathized with by the staff. This generates a good recall of the positive incident in the minds of the customers and builds up their overall dining experience.

It is important to comprehend why customer satisfaction holds a lot of importance. According to Ladhari et al. (2008), customer satisfaction is a key determinant of customer loyalty. In the present study, customer satisfaction has shown to exert a strong and positive influence on customer loyalty. Customer loyalty is all about revisiting the restaurant premises to enjoy their service experience. Most customers tend to revisit their favorite restaurant if they are satisfied with the service experience. Further, if the customers spend more time in the restaurant premises or they tend to try out new dishes, it reflects their loyalty to a large extent.

WOM intentions are also influenced by customer satisfaction. Customer satisfaction is the key basis for them to make recommendations on a particular restaurant's services to their peer groups (Ladhari et al., 2008). WOM is important because it has a significant impact on the decision-making of the potential restaurant customers. It is also a key source of information for prospective customers. In case of dissatisfaction, customers tend to spread criticism more rapidly amongst their social group. However, satisfied customers tend to express their delight with the service experience more readily with others.

The broad issue related to WOM communications and customer loyalty is their capability to reflect competitive advantage. Obviously, they are not the core reasons for gaining competitive advantage, however; they help in building competitive advantage over a period of time. Customers revisit a restaurant and refer it to others, because they were satisfied with the service experience. The service experience was dependent upon the SQ delivered during the entire service process, which had both tangible and elusive aspects. The restaurant makes innovative efforts to comfort their customers with unique ambient settings such that they make positive evaluations of their SQ aspects. Importantly, the restaurants can gain competitive advantage by logical alterations to these factors because they are under their control. The mood and behavior of the customers cannot be controlled for all the customers and hence the important role of ambient settings in building up the mood and bringing in tranquility becomes essential. In fact, it helps to minimize the effect of any external personal thought process occupying the minds of customers. This advantage if gained in the longer run would automatically convert into sustainable competitive advantage. This is strongly related to the basic principles of customer relationship management, which suggests that it is difficult to gain new customers than to maintain an existing one.

9.7   CONCLUSIONS, LIMITATIONS, AND SCOPE FOR FURTHER RESEARCH

In the present study, the role of SQ factors delivered in a restaurant in gaining sustainable competitive advantage is analyzed and discussed. This is carried out using structural equation modeling and confirmatory factors analysis. The research is based on the data collected using structured questionnaires from the patrons of fine dine restaurants. The analysis involves finding out how the ambient settings help in positive evaluation of the SQ of in fine dine restaurant. The influence of restaurant SQ factors in building up the customer experience is also analyzed. Three factors such as aesthetics, empathy and reliability and responsiveness are found to significantly and positively influence the customer experience (see Fig. A9.1 in Appendix). As mentioned previously that the quality of customer experience is more important than the SQ itself, it is important for the restaurant managers to look at how the SQ dimensions translate into customer experience. Customer experience will lead to customer satisfaction and behavioral intentions and hence these three dimensions are important for sustainability of profitable business. It is worth noting that reliability, responsiveness, and empathy are related to human factors; however, aesthetics can only be related to the quality of physical assets. SQ can be understood as the baseline for any restaurant. However, exceptional perception about those SQ dimensions defines the quality of customer experience which is of utmost importance.

Customer experience is found to positively impact the customer satisfaction. If the customer experience is in line with the customers' expectations, then customer satisfaction is achieved. Customer satisfaction has a key role in increasing revenues, as it is responsible for customer loyalty and WOM intentions. The fine-dining restaurant business in particular is a capital intensive business, which is evident from the kind of investments which are being made. The size of the outlet and the location adds to the cost in a significant way. The fine-dining business largely caters to the urban and metro regions and hence the cost is high. In places like Delhi, Gurgaon, and Noida, such restaurants are in plenty. Customers have several options to switch from one outlet to other if they are dissatisfied. They choose to revisit upon satisfaction and having an enriching experience and go further in recommending the services of the restaurants to others. Hence, food quality and SQ are just the baseline expectations, which translate into a memorable experience. Restaurants with low success are unable to balance their costs with their revenues and hence go into losses. Customer visits are low and gradually investors move out of the loss making venture. Hence, it is essential to focus on a strong customer experience arising out of SQ factors mentioned earlier which has positive linkages to increased customer satisfaction. The restaurant should focus on three SQ factors, reliability, responsiveness, empathy and aesthetics, which have a significant influence on customer experience. Among these factors, the former two are intangible dimensions of restaurant SQ. This will help increase customer satisfaction which would result in positive behavioral intentions of the patrons. Hence, it can be concluded that these three SQ factors are essential for fine-dining restaurants, to gain competitive advantage which will help in attaining sustainable profitability.

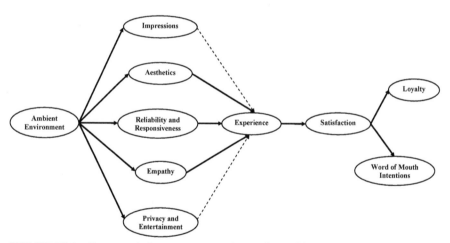

FIGURE A9.1   Framework for restaurant service quality and its consequences.

The present study is conducted in the major urban localities of the national capital region, where most of the customers of fine-dining restaurants dwell. It is worth noting that although India is a culturally diverse country, however, the behavior and expectations of urban fine-dining customers are likely to be similar across high growth and cosmopolitan cities, Bangalore, Hyderabad, Mumbai, Pune, etc. The study limits its scope to fine-dining restaurants, which could also be expanded to fast food service restaurants.

Further research work should be carried out toward comparison of the relationships between different factors based on consumer profiles.

In addition, psychographic profiling can also be used for research to gain deeper insight into the affective or rational behavior of consumers while selecting, repeating, and referring the services of a fine-dining restaurant. Research on SQ and customer experience is useful for restaurant management. The deployment of *mystery shoppers* is worth noting in the works of Lai and Chang (2013). These customers were the complaining customers who had agreed to become mystery shoppers and the experience was useful in improving the SQ and the quality of customer experience. Similar studies should be planned in the Indian context, where such negative experiences are very readily shared via social media to facilitate sharing of hands on knowledge.

9.8 MANAGERIAL IMPLICATIONS

Sustainable competitive advantage in the fine dining restaurant business is contingent to strong relationships with the patrons. If the relationships are strong they would visit the restaurant more frequently, and would also consume more items from the menu. They would also love to stay longer and would not mind eating more even if it requires them to work out a bit more in the gym. They would also bring along their friends sometime and even quite often. They would suggest their peers to visit the restaurant. They would also write positive reviews on social media channels. But what if they don't show such positive behavioral intentions? The question is quite relevant for urban regions in Delhi-NCR where restaurants are flooded in the major markets and malls of the urban localities. Many restaurants attempt to launch referral schemes to lure new customers. This would require the patrons to send discount coupon codes to their peers. By redeeming the code, the referred customers would receive a discount and so will the customers who are referring. But how often does it happen and how often will it happen? The customers in fine-dining settings are not young people generally. They would not like to make efforts to get petty discount in the name of luxury and experience. These set of patrons are affluent and do not mind paying more for better services experiences.

Full service restaurants operate in a different mode than QSRs. The customers at times go on social media and hit the "like" button in favor of the restaurant which they frequently patronize. However, this phenomenon is not as relevant for fine-dining customers as they won't look forward to gaining a petty amount by referring the restaurant to their peers. However, though mistakenly, the restaurants look forward to gaining more likes which might be more suitable for QSRs. However, fine-dining restaurants should look forward to gaining quality customer who should hit "like" in a more tangible way, and not just for gaining the benefits of an ongoing offer. In addition, customers hit like because they might find home delivery a very efficient option. Hitting "like" does not indicate that the customer has gone for a home delivery option, as against physically visiting to the restaurant. For a fine-dining experience, a physical visit is essential. The food may lose its temperature and appearance in the delivery format and that's why many high-quality fine-dining restaurants avoid offering home delivery.

Similarly, the restaurant expects new customers to visit and achieve a full occupancy on most occasions. However, this is not the reality due to the high competition in the marketplace. Many a times offers are available for new customers or the offers are for the current patrons to help gain newer customers. Overall, the focus is on maximizing the customer base. It is very difficult and costly to gain new customers, as compared to retaining an existing one. However, newer customers add to the market share and with the support from the current customers gaining them becomes easier. However, maintaining them is far more difficult. The critical question for the restaurants is to ponder on the frequency of revisit for the newer customers. If they don't tend to show a minimum level of expected frequency of revisit, the fine-dining restaurant should also reduce communication to those customers. If this is continued, the exclusive image of the fine-dining restaurant would deteriorate. In the long run, this phenomenon would have a negative effect and might affect sustainability of the restaurant's business. Hence, the focus should be on the quality customers, who would not only provide maximization of revenues, but also contribute lion's share of the profits, they would also help in maintaining the high-quality image of the restaurant. Fine-dining restaurants should not forget that they are into a business which is highly customized, offers high-quality service and gives a feel of luxury to its patrons. It is their core competence. The high-quality service offerings will provide a rich and exclusive customer experience leading to customer satisfaction. Satisfied customers in a fine-dining setting are not budget customers who look for discounts. Rather they don't look for prices as thoroughly as they care for luxury, comfort and experience. Hence, price increase is not a critical issue due to rising costs. The SQ dimensions, which add to customer experience, should not be compromised in the name of the cost. Among the three SQ dimensions which significantly influence customer experience, aesthetics is the tangible aspect which needs investment while reliability, responsiveness, and empathy can be developed via training and even hiring employees who possess such soft skills. Hence, the role of recruitment and selection is critical for the two dimensions linked to human resources.

KEYWORDS

- **fine dine restaurants**
- **service quality**
- **customer experience**
- **sustainable competitive advantage**
- **customer experience**

REFERENCES

Ajzen, I.; Fishbein, M. *Understanding Attitudes and Predicting Social Behavior*. Prentice-Hall: Englewood Cliffs, NJ, 1980.

Anderson, E. W.; Fornell, C.; Lehmann, D. R. Customer Satisfaction, Market Share, and Profitability: Findings from Sweden. *J. Mark.* **1994,** *58*(3), 53–66.

Anderson, J. C.; Gerbing D. W. Structural Equation Modeling in Practice: A Review and Recommended Two-step Approach. *Psychol. Bul*. **1988,** *103*(3), 411–423.

Baker, J.; Grewal, D.; Parasuraman, A. The Influence of Store Environment on Quality Inferences and Store Image. *J. Acad. Mark. Sci.* **1994,** *22*(4), 328–339.

Bennett, R.; Bove, L. Identifying the Key Issues for Measuring Loyalty. *Australas. J. Mark. Res.* **2002,** *9*(2), 27–44.

Bentler, P. M.; Chou, C. P. Practical Issues in Structural Modeling. *Sociol. Methods Res*. **1987,** *16*(1), 78–117.

Bharadwaj, S. G.; Varadarajan, P. R.; Fahy, J. Sustainable Competitive Advantage in Service Industries: A Conceptual Model and Research Propositions. *J. Mark.* **1993,** *57*(4), 83–99.

Bitner, M. J. Evaluating Service Encounters: The Effects of Physical Surroundings and Employee Responses. *J. Mark.* **1990,** *54*(2), 69–82.

Boulding, W.; Kalra, A.; Staelin, R.; Zeithaml, V. A. A Dynamic Process Model of Service Quality: From Expectations to Behavioral Intentions. *J. Mark. Res.* **1993,** *30*(1), 7–27.

Bowden, J. L.; Dagger, T. S. To Delight or Not to Delight? An Investigation of Loyalty Formation in the Restaurant Industry. *J. Hosp. Mark. Manage.* **2011,** *20*(5), 501–524.

Bowden-Everson, J. L. H.; Dagger, T. S.; Elliott, G. Engaging Customers for Loyalty in the Restaurant Industry: The Role of Satisfaction, Trust, and Delight. *J. Foodserv. Bus. Res.* **2013,** *16*(1), 52–75.

Braithwaite, R. W. Five Meals in the Forties: Perspectives on Hospitality under Extreme Circumstances. *Tour. Rev. Int.* **2003,** *7*(2), 61–66.

Bujisic, M. *Antecedents and Consequences of Customer Experience in Beverage Establishments.* Doctoral Dissertation, University of Central Florida Orlando, Florida, 2014 [Online].   http://etd.fcla.edu/CF/CFE0005309/Dissertation_Milos_Bujisic_June_30.pdf (accessed 29 August 2015).

Bujisic, M.; J. Hutchinson; Parsa, H. G. The Effects of Restaurant Quality Attributes on Customer Behavioral Intentions. *Int. J. Contemporary Hosp. Manage.* **2014**, *26*(8), 1270–1291.

Byrne, B. M. *Structural Equation Modeling with AMOS: Basic Concepts, Applications and Programming.* Lawrence Erlbaum Associates: Mahwah, NJ, 2001.

Campbell-Smith, G. *Marketing of the Meal Experience: A Fundamental Approach,* University of Surrey, Department of Hotel and Catering Management Research Unit, 1967.

Cardozo, R. N. An Experimental Study of Customer Effort, Expectation, and Satisfaction. *J. Mark. Res.* **1965**, *2*(3), 244–249.

Cole, S. T.; Chancellor, H. C. Examining the Festival Attributes that Impact Visitor Experience, Satisfaction and Re-visit Intention. *J. Vacat. Mark.* **2009**, *15*(4), 323–333.

Cole, S. T.; Scott, D. Examining the Mediating Role of Experience Quality in a Model of Tourist Experiences. *J. Trav. Tour. Mark.* **2004**, *16*(1), 79–90.

Crim, S. J. *Developing a Theory of Nightclub Location Choice.* Doctoral Dissertation, Massachusetts Institute of Technology, 2008 [Online]. dspace.mit.edu/bitstream/handle/1721.1/44354/276778029-MIT.pdf?sequence=2 (accessed 29 August 2015).

Cronin, Jr., J. J.; Taylor, S. A. Measuring Service Quality: A Re-examination and Extension. *J. Mark.* **1992**, *56*(3), 55–68.

Czepiel, J. A.; Gilmore, R. Exploring the Concept of Loyalty in Services. *The Services Challenge: Integrating for Competitive Advantage;* 1987; pp 91–94.

Dick, A. S.; Basu, K. Customer Loyalty: Toward an Integrated Conceptual Framework. *J. Acad. Mark. Sci.* **1994**, *22*(2), 99–113.

Economic Times. *Paylo.in Acquires In-restaurant Payment App Ruplee,* 21 March 2016b [Online].   http://articles.economictimes.indiatimes.com/2016-03-21/news/71705481_1_payment-foodpanda-app (accessed 30 March 2016).

Economic Times. Working for Round-the-clock Permit for Restaurants, Bars: Delhi Government, 23 March 2016a [Online]. http://articles.economictimes.indiatimes.com/2016-03-23/news/71758871_1_bars-round-the-clock-delhi-government (accessed 30 March 2016).

Edvardson, B. Service Quality: Beyond Cognitive Assessment, *Manage. Serv. Qual.* **2005**, *15*(2), 127–131.

Engel, J. F.; Blackwell, R. D. *Consumer Behavior;* Dryden Presee: New York, NY, 1982.

Euromonitor. *Full Service Restaurants in India,* 2015 [Online]. http://www.euromonitor.com/.

Fishbein, M.; Ajzen, I. *Belief, Attitude, Intention and Behavior: An Introduction to Theory and Research;* Addison-Wesley: Reading, MA, 1975.

Fong, J.; Burton, S. Electronic Word-of-Mouth: A Comparison of Stated and Revealed Behavior on Electronic Discussion Boards. *J. Interact. Advertis.* **2006**, *6*(2), 7–62.

Fornell, C.; Larcker, D. F. Evaluating Structural Equation Models with Unobservable Variables and Measurement Error. *J. Mark. Res.* **1981**, *18*(1), 39–50.

Grönroos, C. A Service Quality Model and Its Marketing Implications. *Eur. J. Mark.* **1984**, *18*(4), 36–44.

Ha, J.; Jang, S. The Effects of Dining Atmospherics on Behavioral Intentions through Quality Perception. *J. Serv. Mark.* **2012**, *26*(3), 204–215.

Hair, Jr., J. F.; Black, C. W.; Babin, J. B.; Anderson, R. E.; Tatham, L. R. *Multivariate Data Analysis,* 6th ed.; Pearson: Upper Saddle River: NJ, 2006.

Hansen, K. V.; Jensen, Ø.; Gustafsson, I. B. Payment—An Undervalued Part of the Meal Experience? *Food Serv. Technol.* **2004**, *4*(2), 85–91.

Harr, K. K. L. Service Dimensions of Service Quality Impacting Customer Satisfaction of Fine Dining Restaurants in Singapore UNLV, 2008 [Online]. Theses/Dissertations/Professional Papers/Capstones, Paper 686. University of Nevada: Las Vegas, CA. http://digitalcommons.library.unlv.edu/thesesdissertations/686/ (accessed 28 September 2015).

Heide, M.; Grønhaug, K. Atmosphere: Conceptual Issues and Implications for Hospitality Management. *Scand. J. Hosp. Tour.* **2006**, *6*(4), 271–286.

Hemmington, N. From Service to Experience: Understanding and Defining the Hospitality Business. *Serv. Ind. J.* **2007**, *27*(6), 747–755.

Jayawardena, C. International Hotel Manager. *Int. J. Contemporary Hosp. Manage.* **2000**, *12*(1), 67–70.

Johns, N.; Pine, R. Consumer Behaviour in the Food Service Industry: A Review. *Int. J. Hosp. Manage.* **2002**, *21*(2), 119–134.

Johnson, M. D.; Fornell, C. A Framework for Comparing Customer Satisfaction across Individuals and Product Categories. *J. Econ. Psychol.* **1991**, *12*(2), 267–286.

Kim, W. Customer Share of Visits to Full-service Restaurants in Response to Perceived Value and Contingency Variables, Doctoral Dissertation, Kansas State University, 2009 [Online]. http://krex.k-state.edu/dspace/bitstream/handle/2097/1365/WansooKim2009.pdf?sequence=1&isAllowed=y (accessed 29 August 2015).

Kim, W. G.; Lee, Y. K.; Yoo, Y. J. Predictors of Relationship Quality and Relationship Outcomes in Luxury Restaurants. *J. Hosp. Tour. Res.* **2006**, *30*(2), 143–169.

Kivela, J.; Inbakaran, R.; Reece, J. Consumer Research in the Restaurant Environment, Part 1: A Conceptual Model of Dining Satisfaction and Return Patronage. *Int. J. Contemporary Hosp. Manage.* **1999**, *11*(5), 205–222.

Kivela, J.; Inbakaran, R.; Reece, J. Consumer Research in the Restaurant Environment. Part 3: Analysis, Findings and Conclusions. *Int. J. Contemporary Hosp. Manage.* **2000**, *12*(1), 13–30.

Ladhari, R.; Brun, I.; Morales, M. Determinants of Dining Satisfaction and Post-dining Behavioral Intentions. *Int. J. Hosp. Manage.* **2008**, *27*(4), 563–573.

Lai, Y. L.; Chang, S. C. How Improving the Customer Experience Quality and Business Performance? A Case Study by Mystery Shopper Practices. *Int. J. Mark. Stud.* **2013**, *5*(6), 52–61.

Lashley, C. Towards Theoretical Understanding of Hospitality. In: *In Search of Hospitality*; Lashley, C., Morrison, A., Eds.; Butterworth-Heinemann: Oxford, 2000; pp 157–176.

Lemke, F.; Clark, M.; Wilson, H. Customer Experience Quality: An Exploration in Business and Consumer Contexts Using Repertory Grid Technique. *J. Acad. Mark. Sci.* **2011**, *39*(6), 846–869.

Liang, R. D.; Zhang, J. S. The Effect of Service Interaction Orientation on Customer Satisfaction and Behavioral Intention: The Moderating Effect of Dining Frequency. *Asia-Pac. J. Mark. Logistics* **2012**, *24*(1), 153–170.

Mangold, W. G.; Miller, F.; Brockway, G. R. Word-of-mouth Communication in the Service Marketplace. *J. Serv. Mark.* **1999**, *13*(1), 73–89.

Meng, J. G.; Elliott, K. M. Predictors of Relationship Quality for Luxury Restaurants. *J. Retail. Consum. Serv.* **2008**, *15*(6), 509–515.

Meyer, C.; Schwager, A. Understanding Customer Experience. *Harv. Bus. Rev.* **2007**, *85*(2), 116–126.

Muller, C. C. A Simple Measure of Restaurant Efficiency. *Cornell Hot. Restaur. Adm. Q.* **1999,** *40*(3), 31–37.

Naumann, E.; Giel, K. *Customer Satisfaction Measurement and Management: Using the Voice of the Customer*; Van Nostrand Reinhold, 1995.

Ng, S.; David, M. E.; Dagger, T. S. Generating positive word-of-mouth in the service experience, *Manage. Serv. Qual.* **2011,** *21*(2), 133–151.

Nusra. *Food industry, Then, Now, Forever!* Restaurantindia.in, 28 March 2016c [Online]. http://www.restaurantindia.in/article/f-and-b-format/menu-trends/Food-industry-Then-Now-Forever.a682/ (accessed 30 March 2016).

Nusra. *Gurgaon Based Italiano to Open 20 Restaurants in Next Five Years.* Restaurantindia. in, 28 March 2016a [Online]. http://www.restaurantindia.in/interview/starting-up/restaurant/Gurgaon-based-Italiano-to-open-20-restaurants-in-next-five-years.i398/ (accessed 30 March 2016).

Nusra. *We Will Open Not More than One to Two Outlets per City.* Restaurantindia.in, 29 March 2016b [Online]. http://www.restaurantindia.in/interview/people/entrepreneurs/We-will-open-not-more-than-one-to-two-outlets-per-city.i404/ (accessed 30 March 2016).

O'Cass, A.; Grace, D. Understanding the Role of Retail Store Service in Light of Self-image–Store Image Congruence. *Psychol. Mark.* **2008,** *25*(6), 521–537.

Oh, H.; Fiore, A. M.; Jeoung, M. Measuring Experience Economy Concepts: Tourism Applications. *J. Trav. Res.* **2007,** *46*(2), 119–132.

Olson, J. C.; Jacoby, J. Cue Utilization in the Quality Perception Process. In: *Proceedings of the Third Annual Conference of the Association for Consumer Research*; Association for Consumer Research, Ann Arbor, MI, 1972; pp 167–179.

Pine, B. J.; Gilmore, J. H. *The Experience Economy.* Harvard Business School Press: Boston, 1999, p 63.

Pine, B. J.; Gilmore, J. H. Welcome to the Experience Economy, *Harv. Bus. Rev.* **1998,** *76*(4), 97–105.

Prasad, C. J.; Aryasri, A. R. Effect of Shopper Attributes on Retail Format Choice Behaviour for Food and Grocery Retailing in India. *Int. J. Retail Distrib. Manage.* **2011,** *39*(1), 68–86.

Prayag, G.; Hosany, S.; Odeh, K. The Role of Tourists' Emotional Experiences and Satisfaction in Understanding Behavioral Intentions. *J. Destinat. Mark. Manage.* **2013,** *2*(2), 118–127.

Reimer, A.; Kuehn, R. The impact of Servicescape on Quality Perception. *Eur. J. Mark.* **2005,** *39*(7/8), 785–808.

Robson, S. K. Turning the Tables. *Cornell Hotel Restaurant Adm. Q.* **1999,** *40*(3), 56–63.

Rust, R. T.; Oliver, R. L. *Service Quality: New Directions in Theory and Practice.* Sage Publications: Thousand Oaks, CA, 1994.

Rust, R. T.; Zahorik, A. J.; Keiningham, T. L. Return on Quality (ROQ): Making Service Quality Financially Accountable. *J. Mark.* **1995,** *59*(2), 58–70.

Sathyanarayanan, D.; Babar, K. PEs Find Restaurant Chains too Hot to Resist. *Economic Times*, 18 August 2015 [Online]. http://articles.economictimes.indiatimes.com/2015-08-18/news/65530341_1_everstone-capital-samara-capital-jaspal-singh-sabharwal (accessed 30 March 2016).

Schumacker R. E.; Lomax, R. G. *A Beginner's Guide to Structural Equation Modeling.* Lawrence Erlbaum Press: New Jersey, 2004.

Stevens, P.; Knutson, B.; Patton, M. DINESERV: A Tool for Measuring Service Quality in Restaurants. *Cornell Hotel Restaurant Adm. Q.* **1995,** *36*(2), 56–60.

Sulek, J. M.; Hensley, R. L. The Relative Importance of Food, Atmosphere, and Fairness of Wait the Case of a Full-service Restaurant. *Cornell Hotel Restaurant Adm. Q.* **2004,** *45*(3), 235–247.

Swanson, S. R.; Davis, J. C. The Relationship of Differential Loci with Perceived Quality and Behavioral Intentions. *J. Serv. Mark.* **2003,** *17*(2), 202–219.

Tiwari, A. K. Jiggs Kalra Dishes Out a New Restaurant Venture, 13 December 2012 [Online]. http://www.dnaindia.com/money/report-jiggs-kalra-dishes-out-a-new-restaurant-venture-1776888 (accessed 30 March 2016).

Tombs, A.; McColl-Kennedy, J. R. Social–Servicescape Conceptual Model. *Mark. Theory* **2003,** *3*(4), 447–475.

Tripathi, G.; Dave, K. Exploration of Service Quality Factors in Restaurant Industry: A Study of Selected Restaurants in New Delhi Region. *J. Serv. Res.* **2014,** *14*(1), 9–26.

Vavra, T. G. *Improving Your Measurement of Customer Satisfaction: A Guide to Creating, Conducting, Analyzing, and Reporting Customer Satisfaction Measurement Programs*; ASQ Quality Press: Milwaukee, WI, 1997.

Verma, H. V. *Services Marketing: Text and Cases, 2/e.*; Pearson Education: India, 2012.

Wall, E. A.; Berry, L. L. The Combined Effects of the Physical Environment and Employee Behavior on Customer Perception of Restaurant Service Quality. *Cornell Hotel Restaurant Adm. Q.* **2007,** *48*(1), 59–69.

Winsted, K. F. Service Behaviors that Lead to Satisfied Customers. *Eur. J. Mark.* **2000,** *34*(3/4), 399–417.

Yi, Y. A Critical Review of Consumer Satisfaction. *Rev. Mark.* **1990,** *4*(1), 68–123.

Yüksel, A.; Yüksel, F. Measurement of Tourist Satisfaction with Restaurant Services: A Segment-based Approach. *J. Vacat. Mark.* **2002,** *9*(1), 52–68.

Zeithaml, V. A. Consumer perceptions of Price, Quality, and Value: A Means-end Model and Synthesis of Evidence. *J. Mark.* **1988,** *52*(3), 2–22.

Zeithaml, V. A.; Berry, L. L.; Parasuraman, A. The Behavioral Consequences of Service Quality. *J. Mark.* **1996,** *60*(2), 31–46.

Zeithaml, V. A. How Consumer Evaluation Processes Differ between Goods and Services. In: *Marketing of Services Proceedings Series*; Donnelly, J., George, W., Eds.; American Marketing Association: Chicago, IL, 1981; pp. 186–190.

APPENDIX

TABLE A9.1 Validity for SQ Factors.

	CR	AVE	MSV	ASV	Empathy	Impression	Aesthetics	Reliability and responsiveness	Privacy and entertainment
Empathy	0.824	0.610	0.372	0.346	0.781				
Impression	0.827	0.614	0.578	0.386	0.600	0.784			
Aesthetics	0.833	0.624	0.578	0.452	0.610	0.760	0.790		
Reliability and responsiveness	0.814	0.593	0.397	0.308	0.560	0.520	0.630	0.770	
Privacy and entertainment	0.802	0.575	0.462	0.346	0.580	0.580	0.680	0.500	0.759

TABLE A9.2 Validity for All Factors Combined.

	CR	AVE	MSV	ASV	WOM intentions	Impression	Aesthetics	Reliability and responsiveness	Empathy	Privacy and entertainment	Experience	Satisfaction	Loyalty	Ambient environment
WOM intentions	0.822	0.698	0.533	0.307	0.835									
Impression	0.827	0.614	0.578	0.284	0.410	0.784								
Aesthetics	0.833	0.625	0.578	0.374	0.480	0.760	0.791							
Reliability and responsiveness	0.811	0.588	0.548	0.328	0.620	0.520	0.640	0.767						
Empathy	0.824	0.610	0.372	0.308	0.480	0.600	0.610	0.550	0.781					
Privacy and entertainment	0.801	0.574	0.504	0.300	0.400	0.590	0.680	0.500	0.580	0.758				
Experience	0.764	0.619	0.384	0.223	0.550	0.320	0.440	0.440	0.450	0.410	0.787			
Satisfaction	0.856	0.600	0.548	0.389	0.730	0.470	0.590	0.740	0.580	0.530	0.620	0.774		
Loyalty	0.799	0.571	0.490	0.292	0.680	0.410	0.490	0.520	0.550	0.440	0.510	0.700	0.756	
Ambient	0.808	0.585	0.533	0.346	0.540	0.580	0.730	0.570	0.570	0.710	0.450	0.600	0.490	0.765

TABLE A9.3 Hypotheses Testing.

Hypotheses paths		Standard-ized path coefficients	*p*-Value	Results (sig-nificance of hypotheses)
Dependent latent variable	**Independent latent variable**			
Impression	Ambient environment	0.95	***	Significant
Aesthetics	Ambient environment	1.08	***	Significant
Reliability and responsiveness	Ambient environment	0.75	***	Significant
Empathy	Ambient environment	0.84	***	Significant
Privacy and entertainment	Ambient environment	1.11	***	Significant
Customer experience	Aesthetics	0.14	0.04	Significant
Customer experience	Reliability and responsiveness	0.5	***	Significant
Customer experience	Empathy	0.24	***	Significant
Customer experience	*Impression*	*-0.07*	*0.18*	*Not significant*
Customer experience	*Privacy and entertainment*	*0.09*	*0.09*	*Not significant*
Customer satisfaction	Customer experience	0.94	***	Significant
Customer loyalty	Customer satisfaction	0.8	***	Significant
WOM intentions	Customer satisfaction	0.9	***	Significant

CHAPTER 10

PUSH FOR THE FOOD AND BEVERAGES SEGMENT TO DRIVE REVENUE GROWTH IN INDIAN HOTELS

DEBPRIYA DE* and SANDEEP MUNJAL

School of Hospitality and Tourism Management, Vedatya Institute, Gurgaon, India

*Corresponding author. E-mail: debpriya.de@vedatya.ac.in

CONTENTS

Abstract 228

10.1　Introduction 229

10.2　Methodology 230

10.3　Findings from the F&B Leaders Roundtable 237

10.4　Challenges on the Road to Growth in Revenues
　　　and Profitability 247

10.5　Implications and the Way Forward 248

Keywords 249

References 250

ABSTRACT

Food and beverage (F&B) as a business segment is a value proposition for the Indian hotel industry and is considered a key factor contributing to potential revenue growth at large. The Indian hotel industry has been on a strong growth spiral since the late 1990s; but there has always been a debate around whether the F&B as a segment is contributing enough to generate revenue growth for the hotels. Times have changed over the past few years, accommodation-driven revenue that constituted almost 80–85% of the total revenue and nearly 90% of the net profit is under pressure in an oversupply market. Hotels have been able to respond to this emerging trend by focusing on F&B as one of the key drivers to growing operating revenue.

The chapter offers a perspective on various aspects of the F&B segment in the Indian hotel Industry that are reshaping the traditional revenue model, driven by the growth in F&B revenue. The "F&B push" is evaluated on various parameters that are considered significant. As the paper engages with this new found focus, it probes into the new methods that the hotels are adopting to seek higher revenue contribution from the F&B segment. The study will focus on how different segments of the hotel industry in India have responded to, the challenge of weakening ARRs (average room rate) and struggling occupancy percentages, to find support in the food and beverages component to bolster revenues and faltering bottom lines. Using the "Price Bundling" strategy wherein "F&Bs" have been bundled with rooms to create an overall "value deal" for the customers has become significant.

Within the F&B space also there is a turmoil of sorts, "alcoholic beverages" have become a strong volume growth as well as highly profitable component of the overall F&B revenue mix. New cuisine trends developed by hotels to seek changes in the food habits of consumers and to match them with the current trends are today critical to sustainability.

"IRD (In room Dining)" or what is typically mentioned as room service is a facility that has the potential to drive revenue growth and it is interesting to see how hotels are currently managing this segment of the F&B offerings, in order to give a push for revenue growth. The hotels today have also added "Events" as a F&B portfolio component and the chapter covers the impact of events in the F&B revenue growth story.

The hotels have not only been able to recognize the F&B business as a revenue growth driver but have also incorporated major changes in their outlook toward the staffing of the F&B divisions. The HR aspects around the F&B department staffing have seen a shift given the focus and attention that the function has received. The Indian hotel industry faces multiple challenges in terms of the government policies and regulations that can possibly become a hindrance, for the revenue growth aspects of F&B and impact guest experience at large.

10.1 INTRODUCTION

Traditionally, it has been the "rooms division" or the "accommodations" function of a hotel that contributed a major part of the overall hotel revenue. F&B as an operational function (production and service) was a quintessential part of the "operational squad." While the revenue contribution to the overall pie ranged from 25% to 15% depending on the hotel segment, it was never the focus of a revenue growth strategy for hotel businesses in India. With limited number of hotel chains, demand was always ahead of the supply; all this started to change over the last decade or so. Economic liberalization, along with sociocultural shifts, saw Indians travel internally for leisure and business purposes like never before. The demand caused the investor interest to grow and soon enough there was huge capacity addition at the luxury, mid-segment, and budget hotel categories. This capacity expansion included new Indian brands like Lemon Tree, Sarovar Hotels, Golden Tulip, Keys (to name a few) as well as nearly all prominent International hotel brands like the Carlson Rezidor, Hilton, Marriott, Hyatt, Accor, IHG, Dusit Devrana, etc. Interestingly, the maximum capacity addition came from the "Tier 1" cities, and the result was a sudden oversupply situation across all hotel segments in every major Indian city.

The obvious impact of the abovementioned situation has been a decline in ARRs, and a struggle to keep occupancy levels healthy in a rather competitive business environment. A slowing economy in the 2009–2010 made matters worse. All major Indian hotel companies have struggled to remain profitable, IHCL (Indian Hotels Company Limited) has been incurring losses for the last 5 years; the EIH (East India Hotels) with a sub-par 5% net profit over the same period is also feeling the heat. Leela Ventures is another story of negative returns on investment. Amidst this mayhem, the F&B department seems to have come to the rescue of the Indian hotel industry, contributing a stronger revenue share in the overall revenue collection. There has been a steady increase in the share of F&B revenue and some of the industry's most respected names have reiterated this fact.

This revenue contribution shift is a result of a deliberate strategic shift that was a response to multiple factors, some systemic, others a result of changes in the macro-business environment that the Indian hospitality industry had to respond to. It is no secret that every rupee in revenue from "rooms' sales" is significantly more profitable than the rupee in revenue from "F&B sales." The cost of sales for a room product is around 10–15% based on the business segment and brand's specific standards, but the same is 20–30% or even higher for F&B products. The room product did not just contribute majority of hotel revenues, it was also contributing to stronger profitability at a gross level to support the fixed costs of the business, ensuring healthy profitability at the net margin level.

An oversupply market changed that positioning, as hotels struggled to stay afloat, they saw the F&B segment as the olive branch. Since 2011, in Delhi alone, there has been an increase of 200 hotels across all segments in a span of 3–4 years (Khosla, 2014).

10.2   METHODOLOGY

A qualitative approach forms the basis of this research. A round table discussion format was used to bring F&B leaders from a broad spectrum of hospitality brands in India at the discussion table; a semi-structured questionnaire deployed to elicit responses. The panel of industry leaders and experts discussed a range of seven thematic aspects around the Indian F&B sector's growth story and challenges. The findings from the discussion are documented and summarized. Existing literature reviewed constitutes the secondary research that supports the ongoing discussion throughout the chapter.

10.2.1   FOOD AND BEVERAGES REVENUE GROWTH STORY

One of the most recognized personalities in the Indian hospitality industry, Rai Bahaur M.S. Oberoi, believed that hotels are in the business of selling rooms and little else. This statement seems to be losing ground today. The recent FHRAI (Federation of Hotel and Restaurant Association of India) hotel survey reveals that the revenue contribution of the "rooms division" (hotel industry in India as a whole) as an average for past 5 years has dropped steadily from 60.5% in 2008–2009 to 52.2% in 2012–2013. In contrast, during the same period, the F&B revenue share has gone up from 25.6% to 29% and if we add the banquet business component then the contribution of F&B actually jumps from 34.4% to 41.2% (Bhattacharya, 2014). The F&B departments at hotels have been clearly performing better in terms of percentile revenue growth as compared to the rooms department. The share of F&B in total revenue for some luxury hotels had gone up to nearly 45% during the financial year 2013, as a result, the ratio of room to F&B revenue moved from a traditional 70:30–60:40. This demonstrates a strong shift toward food and beverage-driven revenue growth, as stated by Tarun Thakral (CEO), The Le Meridian New Delhi (Khosla, 2014).

The F&B revenues from the Carlson Group in 2014 also saw an increase of over 5% when they compared it with the last financial year. The ARRs have fallen over the past 6 years, while F&B demand has grown. FHRAI data clearly indicate that hotels have tried to cover lost ground in revenue terms by switching focus to the F&B segment (Khosla, 2014). Four seasons witnessed an increase of 10% in the revenue of F&B while the rooms division was stagnant.

Increase in food and beverage revenue is attributed in part to an increase in banquets and conference-related business segment. This segment recorded an increase of 17.3% in 2012–2013 and has continued to chart a double-digit growth, while the overall F&B revenues grew by 4.2%. Hotels across India have added large meeting spaces, which have facilitated the growth of MICE (Meetings, Incentives, Conferences, and Events), in the country (FHRAI Indian Hotel Industry Survey 2012–13, 2013). Hotels have latched on to the opportunity by developing interesting banquet menus and promoting them at attractive prices, to compete with the stand-alone restaurants and banquets. The banquets are doing well as most of the Indians love hosting their marriages and special events in 5-star hotels as a status symbol, and this notion has led to increase in banquet revenues thus contributing in an overall growth of F&B revenues (Khosla, 2014). Hotels have also made significant capital investments to ensure that they offer superior quality function spaces for business as well as other events, given the growth in demand that the segment offers. This trend is now also moving to Tier 2 and 3 cities in the country.

Mr. Dilip Puri (VP South Asia), Starwoods Asia Pacific Hotels & Resorts, acknowledges the importance of F&B today for guests. In Starwoods Hotels, F&B operates at a massive scale and accounts for nearly one-third of the chain's entire revenue globally. It is a vital part of their business and F&B has been the driving force for both their top and bottom line profits. The potential of F&B is well recognized and the brand sees F&B as a ripe area for innovation.

According to Mr. Ashish Shome (F&B Director), Hyatt Regency Mumbai, the revolution in F&B has been mainly due to the growing awareness and the demand from a discerning clientele, which has traveled across the globe and has been exposed to some of the world's best in dining experience. The customers are ready to shell out extra money for quality and hence the hotels have innovated to offer new F&B concepts. The growth of F&B is not about the revenue footprint alone, but about "food" as a part of the "experience" that the guests receive. The liberation of F&B took place due to new entrants from international brands arriving in India, triggering a modernization of local brands.

F&B sales have risen because of rise in spending power of consumers that further led to an increase in discretionary spending. There is a growing trend to eat out, and this has been influenced by the entrance of international brands in India and being exposed to foreign cultures through movies, internet, and the TV. As per KPMG, the key to success for any F&B business has been achieved through customer-driven innovation. The gradual evolution of cuisines has seen chefs and patrons develop innovation in culinary arts to woo their customers. Some of the prominent restaurant owners feel they do not have to look toward the West to be successful, relying on old age recipes and traditional ways of cooking to create new experience for the guests is attracting customer interest. The surge in F&B sales is also driven by the newfound desire to travel and experience food that is symbolic of local culture and ethnicity. This "need" gives the "F&B" function an opportunity to use this as a tool to innovate and create an experience to increase the F&B sales. Another reason of F&B revenues getting a push is that today's bars are not only limited to being a place to "drink" but also add "food" in the mix thereby increasing revenues. Food-related experimentation with an objective to create new menu items that are complementary, with alcoholic as well as nonalcoholic beverages, is in. The availability of new and organic raw ingredients has also contributed to the revolution of F&B and as a result helped to boost sales (Munjal et al., 2016).

Clearly, the driving force for the F&B segment has been the sociocultural shift; as a result, the size of F&B market (hotels and restaurants) in India has grown to $13 billion and is forecasted to become $78 billion as per the NRAI (National Restaurant Association of India). Business will be profitable only if the Indian hotels are able to attract the nonresident guests in addition to the hotel guests. Banqueting has been one of the key forces that have driven the F&B business. Fifty percent of the total F&B business is contributed through banquets in most of the hotels in India. Whether it is Tier I, Tier II of Tier III cities, guests are spending huge sums on marriages, holidays, anniversaries, birthdays, and other celebrations (NRAI, 3013).

F&B service delivery models have gone an extra mile by giving an interactive experience to the guest, thus ensuring greater revenues. With globalization and international brands venturing into India, some of the best practices have been adopted by the Indian hotels, especially in the F&B domain. Consumers are willing to shell out extra money for eating out, but the expectations are set quite high. Some of the prominent restaurateurs quote that as the economy has grown in the last decade, the rise in disposable incomes has really helped the F&B business to flourish. The market size has increased, but there is also a big challenge in front of the F&B businesses to convert the growing revenues into profits proportionately, given the rise in commodity, real estate, manpower, and energy cost (hotelierindia.com, 2014).

10.2.2 DEPENDENCE ON F&B REVENUES

The F&B revenues are very important for the Indian hotels as they alone contribute nearly 50% of the hotel's total revenue; thus, as a profit center, F&B is equally significant when compared to the "rooms division." Mr. Megh Vinayak (Corporate Manager, Revenue) of The Lalit Suri Hospitality Group echoes the above stated reality when he states that "the revenue which they earn from F&B is about 50% of the hotel's total revenue, hence they promote F&B aggressively. The importance of F&B has grown over the years because there has been a steady decline in rooms driven revenue and profitability." Mr. Vinesh Gupta (GM, Movenpick Hotels, Bangalore) quotes that "nearly a decade ago the rooms revenue profitability was as high as 92% and even the ARRs were pretty high. But now the profitability has declined to 75%; the operating expenses are going up including manpower costs."

Mr. Gupta also points out that there has to be a huge thought process shift to conceptualize and market the hotel restaurants. A mid-size hotel of 150–200 rooms can have typically 4 F&B zones, restaurants, and bars in permutation and combination. The covers available are typically twice the number of rooms. The investment varies between Rs. 3 and 4 crores. Each outlet typically represents 2.5–5% of the hotel's total cost of development; hence, it is very important to focus on return on investment and the overall profitability. According to him, "If we market and conceptualize properly then an F&B outlet in a hotel can make operating profits in six months." Marketing the products on social media platforms helps the hotels to compete with the stand-alone restaurants. The choice of the type of restaurant with cuisine or a bar will totally depend on the size of the hotel, clientele in the vicinity, and the cuisine popular in the city. It is a very dynamic environment and it will see more focus in coming days. The future of Indian hotel restaurants will be the concept of branded in-house restaurants, wherein the hotels will treat them as separate profit and loss centers managed internally or through an outside restaurateur (hotelnewsnow.com, 2015).

Vikas Malik, Regional Director F&B South Asia, Starwood, recognizes that the F&B department has become an integral part of the Indian hotels strategy in terms of generating and growing revenue. Malik states that the hotels are innovating to woo the guests by giving an exclusive F&B offering. The contribution from F&B has seen a positive change in the last 5 years. Starwood Hotels have added around 75% of their new restaurants and bars in China and India. Elaborating more, Malik mentions that the F&B offering is central to a hotel experience and will remain a key revenue driver. This ratio will certainly see a positive change in contribution from this sector. With urbanization and globalization happening, the sophisticated consumers have an interest in fine-dining options, new cuisines, and wines. Media has played an important role in creating awareness about food and wines through food magazines and TV programs that are focused toward this segment. Thus, the hotels need to be more innovative in capturing the societal trends and F&B will play the most important role in enhancing the hotel experience. Malik also expressed that the luxury hotels need to have more than one specialty restaurant, to make the most of the current trend (hospitalitybizindia.com, 2012).

The IHCL analyst meet held in 2014 recognized that the trends are changing in the Indian hotel industry, with respect to the role of the F&B segment. There are specific marketing campaigns being run that are focused toward restaurants to give F&B revenues a push. The sales and marketing strategies are promoting "Taj Hotels" as a wedding destination, as this segment has grown to become a large business segment over the years. The hotels also promote themselves by concentrating their efforts toward highlighting their restaurants as the signature product. The annual reports evidence that there was a decline of 1% in the revenue earnings of the "rooms division" in 2013–2014, while in contrast, the F&B revenue in 2012–2013 was Rs. 732.4 crores and there was increase of 6% in the revenue of F&B in the next financial year of 2013–2014 to Rs. 774.2 crores. The room revenues had gone down because there was oversupply in the recessionary market, while there was a healthy increase in restaurant sales and the banqueting business (Corporate, 2014).

10.2.3 THE TECHNOLOGY IMPACT

Technology has played an important role in promoting F&B and in turn boosting revenues. The use of tablets to offer menus, innovative live stations using induction cooking tops for banquet functions, has helped food to be served hygienically and safely. An excellent example of technology play in F&B is the cold-gel bath that is used to serve salads, seafood, and cold meats in many brunches. This has created an opportunity for F&B to boost their sales. Technology plays a vital role in F&B as it helps in changing the operational scope, allowing innovation with food and beverages that was not feasible earlier. It has also helped in decreasing costs and in increasing shelf life, thus making products and ideas more accessible. Technology has also helped to innovate new techniques in cooking giving the guests a superior taste and product quality and ensuring that the nutritional value of the food is kept intact. Some of the examples are molecular mixology, molecular cooking, under vacuum, etc. (Munjal & Sharma, 2012).

10.2.4   THE HYGIENE AND FOOD SAFETY CONCERN

The success of any F&B outlet depends on food safety and hygiene and this plays a very important role in terms of consumer confidence. Consumers have many options while eating out, unlike the past. If the outlet is ignorant about hygiene, then the consumer would go to some other place, one that is sensitive toward their hygiene concerns. The government is also now enforcing strict guidelines on hygiene and food safety. Today "food" is not just consumed, it is experienced. The look and feel of the outlet, the crockery used, décor, ambience, etc. all add up to create overall dining experience.

10.2.5   THE PRICING SPIN

Pricing strategies developed by hospitality managers across hotel chains have responded to the fierce competition from stand-alone food, beverage outlets, and banquet operations by offering attractive discounts; and other price bundling offers to attract customers. The hotels are attracting customers inside their "bars" by giving hefty discounts on alcoholic beverages including whiskies and wines in order to boost sales. Another factor that has led to change in the pricing strategies by hotels is the mushrooming of standalones near the hotels which give the hotels immense competition. Today, the customers go out to eat more often, but they want value for every rupee they spend. They may not always be looking at discounts or special offers but they do want a fulfilling experience and are ready to pay for it.

The hotel management team need to think about strategies to satisfy the unique expectations of specific target markets. Restaurants and bars at hotels also have generated customer interest through activities like limited edition pairing of whisky with cigars, ladies evening, Caribbean nights, etc. Through a mix of innovative pricing and generating customer interest through interesting themes that offer a unique experience of food, beverages, music, entertainment, ambiance and service, the restaurants in hotels are now attracting a wider range of demographic groups, including a rather young crowd along with their regular patrons. The outlets across hotel chains saw a substantial increase in the number of covers per meal period, along with the average check per cover, indicating success with their strategic approach (Hospitalitytimes.com, 2015). That said it is also apparent that the profitability impact of the revenue shift is not what the industry aspired for, the contribution margin from a room revenue rupee being 90% as against the typical 70% for each rupee of F&B revenue earned. As a result, the revenue growth in F&B generates a stunted profit growth.

10.2.6 THE HUMAN RESOURCE IMPACT

The increase in F&B revenues may or may not have had significant direct impact on earnings of the hotels, but the demand for young, qualified chefs and service professionals is definitely on the rise. Chef Manjit Gill, corporate Chef of ITC, says that they had hired 55 young chefs in 2013. He also stated that there has been a 50% increase in the kitchen workforce. Young chefs are being hired as the hotels are coming up with interactive kitchens, live counters, multi-cuisine buffets, etc. and the guests like to see culinary innovation at display. Key hotel brands like The Leela, ITC, The Taj, The Marriotts, The Park are all recruiting culinary talents (Chefs). The "concept cooking" trend is also driving the increased demand for culinary staff and demand for service staff, to manage the increasing load on the food and beverage operations, which has also grown in parallel. The dining concepts are changing at a fast pace and this is resulting in demand for specialized people in this trade. New concepts like gastronomy, pretty plating, fusion cooking are in, and hotels are trying to attract customers toward these concepts. The distribution of F&B staff between kitchen and service has also seen a change in the recent times as compared to a few years back, the number of servers was much more than chefs. But since the induction of new concepts discussed above, the ratio of chef to server is now 1:1. With a growing demand, the salaries of F&B staff have also seen a surge in recent times (Khosla & Sathyanarayanan, 2014).

The F&B segment has been dynamic, responding to the changing trends of customer eating habits and demand. Since the customers have welcomed newer and innovative cuisines, both the service and kitchen operators have turned themselves into progressive thinkers, constantly trying out new ways of enthralling the guest. Guest has always been the focal point of the industry, and the changes have been a result of the customer centric approach of the sector. Technology has become the most important tool in bringing about these changes and hence tapping of new opportunities is essential for getting business and engaging with consumers, while giving "cooking" a new dimension. Hence, this has led to the belief that F&B has emerged as an important source of revenue (hotelierindia.com, 2014).

10.3   FINDINGS FROM THE F&B LEADERS ROUNDTABLE

F&B Leaders "Roundtable" was organized on the October 5, 2015 at Vedatya Institute, Gurgaon, with a purpose of bringing industry experts from the food and beverage domain together to get their views on various aspects around the F&B segment's status and growth prospects in India. The participants included industry professionals in the field of F&B operations. Some of the prominent participants representing nearly every significant hotel brand in India were Liam Crotty (Executive Chef—Hyatt Regency), Supreet Ranjan Roy (Director F&B—Hyatt Regency), Girish Chimwal (Asst. Manager F&B—Carlson Rezidor), Mansi Nijhawan (Event Concierge—Carlson Rezidor), Indrashish Sinha (Director F&B—IHG), Bhoj Raj Sharma (F&B Manager—Marriott), and Jayant Sharma (Restaurant Manager-Hilton) to name a few.

Discussion was guided through a series of theme specific questions, moderated and transcribed to document the inputs shared by the participants.

1.   **What are the emergent trends with respect to performance of the F&B segment in hotels and any strategy or approach that the Indian hotels may have adopted to give a "push" to F&B revenue growth?**

Key findings:

- There is shift of focus from the rooms Division to the F&B function with respect to revenue growth.

- Emergence of new cuisines in India like Japanese, Thai, Burmese, Brazilian, etc., which many of the hotels are offering is playing a positive role.
- Room service (IRD) is still not a major contributor in terms of revenue contribution, but efforts are being directed toward improving both number of covers as well as average check from this sub segment.
- New tax regulation implemented by the government has adversely affected "Bar" sales at hotels.
- The hotel industry is facing huge competition from the stand-alone and chain restaurants, as there were fewer options available for the guest to dine out earlier. Today, they have far too many options.
- Luxury hotels have a high fixed cost toward offering multiple F&B outlets, resulting in a pricing challenge when it comes to competing with stand-alone outlets.
- Hotels are making efforts to attract in house guests to patronize the F&B outlets through theme-based events, price bundling, etc. so that they can hold back the guests from dining outside the hotel.
- The MICE business segment is on the radar of every major hotel chain in India. Hotels are building additional capacity, as there is an increase in the demand for MICE facilities in the country. This is another reason for F&B contribution in the growth of the total revenue of the hotel.
- Breakfast as a meal category in hotels was traditionally restricted more or less to the in house guests, but the hotels are exploring the new opportunities by promoting their "breakfast buffets" and "brunch buffets" to outsiders and this has helped the hotels to increase their F&B revenues.
- The concept of "all day dining" is not recognized merely as a café theme but more as a differentiator; hotels are now focusing to giving more food and beverage options to the guests 24/7 so that they can offer more than what any ordinary café has to offer.
- Hotels in India have reacted to the growth in numbers of travelers and their cultural diversity, through globalization of cuisines and innovative food and beverage products to meet the needs of a highly segmented market. Many are experimenting with "regional Indian" cuisines, while others are looking to offer international fare. Either way, it is clear that the "tourism inspired" volume growth is what every chain intends to exploit to the most.

The panel lists mentioned that the competition is increasing in the market not only among the hotels but also through the surge in stand-alone restaurants and fast food chains. The customers have more option to choose from than they ever did, this means that hotels and restaurant chains alike will have to fight for their share of the growing market. The revenue growth cannot be seen in isolation, the F&B inventory costs have increased due to multiple factors, this affects the pricing and eventually the profit contribution of the F&B department. In India, much of the F&B sector is still unorganized and unstructured, but the hotels have got a well-structured approach toward F&B, which enables them to increase their presence in this domain.

The developmental activities, which have taken place in the tourism sector in India, have tremendous potential to expand the market. The hotels need to leverage this opportunity more effectively.

2.   **How is the F&B department or function being perceived by the hotel's management as a potential revenue growth driver, in contrast to the "accommodations" focused mindset?**

Key findings:

- The F&B leaders from IHG narrated that their group is currently focusing more on F&B as a prime revenue driver in contrast to the accommodations division. In their budget meetings, the management is allocating more funds to the F&B department than the rooms division. The emphasis has shifted toward F&B.
- In order to give their F&B outlets a boost, the hotels are exploring options of franchising. They let out one of their outlets to any other restaurant or bar chain or brand so that the customers loyal to that brand do not have to go looking out. This also brings in footfall that can potentially enable a hotel to market its other F&B outlets.
- Hotels are selling rooms through various packages, which are including F&B offerings as the value proposition or a key differentiator. Many hotels are promoting F&B offerings ahead of the room product, a clear shift from the past.
- Some hotel brands still feel that the accommodation division is the key driver of revenue and mention that the current rooms related over supply situation will pass given the higher contribution to profitability; rooms will remain central to a hotel businesses growth strategy.

- Other hotel chains have a different opinion given that the F&B contributes about 40–45% of the total revenue earnings of the hotel.

There was broad consensus that given that the operating costs of the F&B segment are much higher than the rooms division, the significance of room revenue growth through higher ARRs and stronger occupancy statistics will remain critical for any hotel to achieve a strong fiscal performance. That said with large capacity addition coming through, it is a strategic imperative for the hotel's managements to look toward support from the F&B segment to not only sustain revenue growth but, as mentioned earlier, deploy F&B offerings as a key differentiator for the consumer to choose their hotel as against others. The rooms division can only do brisk business if it has a strong backing from the F&B department in today's economic scenario.

3.   **What are your views on cost-reduction approaches with respect to F&B and their potential to impact the profit margin?**

Key findings:

The F&B department operates at a higher cost of sales, and hence the gross profit margin is weaker as compared to the rooms division. The average food and beverage cost varies from a typical 25% for cafe style outlets in hotels, to even as high as 45–50%. The higher inflation in food index compounds this further. On the whole the at the operating level, the profitability is weakened further due to higher labor cost, license cost, etc. The competition from standalones limits the capacity of food and beverage outlets in hotels to raise their menu prices. The hotel management is deploying innovative practices to reduce their operating costs. They are as follows:

- The hotels have entered into agreements with global HR contractors, where they hire staffs on contract, thereby reducing their workforce costs.
- The emphasis has been on the F&B purchase cycle, ordering of material and following FIFO/LIFO has bought down the overall inventory costs; thereby reducing the cost of carrying inventory, wastage, pilferage, etc.
- The staff is trained to review the banquet order book, function prospectus carefully and check their inventory before ordering so that they do not over order.

- Chefs held accountable with respect to purchase, inventory decisions and expected to innovate through menus that use seasonal, lower cost ingredients.
- Order in volumes where volume-based discounts are available. The hotels have tie ups with various beverage companies which has helped to reduce beverage costs substantially.
- Using green fuels is finding support, this not only helps reduce the carbon footprint but also to bring down the costs as these fuels are relatively cheaper than the traditional fuels. The engineering department played a vital role, by using PNG/CNG/solar power to bring down the costs as well as emissions.
- The food waste from the kitchen and other F&B outlets is diverted toward manufacturing organic fertilizers, which the hotels can sell to agro companies, thereby contributing in cost reduction.
- Some hotels have out sourced their "kitchen stewarding" department, thereby reducing the labor costs and cleaning costs to a great level.
- The use of LED lights in various F&B outlets has bought down the electricity costs, thereby improving the F&B unit level profitability.
- Hotel kitchens have started buying coal strategically and use cheaper versions of burning fuels like coal stones and natural gas which have bought down energy cost.
- The hotels have started giving training and creating awareness in the staff about ways to control costs, wastages, following LIFO/FIFO, etc. to help reduce costs.
- Some of the chains have started using the concept "farm to fork," which means that most of their raw material is from their own produce. This backward integration is helping in reducing costs.
- The management has started "track meetings" where they micromanage the costs through tracking usage of silver foil, films, paper rolls, etc. which has bought the expense to nearly one-third of its historical levels.
- The kitchens have started using new energy efficient ovens for bakery, even though the initial installation cost is high as the overall cost reduction pays off for the initial investment quickly.
- The management of many hotels promoted effort to minimize wastage introducing "no bin day" in staff cafeterias to reduce food wastage is an example. The hotels have regulated laundry timings and allocation, thereby reducing cleaning costs of uniforms other linen items.

4. **What is the contribution of "beverage" component in general and alcoholic beverages in particular, to the overall revenue performance of the F&B function in hotels? Any best practice?**

Key findings:

There has been a shift in the drinking habits of customers in line with a sociocultural change sweeping the country. Consumption of beverages in general and alcoholic beverages is almost a part of any social gathering or event. From the growth in the number of coffee shops to branded milk shake bars like "Keventers," etc., the demand and supply are both growing rapidly. The bars and pubs in Tier 1 and 2 cities are mushrooming at a rapid pace; this trend presents a potential opportunity for hotels but not without meeting the challenge from the stand-alone businesses also fighting for the same market share.

- The guests look for innovative drinks, rather than traditional straight drinks; interesting cocktails offering creatively are in.
- Hotels offer a huge variety of beers (bottled as well as freshly brewed) and any and every brand international or domestic is available on the menu, the guest can find his choice easily.
- There is huge demand for trained bartenders and mixologists as guests are aware of the beverages and they would expect the same standard of knowledge from the service staff. Hence, hotels are hiring trained bartenders and mixologists increasingly.
- Pairing of food with an appropriate beverage alcoholic or otherwise is a requirement and the hotels are putting a lot behind this trend to make sure that the guest gets the best combination of food and drink, which adds to his other experience. The positive resultant impact on average checks is off course welcome.
- Hotels are building transparent relationship with suppliers which allows them to negotiate prices and other contractual terms.
- There is renewed focus on training of each level of staff to use this as a tool, to remain competitive, build capacity to grow customer satisfaction, and eventually boost F&B sales.
- Hotels are coming up with unique "Cocktail Menus" which are mostly innovated by their own bartenders or mixologist, and they use this as tool to increase sales.

- The recent surge in consumption of alcoholic beverages by guests has impacted revenue opportunity from nonalcoholic beverages. There is clear potential of tapping those who are teetotallers.
- There has been a phenomenal change in the training tactics of the hotels; sales teams are informed and trained to promote food and beverages as a unique selling proposition of the hotel. To boost beverage sales, the hotels are offering incentive-based schemes for the staff to motivate them to up-sell rather than just take food orders and deliver the same to the guests.
- The bars are being upgraded and constantly introducing new products to increase their sales and product variety.

The feedback from the roundtable participants indicated that nearly 30% of the total F&B revenue contribution can typically be attributed to beverage sales. The nonalcoholic beverages are in focus and the knowledge and skills of trained bartenders and mixologists are being upgraded to create innovative nonalcoholic drinks for the guests. Guests are demanding in the snacks menu, bars and the hotels have made the most of this opportunity to increase revenue as well as customer satisfaction by introducing new varieties of snacks in their menus. Hotels generate better margins on IMFL (Indian made foreign liquor) as compared to imported liquor; hence, the hotels have started promoting IMFLs more by applying package deals and price bundling strategies.

5. **Is there a shift in the service delivery model with respect to the F&B function? If yes, do you think that this shift has enabled the F&B department to grow revenue and profitability?**

Key findings:

Participating F&B leaders expressed that service delivery approaches and standard operating processes need to change with the changing trends, as today's guests are widely traveled and well aware of the current trends in hospitality. Service delivery models are changing along with food concepts and the style of delivering service has responded to changes in sociocultural settings, emergence of new dining concepts, and food innovation in the recent times. The service styles breaking the historical stereotype service models are the new reality. As the international brands get established in the Indian market, there is access to international standards and the same standards are brought into practice by giving training to the staff and ensuring that the guests get the same service, as they might have experienced out of the country.

- Time is the biggest constraint for certain guests, as they want to experience quick service with wide variety but without any compromise on quality. This has helped the "buffets" to get more popular among guests as they offer variety, quality, and quantity without any waiting time.
- The service styles have changed and it is not rigid as it was in the past, because today the guests are looking for experience and more personalization of service delivery models.
- Convergence of two or more service styles is well received; it makes a difference in planning of staff, thereby reducing labor costs and increasing profits.
- Cost sensitivity is cited as another key reason for the shift of service delivery models across chains. Introduction of new technology has made a direct impact on such service delivery models. Advanced equipment reduces the production time and therefore there is a direct impact on the service delivery model, as the process needs to adapt to change in pace with the production cycle that works.
- There has been a push for ancillary and secondary service to increase revenue through offerings like "packed lunch boxes," "to go beverages," and ODCs (outdoor caterings), etc.

Though the shift in terms of service delivery models has taken place, the pace of adoption or response varies from one brand to another. There are some chains which still follow the traditional service styles and have been slow to respond to the changing sociocultural trends and customer expectations.

6. **Discuss any cuisine trend that is potentially going to "impact" the hospitality businesses in the years to come?**

Key findings:

There was unanimity in terms of stating that cuisine-related innovation is sweeping the Indian hospitality sector in all segments and formats. As people are becoming more inquisitive about food and other cultures, traveling more abandoning culturally motivated limitations; they are looking for change in terms of where they dine, what they eat. This has forced hotels to adapt to the needs of a new discerning customer. New cuisine trends are finding traction and this is likely to continue over the next few years.

- The demography of the "location" also plays a very important role in cuisine trends that find play. Metropolitan cities being more diverse are more open to new cuisines and food-related trends, as compared to smaller cities with a more homogenous demographic status.
- India is becoming a popular destination for Japanese, Peruvian, Brazilian, and Vietnamese cuisine. These are in addition to other international cuisines that are already popular and established in the Indian market like the Chinese, Lebanese, Italian, and Continental spreads.
- Customers are becoming health conscious and this reflects in the menus now being designed keeping in mind the calorie count of a dish. The use of organic vegetables, fat-free options, offering diabetic meals, indicates that hotels are changing the menus keeping in mind the changing requirements of the guests.
- Following mentioned trends are expected to gain popularity:
  - People want to have healthy grains other than corn and wheat, which are very common.
  - Informal dining will gain popularity like eating at the bar, open kitchen, and simple dishes.
  - High teas will make a comeback.
  - The focus will shift from lunch and dinner to breakfast.
  - Fish and seafood will gain popularity.
  - Kids menu will have healthier options as against the fast food driven options like pizza and burgers.
  - Ipads and tablets will replace traditional menu for ordering.
  - Chefs will cut down on the production cost by creating more combo meals.
  - Local flavors will find its way into the restaurant menus.
  - Concept slow food and its sustainability impact will find interest among both customers and professionals.
  - "Flair chefs" is a new concept that will gain traction, where in the chef takes the center stage; skills display like Pizza acrobats, sashimi slicers, and noodle pullers will draw customer interest.

7.   What are the new approaches that the Indian hotels are adopting with respect to the "IRD" segment to maximize revenue growth for the F&B department?

Key findings

There is renewed focus on growing the F&B revenue from IRD as it is recognized as a value added, personalized service that a hotel can offer at a premium price. The Indian hotel industry saw this service (room service) as a competitive necessity is beginning to recognize its untapped potential for revenue growth and superior profitability.

- IRD menu, which includes that items from almost all the other F&B outlets of a hotel are getting a makeover. The specialty restaurant menus are now included in the IRD menu so that the same food can be made available to those guests who want their privacy. The other important area that the hotels have improvised is on the training aspects, especially of the order takers of IRD so that they are able to "up-sell," thus impacting the overall revenue from IRD.
- Some hotels have also considered offering specialized menus for specific market segments that they attract business from, which means that if the hotel has a group booking of a particular culture or community, they can modify menu and provide them a specialized menu as per the guest's requirement.
- Putting technology to use, hotels use Wi-Fi to cater to the needs of the customers by providing the menu of F&B outlets on mobile and tablets in the room so that they can view each product that is being offered by the hotel.

Some of the hotels have used new promotions that help IRD to boost their revenues; IHG offers "15 minute Menus" which means that the guest can get his ordered food and beverages within 15 minutes. Hyatt uses "Crave Menu" as a tool to create interest in the minds of customers. The hotels however still need to upgrade IRD by providing greater experience to the guests by improvising on technology, service, and finally the product. The pricing of IRD menus is usually 10–15% higher; this creates an opportunity for improving profit margin, and the hotels are refocusing on this segment to make the most of the opportunity.

10.4   CHALLENGES ON THE ROAD TO GROWTH IN REVENUES AND PROFITABILITY

The F&B operations at hotels are keen to expand their revenue footprint and profitability contribution. There is evidence of a renewed focus on F&B performance, given the struggle to build room revenue growth in an oversupply market. As has been stated earlier, the results are promising, but having said that, there are many challenges and issues at the macro-level which continue to affect the segment. The major concerns are as follows:

- The tax structure in India has been changing rapidly which impacts the eating out trends directly, as the potential customers have to shell out more money due to high taxation rates. The overall tax component in some cities is as high as 23%. In addition to this, many operators add a service charge of another 5–10%, and this is a huge negative for the sector. The inability of successive governments to pass the good and service tax bill is a setback toward any effort to offer a consistent tax policy across the country.
- Another impact of taxation-related anomaly has been the alcoholic and liquor procurement cost. As the taxes have been on the rise, the purchase cost itself goes up and the additional cost burden either has to be mitigated through increase in the selling price or absorbed resulting in diminished profit margins. Either way, the F&B department gets impacted, because the guests avoid drinking out due to higher prices, thereby impacting the beverage sales. Lower contribution margins result due to the additional cost of procurement being absorbed, without a parallel increase in selling prices.
- There is no proper information that is available to the management which clearly states that the rules, regulations, and laws need to be adhered, as there has been frequent changes of tax laws with the change of governments.
- Lack of updated, information being made available that clearly states the number or type of licenses one requires for operating any F&B outlet across the country is a hindrance. There are so many licenses that one has to get to start any food establishment, which it creates an entry barrier on one hand and ensures complications for those in business on the other.
- Therefore, there is no uniformity in laws and regulations across states. States are often guided by political compulsions, resulting in laws

that ban consumption of alcohol across the state. Recently, the state of Bihar was declared a "dry state," the impact of such legislations on the F&B segment is quite sweeping.

- The labeling regulations that have been changed in the recent times (FSSAI) have made it more difficult for international labels to comply with the changes. Few are even ready to pull out of the Indian market to avoid the compulsion of products being especially labeled for India. This has affected the availability of product variety that the guest demands and hence impacts the ability of F&B operations to offer products that meet customer expectations.
- The rapid technological changes have come at a steep cost; the cost of upgrading or replacing an existing technology needs high investment that impacts the financial viability of F&B-based businesses already under fiscal stress.

10.5 IMPLICATIONS AND THE WAY FORWARD

The F&B segment is one the key areas that will determine the success of a hotel in financial and guest satisfaction terms. While trends in business keep on changing, staying with, if not ahead of, time becomes very vital. The past decade has witnessed a significant change in the role of the F&B function as a driver of revenue growth and profitability. Hotels need to continuously improve their F&B operations by expanding and refreshing the menus to creating unique offerings for the customers.

As is clearly stated by the FRAI, the industry mouthpiece, the F&B sector in India, is at the cusp of a growth explosion of sorts; the current size of the Indian food service industry is slated to be Rs. 247,680 crores and is projected to grow to Rs. 408,040 crores by 2018 at 11%.

In terms of market segments, quick service restaurants and casual dine-in formats account for 74% of the total chain market, while cafés make up for 12% with fine dining and pubs, bars, clubs, and lounges comprising the rest. The chain and licensed segment of the stand-alone restaurant space is expected to contribute an estimated Rs. 24,600–25,000 crores by 2018.

Share of delivery and take-away formats, with a focus on convenience, is expected to grow. As discussed earlier and validated by industry experts, experimentation with new formats, themes, and menus is likely to drive the growth story broadly. International interest through entrepreneurial ventures driven by FDI (foreign direct investment) will further intensify the competition. This may not be a one sided activity as many established Indian F&B brands are planning to expand internationally. Increasing interest from private equity and venture capital investors in the industry will continue to expand the supply side of the business.

Tech-savvy consumers will redefine approaches to market the F&B product, increasing the importance of online social media, food websites and mobile applications.

The Indian hotel industry recognizes the potential of the F&B segment. However, it is also clear that to make the most of the opportunity, the industry will have to compete with the "broader F&B sector" that includes organized and unorganized components. Equally relevant will be the capacity of hotel businesses to respond to economic and market factors, such as high food cost inflation, a fragmented market, and increasing competition. Operational challenges including real estate cost, manpower, fragmented supply chain, and liquor sourcing are another set of challenges for all players. Regulatory concerns such as existing high taxes, burden of new taxes, and over-licensing that have been discussed earlier in the chapter are significant road blocks in the journey.

How hotel management teams respond to the challenges and issues will determine their ability to build a sustainable competitive advantage. The way they position their F&B offerings, deploying the same as a differentiator to only selling rooms, growing revenues on both sides of the aisle and eventually offering impressive returns to investors through superior profitability is the need of the hour.

KEYWORDS

- **F&B**
- **revenue growth**
- **Indian hotels**
- **catering**
- **banquet sales**
- **F&B revenue**

REFERENCES

Bhattacharya, S. *Chefs, F&B Managers Rejoice! Revenue Share of F&B Rises Steadily as Room Revenues Show A Slide: Survey | Indian Restaurant Spy*, 2014 [Online]. Indianrestaurantspy.com. Available at: http://indianrestaurantspy.com/blogpost/chefs-fb-managers-rejoice-revenue-share-fb-rises-steadily-room-revenues-show-slide-survey (accessed 10 May 2016).

Corporate. *Financial Reports*, 2014 [Online]. Available at https://www.tajhotels.com/en-in/about-taj-group/investors/financial-reports/ (accessed 12 May 2016).

FHRAI Indian Hotel Industry Survey 2012–13. *FHRAI Indian Hotel Industry Survey 2012–13*. FHRAI: New Delhi, 2013.

Hospitalitybizindia.com. *Hospitality Biz India: Food for Thought!*, 2013 [Online]. Available at: http://www.hospitalitybizindia.com/detailNews.aspx?aid=16467&sid=5 (accessed 12 May 2016).

Hospitalitytimes.com. *Food and Beverage Revenues in Hotels Growing across Chains in India*, 2015 [Online]. Available at: http://www.ehospitalitytimes.com/?p=81808 (accessed 10 May 2016).

Hotelierindia.com. *Dishing It Out*, 2014 [Online]. Available at: http://www.hotelierindia.com/article-19717-dishing_it_out/ [accessed 10 May 2016].

Hotelnewsnow.com. *HNN*, 2015 [Online]. Available at: http://www.hotelnewsnow.com/Articles/24931/In-India-FandB-revenues-critical-to-hotels (accessed 12 May 2016).

Khosla, V. *F&B Revenues May Soon Beat Room Revenues at Hotels—The Economic Times*, 2014 [Online]. The Economic Times. Available at http://economictimes.indiatimes.com/industry/services/hotels-/-restaurants/fb-revenues-may-soon-beat-room-revenues-at-hotels/articleshow/28768193.cms?intenttarget=no (accessed 12 May 2016).

Khosla, V.; Sathyanarayanan, D. *Demand for Young Chefs on Rise as Hotels Bank on Rising F&B Revenues*, 2014 [Online]. The Economic Times. Available at http://economictimes.indiatimes.com/industry/services/hotels-/-restaurants/demand-for-young-chefs-on-rise-as-hotels-bank-on-rising-fb-revenues/articleshow/29832728.cms (accessed 12 May 2016).

Munjal, S.; Sharma, S.; Menon, P. Moving Towards 'Slow Food', the New Frontier of Culinary Innovation in India: The Vedatya Experience. *Worldw. Hosp. Tour. Themes, Int. J.—Emerald Insight* **2016,** *9*(4), 444–460.

Munjal, S.; Sharma, S. Application of Innovative Food Cost Management Practices in Inflationary Times: Indian Budget Hospitality Segment Experiences. *Worldw. Hosp. Tour. Themes, Int. J.—Emerald Insight* **2012,** *4*(3), pp. 463–477.

NRAI. *Food Service Report*, 2013 [Online]. Available at: https://http://nrai.org/downloads/rep orts/ (accessed 15 May 2016).

CHAPTER 11

CULINARY INNOVATION IN INDIAN HOTELS AND BUILDING COST EFFICIENCIES THAT SPUR PROFITABILITY GROWTH

SANJAY SHARMA*

School of Hospitality and Tourism Management (SHTM), Vedatya Institute, Gurgaon, India

*E-mail: sanjay.sharma@vedatya.ac.in

CONTENTS

Abstract 252

11.1   Introduction 252

11.2   Methodology and Purpose 254

11.3   Creativity, Innovation, and Profitability 254

11.4   Indian Hotels, Restaurants, and Culinary Innovation 259

11.5   Findings and Discussion 261

11.6   Implications...269

11.7   Recommendations...270

11.8   Limitations and Future Research 272

11.9   Conclusion 272

Keywords 273

References..273

ABSTRACT

In a country with the second largest growing economy and more than a billion people, hospitality-related business opportunities are immense. The Indian food service industry is projected to grow at a rate of 11%, where quick service restaurants and casual dining accounts for 74% of the overall market size, while cafés are at 12%, rest of the pie is attributed to the fine-dining restaurant segment. The growing population, increased disposable income, and changes in the sociocultural attitudes toward dining out have resulting in an increase of demand for the Indian restaurant sector. However, it is also true that at the same time, a significant number of restaurants have been running out of business or are finding it difficult to survive or achieve even an operating break even. In such a scenario, despite the opportunity, what is more important is to recognize the issues and challenges, find innovative solutions that lead to efficiencies and eventually profitable businesses. It is in this context that culinary innovation could play a pivotal role in food and beverage operations achieving success. This research is an attempt to understand the efforts, issues, and challenges faced by the food and beverage businesses in terms of innovative practices and approaches from a culinary dimension, and to share the same for potential emulation by the hotel industry at large.

11.1   INTRODUCTION

The significance of innovation as a catalyst for increased profitability and sustained success has been well documented in hospitality research. Numerous researches have recognized the success factors associated with product and service innovation. Majority of the work has been carried out considering four types of innovation, that is, product innovations, process innovations, enhanced knowledge of the market, and management innovations, and most of them deal with enhanced knowledge of the market and communication improvement (Vila et al., 2012). Few of these studies, however, have dealt with culinary innovations.

Hotels innovate with respect to products and services in alignment with their goals and objectives and have specific approaches to measure performance. The hospitality product is considered to be complex, from its production to marketing and distribution; it involves many activities which are diagonally, vertically, and horizontally integrated in varying degrees. Both orthodox and nonorthodox economists agree that innovations will only be undertaken when there is sufficiently high innovation dividend paid for the added cost and risk of innovation. Thus, profitability appears to be the strongest explanatory variable both behind investment and innovation (Weiermair, 2008). Innovation in the hospitality sector, especially technology-based innovation is considered to be singular and often hard to imitate (Vila et al., 2012).

Indian food service industry is projected to grow at a rate of 11%; the current size of the industry is Rs. 247,680 crores and is expected to reach Rs. 408,040 crores by 2018. Quick service restaurants and casual dining accounts for 74% of the market share, while cafés are at 12% and rest of the pie is been shared by fine-dining restaurants. The unorganized sector is not yet tapped; however, it provides an opportunity to collect additional tax by close monitoring (NRAI, 2013). There are several key drivers for such trends; convenience food, take away formats, experiments with menus, innovative themes and décor, increasing use of online, and social media occupying the social center stage. On the other hand, there are factors like high food inflation, fragmented market, increasing competition, shortage of skilled manpower, soaring, real estate cost (lease/rentals), existing high tax policy, with a burden of new taxes on the anvil. These are some of the issues and challenges that are being faced by the industry. In such a scenario while there is an opportunity for tremendous growth, there are also serious issues and challenges that make the task of realizing the stated growth potential difficult. Innovative practices and approaches toward improving efficiencies resulting in lower costs and growth in profitability could prove to be a key critical success factor for the sector.

The chapter draws from research that documents efforts by various F&B outlets (as a part of a hotel's F&B offering) as they practice innovation. It analyses the relationship between culinary innovations based on services, products and technology and evaluates their performance impact at the outlet level. Data received through empirical investigation from Indian restaurants show that constant product innovation and use of latest technology are important drivers of performance. It was found that product innovation and induction of technology are positively associated with employee turnover, their motivation and growth. It addressed the relationship between culinary innovation in restaurants and their profitability. The study suggests that culinary innovation and its benefits visible to customers serve as endogenous variables. These may result in a unique selling proposition that can drive sales growth and render potentially sustainable competitive advantage. Culinary innovation in some forms can impact sales promotions and thus also positively impact capacity utilization for the outlet. It was apparent that culinary innovation when successful resulted in higher profitability; it also has a positive impact on customer retention and brings forth multiple tangible and non-tangible benefits. In addition to natural benefits of increased profits and reduced costs, other dimensions such as economies of scale, restaurant size, authenticity, knowledge of technology innovation, human capital, and latest culinary trends are equally taken into consideration while applying the research.

11.2 METHODOLOGY AND PURPOSE

A qualitative approach has been adopted for this research. Existing literature on creativity and its impact on profitability from the international and Indian context is reviewed and analyzed. The secondary research has helped to offer a perspective on innovation; in terms of product, process, and technology that is been experienced in the Indian restaurant sector and its relevance for future culinary innovation. Unstructured in-depth interviews and field notes capturing the subjective experiences of the researcher were employed, to explain the experiences of senior experienced chefs and F&B managers from all over the country. The unstructured style of interview was possible due to the researcher's previous industry experience. It builds trust and facilitates in-depth conversation between the hoteliers. During the interviews, a lot of metaphors and industry jargons was used to define the product and services.

The context of Indian hotels and restaurants was chosen for three reasons. First, with respect to specialty restaurants, the expert judgment and opinions on creative and innovative performance are formally documented and is publicly available through online and other published sources. Second, Indian restaurants have attracted little systematic research on its innovativeness and profitability (Lane, 2010), and third, the author has professional experience as a chef in various specialty restaurants in India, which would contribute to an understanding of the nature of innovation and creativity in the Indian restaurant sector. The purpose of this paper is to understand the culinary innovations experienced in Indian hotels and restaurant sector, which helps reduce cost and increase profitability.

11.3 CREATIVITY, INNOVATION, AND PROFITABILITY

Innovation is generation of ideas which are novel, yet useful and practical (Amabile et al., 1996). The idea of creativity and innovation has generated continued interest amongst the professionals and the academic fraternity. Existing research has clearly recognized innovation and creativity as two diverse stages of the innovation process; the first stage is creativity where the generation of new idea takes place and is often termed as "brainstorming." The evaluation and practical implementation of a creative thought is the second stage of the process. However, both the stages are rarely analyzed together (Lane & Lup, 2015).

In recent years, there has been a growing interest in the importance of technological development and innovation (Pechlaner & Osti, 2001). Very few studies have analyzed the culinary innovation activities in the hospitality sector in general, and in the Indian restaurant sector in particular. Glaeser et al. (1992) bring up the importance of technology dispersion in the growth of regions and the fundamental role that externalities play in the dispersion of innovation. The concept can also be functional in the hotel sector in general, as there are proven records to demonstrate links between technology innovation and growth of hotels (Connor & Frew, 2001). Managing innovation requires an overall perspective of the factors that may potentially influence the various stages of innovation; a deep understanding would help the management in devising strategy that supports innovation. The management will need to understand the contradictions involved between the generation of idea and its implementation. The challenge becomes even more complex with small organizations, where idea generation and implementation is achieved by the employees themselves (Damanpour, 1992). Therefore, the concept is even more significant to smaller firms, where less number of employees may imply a lower level of exposure to knowledge diversity. It is also evidenced that when employees from diverse backgrounds pool ideas there is an enhanced level of trust, and it makes employees more comfortable to discuss new thoughts without the fear of being rejected (Reagans & Zuckerman, 2001).

The leadership of organizations plays a pivotal role in affecting the innovation process, majorly through their attitude and influence at the workplace (Shalley & Gilson, 2004). During the idea generation phase, the leaders play a crucial role in idea generation and development. If the employees are given autonomy to discuss and experiment with alternate ideas, the impact is positive and more fruitful (Oldham & Cummings, 1996). However, autocratic leadership negatively influences idea generation and its implementation. It is also observed that, as compared to a lean hierarchy, an extended hierarchal organization structure may discourage employees to be creative at work. The bigger the hierarchy, the less motivated employees feel to share, explore, and experiment with new ideas (Shalley & Gilson, 2004).

There are contrasting views on culinary innovation and its impact on reducing cost and increased profitability. However, majority of the studies report that the innovation process has a largely positive impact in terms of profitability growth and improvement in cost efficiencies. Innovation results in greater productivity, often resulting in reducing cost, which leads to financial stability in the organization, irrespective of geographic area where the organization is located (Munjal & Sharma, 2012). Innovation process frameworks are treated as a roadmap from the development of food item to its menu introduction and beyond. Although using such frameworks does not always guarantee financial success, it does increase the chance of being successful (Cooper, 2001). Service industry innovation includes two main concepts, new product development (NPD) and new service development (NSP). The NPD caters to creation of tangible goods, whereas, NPS focuses on development of innovative service related aspects (Johne & Storey, 1998). An exciting component of the restaurant business is its product; it constantly needs innovation which requires to be successfully driven by its leaders (Harrington, 2004). In general, the creativity and innovation process in the restaurant segment in India has received little consideration. Recent studies of the culinary innovation process have used a single case study approach (Svejenova et al., 2007) or archival data to infer organizational performance (Ottenbacher & Harrington, 2007).

Numerous models exist for the development of the innovation process; most of them involve from generation of idea to its implementation and post analysis. One such predominantly used six steps model proposed by Cooper (2001) and Urban and Hauser (1993) consists of

1. idea generation,
2. screening,
3. business analysis,
4. concept development,
5. final testing, and
6. commercialization.

Another similar model by Feltenstein (1986) provided a different perspective to the innovation process from a culinary context. His framework focuses on the development of new menu items to increase market share and hence profitability. The six key steps proposed by him include

1. assemble a new product task force,
2. set new product priorities,

3. generate new product ideas,
4. screen and select ideas,
5. develop products, and
6. Plan marketing and rollout campaigns.

Improvising on the model proposed by Feltenstein (1986); Cooper (2001) tried to mitigate the risks involved in NPD. He proposed a more structured and carefully developed process, to increase the chances of being successful. Adding further to existing models, Harrington (2004) proposed a product innovation model which looks to be derived from the earlier two food-related innovation' models. This four-stage model looks more balanced as it integrates both internal and external factors.

The four phases are

1. culinary innovation formulation,
2. culinary innovation implementation,
3. evaluation and control, and
4. Innovation introduction.

Consequently, he suggests the need for a more refined model that integrates culinary knowledge, food science, implementation, and marketing strategies together. Similarly, based on the experiences of one, two and three star Michelin chefs, Ottenbacher and Harrington (2007), commented on the food innovation and development process. They recommended that restaurant innovation processes has both similarities and differences to traditional food product development. Michelin chefs are less prone to use various traditional steps, which are considered as conventional wisdom in their new menu development. Further, they pay more emphasis on service staff in the restaurant due to the simultaneous nature of food production and its consumption and also on the importance of the human factor in service delivery. Moreover, leadership guidance, support, and commitment are also seen as crucial aspects in the success of any innovative product. This however is now how a typical restaurant would approach its daily business operation. To avoid a high-risk situation that creative freedom and experimentation brings forth, focus usually shifts toward a need to control the operational process, thereby minimizing risk and generating workable returns.

Considering the above models and the Michelin starred chef's description, the culinary innovation process is formulated in seven core steps (Ottenbacher & Harrington, 2007) (Fig. 11.1):

1. idea generation,
2. screening,
3. trial and error,
4. concept development,
5. final testing,
6. training, and
7. commercialization.

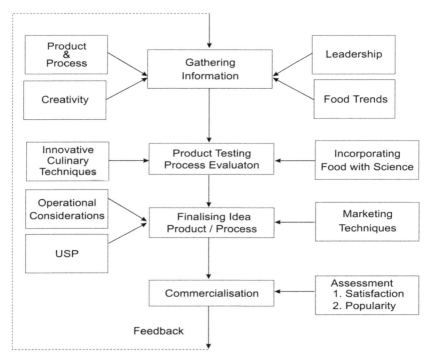

FIGURE 11.1   Culinary innovation process (adapted from Ottenbacher & Harrington, 2007).

Usually, Michelin chef-led innovation process is more natural, less formal and less dependent on financial and market analysis. Largely, their success is achieved through culinary skills of the chefs and their reputation build over time. This, however, restricts competitors wanting to enter the culinary space of fine-dining restaurants of repute. Apart from culinary innovation, technological advancement too plays a crucial role in reducing cost and increasing profitability. For instance, induction cooking is often considered as one of the most efficient cooking technologies, with this technology, up to 90% of the energy consumed is transferred to the food, compared to about 74% from traditional electric systems and 40% from gas. This technology has become popular in Europe, but other continents seem less enthusiastic in adopting such cooking methods. While there is an interest in the technology, but several barriers exist for adopting the technology. Some of the barriers include high initial cost, requirement of compatible cookware, and low perceived reliability of the equipment (Sweeney et al., 2014).

11.4   INDIAN HOTELS, RESTAURANTS, AND CULINARY INNOVATION

Indian cuisine roots back to some five thousand years and together, with some other Asian cuisines, it forms the foundation and inspiration for many traditional food cultures. Many connoisseurs believe that something so classical and influential like Indian cuisine should not be diluted or fused with any other cuisine; Indian cuisine should take pride in its tradition and authenticity, however, to retain customers and increase profitability, food innovation has always been an integral part of hotels and restaurants (Tyler, 2014).

Culinary innovation has always been at the heart of the Taj Hotels (IHCL) dining experience. In many instances, it has been a Taj Hotel that has introduced the city to exotic cuisines such as Thai or Schezuan. Even the regional cuisines of India have surpassed their traditional borders. Favorite dishes from all over the subcontinent are reinvented at Masala Kraft, Masala Klub, and Masala Art, with an emphasis on flavor and freshness, using lighter, healthier cooking techniques. At Varq, Chef Hemant Oberoi introduces new techniques, organic produce and spices to reinvent Indian food with unusual creations and pairings. Creating drama on a plate is achieved through the perfect combination of flavors, colors, tastes, aromas and textures. Excellent ingredients are the starting point.

There is a growing demand worldwide for everything that is "organic" and culinary domain is no exception. Organic food products, and food served in restaurants that is produced from organic ingredients, are being sold at a premium. Consumers are willing to pay four times the price of nonorganic substitutes, and the demand is out pacing supply (Munjal et al., 2016). As a complementary practice, the Taj chefs like to work with local farmers to obtain the local organic products they need. One of the Taj Hotels even has its own nursery to produce the fresh essentials that make all the difference to each dish they serve. At *Varq*, an Indian specialty restaurant of the Taj Mahal, Delhi, Chef Hemant Oberoi, with his new techniques, innovative presentations and usage of organic produce and spices, has given Indian food a different dimension. He has reinvented Indian food with unusual creations and pairings. The menu is a rich accumulation of Indian recipes evolved to the next level. Varq retains the Indian traditional way of cooking while, using exotic ingredients like sea bass, sand crab, black cod, morels, and Iranian berries (Taj Hotel, 2015). On the other hand, Chef Manjit Singh Gill, Corporate Chef, ITC hotels, has documented traditional Indian cuisine to preserve its authenticity and rich traditions. "It is not that I am against innovation" says chef Gill. "But young chefs need to understand a cuisine before they start adapting it. They need to know the roots of the cuisine and in India which, many of them do not."

Chef Jerson Fernandes, Corporate Chef, Keys Hotel believes that experimentation and innovation are the key elements to culinary evolution. The roots of a particular cuisine should not be forgotten. However, Chef Fernandes is a big fan of fusion cooking and techniques. Chefs all across the world are being innovative with food and use various quirky items to serve food to attract guests. People have increasingly become more open toward these experiments. At Keys Hotels innovative food is the crux of the F&B services (hospitality biz India). One of the common things amongst all the Indian chefs to innovate is to adopt fusion cuisine. However, Chef Manish Mehrotra of Indian Accent in Delhi, feels "If we really stick to tradition, then we should not use potatoes, or tomatoes, or chili," items brought to India with the Portuguese in the 16th century and now essential parts of the Indian pantry. Chef Mehrotra's innovative, ambitious cuisine has an identity of its own. He showcased his creativity by the unique amalgamation of the freshest local produce, combining home style nostalgic tastes with unusual ingredients from across the world, introducing dishes like the tuna bhel ceviche, strawberry green chilli chutney, meetha achaar chilean spare ribs, sun dried mango, toasted kalonji seeds and warm doda burfi treacle tart, homemade vanilla bean ice cream to name a few (Indian accent). Such food innovations have not only helped in reducing food cost through ingredient localization but have also given healthier and fresher menu options to the customers. The fusion of skills, concepts, cooking methods with the use of local ingredients, gives an opportunity to customers to experience international cooking styles and trends while retaining basic authenticity.

Indian food industry has observed several new food trends in past couple of years; year 2013 was the year of *Molecular Gastronomy* for Indian hotels and 2014 was viewed as *year of innovation* (Nusra, 2015). According to Restaurant India Research, year 2015 was all about food-tech innovations focused on healthy food, prompt delivery, and structured supply chain. There were different opinions on the trends that dominated the Indian restaurant sector in the past few years. However, Restaurant India researched the culinary fraternity to list top trends that ruled the Indian palate in last 2 years:

1. startups (Chef's initiative),
2. packaged food trend,
3. Indian cuisine with a modern twist,
4. healthy meals,
5. locally sourced fresh ingredients,
6. online food ordering,
7. meals on wheel, and
8. sharing meal experiences on social media.

Another visible trend is to increase profitability through efforts to achieve economies of scale. The Indian Restaurants Association of Singapore launched central processing units (CPU) to collectively procure, prepare, and produce vegetarian and nonvegetarian food. Whether it is centralized production, implementing new dining formats, ready to eat meals, vending machines or grab and go. The businesses are working to improve efficiency to reduce costs, grow profitability, and achieve business objectives (Lim, 2015). A government official from Singapore said; key *initiatives such as the CPUs are helping businesses reap productivity gains, improve job quality, and provide better service for customers.* The chefs however must retain focus not only on not just process efficiencies, but also on improving their product. This will ensure product differentiation that will help achieve competitive advantage, as customers will be able to enjoy high quality services as well as products.

11.5   FINDINGS AND DISCUSSION

11.5.1   CITY VS. RESORT HOTELS

The operations manager at The Park, Delhi, compares the food and beverages revenue trends of city hotels to resort properties. According to him the "city hotels" predominantly target corporate clients, whereas "resorts" focus on the leisure segment. The food and beverages revenue in a city hotel is usually 20–25% of the total revenues. This is probably because the corporate clients are usually out during lunch and they may even prefer to go out for dinner; whereas in a resort, the major source of revenue is the food and accompanying entertainment. This pattern significantly reduces the food revenue growth opportunity for city hotels, thereby making a significant difference in the overall profitability of food and beverage outlets. Tremendous growth in the number of stand-alone restaurants in the cities pan India has further enlarged this impact.

11.5.2 INVENTORY RULES

The food and beverage manager at The Taj, Delhi, feels, inventory management is a key to profitability, it may not have any direct impact on the customers, but it certainly adds to the bottom line, and is eventually reflected in the financial statements. A lot of money can be saved just by not maintaining a large inventory; the idea is to not order the inventory items (SKUs) in excess quantities and to maintain an optimum number (usually guided by weeks on hand based par values) that works from an operational as well as asset utilization perspective. Hotels that get good (volume based) business from banqueting recognize that managing food costs is critical, hence the focus on inventory management. A stand-alone restaurant or a small food outlet may still manage to store some extra inventory, but a large hotel or a chain of restaurants, where daily ordering reflects a significantly big number financially, needs to manage inventory optimally. The approach ensures minimal losses due to wastage, pilferage, theft, or even deterioration and expiry of stored materials.

11.5.3 FRESH IS FRESH

In one of the biggest formal gatherings of executive chefs in India, 30 head chefs of J. W. Marriott hotels gathered together recently to discuss culinary trends and its impact on profitability. They emphasized on the need for a customer centric orientation, wherein following customer's demands and feedback were seen as instrumental for business success. In keeping with the above guidance, the Marriott F&B leaders are focusing on fresh, healthy, and organic menu items, along with healthy "kids meal" options. The chefs also agreed that when it comes to food, the customers are looking for an overall experience; which includes taste, color, texture, and aroma. The importance of ensuring that the food looked more appealing to the eye along with its taste was also restated, mentioning that such a holistic culinary approach would help to get repeat business resulting in improved profitability.

11.5.4 INDIVIDUALITY OF RESTAURANTS IN HOTELS

A senior manager at the Regency was categorical that the best approach for restaurants in hotels is to maintain their individuality. He also suggested a push toward the local supply chain and a customer centric approach. He emphasized that given the increasing competition from local and stand-alone specialty restaurants, "the need of the hour is to take the hotel out of our restaurants and bars and compete locally;" which means consider restaurant and bars as separate "profit centers" allowed to devise strategies and compete.

11.5.5 GOING DIGITAL

In the era of technological advancement, where everyone is encouraged to go green, the use of printed material is being avoided to save costs as well as to demonstrate an environmental focus. Online tools, digital media, social networking sites are being used as tools for promotion, even the menu cards at the restaurants are being replaced by digital menus. At the "Barbeque Nation" (a chain of restaurants), the company has moved away from the traditional printed guest feedback forms and replaced them with digital notepads. Order taking, order placing, in-house promotion is all being done digitally. Some of their outlets even use digital menus. A senior manager however mentioned that largely guests still look for printed menu cards and they have thus retained them. The use of digital platform was seen as trendy, cost saving, and an efficient marketing tool.

11.5.6 REVENUE MANAGEMENT PRACTICE

The restaurant manager at The Taj, Delhi, expressed his concern with respect to poor understanding and focus on restaurant revenue management. "We do manage cost across all distribution channels; we talk revenue management across departments, but what about revenue management in restaurants? Just as we manage room rates, room inventory, similarly, can't the diners be charged little extra for peak hour booking or signature items could be priced more during those specific hours?" An up market Bar and Restaurant – Manhattan Brewery, recently launched a "bar exchange" concept, the customers can see changes in prices of beverages by the minute, almost like stocks on an exchange. Based out of Gurgaon (NCR), this restaurant is setting the tone for RM practice in the food and beverage domain.

11.5.7 EDIBLE ROOFTOPS ARE IN

The concept of growing fresh organic vegetables on the roof started in Delhi NCR. The idea was to grow and eat healthy and is been well received by the people around the city. On similar lines, a lot of stand-alone restaurants have started to grow exotic herbs and vegetables organically (Olive Delhi). This not only helps to get repeat business but also reduces cost and improves profitability. There is evidence that an effort toward backward integration of the supply chain is being attempted by many hotel and restaurant chains.

11.5.8 SUPPLIER'S CONTRACTS

At the Radisson Delhi, the Chef stated "We have moved away from multiple year contracts for almost all commodities now. It has been observed and realized that multiple year contracts helps the vendor eventually." For hotels and restaurant operators alike, annual contracts are being found to work best. It keeps the vendors on their toes, ensuring they deliver food items as per the standard specifications. The approach of not holding contracts for more than a year, enforcing annual bidding for the supplies, is being accepted as a practice that is delivering cost benefits, especially given that food-related inflation is still worrisome.

11.5.9 SLOW FOOD AND SUSTAINABILITY FIND FOCUS

Slow food and sustainability are themes that will continue to dominate the food and beverages segment of the hotel and restaurant sector in the coming years; concepts around local, healthy, 50 miles, traditional, slow food, will continue to feature on menu items across the sector. Throughout the country, healthy and local seem to go together; hoteliers, restaurateurs are increasingly tying-up with local producers and farmers. This backward integration offers a win-win situation for both the parties involved. One such unique tie-up is between Vedatya Institute, Gurgaon, and Radisson Blu Plaza, Delhi. The institute produces fresh herbs and vegetables, which, are consumed by the institute and are also supplied to the hotel. The vegetables are organic and have superior taste and freshness. The concept of the farmers market is also catching up in Delhi. These markets witness hoteliers, restaurateurs, and chefs picking up fresh produce for the day or for the week. Such initiatives provide healthy, fresh options to the customers, help businesses in reducing inventory cost and food cost, and also increase profitability.

11.5.10 FOOD IS NOT TRASH

According to many chefs in the industry, food wastage is an issue that needs attention, "We cannot do much for the food left on the customer's plate, except for processing it further, however, the leftover of the staff meals or the cafeteria can be handled better." Efforts in this direction do have significant impact on the food cost and eventually impacts the overall profitability. "We keep an eye on what gets wasted; we weigh it daily and share it with the staff members. This has helped to control food wastage, reduce cost hence, increase profitability" (Chefs at Oberoi, Mariott).

11.5.11 APTLY APP

The coming year seems to be another big year for the Indian restaurant business. With the customers moving toward phone app-based purchase behavior, the restaurant sector has also integrated applications into their services. Food Panda, Yumist, Doordash, Dominos, and Zomato have revolutionized the service model. The 5-star hotels have not yet adopted similar model, but with increasing pressure, one needs to think of ways to adopt similar technology and keep pace with the competition.

11.5.12 FOOD INFLATION

In 2015, the prices of poultry and meat items increased drastically. Such increase put pressure on the operator to either increase the cost or look for ways to maintain overall food cost. The food inflation compelled chefs to use more of vegetables dishes across menus, some of the chefs even used underutilized fish to cope with seafood supply and maintain overall food costs (Barbeque Nation).

There are numerous factors responsible for reducing cost and increasing profitability. However, the Indian hotel and restaurant sector is actively engaged in culinary innovation and creativity, both in terms of product and process innovations. Some of the direct effects of innovation involve customer satisfaction and repeat business. However, internal factors like employee development, reducing turnover ratio, and motivation of the employees are positive impacts of culinary innovation. Hu (2010) derived an innovative culinary competency model, which covers several dimensions of culinary innovation that significantly reduces costs and improves profitability (Fig. 11.2).

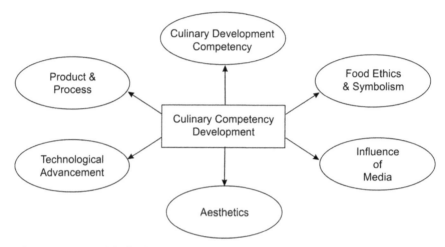

FIGURE 11.2   Model of culinary competency development (adapted from Hu, 2010).

Each of the aspects covered by Hu (2010) has further sub-dimensions, which are summarized in the following table. Having in-depth knowledge and understanding of these dimensions would help hoteliers to improve the restaurant's performance in general and would promote development of creative culture within the restaurants in particular.

Dimension	Items
1. Culture (9 items)	• Knowledge of ingredients' characteristics
	• Knowledge of cooking culture
	• Knowledge of cultural history of the place of origin
	• Knowledge of dietary habits
	• Skilled at fusion cooking
	• Skilled at a variety of culinary techniques
	• Positive attitude toward understanding overseas diets
	• Positive attitude toward internationalization
	• Positive attitude toward innovation diffusion

(Continued)

Dimension	Items
2. Esthetic (9 items)	• Knowledge of basic esthetic concepts and literacy
	• Knowledge of current trends of food design
	• Ability to admire art and beauty
	• Ability to make a harmonious product
	• Skilled al the sensibility of fashion
	• Skilled at the sensibility of color experience
	• Skilled at deploying size, amount and location of products
	• Positive attitude toward preserving beauty
	• Positive attitude toward presenting esthetic value
3. Technology (9 items)	• Knowledge of principles of food science
	• Knowledge of cooking chemistry
	• Knowledge of molecular cuisine
	• Ability to use technology to keep food fresh
	• Ability to use technology to enhance cooking speed
	• Ability to use technology to enhance service speed
	• Ability to use technology to enhance food quality
	• Positive attitude toward using new cooking equipment
	• Positive attitude toward using new technology to communicate with customers
4. Product (11 items)	• Knowledge of presenting products with an original flavor
	• Knowledge of presenting healthy products
	• Knowledge of products with a harmonious flavor
	• Ability to create commercial products
	• Ability to make products with "wow" feeling
	• Ability to make products with vitality
	• Ability to make products safe and hygienic
	• Positive attitude toward using new ingredients and recipes
	• Positive attitude toward new value of products
	• Positive attitude toward using unique ingredients
	• Positive attitude toward new product development

(Continued)

Dimension	Items
5. Service (8 items)	• Knowledge of matching food and beverage
	• Knowledge of designing a unique dining experience
	• Ability to cooperate with servers
	• Ability to communicate with customers
	• Ability to develop a new culinary service
	• Skills at handling guest complaints and service recovery
	• Positive attitude toward control service
	• Positive attitude toward adding new value during service delivery
6. Management (13 items)	• Knowledge of innovation process management
	• Knowledge of cost during innovation management
	• Knowledge of current and future food trends
	• Ability to present marketing skills during innovation management
	• Ability to collect and manage information
	• Ability to control culinary innovation process
	• Ability to open up a new market
	• Ability to handle team management
	• Ability to present leadership management
	• Ability to handle interpersonal management
	• Positive attitude toward change
	• Positive attitude toward crisis
	• Positive attitude toward self-learning
7. Creativity (10 items)	• Knowledge of basic culinary science
	• Knowledge of making decisions
	• Ability to use divergent thinking
	• Ability to find creative idea
	• Skilled at basic culinary techniques
	• Skilled at problem solving
	• Positive attitude toward creating new ideas
	• Positive attitude toward accept others' opinions
	• Positive attitude toward using new ways to resolve questions
	• Positive attitude toward being optimistic

11.6 IMPLICATIONS

One of the key processes driven aspect of restaurant operation is purchasing and receiving. The basic process of ordering, receiving, storing, processing, and serving food is relatively complex; the fundamentals of the ordering cycle have evolved from a simple comparative market pricing to management of an extended supply chain. The hotels are now working with primary producers to reduce cost and improve quality and profitability. This development is been greatly helped by the use of technology and the internet. However, at the same time, we also evidence a horizontal integration of hotels with the suppliers that supply the complete range of food and other hospitality products on a contractual basis. Such integration brings the benefit of economies of scale and helps alleviate the pressures of inflation.

Despite technological advancements, standard purchase specifications have to be formulated and checked manually, still depending on human expertise and decision making. Computerized inventory management with strong integration of accounting and forecasting systems has made stock management easier. However, the need of physical stock taking still exists. Similarly, the use of standard recipes and menu costing has, with computerization, become a budgetary control process. Again, performance against budget is determined by the willingness of cooks to actually use standard recipes. The primary issue of cost reduction and improved profitability constantly needs management supervision, irrespective of the use of advanced technologies.

Not just the inventory management systems and purchasing systems have changed but the technology has also changed the way we cook in commercial kitchens, use of microwave ovens, induction cookers, cook chill methods, and many other labor-saving technologies have been inducted to reduce costs and increase productivity. Another concept which is gaining popularity amongst hotels and restaurants is the concept of outsourcing. The culinary professionals are outsourcing prepared food from outside instead of cooking them in-house. The consequences of ready to eat food are that on one side, it saves labor cost but on the other, it reduces staff skills and training opportunities. Some of the hotels are partly outsourcing food items especially bakery products and sauces. The chef manager needs to decide whether to surrender creativity, freshness, and skills over readymade products, which offer a workable product, and also reduce cost. The industry versus the individual establishment is a crucial dimension as related to the issue of culinary skill development versus de-skilling through outsourcing (Riley, 1981).

Radical changes in the eating habits are market driven, hoteliers seems to be chasing the market trends. With the increase of disposal income and other sociocultural changes, more people are eating out than ever before and they demand variety, quality, and more. In the quest to cater to the need of customers, chefs and restaurant managers seem to be in dilemma of whether to meet the demand of the customers by partly outsourcing or to offer variety in menu keeping freshness and creativity alive. The dilemma remains; is the variety enough? Is it attractive to customers? The wide range of dishes may attract customers but what if they choose narrowly. Avoiding wastage becomes a challenge for operators as they try and balance multiple expectations. The solution lies in deploying technology in food production, storage, and regeneration. The alternative to offering variety in menu is to offer variety in controlled quantities. It would be cost-effective and would also segment the market appropriately.

Unlike, in some of the industries where product innovation is considered to be a team effort, in the restaurant sector, it is expected from the Executive Chef or Chef De Cuisine. The innovative "signature dish" is also expected to be the main draw, with a philosophy behind each signature dish. Therefore, it can only be developed by the head chef with slight assistance of some additional chefs. Sometimes the head chef goes solo, not involving staff in research and development, the expectation from junior staff is to replicate the "innovative menu items" as directed. However, brainstorming always helps in creativity and it also develops an environment conducive for innovation. While interacting with the executive chefs, some chefs welcomed the idea of taking inputs from the staff regarding techniques and processes but not on the "menu selections." For menu enhancements, the head chefs prefer to conceptualize and take a lead. It is challenging for the head chefs to constantly plan and innovate as they are usually under a lot of work pressure. They work for long hours and on odd timings, their work environment is full of noise, heat and pressure for consistency and quality. Apart from being creative, chefs are also responsible for managing kitchen staff and day-to-day operation; together all these factors add to the pressure on head chefs and sous chefs which negatively impacts creativity and innovation.

11.7 RECOMMENDATIONS

The restaurant sector would continue to grow in size. With investor funding, existing restaurant chains will grow, new brands will come to market.

Profitability will remain a challenge and customer satisfaction a priority. F&B outlets in hotels will have to ideate to remain relevant in a market where options galore for the discerning customers.

Culinary innovation is more of an imperative for the Indian hospitality sector. Based on the discussion and review, there are certain key recommendations which if, implemented would help reduce cost, increase profitability, and yet maintain quality with consistency.

- Culinary creativity in a restaurant setting can relate to cooking methods, tastes and new flavor combinations, smell, visual esthetics and composition, textures, presentation methods, and even sound.
- Focus on new approaches toward supply chain management that allow initiatives that bring sustainable practices, eliminate middlemen, and reduce costs.
- Slow food has a future, industry will do well to embrace the "Indian culinary heritage" and give authentic, traditional Indian food more space on the menus.
- Sous-vide cooking, where the food item is vacuum packed and cooked in water bath has superior quality and saves time, labor, and cost.
- The efficiency of conventional electric cooking depends on the size of the cookware. However, induction cooking technology was found to maintain high efficiency regardless of cookware size.
- Conduction griddles in kitchen increases surface area and reduces cost of production.
- Use of infrared for restaurant boilers, deep fat fryers, hot plates, and even dishwashing reduces cost by almost 40%.
- Using wireless point of sales, where the food order can directly be placed to the kitchen reduces time and saves labor.
- Hospitality education is focused on hotel operations, safety, and sanitation; however, the use of modern tools and technology is often overlooked. There is need to rework the approach toward culinary training and skilling to make it contemporary and industry relevant.
- Modern Indian culinary education hopes to produce food connoisseurs with an ability to use their imagination, to be more creative and incorporating latest practices. Upgrading the academic curriculum would help achieve this objective.
- Developing a friendly work environment would help ease pressure, increase creativity and results in better performance.

11.8   LIMITATIONS AND FUTURE RESEARCH

This study has a number of limitations that must be taken into consideration. The study is an exploratory study where the results are valid in the current situation and may vary with time, location, and the sector analyzed. These results are based on the personal experiences and discussion between the professional chefs and the managers which is valid and reliable; however, it may have possible biases. While this study provides much insight into the innovation process used by chefs in the restaurant industry, further research could be more specific or conducted at the micro level, where individual menu items and each equipment is examined to see its impact on cost and profitability.

11.9   CONCLUSION

Culinary innovation in the form of product, process, and technology would lead to reducing costs and increase profitability. Investments in technology and equipment will require a long-term view from a cost–benefit standpoint. The Indian restaurant sector is currently defined by product innovation; most of the culinary innovation in restaurants is focused on food and its presentation. Food trends are been set on traditional and contemporary styles of food. Hotels and apex bodies reward chefs based on their culinary innovation; which in turn acts as a positive inducement to introduce and implement new product ideas. The other aspect of culinary innovation is adopting latest tools and techniques in professional kitchens. It is observed that culinary managers have a low tendency to adopt technological innovation. Cost of implementation and training is the main hindrance in adopting such techniques, technical knowhow and impact of migration on a running operation has an adverse impact on decisions to move forward. Industrial cuisine and outsourcing of the product has caught up well and looks like it is the future of the food sector. Cost leadership brings the elements of industrial cuisine in sharp contrast with slow and fresh food, as it lacks aspects of health, personal touch, customization, and scope for innovation.

Technology advancements have a major impact on the hospitality industry in general and more specifically on the restaurant sector. In the past couple of years, the restaurant sector has seen great possibilities that technology has to offer and this generates opportunities to motivate hoteliers toward innovation. Despite this, professional cooking is still governed by traditional, low tech approaches, even the elitist restaurants still evade technological advancements, it is these restaurants that are market leaders and are responsible for setting up trends regarding adoption of innovative approaches for the cuisine they specialize in. As the sector grapples with issues and challenges, it is quite apparent that growth and profitability will be achieved only through persistent efforts to innovate and adapt.

KEYWORDS

- culinary innovation
- food trends
- inventory management
- culinary creativity
- fresh food

REFERENCES

Amabile, M.; Conti, R.; Coon, H.; Lazenby, L.; Herron, M. *Assessing The Work Environment For Creativity. Acad. Manage. J.* **1996,** *39,* 1154–1184.

Connor, P.; Frew, A. J. Expert Perceptions on the Future of Hotel Electronic Distribution Channels. In: *Information and Communication Technologies in Tourism*; Sheldon, P. J., Wober, K. W., Fesenmaier, D. R., Eds.; Sprinter Computer Science: Vienna, New York, 2001; 294–302.

Cooper, R. G. Winning at New Products. In: *Accelerating the Process from Idea to Launch,* 3rd ed., Perseus Books: New York, 2001.

Damanpour, F. Organizational Size and Innovation. *Organ. Stud.* **1992,** *13*(3), 375–402.

Feltenstein, T. New-Product Development in Food Service: A Structured Approach. *Cornell Hotel Restaurant Adm. Q.* **1986,** *27*(3), 62–71.

Glaeser, E.; Kallal, H.; Scheinkman, J.; Shleifer, A. Growth in Cities. *J. Polit. Econ.* **1992,** *100*(6), 1126–1115.

Harrington, R. J. The Culinary Innovation Process: A Barrier to Imitation. *J. Foodserv. Bus. Res.* **2004,** *3,* 35–57.

Hu, M.-L. Discovering Culinary Competency: An Innovative Approach. *J. Hosp., Leis., Sport Tour. Educ.* **2010,** *9*(1), 67–69.

Johne, A.; Storey, C. New Service Development: A Review of Literature and Annotated Bibliography. *Eur. J. Mark.* **1998,** *32*(3/4), 184–251.

Lane, C. The Michelin-starred Restaurant Sector as a Cultural Industry: A Cross-national Comparison of Restaurants in the UK and Germany. *Food, Cult. Soc.* **2010,** *13,* 493–519.

Lane, C. Lup, D. Cooking under Fire: Managing Multilevel Tensions between Creativity and Innovation in Haute Cuisine. *Ind. Innov.* **2015,** *22*(8), 654–676.

Lim, P. J. *Indian Restaurants*, 14 November 2015. Retrieved from http://www.channelnews-asia.com/news/business/singapore/indian-restaurants-band/2228664.html.

Munjal, S.; Sharma, S. Applying Innovative Food Cost Management Practices in Inflationary Times Indian Budget Restaurant Segment Experiences. *Worldw. Hosp. Tour. Themes* **2012,** *4*(5), 463–477.

Munjal, S.; Sharma, S.; Menon, P. Moving towards 'Slow Food,' The New Frontier of Culinary Innovation in India: The Vedatya Experience. *Worldw. Hosp. Tour. Themes* **2016,** *8*(4), 444–460.

NRAI (National Restaurant Association of India), 2013. Retrieved from http://nrai.org/downloads/reports/ (last accessed 12 May 2016).

Nusra. *Top Food Trends that Ruled India in 2015*, 14 November 2015. Retrieved from http://www.restaurantindia.in/article/f-and-b-format/menu-trends/Top-food-trends-that-ruled-India-in-2015.a237/.

Oldham, G. R.; Cummings, A. Employee Creativity: Personal And Contextual Factors at Work. *Acad. Manage. J.* **1996,** *39*, 607–634.

Ottenbacher, M.; Harrington, R. J. The Innovation Development Process of Michelin-Starred Chefs. *Int. J. Contemp. Hosp. Manage.* **2007,** *19*(6), 444–460.

Pechlaner, H.; Osti, L. Reengineering the Role of Culture in Tourism's Value Chain and the Challenges for Destination Management Systems: The Case of Tyrol. Paper Presented at Information and Communication Technologies in Tourism. In: *Information and Communication Technologies in Tourism*; Wober, P., Fesenmaier, D. R., Eds.; Springer Computer Science: Vienna, New York, 2001; pp 294–302.

Reagans, R.; Zuckerman, E. W. Networks, Diversity, and Productivity: The Social Capital of Corporate R&D Teams. *Organ. Sci.* **2001,** *12*, 502–517.

Riley, M. Declining Hotel Standards and the Skill Trap. *Int. J. Tour. Manage.* **1981,** *2*(2). 95–104.

Shalley, C. E.; Gilbson, L. L. What Leaders Need to Know: A Review of Social and Contextual Factors That Can Foster or Hinder Creativity. *Leadersh. Q.* **2004,** *15*(1), 33–53.

Svejenova, S.; Mazza, C.; Planellas, M. Cooking Up Change in Haute Cuisine: Ferran Adria as an Institutional Entrepreneur. *J. Organ. Behav.* **2007,** *28*, 539–561.

Sweeney, M.; Dols, J.; Fortenbery, B.; Sharp, F. *Induction Cooking Technology Design and Assessment*. Electric Power Research Institute (EPRI), *ACEEE Summer Study Energy Effic. Build.* **2014,** *9*, 370.

Taj Hotels, 23 November 2015. Retrieved from http://www.tajhotels.com/luxury/food-and-wine/philosophy.html.

Tyler, L. *India's Restaurant Rules: Tradition vs. Innovation*, 19 November 2014. Retrieved from https://www.finedininglovers.com/stories/indian-food-restaurant-rules/.

Urban, G. L.; Hauser, J. R. *Design and Marketing of New Products*, 2nd ed., Prentice-Hall: Upper Saddle River, NJ, 1993.

Vila, M.; Enz, C.; Costa, G. Innovative Practices in the Spanish Hotel Industry. *Cornell Hosp. Q.* **2012,** *51*(1), 75–85.

Weiermair, K. Prospects for Innovation in Tourism Analyzing the Innovation Potential throughout the Tourism Value Chain. *J. Quality Assuran. Hosp. Tour.* **2008,** *6*(3–4), 59–72.

CHAPTER 12

EVENTS AND CATERING BUSINESS: SHIFT FROM UNORGANIZED TO ORGANIZED

KAVERI VIJ*

Designer Events Inc., New Delhi, India

*E-mail: kaverivij26@gmail.com

CONTENTS

Abstract 276
12.1   The Event and Catering Industry 276
12.2   How to Start a Catering Business in India 283
12.3   Event Industry 287
12.4   The Future of the Events and Catering Industry in India 294
Keywords 296
References 296

ABSTRACT

This chapter aims to identify the shift in the event and catering business, from the unorganized to organized sector in India. The chapter highlights the various reasons for the unorganized nature of these industries and the influences which brought about the radical change to transform them into becoming organized. The change of mindset, the shift in lifestyles, and the increase in disposable income have been big influences in changing the nature of these industries. Time has actually given these two industries a different perspective and a self-identity. Households previously have been organizing events and making their own food as a part of their family duty. Much of this demand is now being outsourced either to catering businesses or event management firms. There is an impact of macroeconomic fundamentals on these industries and it is interesting to note, how the two industries coexist depending on each other. The easing of government regulations toward opening new companies in India is identified as one of the key reasons for the increase in competition in these two industries. However, an explicit tax and legal structure shows the disparity in the business patterns amongst the industry players. A specific skill set for these industries has been identified and the seasonal nature of these industries is inherent, which explains why human resource is so easily available during peak business. Both the industries, centered in creativity, are increasing the top line of a number of other businesses. Technical advancements are also acting as a catalyst to the growth of these industries. The latter part of the chapter addresses, what are the current factors which are influencing further growth, as well as limiting its double digit revenue trajectory. A detailed SWOT analysis showcases the real picture of the two industries in this dynamic business environment.

12.1 THE EVENT AND CATERING INDUSTRY

12.1.1 AN INTRODUCTION TO THE CATERING INDUSTRY IN INDIA

Food forms a very crucial part of every event. Food is also given the top most priority in India while organizing events. The food service industry in India includes those places that provide meals away from home. One key niche of this industry is the catering industry. Catering primarily refers to offering meals to people in bulk. Catering is a multifaceted segment of the food industry. Catering management can be defined as the art of planning, procuring, organizing, controlling and executing production, and service of food in some form or the other. It represents a rapidly expanding segment of the food industry. It is also not only about providing food to a customer but also providing the right kind of atmosphere to the customer. A lot of detailing goes in every catering assignment—from how each dish is served to what crockery which meal would be served in and much more.

12.1.2 FROM ANCIENT TO MODERN TIMES

Dating back to old times in the Indian cultural context, there was a concept of mass cooking due to the existence of large sized families. Each family would prepare maybe two dishes, but were made in abundance to cater to all the members of the family. Thus, these families were so accustomed to cooking large quantities of food at home. Families would cook one meal and the same would be consumed in the day and night time. One more reason for this lifestyle was also financial constraints. Food being on the table wasn't a given element in these times, and thus, it was a medium to fill one's stomach. There wasn't a lot of innovation and dishes were kept simple. More stress was given on food which had higher calorific and nutrient value. Considering occasions where large-scale cooking would be required, the family members would divide their chores and different dishes would be made and consumed within the household itself. It was a very "do it on your own" affair. People weren't accustomed to outsourcing and considered it as a family obligation to be a part of such duties.

In the next stage of cultural transition, larger families broke up into nuclear families. More and more families decided to live on their own and fend for themselves. This gave a reason for these families to come together on occasions or for specific purposes. Nuclear families having no additional help would thus want external help to organize and manage even a small get together. Slowly and steadily, progressing further every family would have a *halvai* for every occasion or celebration. The *halvai* would come with his setup and cook within the premises of the house for the occasion. The *halvai* would get all raw materials or ask the house to give him the same, to perform their task. This gave the family escape from the stress of cooking bulk food. While these *halvais* were becoming popular, another transitional wave shifted focus on hygiene and cleanliness, caused concern with respect *to deploying this rather unprofessional catering channel.* These two factors made families consider *halvais* as a less preferred option.

Responding to the earlier mentioned concerns around hygiene and cleanliness, soon enough there were fully fledged catering companies offering catered food in a much more hygienic manner. During the 1990s, there were very few market leaders. Both *halvais* and catering companies offered food; however, the catering companies captured bulk of the business leveraging their focus on hygienic cooking and menu innovation. The catering companies would also come to the location, set up their kitchen, and offer food and service. By maintaining a higher standard of operation, their popularity showed a vertical growth. These companies would ensure any person handling food preparation and serving, would need to wear gloves, meat, and vegetables to be treated differently, etc. All these factors enabled these companies to be chosen over the traditional *halvais*. The next level innovation that these companies got on the ground was to introduce new dishes to the market which were earlier unheard of. It wasn't the regular Paneer-based (cottage cheese) or Aloo-based (potato) dishes, but the same recipes cooked or simmered in a different style. The chefs were now avoiding the use of *ghee* which was a patent style of the *halvais* and, instead, used healthier alternatives. With the restaurant industry growing and booming side by side, every guest wanted the best of the best dishes at their events. That's when these catering companies started roping in famous chefs to head these companies. The market saw a new style of catering emerge, with innovation in the way food is served and the manner in which it is prepared. Initially, catering companies would have a standard buffet spread for snacks, salads, main course, and desserts. Based on increased paying capacity of the consumers, today it's common to see that catered events have live stations where chefs showcase their talent and cook live for the guests. The *done to death* salads like Russian Salads, Kachumbar Salad, etc. don't exist anymore but have names inspired by the French as an integral part of the buffet.

As eating "healthy" has gained momentum, so did healthy options on the caterers menus, the caterers now include "size zero" snacks and healthy items as a quintessential part of food options made available. There is a continuous pressure to innovate and be abreast with the market food trends, to offer unique options to the guests for the special occasions.

The caterers have also transformed how food looks like. The chefs at these companies believe that people consume food with their eyes first. The presentation of buffets at these events has gone to another level. There are unique and creative ways of serving dishes and displaying the buffet. Earlier there was the regular basic crockery and cutlery to serve food to the guests, and now these companies are investing a lot more into the use of fine cutlery and crockery. The bigger players of the market request a cutlery and crockery selection from each customer. There are certain catering companies who now specialize in a certain type of a cuisine and offer the same to the market. However, the broad market demands to have all kinds of cuisines in one event, food being such a critical and central part of each event.

Given the nature of business, the catering industry has largely remained unaffected by the economic slowdown and has, in fact, maintained a 15–20% growth rate year on year. The only change this industry has witnessed after the advent of the economic slowdown is, customers trimming their guest list or cutting the menu prices to save cost.

12.1.3 THE UNORGANIZED CHAOS

The catered food industry in India has gained momentum in the past few years attributed to the changing lifestyle. More and more people want to venture out with families to enjoy a meal. There are restaurants small and big sprouting all over the country. Catering however still remains largely unorganized. There are multiple players catering to different segments of the society. One caterer would cater at INR 250 per head and another one at INR 2500 per head. In a lot of cases, having catering for a smaller function works out much more economical than ordering in a meal from a restaurant. While smaller towns in the country are ridden with local cooks, chefs, and small operators, bigger cities have seen an increase in established names in the catered food and restaurant space. In the west, any catering at an event is often more expensive than going to a restaurant, because it offers a premium service as opposed to the situation in India.

The catering industry in India is dominated by a number of players, some are established and some who run the business from the comfort of their homes. A number of restaurants have also expanded into catering including few well-known hotel chains who term this service as "Outdoor Catering—ODC." With the introduction of new laws, taxation and food becoming a fashion statement for each and every event, a lot of organized operators comprising international catering companies and big restaurant chains have also started taking this business seriously. Catering not only is more limited to weddings and birthday parties in the country but also includes corporate events, fashion show, sporting events, and much more. Moreover, the demanding customer of today who is even more aware and wants to ape the west in every way requires diverse choices which is also resulting in the growth of the organized professional catering business.

Analyzing the transition in this industry, there are plenty of players operating at various quality levels and scales. Progressing, with the need of having cleaner options for catering and considering other elements; there are government regulations that came into play with respect to the formation of such companies, requiring compliance to with a range of legal requirements. Every company would have to be identified under a certain section and apply for a license to be able to serve food. This brought in some form of professional organization into this sector and more and more catering companies started abiding to the guidelines. On the other side, as this is still not a distinguished industry, there are a lot of players in the market who would still operate without registration. The ease of forming a company and getting it registered has been seen as a factor for increased competition amongst these companies. With the increasing demand of catering requirements, a lot of catering firms have emerged owing to the ease in regulations. This competition still leaves the market place in an unorganized chaos, as every customer has so many options to choose from. Though the industry is inching toward an organized status, it still remains unorganized in a lot of ways.

Very similar to the hospitality industry, catering companies are also predominantly labor intensive. They need skilled labor in terms of cooks, chefs, and servers, although these resources are not necessarily hotel management graduates. The catering industry takes in people based on experience too and thus is able to widen the pool of labor to choose from. Service operations are not starved for labor which is available in abundance for this sector; the level of skills is the main challenge faced by business owners. Companies have certain people on their payroll and also hire certain percentage of labor such as waiters, cleaners, helpers, cooks, chefs on a contractual basis. A lot of college students also show keenness to work with these companies, to earn extra pocket money, thus solving the problem of sourcing labor. Despite the immense competition, each company has enough manpower to work and grow the reach of their business. The owners of these companies are ex-hoteliers or graduates of hospitality, but the degree of education diminishes as one percolates down the hierarchy. It is interesting to note, how these contractual labor are just trained at times, in just 1 h of briefing on serving snacks and managing the buffet, and then left to manage the show. Very little importance is given to the training aspect of manpower and hence the quality of service offered gets short changed. However, the established players in the industry take care of these finer details and have major of their employees on permanent payroll, offering a world of difference in their service levels through investment in training of teams.

Another factor which plays a major role in this industry is the seasonality of the business. Though these companies are busy throughout the year as they cater to different segments, the wedding season is the busiest. This season is a real test of quality and performance of these companies, as they perform day and night without rest. The true test of their standards can be judged in these seasons. Though every caterer offers food trials before booking them, when food is made on a super large scale; it defines the actual test of quality and management.

Initially, people would call a chef from a specific region of the country to cater to the regional taste buds of their guests. However, the established firms today hire chefs who are trained to cook multi-cuisine food including regional delicacies, which not only helps them to serve all types of guests, it also gives them an opportunity to target multiple market segments. With the increase in the number of players, every catering company has a geographical area they cater to in addition to their regular customers. This gives them ample amount of business, to cover their costs and run their business with profits.

Sociocultural changes resulting in busier lifestyles require professionals to handle events, where services are pre-decided and executed on the relevant day without any hitches. Since food is given the most importance in India, it's the highlight of any event that is organized. Thus, having a lot of variety is essential. Having so many suppliers in the market makes it very easy for the customer to choose from, as there would be marginal differences between one caterer and another. The increase in the number of the service providers has made the market scenario very price competitive. On a positive note, while people have a huge variety to choose from, those with reputation of quality delivery can demand a price premium for their reliability. Though it is largely a saturated market, with many players catering to low, medium, and high budgets, there is enough business for all as the market is growing at 20% or more year on year. This growth in demand fuels the entry of new players every day, leaving the buyer to call the shots.

It is quite clear that the catering scenario in India is only getting more competitive, riding on various factors that are propelling its growth. This spells good news for the consumer, who is going to get good quality hygienic food at a very well-structured price. But it is yet to be seen, how this industry shapes itself in the coming future.

The challenge still remains to make this industry organized and driven by quality and innovation. Every new player who enters this market feels it is a piece of cake. Catering is just mere organization of food. But in reality, it is a lot more. Caterers often take on bulk orders, and when they fail to deliver, they are driven out of the market. But as the market has so many players, when these players vanish, no one notices or realizes this churn.

Hygiene is another big challenge the caterers need to deal with continuously. It encompasses hiring experienced chefs and trained staff, bringing in the latest equipment in the kitchen, and ensuring each and every aspect passes the hygiene standards. Emphasis also has to be on choosing safe ingredients and preparing food within the hygiene regulations. Segregation of vegetarian and nonvegetarian, cooked and raw food, dairy, and bakery helps to avoid cross contamination during food preparation. The food also needs to be transported to the venue in hygienic air-conditioned mobile vans, which are fast becoming the norm. Though these are mandatory, there is no checkpoint ensuring adherence to these regulations. Compromises on these aspects by the smaller players are not uncommon. The smaller players of the industry at times cannot even afford proper equipment, needed to pass the basic health hazard audit test.

On the bright side, the start-up cost for a catering service business is relatively low and the premises don't necessarily have to be in a prime real estate location. This helps save on the investment required to get started. The catering location can be far away, and the company can still cater to customers in the entire city. Joint venture partners and banks are also recognizing the potential of this business and are offering financial credit, for setting up the business and funding its expansion.

The catering business may be covered under the service tax and sales tax act, based on the annual sales turnover and state of operations. Based on the State's value added tax (VAT) regulation, a VAT registration may also be applicable based on turnover of the catering business. This works out more economical than the taxes charged at restaurants. As compared to employing catering from a restaurant or a hotel, the taxes charged are far higher than those by a catering company. This propels customers to choose an established catering firm than an established hotel brand. Few people still go in for the branded service provider, but this trend is gradually shifting in favor of the caterers.

The players of this industry need to realize the value of quality, driven by the team's skill set. The industry is moving toward this; however, a more dedicated effort is required to enhance the skills of the team employed. The companies need to be more aware of the global food trends and develop the ability to create unique offerings, to establish their place in this competitive market. Innovation and creativity are the keys to success in this business, along with immaculate execution.

The newer and the established players are bringing in better quality by hospitality professionals and trained chefs to set up industrial kitchens, to service their clients in a hygienic, professional, and systematic manner. Few dominant key players in the market are F&B Catering, Grand F&B, F&B by Amit Dua, Creative Cuisines Inc., Karims, Harrison Nandi Caterers, and Cawasji Behramji Catering Services Limited.

It is interesting to note that Cawasji Behramji Catering Services Limited is the only catering services company that filed for an IPO in September 2015. Incorporated on April 3, 2009, by Alfred Micheal Arambhan and Nalini Maria Arambhan, the company provides offshore catering and house-keeping services to various Indian and international oil exploration and shipping companies. This includes operating and managing staff cafeterias on a contractual basis. The company is also into the business of food catering for corporate clients, banquets, parties and events, and gymkhanas, besides running a fine dining restaurant called "Me So Happi" in Mumbai. The company's prominent clients include ONGC, Great Offshore, Hind Offshore, L&T, Punj Lloyd, and Essar Projects. They have setup a central-ized warehouse in Mumbai, which hosts a cold storage facility and a blast freezer to avoid spoilage of raw materials. The company also owns a fleet of four reefers and a pick up van for cold chain transport and handling, to ensure timely procurement and movement of supplies. The company's total income for 2015 was INR 64.16 crores and net profit was INR 82.21 lakh. It's top line and bottom line for 2014 stood at INR 72.89 crores and INR 2.21 crores, respectively (Business Line, 2015).

12.2   HOW TO START A CATERING BUSINESS IN INDIA

This section gives an insight on the road map and blueprint on how to start a catering business in India.

1. The operations of a catering business in India are covered under the FSSAI Act (Food Safety and Standards Authority of India). It is recommended that the company be laid down as a private limited company or a limited liability partnership (LLP) company, or as a one person company. The abovementioned companies are trans-ferable to any person for a consideration. Since these entities offer limited liability protection and are transferable, it makes them ideal for a starting a catering business.

2. The catering business can be set up as a LLP if the annual sales turnover is expected to be less than INR 40 lakhs and capital less than INR 25 lakhs. If the LLP is expected to have a sales turnover in excess of INR 40 lakhs, and a capital contribution in excess of INR 25 lakhs, then it is best to start a private limited company.

3. It is advisable not to start a one person company, as it would mandatorily have to be converted to a private limited company, when the annual sales turnover crosses INR 2 crores.

4. *Obtaining an FSSAI license*: A food business operator license is a license granted by the FSSAI that allows the entity to carry on activities related to any stage of manufacturing, processing, packaging, storage, transportation, distribution of food, and imports and includes food services such as catering services, sale of food, and food ingredients. To obtain a FSSAI food business license, the incorporation documents of the business must be submitted along with proof of address, identity or resident proof of the promoters and details as per the application form. The FSSAI food business license for catering businesses is granted by the state government and must be submitted to the local FSSAI office.

5. *Tax registration*: The catering business may be covered under the service tax and sales tax acts, based on the annual sales turnover and state of operations. The services of a catering business will be covered under service tax, if annual services provided by the catering business exceed INR 10 lakhs. When the catering business exceeds a turnover of INR 9 lakhs, service tax registration must be obtained and service tax collection and payment should start once the turnover exceeds INR 10 lakhs.

6. *VAT*: Based on the State's VAT regulation, a VAT registration may also be applicable based on the turnover of the catering business. Since VAT regulations differ from state to state, it is best to consult the local VAT authorities to determine the correct applicability.

7. *Human resource*: Based on the size of the company, the team needs to be employed which includes the kitchen team, the-head Chef, the Sous Chef, and an operations team to manage service operations.

8. *Menu planning*: Menu offerings vary on what the company wishes to offer to the market. Is the company a one cuisine specialty service provider or has a multi cuisine offering? Most of the menus are customized as per the guests' needs; however, some standard menus are designed for the guests to choose from.

9. *Pricing strategy*: Each dish is priced after assessing the raw material costs and adding a markup on the same. However, since catering is not specifically a restaurant offering instead a combined menu offering, the final pricing varies on the choice of menu items. For instance, a menu with prawns would necessarily be more expensive than one with chicken or compared to a vegetarian one. Labor costs and rental costs are usually not added to derive the final menu costs, as the catering business is more of a number game rather than a single dish seller. The ideal food costs for a full service caterer varies between 25 and 28%.

10. *Inventory management*: The company needs to maintain the necessary inventory of kitchen equipment, high-end service ware, table ware, china ware, glasses, etc. The company should own different service ware for different types of cuisine offering to make a differentiation.

11. *The production place*: The base kitchen needs to be set up in a clean and hygiene manner. They also need a small place to set up a table seating, for guests to facilitate menu tastings.

12. *The unique selling proposition*: The innovation in dishes and the offering is what can make the product offering unique. The new trends and the innovation in serving of food are also a differentiation point. Molecular gastronomy has been as a major trend experienced at events.

—Cited from India Fillings (2015) and from the author's own studies and experience.

It is interesting to note that many believe that there is little need of any special training and education to start a catering business. That is however debatable. For instance, if someone aspires to be a chef for a 5-star property, they would be expected to have a hotel management graduate degree as a minimum qualification. However, the same is not believed to be the case when being considered for a catering business. It is assumed anyone who has even basic culinary skills can start a catering company. In reality, that does not work, as a lot of planning and organizational skills are required to manage the business. Thus, it is necessary for any potential entrant to have a certain level of skills and education to be effective in this industry. The people hired should have specific experience to handle their specific job roles. This could range from a necessary culinary course or a hotel management course, having worked with a catering firm or a professionally managed hotel chain. For instance, one of the leading caterers in Delhi, F&B by Amit Dua started his career with the Oberoi Intercontinental, New Delhi, in 1976 and thereafter held various roles in organizations such as the international trade fair authority, the Bistro and Gaylord to name a few. After learning the tricks of the trade, he started his own venture.

Though it is a highly competitive market having a large number of players, this is also a high growth market, where demand for good food for an Indian event will never diminish. This industry is expected to continue to grow, but the demanding customers will require innovation and professionalism increasingly. As the very famous saying goes *"Khaana tho sabse zaroori hai"* translating to food is the most important (Ernst & Young, 2015).

12.2.1 OVERALL ANALYSIS

12.2.1.1 OPPORTUNITY

- The average guest list for large events in India ranges from 500 to 2000, which forces people to have events in farm houses rather than hotels which have limited capacity. All farm houses demand to have outside catering, which generates a huge demand for this industry.
- Increase in disposable income of the people has resulted in investments in real estate, bigger houses, or farm houses (Ernst & Young, 2015). Such people require professional services to organize catering services.
- Every event requires food; no event is complete without food, explaining the huge demand generated by this industry.
- Apart from social gatherings and festive occasions, formal events, conferences, seminars, exhibitions, and other business-related events generate demand for professional catering services adding to the growing opportunity (MyNewsDesk, 2010).
- *Supplier bargaining power*: A company offering a special type of catering or cuisine in its offering has a higher bargaining power compared to its competitors offering multi cuisine options.
- Huge demand generated from destination weddings is a great opportunity for caterers in one city to flaunt their skills in another city, which gives them a greater geographical coverage.
- The rise in disposable income and the willingness to spend has created a huge demand in Tier-2 and Tier-3 cities. Technology acts as a big catalyst to reach out to new customers and increase the potential customer database.

12.2.1.2 ISSUES AND CHALLENGES

- *Suppliers bargaining power:* The market infused with so many competitors leaves the suppliers in a poor bargaining situation. The customers are spoilt for choice, and without a unique selling proposition, it's a tough business to be in.
- The service and bar staff at each event organized by these catering companies is usually hired on an event to event basis, which affects the quality of service delivered. No company can afford to have such high payroll costs and hence depends on part time resources to ensure profitability.
- Most of the venues do not provide any dedicated area for the caterers to set up their kitchen. The production area is temporarily made with tents for the required number of cooking days. This poses a threat to cleanliness, sanitation, and health.
- The new players in the market usually end up taking on bigger assignments, which often results in shortage of small wares and equipment. A newly established firm usually ends up renting their service ware rather than investing in the high-end service ware, at such initial levels. This again poses a threat to the quality of display and service of food.
- The players who have existed in the market for years have established their clientele and a brand name, which lessens the demand for new entrants as no one wants to take the risk of hiring a wrong caterer, food being such a critical element.
- Fluctuations in the prices of raw material can pose a threat which directly affects the pricing strategy and profit margins. In an inflationary economy, this becomes a critical issue.
- A lot of venues offer their own catering. This reduces the need to hire catering from outside. Five-star hotels, large number of banquet venues, and few reputed venues have their own food production team and do not allow the option to get catering done externally.

12.3 EVENT INDUSTRY

12.3.1 INTRODUCTION

The word "events" is a big umbrella term which encompasses a number of dimensions within it. The word event as per the Oxford Dictionary is

defined as "a thing that happens or takes place, especially one of importance." The word organization is synonymous with event management. The
popular formats of events that are managed by event management businesses range from social events like weddings or corporate events like meetings, conferences, annual general meetings, etc. Initially, the word event
meant getting together of certain number of people at a certain location for
a certain purpose. With the advancements in time, MICE (meetings, incentives, conferences, and exhibitions), as a terminology, has become synonymous with all types of events being organized and managed by the event
management and hospitality companies. Broadly, events can be classified as

1. *Social events*: This dimension includes events organized by family
    and friends and would feature weddings, birthdays, anniversaries,
    pre-wedding functions, house parties, baby showers, etc.
2. *Corporate events*: Any event organized by a corporate entity with an
    official purpose is categorized as corporate events.
3. *Exhibitions*: Events that exhibit products and services fall into this
    category. Exhibitions usually have a defined area of exhibit and
    showcase one kind of products hailing from the same industry.
4. *PR events*: Any promotional event falls into this category. For
    instance, promoting a movie or a hotel can be termed as a promo-
    tional event.
5. *Events for a social cause*: Any event which is organized with a social
    motive falls under this category, for instance, a blood donation camp.
6. *Activations*: These are usually carried out for the promotion and
    sales of a product or a service at multiple locations.

The events industry is one of the fastest growing industries in India. It is
expected to grow at 25% annually and estimated to reach $996 million by
2015–2016. This industry with a double digit growth has travelled a journey
from zero requirement in a household to a requirement in every household.
With a compounded annual growth of 14%, this industry is projected to be
worth INR 5000 crores by 2015 (Sanjay Kankaria, Director, Rachnoutsav
Events Academy). The phenomenal growth of this industry is coupled with
transition from unorganized to an organized sector.

The events and activations industry has grown at 15% annually from
INR 2800 crores in 2011–2012 to INR 4258 crores in 2014–2015 according
to an EY-EEMA (Event and Entertainment Management Association) report
titled "Making Experiences in India: The events and activations industry."
If one were to include the unorganized segment as well, the industry grew

from INR 728 billion in 2011 to INR 821 billion in 2012, an overall growth of 12.6%. The industry has achieved a growth of 11.8% in 2013 to touch INR 917 billion. The sector is projected to grow at a CAGR of 15.2% to reach INR 1661 billion by 2017, as per the Ernst and Young Report (2015).

The unorganized segment of this industry is still quite significant in size, the reason being that there is practically no entry barrier to commencing operations as an event management company. These companies have no defined business processes or policies and are easy to be constituted as per the laws of the country.

12.3.2 FROM ANCIENT TO MODERN TIMES

Till a couple of decades back, the event industry did not play any major role in the Indian society. Families would typically get together and organize the events. Every family person was given a key responsibility to take care at the event. The family would plan the entire get together and these events would usually take place at home.

Gradually, families started expanding and having events at open spaces, for example, parks and open space next to houses. This period saw a growth of "tent houses," these businesses would provide the necessary set up requirements like seating, music, covered carpeted area, etc. Food was catered by "halwais" as mentioned earlier in the chapter.

With sociocultural changes sweeping the nation, families started getting busier in their routines and like explained earlier, nuclear families started emerging. This resulted in a demand-driven growth in the form of a few professional event management companies. Families started requiring professional help for managing and organizing events. This period also saw an increase in corporate companies, which also increased the demand to organize various corporate events. Gradually, corporate companies also started hiring professionals to organize their events.

Moving forward, there was mushrooming of various companies in this industry. A sudden increase in the demand in this industry was the reason for this mushrooming. The industry leaders and these players assumed this not to be a "skills heavy" industry. The general consensus was that anyone with organization skills could start an event management company. Since the capital investment required was minimal, soon enough a large unorganized industry emerged.

Another trend this industry has witnessed is that of *wedding planners*. The wedding-related events being huge in India have seen a dramatic growth in wedding planners. Wedding planners handle every wedding like a project and the family members can enjoy the wedding stress free, without having to deal with any organizational aspects, once key decisions are made. The wedding industry in India is estimated to be worth $40 billion. As per a survey conducted by Ernst and Young, Indian families save the most for the education of their children, followed by their marriages. Hence, weddings are lavish in India. Dating back, weddings were very simple and did not involve much flare. Today, every family wants their weddings to be the talk of the town. Many a couple wants a unique wedding and also have a big budget to spend on this. Thanks to the influence of media and a big influence from Bollywood, Indian brides often dream for larger than life weddings. Economic liberalization and the rise of the middle class too have prompted a change in spending patterns. This growing demand explains the increasing number of wedding planners operating in the country. With most people busy with their careers and the joint family system declining, there is neither time nor the bandwidth to organize weddings. Nuclear family setups are readily willing to hire professional help, to plan and organize weddings, as per their aspirations.

There are event management companies catering to every type of budget, for families organizing events, including weddings. There is competition, but it is balanced by the growth in terms of market size that this industry is experiencing. Nearly all companies survive this seasonal industry, as the typical "fee" for professional services that wedding planners charge is quite steep. The planners usually charge a commission from 10% to 17.5%. This means that a Rs. 1 crore wedding will leave the planner richer by Rs. 10 lakh. While for most upper class people wedding budgets start at Rs. 70–80 lakh, it can go up to Rs. 10 crore for industrialists and businessmen. Weddings are a much bigger business in India, as compared to some other parts of the world, where events tend to be smaller and more formal. Weddings in India see people compete with each other in terms of opulence and creativity. Also, the rising trend to have more than one event at a wedding is adding to the business for these planners. Every bride wants to have at least five distinguished days of celebration, with every event being a unique one. Another fad is a destination wedding, where the entire family and the invitees move to a destination for 3–4 days and all the wedding functions take place at the destination. A lot of people prefer to trim down their guest list and opt for destinations to plan weddings. This allows guest to have a more intimate affair and enjoy the events with closer friends and family. Destination weddings cannot be handled without professional help, as a lot of planning is required. Air tickets, flights, managing logistics, visa arrangements, local language, managing and dealing with local vendors, food requirements, etc. are some of the key responsibilities for these planners in a destination wedding. Various cities in India are preferred as destinations for weddings, such as Jaipur, Udaipur, Kochi, and Goa. These places are popular because of good infrastructure and availability of big palaces and hotels. However, people are also opting for international locations like Bali, Thailand, Sri Lanka, Bhutan, etc. for their weddings. The expense though a factor is becoming less relevant with the increase in disposable income. A farm house wedding with more number of people works out more economical; however, a destination wedding is more like a fashion statement. Destination weddings can be fun and crazy in their own way. Some of the properties only cater to or run largely on the revenues generated from destination weddings, for instance, Raj Palace at Jaipur or the Leela at Goa. Heritage properties at Jaipur not only organize the *doli* (palanquin) for the bride but also camels, horses, elephants, drummers, and dancers to be a part of the marriage procession. There might be a Bollywood singer or even a Hollywood celebrity like Jenifer Lopez who perform at Jaipur for a private wedding function. Every aspect of the wedding is customized and detailed to each minute element. From the entry of the Baraatis to the cutlery, the linen, every smallest detail is planned. NRIs (non-resident Indians) are the biggest clients for these destination weddings. As they are unfamiliar with India, wedding planners plan and help them with every aspect of the wedding. Every expense almost doubles for a destination wedding, as some resources are locally sourced. However, some resources such as the makeup artist, entertainment artist, etc. may have to be specially flown in from overseas. Despite these high expenses, the Indian wedding industry is a growing industry. The concept of weddings planned and implemented by professional planners and event management companies has still not penetrated Tier-2 and Tier-3 cities in India; once this happens; this industry is expected to grow at a faster pace.

Another revenue generation stream for these planners is from their preferred vendors who they work with. Every planner has specific set of vendors for the mehendi function, photography, entertainment, etc., who pay the planners a commission for allocating them work contracts.

12.3.3 IMMUNITY FROM ECONOMIC SLOWDOWN

The impact of economic slowdown and the associated uncertainty primarily affects those corporate events that are limited in spending as well as quantity. However, the wedding segment of the industry is largely not affected by these slowdowns, as weddings happen irrespective of the economic scenario and have been usually financially planned for well in advance by families. In fact, even if it means taking on debt, Indian families would still spend on weddings to their hearts content rather than have a low key affair. Weddings remain a stable business segment, even though they are usually a once in a lifetime event in India. This explains the competition in this business. Irrespective of its seasonal nature, Hindu weddings *happen in consultation with astrology* or the *"mahurat"* taken out by Pandit ji. Event companies usually have ample amount of business to survive the poor business months in this segment. Every year auspicious dates are taken out by Pandit jis, where wedding planners play around with their revenue maximization techniques. A wedding would cost at least twice the price in a non-seasonal month than on a heavy *"saya" or auspicious* date. This seasonality allows the planners to charge a premium during peak season time, as busy season bookings become unavailable very fast. On the contrary, the flip side to this process is, as there is so much competition in the market, guests actually have options which are just few thousand rupees lower than quotes given by another company. Thus, various wedding planning companies sometime lose business just due to price undercutting in the market.

Key players who have dominated the market for the longest time are Percept, E-Factor Entertainment Pvt. Ltd., Shloka Events, Wedding Design Company by Vandana Mohan, Showtime, Wizcraft, Cox and Kings, and DNA Entertainment Networks Pvt. Ltd. The event industry is now nearly 20–25 years old and still has tremendous scope for new players to come in and offer original services. The key is to bring in technology and innovation in the events further, to enhance the experience offered to the customers. Social media is playing a big role in increasing the popularity and focus on this industry. One of India's prime wedding blog, Wedmegood, run by a couple Mehak and Anand Sahni, has gained so much popularity that every wedding guest turns to their website for wedding solutions. This website lists all the necessary vendors required to plan a wedding along with reviews from previous clients. Another interesting feature covered by this website is to showcase real weddings, where the couples share their story and their details of planning the wedding. This gives an insight to others, to choose the right kind of planners and vendors for their wedding.

12.3.4 OVERALL ANALYSIS

12.3.4.1 OPPORTUNITY

- The industry has a number of reputed players who have been game changers, but there is potential for more new entrants.
- Since the industry is still not considered a skill specific industry, there is access to a large pool of labor. A lot of people are inclined toward creative jobs and the industry demands more experience than learning, which explains the relatively easy availability of human resource.
- The organized industry has been documented to grown 15% annually from INR 2800 crore in 2011–12 to INR 4258 crore in 2014–2015 (Ernst & Young, 2015). The growth in the market size of this industry explains the tremendous demand for their services.
- India has a complete array of venues in most of the cities, which makes it a preferred choice for events. India is one of the top 10 destinations to hold weddings at in 2015, as quoted by Conde Nast Traveller (Conde Nast Traveller, 2015).
- India is one of the fastest growing outbound MICE market in Asia Pacific.
- The organized segment of the event industry is expected to grow at a rate of 16–17% for the next 2–4 years. It is expected to touch INR 5779 crore by 2016–2017 (Ernst & Young, 2015).
- Personal events are expected to register the fastest growth in the next 2–4 years. High disposable incomes and the willingness to spend on large scale events will translate into increasing the growth rate of the personal event space. The busier lifestyle of people leaves more room for opportunity for people to opt for professional services (Ernst & Young, 2015).
- More products and companies today prefer to organize events to introduce their products rather than advertising on TV or the radio.
- As per a survey conducted by Ernst and Young, personal events, sports, activation campaigns, and MICE are the categories that will register the fastest growth rates ranging from 18% to 25% in the next 2–4 years.

12.3.4.2 ISSUES AND CHALLENGES

- The industry is still not considered as a skill specific industry. It is defined as a labor intensive field. Thus, there are very few formal education imparting institutes in the country in this sphere.
- There are multiple taxation systems for this industry, which differs depending on the nature of the event. This often creates a gap between the customer and the service provider. This also initiates the use of black money in large events to avoid high taxation amounts (Ernst & Young, 2015).
- A lot of money is pumped into this industry though cash payments, which do not get recorded in real terms and thus accessing the real size of this growing industry is always a difficult number to estimate.
- The government has a number of licenses associated with different kinds of events, which acts as an additional charge for the guest. The attitude of consumers here creates an opportunity for bribery to grow that is dispensed to government officials.
- There is only one convention center in the country built as per international standards, i.e., Hyderabad International Convention Centre, leaving a huge infrastructure gap in this segment.
- The customer has too many options to choose from, which allows them to shift from one company to another. There is hardly any brand loyalty.
- Since the buying power of the customer is higher in this saturated market, this translates into lower profit margins for these companies, especially during the off season.

12.4 THE FUTURE OF THE EVENTS AND CATERING INDUSTRY IN INDIA

- The key strengths of the event and the catering industry remain, in its ability to capitalize on the changing sociocultural context, and the innovation and efficiency with which it operates. These two industries which rely on each other in a very big way need to work on acquiring the right talent pool, managing costs and having transparency in their operations.
- *Human resource*: Improving the quality of talent needs to done by skill identification and choosing appropriate people for every role,

skill development, job security, compensation benchmarking, and implementation of health and safety standards.

- *Non-metro market expansion*: These will be the next focus areas for growth, as marketers look toward Tier-2 and Tier-3 cities for incremental growth. Metro cities are saturated with many players, and non-metro cities are the next target market for all these players.

- *Technology as a driver*: Digital events and activation is also expected to grow significantly on the back of smart phone penetration, internet availability, and the resultant cost efficiency. Service providers need to invest a lot more in technology and introduce technology in their daily operations to improve their efficiency. The turnaround time for each event needs to reduce and the productivity needs to increase. The industry must build robust policies, processes, and information systems to manage business efficiently and safely and implement technology and automation.

- *Taxation*: Taxation is also one of the challenges faced by these industries. Double taxation, taxation across multiple states, and varying and inconsistent application of different taxes, needs to be regularized to introduce organization in these sectors. The regulatory ecosystem needs to be made more conducive, by simplifying taxation, permissions, and copyright issues.

- The industry needs to work on its positioning across key market segments, build a transparent accounting focus and demonstrate financial returns more effectively.

- There is a need to improve the supply chain, by developing quality vendors, implementing a system of vendor accreditation and improving overall risk management.

- *Education and training*: More and more educational institutes need to impart necessary education focused on the events and catering industry, to develop the necessary skill set. The fast growing industry also needs the right minds to steer its future. It is not only hands on creative job but also a methodological calculative planned job which needs a specific skill set.

- Sabbas Joseph, President, EEMA, mentions that India has been doing well economically and there is an interest in its culture and people. As India will grow, this opportunity will grow for every aspect of the Indian events industry. The events industry is best poised to capitalize on this emerging opportunity (Ernst & Young, 2015). He also mentions that India is no longer just a market place for this industry and there is a urgent need for a new world order. The one in which event company's work in sync with the Indian government, to create event calendars that drives tourism and related industries, such as hotels, airlines, retail outlets, etc. (Ernst & Young, 2015).

- There is a need for this industry to work on acquiring the right talent, managing operational costs, demonstrating a high return on investment to marketers and increasing the transparency in operations.
- Profit margins are expected to decline from an average of 16–13% over the next 2 years, pertaining to the growth in the overall costs by 12% and payroll costs by 15%, as the companies are expected to increase their average number of employees from 84 to 104 (Ernst & Young, 2015).

All said and done, event management and catering businesses in India will continue to demonstrate high growth in the coming decade. The momentum in shift toward organized status is also likely to continue. It will be interesting if global event management companies make a move to find foot hold in this emerging market.

KEYWORDS

- catering
- event management
- wedding planners
- Indian wedding
- halwai
- ODC

REFERENCES

Business Line. *IPO of Catering Firm Cawasji Opens Next Week*, 24 September 2015. Available at: http://www.thehindubusinessline.com/markets/stock-markets/ipo-of-catering-firm-cawasji-opens-next-week/article7686053.ece.

CondeNastTraveller. *The Best Wedding Destinations: Where to Say I Do*, 2015. Available at: http://www.cntraveler.com/galleries/2014-12-29/destination-weddings-most-popular-places-to-say-i-do-jamaica-las-vegas-italy/6.

Ernst & Young. *Making Experiences in India, The Indian Events and Activation Industry*, 2015. Available at: http://www.ey.com/Publication/vwLUAssets/EY-making-experiences-in-india/$FILE/EY-making-experiences-in-india.pdf.

India Fillings. *How to Start a Catering Business*, 26 May 2015. Available at: http://www.indiafilings.com/learn/how-to-start-a-catering-business/.

MyNewsDesk. *An Overview of Indian Industry of Catering Services*, 2010. Available at: http://www.mynewsdesk.com/in/pressreleases/an-overview-of-indian-industry-of-catering-services-468222 (last accessed 10 September 2015).

CHAPTER 13

GENERATION Z AND SPECIALIST COFFEE SHOPS IN INDIA: A PERSPECTIVE OF THE NEEDS, MOTIVES, AND ISSUES OF GENERATION Z

DURGAMOHAN MUSUNURI*

Bhavan's Usha & Lakshmi Mittal Institute of Management, New Delhi, India

*E-mail: durgamohan27@gmail.com

CONTENTS

Abstract 300

13.1 Introduction 300

13.2 Liberalization of the Indian Economy 301

13.3 India's Tryst with Coffee 302

13.4 Coffee Drinking in India 303

13.5 Consumer Shopper Typologies 315

13.6 Conclusions and Recommendations 321

Keywords 322

References 322

ABSTRACT

India is an important constituent of the BRICS countries that drives the world economy today. It is not a farfetched idea to say that India will lead the BRICS countries in growth in the next 10 years. It will be driving global economic growth due to its large population, consequent growing demand for goods and services, and most important a government with pragmatic policies.

In this context, any global organization would like to enter the Indian market to set up base and be part of the growth story. Specialist coffee shops are no exception. Several global brands like "Costa Coffee," "Starbucks," Indian brands with pan-Indian presence like "Café Coffee Day," regional brands and local brands all together have a presence in India and compete with each other for a bigger market share.

Generation Z is loosely defined as those born after 1990 and consequently have entered the job market or are still students. This group that was born after the liberalization of the Indian economy is a group of consumers, who have changed consumption patterns, experienced a wide variety of choices available in the market place, are tech-savvy and consequently no strangers to global products and services offered by global corporations.

This chapter explores the current status of the specialist coffee shops in India, the needs, motives of generation Z, and finally the issues this generation has vis-à-vis these coffee shops.

13.1 INTRODUCTION

India, a country that experienced varied conquests and the resulting change in the rulers and ruling elite, had a propounded impact on the way of life and the economic status of the country. These rulers influenced the culture of the country in their own inimitable way leaving a lasting impression on the norms, value systems, customs, and practices of the Indian Society. India was also a host to one of four ancient urban civilizations, namely, the Indus Valley Civilization or Harappan Civilization, which existed between 2500 and 1700 BCE (Indus Civilization, 2015). The present day Indian society is in existence for more than 2500 years based on the fact that Gautama Buddha lived between 563 and 483 BC in the Indo-Nepalese region (The Life of Buddha, 2015).

India was ruled by the Mughals between 1526 and 1858 (Mughal Dynasty, 2015). Thereafter, India came under the direct rule of the British crown after a failed Indian mutiny (called the First war of Independence) in the year 1858. The British ruled India till 1947 (India Profile—Timeline, 2015). She gained independence from the British on the August 15, 1947 and at that time was a major commodity exporter. One of the important commodities that were exported from India was coffee. Even though India's exports have become diverse over all these years, coffee still remains an important export commodity.

In the world's comity of nations, India occupies a unique position as the second most populous country in the world and at the same time is the world's largest democracy. India is also an important member country of the BRICS group of nations. BRICS stands for a group of five major emerging economies namely, Brazil, Russia, India, China, and South Africa. This was originally a group of four countries and in the year 2010 South Africa was included. BRIC the acronym was coined by Jim O'Neill of Goldman Sachs, while referring to the investment opportunities in emerging econo- mies. These five countries constitute 42% of the world population, 26% of the geographical territory, and 27% of the world's Gross Domestic Product, which indicates the importance of these countries in the world economy (BRICS in Numbers, 2015).

13.2 LIBERALIZATION OF THE INDIAN ECONOMY

1991 is a watershed year for the Indian economy in the post independent era as a combination of economic factors, especially the acute balance of payments crisis led to unprecedented economic reforms. Thus, began a new era of liberalization, with the emphasis shifting from import substitution industrialization and the dominance of public sector undertakings, in indus- trial activity to promote and facilitate investments. The reforms were related to the following, which aptly describes the economic policy, trade policy, etc., prior to 1991:

- Dominance of the public sector in industrial activity,
- discretionary controls on industrial investment and capacity expansion,
- trade and exchange controls,
- limited access to foreign investment, and
- public ownership and regulation of the financial sector (India's Economic Reforms, 2016).

The reforms of 1991 were initiated in the areas of industrial policy, trade policy, foreign direct investment, agriculture, infrastructure, and the financial sector. The industrial policy saw a transformation from one of excessive governmental controls of what to produce, where to produce, how to produce, and how much to produce (apart from reserving 18 industries solely for the public sector) to a complete dismantling of the licensing system. Consequently, the government gradually transformed itself from an entrepreneur to regulator and facilitator. Simultaneously, the trade policy was also liberalized, wherein the negative list of items for import have been pruned considerably and at the same time the tariffs were gradually reduced. The import policy licensing was done away, thereby removing the quantitative restrictions on imports. The Indian Rupee was made fully convertible on the current account, facilitating imports. Foreign direct investment was liberalized, that now allows 100% foreign ownership in many industries except certain sectors. Procedures for obtaining permissions have been simplified by listing industries, which are eligible for automatic approval up to a specified level of foreign equity participation (Ahluwalia, 2002).

These reforms have increased the competition in the market and the customer has a wider choice today. Even the liberalization process was a gradual one adopted by the Indian government, and it has had a positive impact on the economy. The Indian economy experienced higher growth rates that were unheard of previously. This liberalization has impacted the restaurant industry including coffee shops too, with a number of global restaurant and coffee shop chains starting their businesses in India.

13.3   INDIA'S TRYST WITH COFFEE

Coffee is not native to India and was introduced 400 years ago by a saint called Baba Budan. The story goes that Baba Budan traveled from India to Mecca on a pilgrimage. He stopped at a street stall in Arab land for some refreshments and had a dark sweet liquid called "Qahwa." The liquid refreshed him so much that he wanted to take it back to his people in India. However, the local law did not allow anyone to carry it. Baba Budan had surreptitiously carried seven seeds strapped to his stomach and brought those seeds to India. He planted these seeds in the hills of Chikmaglur in the state of Karnataka, India. Thus, the coffee plant was born in India (Coffees of India, 2015). In the ensuing period of 400 years since Baba Budan planted those seven coffee seeds, many others have influenced the growth of coffee plantations in India.

The Dutch started growing coffee in the Malabar region in the state of Kerala, in southern India. The British were responsible for setting up an Arabica (a coffee variety) plantations in the hilly regions of South India, as they found the climatic conditions to be suitable for growing the coffee crop. The plantation was started by an enterprising British manager called J. H. Jolly, which led to a proliferation of coffee plantations in South India. Presently, India produces 16 varieties of coffees, which are grown in 13 distinct coffee growing regions. Traditionally, coffee is grown in the Western Ghats region of Karnataka, Tamil Nadu, and Kerala. These are termed as the traditional areas for growing coffee. Nontraditional areas of Andhra Pradesh, Odisha, and the north-eastern regions of India are also cultivating coffee. The liberalization of the Indian economy even touched coffee and coffee growers, wherein the government allowed coffee growers to market their own produce rather than sell to a central pool (Origin of Coffee, 2016).

The two major coffee varieties that are grown in India are Arabica and Robusta. Arabica has a delicate flavor and a balanced aroma with a sharp, sweet taste. Robusta has a strong taste, a grainy essence, and have twice the level of caffeine compared to Arabica. Robusta are preferred in espressos, because of their strong taste and the cream they assist in generating (Coffee Varieties, 2016).

Coffee production in India has reached 327,000 metric tons (MT) in 2014–2015, from 18,893 t in 1950–1951. The Robusta variety accounted for 229,000 MT amounting to 70% of the production and Arabica 98,000 MT making up the balance 30%. With this production, India became the seventh largest producer of coffee in the world (Coffee Statistics, 2015). In the year 2015–2016, coffee production is set to record 355,600 t, which will be the highest till date (India Set to Record Highest Coffee Production in 2015–16, 2015).

13.4 COFFEE DRINKING IN INDIA

India has been a nation of tea drinkers for centuries, except for some states of Southern India like Tamil Nadu, Andhra Pradesh, and parts of Karnataka. Coffee drinking was much lower compared to tea. Figures for 2010 show that Indians drank 837,000 tons of tea compared to 108,000 t of coffee. With the advent of coffee shops, coffee is slowly penetrating the traditional tea drinking regions of India. However, Indians drank 163.7 cups of tea per capita in 2014 and 176.6 cups in 2015, as compared to coffee, which accounted for 15.6 cups per capita in 2014 and 16.6 cups per capita in 2015

(Vaidyanathan, 2012; Chandran, 2015). Nelson (2013) article in the newspaper The Telegraph titles "India's tea and coffee wars" stated that, India has been associated with tea for more than 100 years and the British survived on it. However, the dominance of tea is being challenged in recent years by the Indian middle class love for café latte, with the rise of home grown western style coffee bars. The author quoted, that the head of a major coffee firm, said: "There is no doubt that coffee has gained significant popularity across India in the last few decades. Chains like Coffee Cafe Day, Barista and others have a widespread presence in all Indian cities, which makes it evident that people in India like coffee." The per capita coffee consumption in India is 80 g/year, whereas it is 8 kg/year in developed countries. The size of the café market was estimated at USD 290 million in 2013 and is expected to grow at a CAGR of 20% and reach USD 725 million by 2018 (Nusra, 2013).

13.4.1 SPECIALTY COFFEE

Specialty coffee, a term that originated in the United States, describes the range of coffee products sold in dedicated coffee shops so that their offerings could be differentiated from coffee available in supermarkets and retail outlets. As of today, specialty refers to coffee beverages and coffee bean sold in coffee bars and cafés. The range offered includes high quality coffee of single origin and blends, unconventional coffees and coffees with an unusual background. Due to the proliferation of specialty coffee shops and the expansion of the range of specialty coffee products into supermarkets, the term has lost its specificity. Specialty coffee has become a generic label for coffees that are perceived as different by the consumers or command a premium price (The Meaning of Specialty, 2015).

13.4.2 SPECIALTY COFFEE SHOPS

The concept of a coffee shop is a recent phenomenon in India. Earlier in the 1980s and 1990s, coffee shops existed but were restricted to the 24-h coffee shops in luxury hotels, which were out of bounds for majority of the population due to their exclusivity and very high prices. The new millennium saw the entry of specialty coffee shops into the Indian market, to start with in major cities and then in Tier-II cities. The major coffee chains of the world as well as home-grown ones have established their outlets. Coffee is now competing against tea in these cafes, especially among younger consumers. Increasing disposable incomes and a willingness to consume food and drink outside their homes, are the reasons fueling this growth. Some of the major ones are as follows:

Café Coffee Day: CCD as it is fondly called by its patrons or customers, a home-grown coffee chain, started by V. G. Siddhartha, son of a coffee plantation owner. It opened its first café in Bangalore in 1996. It has over 1550 cafes all over India and growing at around 150 outlets per year, a pace difficult for other coffee chains to catch-up quickly. CCD also has around 25,000 company-owned vending machines at 1000 locations within the premises of firms in 350 cities; that serve a billion cups of beverages per year (Rai, 2016). It is now the largest chain of coffee shops in India and having outlets in Prague, Vienna, and Kuala Lumpur (Siddhartha, 2016).

Costa Coffee: Devyani International Ltd, an Indian company brought Costa Coffee to India in 2005. Two Italian brothers started Costa in 1971 with their unique coffee roasting style, based on their Italian background. Whitbread PLC, UK's leading hospitality chain owns Costa now. Costa Coffee operates 90+ outlets in all formats that cover shopping malls, airports, business hubs, highways, hospitals and the high streets too. The number of outlets is going increase in the coming years under an ambitious growth plan drawn up by Devyani International Ltd (Our Business, 2016).

Barista Lavazza: The chain was established on 2000 as "Barista," Indian in origin was taken over by the Italian coffee products manufacturer "Lavazza" in 2008. It operates a chain of espresso coffee bars (around 160 outlets all over India) under the name: "Barista Lavazza." Apart from the basic coffee, it offers espressos, lattes, cappuccino, and pastries (India Coffee Annual, 2014).

Café Pascucci: Café Pascucci, an Italian coffee brand opened its first outlet in Bangalore in 2013. Madhura Beverages, Bangalore, the master franchisee has plans to set up 60 outlets (India Coffee Annual, 2014) moving forward.

Di Bella Coffee India: The Australian chain is presently operating 11 outlets, 8 in Mumbai, and 3 in Hyderabad and plans to open outlets in 4 more cities soon (Australia's Ultimate Coffee Experience, 2016).

Gloria Jean's: Gloria Jean's Coffees, another Australia-owned specialty coffee company started in 1996, entered the Indian market with the Landmark group of Dubai. It was having 16 outlets before it ended the franchise agreement with Landmark group and most of the outlets have been shut down, others converted to different brands (India Coffee Annual, 2014; Tiwari, 2014).

The Coffee Bean & Tea Leaf: The largest privately held chain of specialty coffee and tea stores in United States; it has 27 outlets in India (India Coffee Annual, 2014; http://locations.coffeebean.com/#/map, 2016).

Starbucks: The American chain entered the Indian market in 2012 as a joint venture with Tata Global Beverages. It has presently 40 outlets in India, and growing fast.

Javagreen: Reliance Group, the Indian Conglomerate, started Javagreen in 2003 this Indian chain of in-store cafes. It has 40 outlets across eight cities in India.

Mocha: Another Indian chain started in Mumbai in December 2001 has 20 outlets.

Brewberrys Café: It has 37 stores across India and started its operations in Vadodara, Gujarat.

Coffee N U: In the year 2008, it opened its first outlet in Bangalore and currently has 35 outlets across India.

BRU World Café: Hindustan Unilever Ltd. started this chain as an extension of its coffee brand BRU. It has six outlets.

Cuppa Joe: Umbrella Hospitality launched Cuppa Joe in 2012 in Mumbai. It has plans of expansion.

Qwiky's Coffee: There are 22 company-owned outlets mostly in South India.

Coffee World: The chain has seven outlets in India (India Coffee Annual, 2014).

13.4.3   COFFEE SHOPS AND COFFEE CULTURE

The coffee café culture is growing in India with hundreds of coffee shops influenced by the developed West setting shop across India, in both metros, mini-metros, and other Tier-II cities. As illustrated above, there are more than 16 coffee chains operating in India with number of outlets ranging from 6 to 1550 (approximately) and offering coffee in its various forms, and tailor-made snacks that go with the coffee and the location of the outlet.

In an article by Vaidyanathan (2012), the author states, that the way Indians socialize has changed with the advent of coffee shops. Students in Mumbai go to coffee shops to just hang out. They don't have many places to hang out and spend hours sitting in these coffee shops, as these outlets have no objection to it. Coffee shops also serve a range of coffees—mochas, lattes, espressos, iced coffees, etc. The bar culture in India is limited and is also not acceptable to the society, coffee shops have provided a safe and socially acceptable place for young people to share a drink. These coffee shops have facilitated the country's dating culture, which are considered as a place away from the prying eyes of the parents. The author quotes a graduate who said, that it is a perfect place to discuss college work than sitting on a bench drinking tea. A leading columnist and social commentator is of the view that these coffee shops have made café culture more accessible and thus attract the young crowd, who could hang out in a relaxed atmosphere. The commentator further stated that these coffee shops are seen as a lifestyle to aspire for and is very popular with the young generation.

Sharma (2015) quoting the CEO of Pan India Food Solutions, the franchisee in India for the US chain Coffee Bean and Tea Leaf (CBTL), commented that coffee consumption is becoming a lifestyle for the young and is largely building café culture. Higher incomes and greater urbanization are the reasons for permeation of the coffee culture. Coffee shops have become the hub for a multitude of people like corporate employees, teenagers, couples, artists, expats, etc. They are used as a meeting place and for holding business meetings, due to their ambience thereby coffee is not an impulse buy for them. A director of Brew Berrys Hospitality that runs "Brewberrys Cafes" is also of the same view, that rising per capita income, increased literacy and rapid urbanization are the reasons for the tremendous growth being experienced by the coffee chains. People expect a gourmet coffee experience due to their global exposure. He further stated that coffee shops serve as social hubs for the youth with steady disposable incomes, serve a basic emotional need of a refuge between office and home, thus becoming a necessity for all. Coffee shops create a meeting place for people and provide the ambience for people to hang out and spend quality time. Nusra (2013) indicates that the COO of Mocha is of the opinion that café culture is growing because it is aspirational, an experience to enjoy, and a meeting place to meet colleagues or have business meetings.

Smith (2015) describes coffee shops as places where intimate groups of well-dressed sophisticated people are in conversation or looking into their computing devices, perched on narrow wooden benches with an unapologetic pretension. He is of the view, that these people are maintaining a well-established English tradition that existed since the 18th century. Coffee houses have been remarkably consistent all these centuries and even today represent fashionable sophistication. They had provided and continue to provide space, where people can meet and converse and that is worth celebrating. The tradition of the 18th century continues to flourish even in India, as the coffee houses in India, be it Indian or global, do follow these traditions and people continue to have the same perceptions about them.

Back in 2005 itself, when coffee houses were still in their infancy in India, coffee houses were considered as places to socialize, to listen to music and read on one side and on the other to discuss and finalize business deals and conduct interviews too. The CEO of Café Mocha points out that call centers and the consequent night shift professionals added to the people working during day time is also one of the factors responsible for the growth of coffee houses. People shifting to big cities from small towns in search of employment are another segment that is fueling the growth. These people need a place to socialize with other who share their interests and are of the same age (Branded Coffee Houses a Rage in India, 2005).

The coffee shops, which started opening in many cities since the late 1990s, have become an integral part of the Indian way of life. The ambience, plush sofas, music, free internet, and casual atmosphere attract people to the coffee shops. A fashion designer and an entrepreneur is a regular at one of the outlets of Coffee Bean and Tea Leaf, even though she drinks tea there. She likes the comfortable environment, wireless connectivity, central location, and the quality of food that is served there. She also holds business meetings there. For an engineering student, it is a place to chill out and he likes to go to coffee shops for the ambience, good seating, and to watch football matches. For an advertising professional going to coffee shops is a change from the office environment. It is a less expensive option compared to restaurants for meeting people. For some school students too, coffee shops have become a meeting place and a part of their social life (Thirani, 2012).

The above literature points out that coffee houses (cafes) are patronized by people due to the following reasons:

1. It is a change from the office atmosphere.
2. It is a convenient meeting place and an integral part of social life.
3. A place to socialize, meet, and listen to music.
4. Suitable to conduct interviews, hold business meetings, and work on business deals.
5. They serve the basic emotional need of a refuge between home and office.
6. It is a place to "just hangout" and spend quality time.
7. It is a safe and socially acceptable place, as the bar culture is not socially widely acceptable in India.
8. They serve good coffee, gourmet coffee, and delicious snacks.
9. The ambience and the environment of the coffee shops is good.
10. They are affordable and cheaper than normal restaurants.

11. Visitors can spend hours in a coffee shop without any hindrance or disturbance.

Coffee shops serve the compelling need to socialize or meet others. In India, it is all the more important, as the Indian culture is a relationship-oriented culture, and consequently Indians lay a lot of importance on establishing and maintaining relationships. In metros and mini-metros socializing as it exists, that is, visiting each other at one's residences has become a herculean task due to the distances one has to travel. Here, coffee shops serve the purpose of a common and easy to access meeting point.

13.4.4   GENERATION X, Y, AND Z

Every generation has its own characteristics. They have been affected by changes in the world and vice versa, they changed the world. Soon a new generation will dominate the world and we need to prepare for it. Huge amount of information is now available on a cell phone. The old standards and ways need to be redesigned and adapted to the new demands. The pessimistic point of view toward the millennial generation is that they are lazy, irresponsible, impatient, apathetic, selfish, disrespectful, and even lost. But from the optimistic view, they are often labeled as open minded, social, innovative, energetic, ambitious, confident, motivated, and smart. There seems to be one common thread; they love to buy. Consumer behavior is the main field and source for customer relationship management (CRM) programs. It is important to evaluate and understand the patterns and motives behind shopping attitudes. The main purpose of this research is to find out, if the shopping patterns of Generation Z are different from other generations. The secondary purpose of this study is to analyze if brand loyalty of Generation Z is associated with any other elements, related to their purchasing behavior.

The changes in consumption patterns can best be understood best by studying the buying behavior of different generations. Generational determined lifestyles and social values, exercise as much influence on buying and purchasing as more commonly understood demographic factors like income, education, and gender do, perhaps, even more. Different generations and demographic consumer groups are exposed to: (a) different social and economic opportunities and the operational barriers, (b) different types of technological activities, (c) different social perceptions, different community norms, and (d) different life experiences and events.

Consumer motivation and purchase engagements often lie below the surface of age. Generational cohorts comprise people who are born during a particular period, and whose life courses correspond to each other.

Generational cohort marketing has become a useful tool in segmenting markets since such members share similar values have different experiences, which influence their values, preferences, and shopping behavior. The buying power of the baby boomer generation in the United States can be taken as an example, since it has been a driver for the economy. Although it is still a dominant market segment, there is another even larger segment that spends a significant amount on consumer goods. This group is called Generation Z and has become a major force in the marketplace.

Generation Z is three times more the size of Generation X or Y and constitutes the largest market since the baby boomers. Determining specific factors that influence Generation Z, their purchasing attitudes and patterns has become an important focus of consumer research due to their potential spending power, their ability to be trendsetters, adoption to new products, and potential for becoming lifetime customers.

The Second World War and the end of the war are important milestones in the history of mankind. It brought about a radical departure in the way the nations of the world resolve their disputes, and the consequent economic development that the world experienced and continues to experience. The war had an indelible impact on the people also. Those who were born after the war were different in their attitudes, thinking and actions from their predecessors. Generation X people were born approximately between 1960s and 1980s, who did not participate in the Second World War but are a witness to the effects of war. They are the children of the baby boomers generation. They were part of the economic reconstruction of their nations and at the same time lived in an era of relative peace, even though cold war existed during that time. There are many subsets among Generation X, depending on the time period they were born into the world.

Generation Y people born approximately between 1981 and 1994, also called the Millennials, are the generation that was a witness to the advent of new digital technologies and to a large extent, their lives are molded by technological advances.

Generation Z is the group that is relevant for the present study and hence dealt with in detail in the subsequent pages.

The need to know understand these generations or demographic segments arises from the fact that they are the consumers for various goods and services. However, their way of thinking, motivation, needs, tastes and preferences, etc., are different and their processes of satisfying these needs are also different.

13.4.4.1   GENERATION Z

Generation Z is loosely defined as those born between the years 1990/1995 and 2012 (Careers, 2016; Schroer, 2015), who consequently have entered the job market, about to enter the job market or are still students. This group that was born in the era of globalization on one hand and the liberalization of the Indian economy, is a group of consumers who have changed consumption patterns, experienced a wide variety of choices available in the market place, who are tech-savvy and consequently no strangers to global products and services offered by global corporations. It is a generation that will form the customer base of any business organization for their products and services. They are an integral part of the internet and IT revolution, and the consequent availability of information at a mouse click, and are adept at using these enormous resources to their advantage.

Kapoor (2012) in an article titled "The desi (indigenous) definition of Gen X, Y, Z" states that the western definition of Generation Z as those born in early 1990s and afterward are not aware of a world without internet or cell phone. The author states further, that the terms Generation X, Y, Z are used incorrectly and interchangeably in India. Most Indians do not understand these terms and are mere euphemisms for the youth of India. Some experts are of the view, that if one has to use these terms they should be restricted to the small urban middleclass population.

However, Dr. Kaur, R. Director, Center of Global South Asian Studies is of the view, that one should not look at the time periods to define Generation X, Y, Z; but should look at the qualities associated with them. Generation Z are those youngsters growing up now with a range of digital possibilities, that were not existing a decade ago. Kakkar gives a different nomenclature to different generations in India as "Silvers" people in their 50s and 60s, Gen Y as people in their 30s and 40s, and Gen X or the generation next, who are in the age group of 17–19 years, finishing college, completing higher studies, and who are taking up jobs. Jodhka, Department of Sociology, Jawaharlal Nehru University (JNU) Delhi is of the view, that Generation X, Y, Z is a completely western concept and pertains to United States and applicable to the entire country. In India, it applies to the urban middle class only, who constitute around 25% of the Indian population.

According to a study carried out concerning hiring and retaining generation Z employees that is those born after 1990, employers should offer flexible timings without communication gaps, better learning and career opportunities. It is challenging and meaningful work that acts as the biggest motivator. Fifty-two percent of the organizations studied stated, that work-life balance matters to Generation Z employees. They seek to make their hobbies their jobs. Forty-one percent of the employers surveyed opined that career growth and learning opportunities will retain employees and money is not the main motivator. They prefer face-to-face communication instead of e-mail and instant messaging. Forty-nine percent of the employers found that the most effective way of communication in the workplace is face-to-face communication. Another expert stated that the Generation Z professional is not aware of a world without internet, mobiles or social networking sites like Facebook. They were born into it and grew in a hyper-connected world with information available at their fingertips (Careers, 2015).

As regards engaging the Generation Z buyers, global brands like Puma, Starbucks, and Lego are actively engaging with this generation in innovative ways. "Creative factory," a shoe-making studio is one initiative, where buyers get hands-on in the creative process and can design their own sneakers. "My Starbucks ideas" is another innovative method to engage Generation Z. Coffee drinkers are invited to make suggestions on how to make Starbucks' products, services, or any other aspect better. The company implements 13–17 suggestions out of the thousands received every year. This shows that Generation Z informs and induces change in large organizations. As Generation Z is very different from other generations, marketers need to refocus their efforts to engage them. By 2020, Generation Z will constitute 40% of the consumers of the United States, Europe, and the BRIC (Brazil, Russia, India, China) countries and 10% of the rest of the world. Another head of business operations is of the view, that Generation Z represents informed buyers and has the tools and techniques to compare products and hunt for the best prices. They have the power to go from one retailer to another, share information on social media, and discuss with friends before making the buying decision. This is the ecosystem they have created, in which marketers need to find their space. This generation wants to be involved from conception, design, creation on one side to marketing and retailing on the other. Customization is the key in attracting Generation Z customers, providing a platform for the customers' individuality and expression. Retailing needs to fundamentally change its way of engaging with Generation Z. The different facets of retail like store design, online operations, marketing, and logistics should not be separate departments, but must be part of a holistic approach to retailing. A new post of Chief Experience Officer needs to be created to manage holistic operations (Rai, 2014).

Generation Z is the first generation that has broken down generational barriers. The same technology is being used in work and personal lives by people of all ages. For the first time, technology is unifying generations. Generation Z is having its impact on social change, education, diversity, collaboration, productivity and ano-sharing (anonymous sharing). Generation Z wants to change the world. Unprecedented access to information makes them one of the most knowledgeable generations in history. They are taking up causes such as environmental issues, social injustices, alleviating poverty, etc. This generation's lingua franca includes words like crowd sourcing, crowd funding, inclusive class rooms, etc., indicating that they thrive in group settings and are better team players than any other generation. The Generation Z workforce will be made up of motivated, resourceful, hard-working individuals, who are more diverse, more technologically savvy and have more information at their fingertips and want to make the world a better place (Schoenberger, 2015).

Generation Z as a group, is born since the start or just before the start of the millennium. They are smarter and more prudent than Generation Y. Quoting a report by a US advertising agency, they are described as the "Screenagers" or "the first tribe of true digital natives." They want to make the world a better place and are also keen to take care of their money (Wallop, 2014).

The Generation Z that exists in the USA is that group of people that were born in the mid-1990s and constitute 68 million people approximately. They display many distinctive characteristics. From the point of view of demographics, they are ethnically more diverse than any other previous generation. Caucasians constitute only 54% of this generation, as per US census projections of 2008. This leads to ethnic foods becoming mainstream foods and the differences between ethnic and nonethnic menus becoming nonexistent. They expect the cuisine to combine various ethnic influences. As they were raised in an era of economic distress, their buying behavior will be different; first, spending will be conservative and measured. They are likely to maintain high value expectations. As their own families experienced financial hardships, they will have a pronounced interest in social justice and philanthropy. The most important characteristic will be their relationship with technology and are aptly described as digital natives. This has an impact on the way companies need to engage with them. They expect more frequent communications through multiple channels, with built-in feedback loops replacing the one way communication that has existed till now. This generation uses technology and information extensively, which leads to well researched and informed purchase decisions. Companies need to practice transparency and provide more information to satisfy them. Real time experience and multitasking define their lifestyles. This generation has started to expect customized experience as new capabilities in filtering, predictive analysis, and adaptive technologies are widely used (Yohn, 2013). According to Crouch (2015) employers should take note of Generation Z, which is as focused and driven as the millenials, but at the same time their aspirations are different from the millenials. Quoting a work survey conducted in the USA, the authors further state that for 53% of the current student view the quantum of education loan a major consideration while deciding their schooling and careers paths. The greatest aspiration for 32% of the Generation Z surveyed is to be in their dream job in 10 years from now. In spite of the debt incurred for education, for 36% growth opportunities rather than salary is an important consideration for taking up the first job. This is followed by fulfilling work and stability (19%), friendly work environments (10%), flexible work schedules (7%), and highest salary (6%) was ranked lower. The author concluded that Generation Z has big aspirations are motivated to climb the ladder and have a desire to learn.

Generation Z is described as hyper-connected consumers, who make up 26% of the US population and have $44 billion to spend with their purchasing power growing increasingly every day. Technology is in their life and blood. At the global level, they are around 2 billion of them and reaching them is a challenge that marketers face, as they have to break through the extreme digital clutter. The author outlines six rules for brands and their marketers to connect with this generation, which are as follows:

1. Show them your true (weird, quirky, funny) brand personality, that is, show them your relatable side.
2. Have no filter—authenticity rules. Create content that is real.
3. Find a cause, because it's important to make a difference. Show them that the brands and marketers care about the issues that Gen Z focuses upon.
4. Get social in the channels where Gen Z lives. Social media engagement on the highest level needs to be perfected by brands. There is an outlet for every facet of their identity. I am reserved on Facebook (if and when I actually use it). I am informed on Twitter. I am a showoff on Snapchat. I am a troll on Reddit. I am creative on Instagram.
5. Find their tribes. Be the conduit, help them find others like them, but on their terms. It is acceptable to ask but never ok to assume.

6. Break through the clutter. They have more opportunities to be distracted, overstimulated, and overscheduled.

Access to everything, everywhere and the expectations that holds for any experience makes Gen Z different from other generations. They have access to massive amounts of information and at the same time absorb it too. Brands need to remember that they don't need you. They want to collaborate with you as long as you speak their language (Alberti, 2015).

Having discussed Generation Z from various perspectives and taken note of the various viewpoints, one can describe or characterize Generation Z as follows:

1. Generation Z is made up of people born after 1990.
2. They are born in the digital age, experienced a wide variety of choices, and are tech-savvy.
3. From an Indian perspective, they are no strangers to global products; the concept of Generation Z applies to the urban middle class and constitute 25% of the Indian population, that is, around 31 million as compared to 68 million in the United States.
4. From an employer's perspective, they prefer face-to-face communication.
5. Brands need to actively engage them in innovative ways.
6. Customization is the key to attract these customers.
7. They thrive in group settings and are better team players.
8. They are motivated, resourceful, and hard-working individuals.
9. They are hyperconnected people.
10. They want to make the world a better place and are keen to take care of their money.

13.5 CONSUMER SHOPPER TYPOLOGIES

Research reveals that at various levels of marketing in theory and in practice, the consumer is central to all activities. It is important for marketers to have an updated knowledge of the various factors influencing the decisions of consumers; in order to facilitate both the successful delivery of products as well as the retention of customers in the marketplace. Shopper typologies define general consumer types, such as price-oriented shoppers, problem-solving shoppers, impulse shoppers, and convenience shoppers. The shopper typologies approach seeks to categorize consumers into groups or types that are related to retail patronage as well as shopping orientations.

Shopping orientations are shopper's styles that place special emphasis on certain activities. Shopping orientation is recognized as a complex social, cultural and economic phenomenon. As such, the examination of an all-inclusive relationship amongst key variables in determining shopping orientations could provide diagnostic value to retailers in determining market segmentation. The basic premise of shopping orientation is that shoppers with different styles have different market behaviors, including the need for different information sources and different store preferences.

It is well established that the first taxonomy of consumer shopping typologies was suggested by Westbrook and Black (1985), which attempted to improve the understanding of motivation-based shopper typologies of adult female shoppers in department stores. This taxonomy stratified shopping styles into four classifications: the economic consumer, the personalizing consumer, the ethical consumer, and the apathetic consumer. Economic shoppers are characterized by a cautious approach to shopping, giving heightened attention to merchandise assortment, price and quality. Personalizing shoppers are those who seek personal relationships with retail personnel, whilst ethical shoppers are those who are willing to forgo lower prices and wider selections of goods in order to behave consistently with their moral beliefs. Finally, apathetic shoppers are those who purchase goods largely out of necessity, with the shopping activity holding no intrinsic interest.

Hafstrom et al. (1992) examined the taxonomy of shoppers and identified "perfectionism," "value consciousness," "brand consciousness," "novelty-fad-fashion consciousness," "shopping avoider-time saver-satisfier," and "confused support-seeking decision-maker" as the dominant shopping orientations amongst consumers. In this taxonomy, perfectionist consumers seek the very best quality products, have high standards and expectations of consumer goods and are concerned with the function and quality of products. Value-conscious consumers are price conscious, they look for the best value for their money and are likely to be comparison shoppers. Brand-conscious consumers are oriented toward expensive and well-known national brands and feel price is an indicator of quality. Novelty-fad-fashion-conscious consumers gain excitement and pleasure from seeking out new things and are conscious of new fashions and fads. Shopping avoider-time saver-satisfier consumers avoid shopping, make shopping trips rapidly, and may forgo some quality for time and convenience. Finally, the confused support-seeking decision-maker finds the marketplace confusing; they find brands alike and seek help from friends to make decisions.

Bae (2004) distinguished eight characteristics of consumer shopping orientations: perfectionist, brand conscious, novelty/fashion conscious, recreational/hedonic, price conscious/value-for-money, impulsive/careless, confused by over-choice, and habitual/loyal consumers. The perfectionist or quality-conscious consumers have a desire for high-quality products and a need to make the best or perfect choice, versus buying the first product or brand that is available. The brand-conscious consumer has the desire to purchase well-known national brands, higher-priced brands or the most advertised brands. The novelty/fashion-conscious consumer can be defined as a shopper who is aware of new styles, changing fashions and attractive styling, as well as having the desire to buy something exciting. The recreational/hedonic consumers are shoppers who enjoy shopping as a leisure-time activity. The price-conscious consumers aspire toward the best value, buying at sale prices or the lowest price. The impulsive/careless consumers can be described as shoppers who tend to make impulsive, unplanned, and careless purchases. The consumer confused by over-choice feels confused by product choices because of a proliferation of brands, stores, and consumer information. Finally, the habitual/brand-loyal consumers are described as consumers who have favorite brands and whose buying habits reveal that they consistently use the same store over time.

Based on the preceding discussion, it can be concluded that there is diversity in consumer shopping typologies. Consumers tend to display different shopping orientations, based upon their individual personalities and characteristics. They may have a unique focus when they enter a store and shop (McDonald, 1993). Some consumers consider a good price and trendy fashion, whilst others are interested in brand names with high quality. Depending on their wants, consumers customize their shopping orientations. Consumer confusion, however, often takes over when they encounter other choices immediately prior to making a specific selection.

13.5.1 METHODOLOGY

In social sciences, qualitative research or quantitative research methods can be used without impacting analysis or drawing conclusions and making recommendations. Qualitative research is used to obtain a deep understanding of an event or a specific organization. It generates data about human groups in social settings. Qualitative research lets meaning emerge from the participants. Firsthand experience, truthful reporting, and quotations of actual conversations are used to gain a better understanding (PPA 696 Research Methods, 2016).

According to a WHO publication, qualitative research is characterized by three features as given below:

1. An approach which seeks to describe and analyze the culture and behavior of humans and their groups from the point of view of those studied.
2. An emphasis on providing a comprehensive or holistic understanding of the social settings in which research is conducted.
3. A research strategy which is flexible and iterative (Resource Paper No. 3, 2015).

Focus group interviews are one of the methods used to get insights into a topic or get information. These focus group interviews are "generally anchored in a qualitative paradigm, reflecting a person-centered, holistic perspective for achieving depth of understanding of the participant's reality" (Hollis et al., 2002). Focus groups are "designed to obtain perceptions on a defined area of interest in a permissive, non-threatening environment" (Krueger, 1994).

Focus groups are group discussion involving people with the express purpose of discussing a specific topic of interest to the researcher. The researcher and/or moderator guide the participants of the focus group to discuss key issues of the research topic with considerable levels of focus and depth. These focus group discussions are very helpful in obtaining answers to questions like how, why, and what (Resource Paper No. 3, 2015).

An insider's view is provided by this methodology. Further inductive processes are used to analyze and interpret the views and opinions of participants. It is particularly useful for obtaining an insight into the participant's knowledge and experiences. This methodology can be used to explore on one hand what people think and on the other to examine how they think and why they think that way (Kitzinger, 1995). Thus, focus group interviews are a valuable means for distinguishing a range of perceptions regarding factors, that makes coffee shops popular among the Generation Z. Focus group interviews were selected over individual interviews keeping in view that "the dynamic interaction afforded by focus groups enables the eliciting of a diversity of views from participants and the immediate clarification of issues that affect this diversity" (Hollis et al., 2002).

Thereby, the study is used a qualitative method of conducting focus group interviews, which provided the researcher with an occasion to explore the stakeholders' perceptions by giving them a forum to express their opinions without the pressure of arriving at a consensus. The population consists of men and women born after 1990 and who are doing their graduation or post-graduation. Nonrandom sampling method (nonprobability sampling method) or snowballing sampling method was used to identify the respondents, who were then invited for the focus group interviews. The names and identities of the respondents were kept anonymous, so that they can interact openly and without any inhibitions and hindrances.

Each focus group was conducted within the broad focus group study parameters outlined by Krueger (1998a) with the help of question, that were developed using protocols and strategies expressed by him. Questions were largely open-ended and probes were used to gather richer details about the participant's experiences. Dichotomous questions and questions which required the participants to make noncontextual judgments were avoided (Hollis et al., 2002).

The focus group interviews were conducted at locations convenient to the participants. In order that the interviews remained focused on the topic, the researcher was the moderator, who also facilitated the group interaction. The proceedings of the discussions were collected by recording the discussions, with prior approval of the participants and then the recordings were transcribed following the principle of being true to the original.

The study parameters outlined by Kruger (1998a) were used for conducting each focus group with the help of questions. The questions were developed based on the inputs given by him. Open-ended questions were used and wherever necessary probed further to gather more information about the participant's views. Questions that are dichotomous and require making contextual judgment were not used (Hollis et al., 2002) at all.

13.5.2 DATA ANALYSIS

Thematic analysis was used to analyze the proceedings of the focus group interviews and to identify the common themes. Thematic analysis is a categorizing strategy for qualitative data. The data is reviewed; notes are made to start sorting the data into categories. It helps in moving the analysis from a broad reading of data to discovering patterns and developing themes (About Thematic Analysis, 2015). The six phases of thematic analysis as enunciated by Braun and Clarke (2006) are familiarizing yourself with the data, generating initial codes, searching for themes, reviewing themes, defining and naming themes, and producing the report. The findings of the data analysis are as follows:

13.5.3   FINDINGS

From the thematic analysis carried on the transcripts of the focus group interviews the following themes were delineated as

The themes are needs, ambience and/or environment, service, and prices.

The key terms and phrases used during the discussions by the participants are tabulated under different themes listed above, which are as follows:

Needs	Ambience and/or environment	Service	Issues	Products
Spending good quality time	Good ambience	Excellent service	Prices are very high	Varieties of coffee
For having fun	Air-conditioned, clean environment	Good customer service	Expensive	World class coffee
Outing with friends	Peaceful	Sophisticated staff	Sometime crowded	Tasty coffee
Chill out with friends	Friendly environment		Cost	Cold coffee and refreshments
Have coffee and talk to friends			Largely crowded	Delicious muffins
Spending time (time pass)			No problems at all	
For formal meetings			Prices have risen	
Simply to hangout				
Meeting friends				
Dating				
To be with friends				
To celebrate with family and friends				

Apart from the above key phrases used to describe their view on coffee shops, most of the participants of the focus group interviews have recommended CCD, because it is the least expensive option. However, few recommended other coffee shops, such as Starbucks and Barista.

The findings point out that coffee shops are frequented by Generation Z to meet friends, celebrate with family and friends, and to be with friends. They are places to chill out and to simply hangout. They consider the ambience as good, peaceful, and friendly. The varieties of coffee and the refreshments on offer are also the other factors that draw Generation Z to coffee shops. However, they also have certain issues like high prices, crowded environment, etc. These findings are largely in consonance with factors identified in published reports and literature as detailed elsewhere in this chapter.

13.6 CONCLUSIONS AND RECOMMENDATIONS

Generation Z is and will constitute the future customers and consumers of products and services offered by coffee shops. This generation is born and brought up in the digital era with easy access to information, and information overload too. As they are very well informed, the buying decisions will be based on facts and figures. Also this generation is very active on social media seeking and giving information, expressing thoughts and opinions, posting their experiences with different products and services on offer. In the light of this, coffee shops will need to be prudent enough to be transparent in their advertising campaign regarding their offerings, and make every effort to identify the changing needs of these customers and satisfy them. To cite an example, the ambience of coffee shops is very important for these customers, and the top management of coffee shops should ensure that the ambience continues to remain friendly, peaceful. Based on Bae's (2004) eight characteristics of consumer shopping orientations, one can conclude that Generation Z in the Indian context is the price conscious/value-for-money type to a large extent.

Some of the issues that came to the fore during the focus group interviews also need to be given due importance. In the Indian context, the perception of Generation Z is that the prices are high to very high. Here, a fine balance that has to be achieved between maintaining the quality of the product, ambience of the outlet, and the prices charged. It is a difficult task but certainly achievable. Most of the coffee shops have a presence on social media, which are used by Generation Z very frequently. Social media is to be used as a tool and vehicle to engage with Generation Z. Given the fact that Generation Z is very active on social media, this will yield benefits to the coffee shops in the long and short run.

Looking at India and the 31 million Generation Z, who is comparable to Generation Z of the United States and other developed countries in many ways, is a sizeable population. For them bars, where liquor is served, is still a taboo place to meet and is also expensive. The taboo aspect will continue to be a force, as it is part of the culture of the Indian society that draws people to coffee shops. Hence, the demand for products and services of coffee shops will continue to be in demand till such time the culture changes. However, changes in the norms and standards prescribed by the culture of a society, do not change as they are passed on from generation to generation and form the very basis of living. The relationship oriented culture of Indian society, where relationships are maintained and nurtured at any cost, coffee shops serve this need especially in big cities, where time is always at a premium. Lastly, coffee shops, Indian or global, will continue to dot the hinterland and thrive in the years to come, because of the unique products and services they offer and serve the needs of Generation Z, who have started earning or will soon have independent income.

KEYWORDS

- coffee shops
- food retail
- Generation Z
- Indian Coffee Shop
- hospitality industry
- consumer behavior

REFERENCES

Ahluwalia, M. S. Economic Reforms in India since 1991: Has Gradualism Worked? *Journal of Economic Perspectives* 2002, *16*(3), 67–88.

Alberti, B. *Still Obsessing over Millennials? Here are 6 Rules for Reaching Generation Z Your Next Best Customer*, 2015 [Online]. Available from: http://www.adweek.com/news/advertising-branding/still-obsessing-over-millennials-here-are-6-rules-reaching-generation-z-164882 (accessed on 26 December 2015).

Australia's Ultimate Coffee Experience, 2016 [Online]. Available from: http://www.dibellacoffee.in/aboutus.html (accessed on 10 January 2016).

Bae, S. *Shopping Pattern Differences of Physically Active Korean and American University Consumers for Athletic Apparel*, Doctoral Thesis, College of Education, Florida State University, 2004.

Branded Coffee Houses a Rage in India, 2005 [Online]. Available from: http://www.rediff.com/money/2005/jul/16spec1.htm (accessed on 01 January 2016).

Braun, V; Clarke, 2006. [Online]. Available from: http://dx.doi.org/10.1191/1478088706qp063oa (accessed on 01 January 2016).

BRICS in Numbers, 2015 [Online]. Available from: http://en.brics2015.ru/ (accessed on 31 December 2015).

Careers. *4 Ways to Attract and Retain Generation Z Employees in India*, 2015. [Online]. Available from: http://www.businessinsider.in/4-ways-to-attract-and-retain-generation-Z-employees-in-India/articleshow/48467727.cms (accessed on 31 December 2015).

Chandran, N. *Chai as it Might, Coffee Can't Topple Tea in India*, 2015 [Online]. Available from: http://www.cnbc.com/2015/12/01/tea-still-top-beverage-in-india-despite-cafe-coffee-days-rising-coffee-culture.html (accessed on 10 January 2016).

Coffee Statistics, 2015 [Online]. Available from: http://www.teacoffeespiceofindia.com/coffee/coffee-statistics (accessed on 02 January 2016).

Coffee Varieties, 2016 [Online]. Available from: http://www.teacoffeespiceofindia.com/coffee/india-coffees-varieties (accessed on 02 January 2016).

Crouch, B. *How will Generation Z Disrupt the Workplace?*, 2015 [Online]. Available from: http://fortune.com/2015/05/22/generation-z-in-the-workplace/ (accessed on 28 December 2015).

Coffees of India. European Coffee Report 2013/14, 2015 [Online]. Available from: www.ecf-coffee.org/images/European_Coffee_Report_2013-14.pdf (accessed on 29 December 2015).

Hafstrom, J. L.; Chae, J. S.; Chung, Y. S. Consumer Decision-making Styles: Comparison between United States and Korean Young Consumers. *J. Consum. Aff.* **1992,** *26*(1), 146–158. http://dx.doi.org/10.1111/j.1745-6606.1992. tb00020.x.

Hollis, V.; et al. Conducting Focus Groups: Purpose and Practicalities. *Br. J. Occup. Ther.* **2002,** *65*(1), 2–8.

http://locations.coffeebean.com/#/map, 2016 [Online] (accessed on 02 January 2016).

India Coffee Annual, 2014 [Online]. Available from: http://gain.fas.usda.gov/.../Coffee%20 Annual_New%20Delhi_India_5-15-2014 *(accessed on 28* December 2015)*.

India Profile—Timeline, 2015 [Online]. Available from: http://www.bbc.com/news/world-south-asia-12641776 (accessed on 02 October 2015).

India Set to Record Highest Coffee Production in 2015–16, 2015 [Online]. Available from: http://www.ndtv.com/india-news/india-set-to-record-highest-coffee-production-in-2015-16-774287 (accessed on 04 October 2015).

India's Economic Reforms, 2016 [Online]. Available from: http://indiainbusiness.nic.in/newdesign/index.php?param=economy_landing/217/2 (accessed on 02 January 2016).

Indus Civilization, 2015 [Online]. Available from: http://www.britannica.com/topic/Indus-civilization (accessed on 17 October 2015).

Kapoor, K. *The Desi Definition of Generation X, Y, Z*, 2012 [Online]. Available from: http://timesofindia.indiatimes.com/life-style/relationships/man-woman/The-desi-definition-of-Gen-X-Y-Z/articleshow/14386670.cms (accessed on 12 December 2015).

Kitzinger, J. Introducing Focus Groups. *BMJ* **1995,** *311*, 299–302.

Krueger, R. *Focus Groups: A Practical Guide for Applied Research*, 2nd ed. Sage Publication: Thousand Oaks, CA, 1994.

Mughal Dynasty, 2015 [Online]. Available from: http://www.britannica.com/topic/Mughal-dynasty (accessed on 02 October 2015).

Nelson, D., 2013 [Online]. *India's Tea and Coffee Wars.* Available from: http://www.telegraph.co.uk/news/worldnews/asia/india/10054158/Indias-tea-and-coffee-wars.html (accessed on 12 January 2016).

Nusra. *Growing Café Culture in India*, 2013 [Online]. Available from: http://www.restaurantindia.in/article/f-and-b-format/beverages/Growing-Cafe-Culture-in-India.a62/ (accessed on 20 January 2016).

Origin of Coffee, 2016 [Online]. Available from: http://www.teacoffeespiceofindia.com/coffee/coffee-origin (accessed on 02 January 2016).

Our Business, 2016 [Online]. Available from: http://www.dil-rjcorp.com/CostaCoffee.aspx (accessed on 12 January 2016).

PPA 696 Research Methods, 2016 [Online]. Available from: http://web.csulb.edu/~msaintg/ppa696/696quali.htm (accessed on 05 January 2016).

Rai, A. *Targeting Gen Z—What Marketers Need to Know*, 2014 [Online]. Available from: http://www.business-standard.com/article/management/targeting-gen-z-what-marketers-need-to-know-114092100690_1.html (accessed on 02 January 2016).

Rai, S. *Cafe Coffee Day, India's Biggest Cafe Chain & Starbucks rival, Headed For An IPO*, 2016 [Online]. Available from: http://www.forbes.com/sites/saritharai/2014/06/04/cafe-coffee-day-indias-biggest-cafe-chain-starbucks-rival-headed-for-an-ipo/ (accessed on January 2016).

Resource Paper No. 3, 1994 [Online]. Available from: www.who.int/tdr/publications/documents/qualitative -research.pdf (accessed on 14 August 2015).

Siddhartha, V. G., 2016 [Online]. Available from: http://www.forbes.com/profile/vg-siddhartha/(Accessed on 10 January 2016).

Schoenberger, A. *Grateful for Gen Z*, 2015 [Online]. Available from: http://www.huffingtonpost.com/entry/grateful-for-gen-z_b_7154278.html?section=india (accessed on 25 December 2015).

Schroer. W. J. *Generation X, Y, Z and Others*, 2015 [Online]. Available from: http://www.socialmarketing.org/newsletter/features/generation1.htm (accessed : 25th June 2015).

Sharma, A., 2015 [Online]. *Smell the Coffee* Available from: http://www.financialexpress.com/article/fhw/cover-story-fhw/smell-the-coffee/50704/ (accessed on 04 January 2016).

Smith,A. J. *Coffee Shops: the Hangout of Choice for 18th Century Hipsters*, 2015 [Online]. Available from: http://www.citymetric.com/horizons/coffee-shops-hangout-choice-18th-century-hipsters-1197 (accessed on 04 January 2016).

The Life of Buddha, 2015 [Online]. Available from: http://www.souledout.org/wesak/story-buddha.html (accessed on 23 October 2015).

The Meaning of Specialty, 2015 [Online]. Available from: http://www.thecoffeeguide.org/coffee-guide/niche-markets-environment-and-social-aspects/the-meaning-of-specialty/ (accessed on 09 October 2015).

Thirani, N. *Indian Chai Drinkers Embrace Coffee*, 2012 [Online]. Available from: http://india.blogs.nytimes.com/2012/01/31/india-nation-of-chai-drinkers-embraces-coffee/?_r=0 (accessed on January 2016).

Tiwari, A. K. *Australia's Gloria Jean's Coffee Ends India Franchise with Landmark group*, 2014 [Online]. Available from: http://www.dnaindia.com/money/report-australia-s-gloria-jean-s-coffee-ends-india-franchise-with-landmark-group-2044923 (accessed on 02 January 2016).

Vaidyanathan, R., 2012 [Online]. Available from: http://www.bbc.com/news/magazine-16932747 (accessed on 10 January 2016).

Wallop, H. *Gen Z, Gen Y, Baby Boomers—A Guide to the Generations*, 2014 [Online]. Available from: http://www.telegraph.co.uk/news/features/11002767/Gen-Z-Gen-Y-baby-boomers-a-guide-to-the-generations.html (accessed on 25 December 2015).

Westbrook, R. A.; Black, W. C. A Motivation Based Shopper Typology. *J. Retail.* **1985,** *61*(1), 78–103.

Yohn, D. L. *Don't Forget Gen Z*, 2013 [Online]. Available from: https://www.qsrmagazine.com/denise-lee-yohn/don-t-forget-gen-z (accessed on 25 December 2015).

CHAPTER 14

EPILOGUE AND FUTURE TRENDS OF THE INDIAN TOURISM AND HOSPITALITY INDUSTRY

SUDHANSHU BHUSHAN*

School of Management and Entrepreneurship, Vedatya Institute, Gurgaon, India

*E-mail: sudhanshusb@gmail.com

CONTENTS

14.1   Future Prospects and Trends of the Indian Hospitality Industry...351

Keywords 361

References...361

Web References...362

The hospitality and tourism industry is a significant revenue and employment generator in India; the massive population base is a huge potential for both inland and outbound travel. The number of departures is expected to touch 24.4 million by 2018, with international tourist arrivals showing a CAGR of 7% during the past 5 years. The Visa on Arrival facility extended to citizens of 180 countries along with the electronic visa authorization across the nine international airports will further boost travel and demand for hospitality services. The depreciating Indian currency against the American Dollar makes India an attractive travel destination for all travelers domestic and international. This chapter covers two distinct subjects in context to the Indian hospitality industry. In the first section, summaries of the 11 chapters have been highlighted, ranging from macro to micro-factors and challenges influencing the industry from the perspective of industry experts. Expected growth trends, innovation in food and beverages, growth of the mid-market budget hotel segment, the human resource and leadership crunch, changing consumer demands and service quality, tools of revenue management, the value of arts in family-run businesses, the contribution of events and catering, and the role of Generation Z are topics that have been examined in the context of India. The second section, traces the sweeping changes taking place on account of technology, social media, financial innovation, etc. and its impact on the way consumers make their buying decisions. Numerous real-life examples have been illustrated that are aiding the improvement of service quality in hotels across the globe and the trends we can expect to see in the future in India.

In Chapter 1 titled "Economics of the Indian Hotel Industry—An Overview: A Global Benchmarking across Different Segments of Hotel Offerings and Mapping the Growth Trajectory of the Industry," the author Dr. Sudhanshu Bhushan traces the significant impact of the hospitality industry across the globe. Special focus has been given to the changing demands of customers in India and the emerging trends exhibited by hotel providers, to meet the changing needs of the industry as a whole. The author compares the developed hospitality markets of the United States and Europe and their prevailing trends, with the emerging market in India. The chapter concludes with pointing out the opportunities available in India, both in terms of hospitality service offerings and financing options to create sustainable brand value.

The World Travel & Tourism Council has quoted that the travel and tourism industry encompasses 266 million jobs and contributes 9.5% of the GDP globally. With the travel and tourism sector growth forecasted to expand by 3.9% during 2015, the sector has been recognized as a key driver of growth. The tourism and hospitality sector's direct contribution to GDP aggregated to US\$ 44.2 billion in 2015 and is expected to register a CAGR of 10.5%. The direct contribution of travel and tourism to GDP is expected to grow at 7.3% per annum to US\$ 88.6 billion by 2025.

The US hospitality industry is the most developed globally. It has approx. 4.9 million hotel rooms in 52,887 properties serving about 318 million population. It generates a revenue of US\$163 billion, with an average occupancy of 62%. The main differentiation across categories lies in the services offered, on account of extremely high payroll costs. The cost of product is relatively low, due to easy financing, cheap infrastructure, and a relatively quick government approval process. The power resides with the brand-owning companies, who ensure a strong top-line with their loyal customer base focusing mainly on customer satisfaction.

The global industry shows the supremacy of the Anglo-American groups. The Inter Continental Hotel Group remains in the first place, with Hilton Worldwide ranked second, Marriott International at the third position and Wyndham Hotel Group at the fourth position. Each of the top four groups worldwide has more than 645,000 rooms in operation. It is especially significant that all the groups in the Top 10 showed growth in their supply. With some 19.5 million rooms on January 1, 2014, the global hotel supply slowed with a growth of 3% in recent years. The Indian market, in contrast, is underdeveloped and lies at the opposite end of the spectrum. The number of member hotels at FHRAI (Federation of Hotel and Restaurant Associations of India) as on March 31, 2014, was 3681 and increased to 3938 as on March 31, 2015. It has increased to 3990 as on August 22, 2015. The pan-India membership of FHRAI accounted for a little over 166,077 rooms.

The Indian hospitality industry contributed 6.88% to the GDP, employing a population of 8.7% (36,695,000 direct and indirect jobs) in 2014, expected to rise by 1.8% in 2015; and further rise by 2% per annum to 45,566,000 jobs in 2025 as per estimates of the World Travel & Tourism Council. The foreign exchange earnings generated from overseas tourists in 2014 equaled US\$ 20.24 billion, indicating an annual growth rate of 9.7%. During the period April 2000–May 2015, this sector attracted around US\$ 8.1 billion of foreign direct investments, as reported by the Department of Industrial Policy and Promotion. The major initiatives taken by the Government of India to give a boost to the tourism and hospitality sector included, covering 150 countries under the e-visa scheme, the Tourist Visa on Arrival scheme enabled by Electronic Travel Authorization, allocating Rs. 500 crores (US\$ 79.17 million) for the first phase of the National Heritage City Development and Augmentation Yojana (HRIDAY), and last but not least, launching Project Mausam.

It is observed that the Indian hotel industry comprises three main participants: the real estate asset investors who own the hotel properties, hotel management companies operating the hotel, and brand-owning companies who provide the brand. Hotels operate across four different price, product, and service points. They are the luxury and deluxe hotels equivalent to the 5-star category and above, upscale, and up-market hotels equivalent to the 4-star category, mid-scale, and mid-market hotels equivalent to the 3-star category; and budget or economy hotels equivalent to the 2 or 1-star category. The main differentiation across Indian categories lies in the quality of product. This is because the cost of product is very high, primarily due to a combination of high land cost, expensive debt, absence of basic infrastructure, and the world's slowest opaque government approval process.

The shortage in supply of lower category rooms is further exaggerated by the absence of a good public transport and price conscious hotel guests. Fifty percent of the classified hotels in the FHRAI's membership list are deluxe, leading to an inverted pyramid of supply meeting the needs of a regular pyramid of demand. It is clear that there is enormous latent demand in India for appropriately priced mid-market and budget hotel products. The advent of online aggregated budget accommodation providers is changing the landscape of the Indian hospitality industry. The market leaders are OYO Rooms and Zo Rooms based on the level of investments raised, followed by Treebo and Vista Rooms. Stayzilla, a start-up specializing in alternative stays like homestays, houseboats, and hostels, along with Yatra.com, has joined the race with the biggest selection of budget properties.

Initially, many domestic and international brands will own and operate hotels; successful brands will over time be able to divest their assets wholly or partially, to move into brand cum operator or just brand players. By 2020, the separation of asset management and brand into distinct business segments will prevail. Hotel companies will increasingly reduce and even exit capital investment in assets, by entering into partnerships, joint ventures, leasing models, and public–private partnerships. Asset investors will expect hotel operators and brands to design, develop, and lease their hotels and offer the owners a combination of a minimum guaranteed return and a revenue share profitability model. Capital appreciation will also accrue to the hotel owners. Life insurance companies, pension funds, and real-estate investment trusts would find such long-term asset investment opportunities ideal, as would hotel companies looking to rapidly develop hotels to their brand specifications in an asset light manner.

The travel industry in India is expected to touch 1747 million travelers by 2021, requiring 188,500 additional hotel rooms as per estimates of HVS.

Mid-market hotels will be the driving force as they can be built faster and cost-effectively. The demand for hotel rooms in India will grow between 9% and 11% annually. The expected trends would encompass partnerships with the government and financial investors, and building powerful brands by addressing high quality yet low priced needs of millions of Indian travelers, at a profit.

In Chapter 2 titled "The Growth Story of Hotels in India—Looking Beyond the Rhetoric," the authors Sandeep Munjal and Anmole Singh discuss the role of brand operators and asset owners in the hospitality industry. This is followed by an analysis of their mode of operations and the areas of growth and profitability expected in the next decade in India. The hospitality industry in India is a capital intensive business, wherein established brands tie up with real-estate asset owners and manage the hotels on management contracts, leases, etc. Greenfield investments in the sector will require realistic assessment of profitable ROIs and investor confidence, based on the fundamentals of growing demand. The government's policies on enabling a favorable visa regime, potential introduction of the GST, and other impetus given to the tourism industry are expected to fuel the growth in this segment.

The hotel companies managing these hotels not only lend their brand name and operating specifications but also are active in managing the performance of the hotels and are responsible for their day-to-day functioning, to deliver strong returns to the hotel ownerships as well as the parent hotel brand company. The hotel brands are generally averse to investing capital to set up new hotel projects and concentrate their resources in building winning operational teams. The real-estate owners invest in the infrastructure and tie up with these brands, to make a hotel asset optimally perform and become profitable.

The key questions influencing expansion in the hospitality industry are the status of room inventory, the direction in which expansion is headed, the profile of the Indian investors, kind of partnerships which are feasible, the expected returns on investments, what is the mix of financing that is profitable, etc. Consolidation and mergers are the route global brands have chosen to grow in India. Room inventory is expected to expand across multiple segments. Every lodging format including hotels, resorts, heritage hotels, service apartments, B&Bs, etc. will see growth in the years to come. Investments made in the sector will attract financial returns that will be competitive globally in the years to come.

In Chapter 3 titled "Corporate Social Responsibility: an Important Aspect of the Indian Hospitality Industry" author Savita Sharma attempts to understand and debate the meaning of corporate social responsibility (CSR) in the context of the hospitality industry in India. The concept of CSR was debated insistently in the early 1990s, but it was not enough to make it mandatory. In recent years, CSR has become the cornerstone of success, for many Indian companies as the government has mandated them to spend at least 2% of their net profits on CSR for companies with at least Rs. 5 crores net profits or Rs 1000 crores turnover or Rs 500 crores net worth under the new Companies Act 2013. The main objective of CSR is that a corporate or business entity should realize their responsibility beyond a mere economic role in society. The key components of CSR may at least include corporate governance, business ethics, workplace and labor relationships, affirmative actions, the supply chain, customers, community, and the natural environment.

The present study has observed that hotels are involved in various philanthropic activities in tune with their corporate philosophy. It has been witnessed that there is a lack of contribution toward promoting gender equality and empowering women. Other areas which need attention are eradicating extreme hunger and poverty, emphasis on education, to name a few. Problems like economic backwardness and poverty in India also exist in magnitude. Corporates require the society to carry on business and the society needs to be nourished to allow businesses to prosper. For a sustainable business growth to happen, the hospitality industry must seek common ground where their CSR principles and actions satisfy the demands of the environment, stakeholders, and the society at large. The industry must work to create a platform, where maximum number of participants can contribute toward a sustainable future irrespective of their size and business presence. Further continued research in this area can assist the hospitality industry to measure the impact of their efforts, as well as their overall CSR footprint in India. Therefore, this chapter helps to understand the range of activities and their benefits accruing to luxury hotels and suggests that getting involved into the CSR activities provides a better platform and reputation for them. The present study is also an effort to identify various policies and activities, followed by the hotels, and how new policies and activities can be merged strategically with the existing structure of organizations.

In Chapter 4 titled "The Indian Hospitality Sector is in a Flux: Changing Trends that Respond to the New Customer," the author Arvind Birdie focuses on factors governing the behavior of Indian consumer such as age, economy, social change, mass media, changing perceptions, lifestyle, and access to more disposable income. The chapter also draws insights from the practitioners, on the challenges and opportunities for providing services, and satisfaction to the aware consumers. The buying behavior of consumers in India has changed, and education, age, income, economic scenario, media, and technology play a predominant role in shaping the way people shop. The fact that a large chunk of these customers are the youth is changing the way people are shopping having a direct implication on various aspects of shopping and a brand led focus. By now, accommodation options throughout India have become extremely diverse, from cozy homestays and tribal huts to stunning heritage mansions and maharaja palaces.

Moreover, the global markets have witnessed major shifts in the consumer behavior that have been much influenced by the change of technology, innovation, research, and development. These changes in the consumer behavior enabled the international retailers, to enter the market in an attempt to gain market share and brand presence in the fast foods segment. Indian culture is based on the philosophy of "Atithi Devo Bhava," meaning "the guest is God" in the Sanskrit language. From this stems the Indian generosity toward guests whether at home or elsewhere. Only during the last decade has the mid-segment gradually developed beyond non-chain properties, with entrants into the field such as Hilton Garden Inns and the Taj Group's Ginger Hotels.

The new entrants in the Indian hospitality industry are varied including financial service providers, such as ICICI Bank and Citi Bank, have teamed up with major Indian tourism players like Thomas Cook and Cox & Kings to offer personal travel loan schemes. Reliance Industries and the Mahindra Group successfully forayed into hospitality, to leverage their brand equity. Others yet engage the hospitality industry to increase their bargaining power, such as eminent IT companies, who count among the biggest clients of hospitality services in India. Metropolitan cities dominate the industry, accounting for 75–80% of total revenues, with Delhi and Mumbai leading the revenue race. Private persons convert their country homes, villagers offer home stays, and agriculturalists as well as pastoralists open their farms to visitors. Beach resorts, diving resorts, river resorts, mountain resorts, ski resorts, family resorts, golf resorts are popular hotel themes in the hospitality industry now.

According to the World Tourism Organization, eco-tourism is the fastest growing market in the entire tourism industry. The environment is a priority in the industry now. Statutory compliances are already in place regarding sewage, energy, products, and water. Upcoming properties often have programs to save water, energy and reduce solid waste in place. Agricultural tourism is widely acknowledged as an instrument for economic development and employment generation, particularly in the remote and backward areas.

Unconventional accommodation options such as religious centers, ashrams, and monasteries are among the popular alternatives to regular accommodation. Spa experiences, healthy eating, opportunities for personal growth, yoga and meditation, fitness, stress reduction, and holistic health are among the experiences sought by wellness travelers, according to the 2013 Global Wellness Tourism Economy Report. Since the 2002, "Incredible India" tourism ad campaign, travel to the country, has been on a fairly steady rise.

With the introduction of a new category of visa, the "Medical Visa," the Indian government seeks to promote medical tourism in India. The expertise of Indian doctors in modern medicine from heart surgery to cataract removal has put India on the world healthcare map. India received 1.1 million medical tourists in 2009, registering a growth of 17% (India Brand Equity Foundation, 2010). The New Industrial Policy in 1998 eased the norms for foreign institutional investors to enter and participate in the Indian economy for their businesses. These new regulations allowed several multinational fast food retailers to start their businesses through joint ventures, alliances, and collaborations with local food chains through foreign direct investment.

Technological innovations might very well be the biggest driver behind sweeping changes in the Indian hospitality industry. Speeding up decision-making, facilitating guest reservations, widening information access, improving payment options, and managing outsourcing processes, technological innovations lead to ever higher efficiency levels. It is reported that by now, 25% of all reservations are made online in India, thus making it a key tool in room occupancy fulfillment. With the advent of third-party travel websites like Hotels.com and Expedia.com, Makemytrip.com and Yatra. com, the information flow between hospitality service providers and their potential clients have improved massively.

Amid growing brand consciousness, companies may also need to cater to strong local tastes of consumers, which may involve tweaking the product, marketing and supply chain as well. The emerging trends in hospitality include the Millennials have become the fastest growing customer segment. Expectation of more international visitors has increased tourist traffic, fueling demand in this segment. Booking more profitable business is critical as more revenues result from strong increases in occupancy levels, average rates and revenue per available room. Airbnb and Uber continue to dominate the revenue conversation in a shared economy.

Real-time marketing and providing content on an ongoing basis will dominate the industry, alongside traditional marketing. Finally, the days of walk-in reservations are dwindling. With mobile apps such as Hotel Tonight and others, guests rarely walk in to inquire about room availability. Instead, they turn to apps and mobile websites, to make confirmed bookings. Innovative concepts of diversification hold the key to survival in the hospitality industry in the long run.

In Chapter 5 titled "Competing for Profitability: The Role of Revenue Management as a Strategic Choice for Indian Hotels," the author Anjana Singh highlights how the management of 5-star hotels are being innovative, in implementing a set of conventions and strategies to achieve higher sustainable revenues. Hotels being significant investments for both the investors and the national economy need long-term strategic planning and management to be successful. Improved customer service, better quality, operational effectiveness, bottom line profits, and ability to engage with customers are essential to survive in this stiff competition. Revenue management has been one of the contributors toward business profitability and its wide adoption by most service organizations especially hotels. The purpose of this research was to explore the existing revenue management practices, emerging opportunities, and the challenges in the luxury segment from the hotel operator's perspective. A qualitative approach was adopted for investigation through personal in-depth interviews with Revenue Managers and General Managers of 5-star luxury hotels. This research helped in identifying the level of achievement of 5-star luxury hotels in applying revenue management practices and also throws light on the knowledge and awareness of Revenue and General Managers. This study also uncovered the challenges faced by Indian hospitality managers while implementing revenue management in 5-star hotels of India. The practical implication of this study was to suggest strategies that Indian hotel managers can adopt to overcome challenges and implement responsible revenue management effectively in all parts of the hotel.

The discipline of revenue management started with the airline industry and was adopted by hotels in the late 1980s. It is effective only with certain characteristics which are fixed capacity and segmented market according to similar characteristics, perishable inventory, fluctuating demand, high fixed cost and advance bookings. Accurate forecasting and controlling inventory for those guests who gives you overall holistic maximum revenue, rather than accepting reservation that is paying higher price only for one night can add significant profits to hotels. The integration of IT with strategy plays an incredible role in areas of productivity and revenue enhancement and helps in gaining competitive advantage. The swift acceptance of social media worldwide gives effective information and platform to users of revenue management to implement strategic revenue management, which eventually will help hotels to be more customers centric and expand their brand

and presence. Online booking account for 50% of the leisure traveler bookings. The emergence of OTAs has made it imperative for revenue management practices to be adjusted and changed to adapt. This has pushed revenue managers to have online business strategies as a big part of their plans.

Gross operating profit per available room would be the preferred metric in the future, with tracking total revenue per available room and total revenue per available per square foot, rather than only revenue per available room. Experts were asked to identify existing revenue management practices that they are using in their hotels, and most of the hotels agreed that they implement following techniques which are managing room inventory, length of stay restrictions, differential pricing according to source and segments, identifying customer value, and demand control. The key performance metrics highlighted by hotels were average daily rate, revenue per available room, occupancy, revenue market share index, targeted budgets and performance against last year, and monitoring costs closely.

The most challenging issues emerged are the shortage of qualified managers, changes in the global economy, increased competition, and pressure to reduce costs and therefore reduce standards of service from variety of stakeholders, Accuracy of data and weak cyber law, expensive revenue software, talented workforce, strong learning, and training processes is in place to stay ahead with the new trends in the market. As more and more international chains are entering the market and segmenting the market into luxury, to upper upscale, upscale, mid-segment, and budget, there is a change in focus, moving from RevPAR to REVPAG, that is, revenue per available guest. As technology evolves analytical pricing models, social networking and mobile technology are going to have a major impact on the future. Revenue management function is going to become more centralized, and the skills required for a successful revenue manager are going to be a combination of analytical and communication abilities.

Revenue management, marketing, sales, and operations are truly dependent on each other for customer satisfaction and profitability. The strategy deals directly with customers and if not handled appropriately, it may lead to short-term revenue but will dilute long term profitability. Sustainable pricing strategies for hotels profitability will be with high RevPAR. Due to intelligent customers, the pressure is on the revenue manager to effectively forecast demand, implement pricing controls and launch promotions at the right time to avoid any direct loss from the competitors. Revenue managers with owners need to review the distribution costs and find ways to divert business to most profitable channels. Understanding the preference of loyal customers to an extent whether they would like to redeem points or avail free nights gives an opportunity to personalize stay packages and services. In the era of empowered consumers, price transparency, technology, domination of OTAs and big data, and revenue managers who will be innovative and proactive will lead business toward success.

In Chapter 6 titled "Skilling India Initiative: Responding to the Critical Need for Skilled, Trained Manpower for the Indian Hospitality Industry," the author Dr. Shweta Tiwari highlights the pressing need for skilled and trained manpower in the industry. India is one of the youngest nations with more than 62% of its population in the working age group of 15–59 years, and more than 54% of people below 25 years of age. To harness this demographic profit, India needs to skill its workforce with employable knowledge, to fuel sustained economic growth. India has around 5.5 million people enrolled in vocational courses, while the number stands at 90 million in China, demonstrating the gaps in availability of skilled workforce. Recognizing the imperative need for skill development, the National Policy for Skill Development and Entrepreneurship 2015, has been operating with the primary objective to meet the challenge of skilling at scale with speed, standard, and sustainability.

India has a target of creating 500 million skilled workers by 2022. Skill development initiatives will harness inclusivity and support initiatives to increase the supply of trained workers, adjustable to the changing demands of employment and technologies. National Vocational Qualification Framework will be created with a flexible system which will permit individuals to accumulate their knowledge and skills and convert them through testing and certification into higher diplomas and degrees. The skill gap study conducted by NSDC over 2010–2014 revealed that there is an additional net incremental requirement of 109.73 million skilled manpower by 2022. The Union Budget 2015 cleared the path for the launch of the National Skills Mission to supplement Prime Minister Narendra Modi's "Skill India" and "Make in India" exhortations. The key objective of Make in India is to advance manufacturing in 25 sectors of the economy, which will lead to job creation and meet the requirement for skilled manpower. Of these 25 sectors, tourism and hospitality is one of the important sector. The current supply of skilled trained manpower is estimated to be a very dismal of 8.92% to the total requirement as per study carried out by Ministry of tourism. As per a recent report revealed by KPMG, the current hospitality and tourism industry workforce of 6.9 million is expected to increase to 13.4 million by 2022.

The hospitality industry is a human-centric industry. Managing the single largest operating expense labor cost (typically 44.6% of total operating costs) without compromising on guest satisfaction is a massive challenge, especially given the constant shortage of skilled, experienced staff. With increasing competition for skilled hospitality employees and high rates of attrition, business success in hospitality organizations is highly dependent on their ability to retain their key employees as well as recruit the right quality of new employees. According to the Aspiring Minds National Employability Report, only 4–11% of the entire hotel management graduates are employable; while other 12–21% candidates can be employed post some training. Soft skills are vital for a hospitality professional. This includes communication skills, teamwork, problem solving, and flexibility, to name a few. Livemint.com recognizes a serious problem that currently 2000 trained people are available to meet the hospitality industry's predicted need for 583,000 professionals till 2017.

Service organizations need intangible knowledge-based resources to achieve a sustainable competitive advantage in an industry, with changing customer expectations. This is the reason why training can be regarded as a new competitiveness area for the hospitality industry. Investing in effective training for the workforce has emerged as the top initiatives toward managing costs in the hospitality industry. There are three basic factors affecting the efficiency of training efforts; first, individual factors such as behaviors toward the job and personality, the educational level of the individuals, training expectations, and motivation levels of the individuals. Second, organizational factors such as top management, support from superiors, and colleagues, practicing of training with enough financial support); and thirdly, training programs such as perception of training, specialties of trainers, etc.

In addition to this, it is also imperative to investigate the training needs from the organizational, the individual, and the program viewpoint. From the organizational level, it is important to recognize training needs such as training cost, training output, and transferability. Also from the individual level, it is important to consider performance evaluation as an important criterion, for activity level job analysis. Researchers observe a big gap in this segment, with dearth of good colleges and lack of quality training. To overcome the situation and due to acute shortage of quality training centers, many hotels are taking the initiative of opening institutes and developing new hotel management programs. The services required in the hospitality and tourism industry are highly personalized, and no amount of mechanization can replace the necessity for trained professionals. Guest contentment is a prerequisite for successful operations in the hotel industry, requiring professionally trained and highly skilled manpower.

There is a need to build effective industry institute interface, and it is the duty and accountability of the industry as well as the institutes to forge necessary tie-ups to build a skilled workforce. Also there should be more craft level institutes to offer skilled jobs in the industry; in addition to this the apprentice scheme being implemented by the Ministry of Labor is another activity that should be enhanced. The government could constitute a board to audit the demand and supply of human resource in the hospitality industry and organize the workforce developmental needs as per industry requirement. Technological innovation can also play an incredible role in guaranteeing quality of delivery at scale.

In Chapter 7 titled "Leadership Development in the Hospitality Industry—Perspectives from India," the author Sonia Bharwani traces the role the senior management of a hospitality business plays, in sustaining their competitive edge and profitability. It is relatively easy for competition to imitate the tangible aspects of the product and service offerings of a hospitality organization. The key to success and differentiation lies in organizing the intangible human capital of an organization. Effective leadership is central to organizational success. Astutely aligning leadership skills and competencies to match the key requirements of the job profile is critical to capturing available growth opportunities. Thus, integrated talent management in terms of recruitment, development, and retention of senior management is one of the key challenges faced by the hospitality industry. This study aims at identifying and mapping the talent management practices adopted by hospitality organizations for leadership recruitment and development.

Competency models gained popularity in the 1980s and are being increasingly used since then as a key tool in human resource management and development, to improve both individual job performance and overall organizational effectiveness. Competencies refer to behavioral dimensions that an individual brings to a position to enable him to perform the job competently. It refers to the willingness and capability to behave in a competent manner and incorporates knowledge, skills, behaviors, and attitudes into a single core unit. As a senior manager and the leader of operations of a hotel, he or she is now expected to wear the hats of an operations expert, a business strategist, a people's champion, and a change catalyst.

Cognitive or conceptual competencies help in understanding and responding to complexities and challenges that are an inbuilt part of the operating environment. They are gathered through systematic knowledge acquisition and include competencies like critical thinking, analytical skills, creativity, strategic thinking, and decision-making. Functional or technical competencies help in performing concrete activities for running the day-to-day business operations and for hotel General Managers include job-specific skills such as guest handling through service orientation, revenue management skills, employee performance appraisal skills, and IT skills. Social or interpersonal competencies are useful in establishing and maintaining relationships with others and include people skills like effective communication, empathy, teamwork orientation, fostering motivation, developing and coaching others. Lastly, meta-competencies are overarching personal competencies such as self-awareness, self-management, achievement orientation which enable an individual to understand, monitor and manage their own performance. They refer to abilities that underpin the development of other competencies such as initiative, openness, and willingness to learn, as well as intrinsic personality traits like emotional resilience, optimism, and diplomacy. Meta-competencies, along with key cognitive abilities, technical skills, and interpersonal skills, help an individual to deliver superior performance.

According to the experts, the competencies which were commonly the focus of leadership development programs for General Managers include strategic thinking, change management, teamwork, and service orientation. Among the functional competencies, training programs are largely held for developing revenue management skills and financial analysis skills. While some hotel chains used competency based performance appraisal systems, others used balanced scorecards for evaluating the performance of its General Managers. The competencies which were commonly used for evaluating a General Manager's performance included people development skills, team building, business ethics, change management, and achievement orientation.

One of the experts commented that though hospitality organizations in India did use competencies in certain aspects of talent management, there was a lack of an integrated approach. All experts concurred that there was lack of an industry-specific leadership competency model for the Indian hospitality sector, which could be used as a blueprint for developing competency frameworks tailored to the needs of individual organizations, aligned with their unique vision, strategies, and culture. A robust leadership competency model would facilitate competency identification and measurement and keep the leaders focused on areas which are crucial for success and development.

The finding of the study revealed that while hospitality organizations in India recognize the importance of a holistic competency-based approach in leadership development, there was a lack of a structured, competency-based training need analysis to assess the developmental needs of General Managers. Further, competency development initiatives for General Managers were usually conducted on an *ad hoc* basis, depending on the availability of suitable external training resources. There was a higher degree of focus on functional and cognitive competencies while designing training initiatives, as these competencies are readily identifiable and measurable. However, there are several other social and meta-competencies that are covert, below the surface, and are more difficult to detect and yet are highly significant.

In Chapter 8 titled "Arts Informed Leadership in Family-Run Business-Arts in Play," the authors Vimal Babu and Amirul Hasan Ansari explain how the artistic process of different art forms affect leadership, involving engagement and decision-making in family-run businesses. Irrespective of the myriad attempts to change status quo, family-run businesses are finding the present adverse situation a lot more challenging than before. Due to macroeconomic factors and industry prone changes, family-run businesses are trying to tackle this difference in terms of deteriorating business conditions and sensing immediate necessity of scaling up of their businesses.

This chapter explores the concept of leadership affecting the decision-making process in family-run fast food businesses in the city of Surat in Gujarat. Researchers have observed the role of past performances, imagination, inspiration, intuition, concentration, and identification as an artistic process in any art form. This has led researchers to understand the connection between arts as an artistic process and leadership behavior in family-run business owners. Arriving at any judicious and satisfactory decision can also be expressed as more of an art.

The methodology of conducting research has been stimulating and comprehensive. Focus group discussions and in-depth interviews were organized. Qualitative data were collected from consumers, family-run business owners, and local civic agency, etc. to develop a complete view on the present study. The Indian hospitality industry represents a business space that is poised for strong growth in terms of top line revenues. This growth is currently riding largely on the capacity addition that is organic in nature. Both domestic as well as international hospitality businesses have reported pressure on their bottom line. While some like IHCL have witnessed steep losses quarter on quarter, others too have struggled to achieve healthy profitability. Reasons for this rather indifferent performance need to be investigated. Is this a result of ill thought investments toward capacity building or is it about operational efficiency?

To study the effectiveness of arts in finding solutions to business issues, there have been many research projects conducted successfully in most of the European countries over the last decade. Some of the prominent studies were The AIRIS (Artists in Residence) program in Sweden, the NyX Innovation

Alliances Program in Denmark, and the Unilever's Catalyst Program. The AIRIS program in Sweden was conducted to understand the possible impact of artists coming in contact with business managers and business related issues. The purpose was to attend to issues from a different and novel perspective of artists. The NyX Innovation Alliances program was also on the same agenda to understand how artists can make significant difference in a business unit. Twenty artists were chosen to pair up with 20 different organizations from different industries, to shed some light on how these artists and business issues could be related in a manner that it could produce some results, helping to understand how and when they jointly work or do not work. The Unilever's Catalyst program stood out amongst the major studies carried out in arts and business in Europe. The idea of having such an arts intervention was proposed to Unilever by Alaistair Creamer, an external arts consultant. There were many arts-based activities introduced along with artists-in-residence projects as well. Based on these studies, it was clear that arts and business have a strong interrelationships. Researchers were motivated to explore further about art forms to see whether there exist any work of artistic process evolving out of different arts forms. Also, efforts were made to see if a novel leadership style could be proposed by incorporating the artistic process of music, dance, drama, painting, etc.

If business behaves erratically on account of industry prone factors or macroeconomic instability with high market volatility, the manager will have to change from a managerial mode to a leadership mode. Due to changing markets, undefined programs, unclear objectives, difficulty in achieving targets, sophisticated and nonuser friendly technology, improper and complex communication channels, indifferent customers, competitors imitating the products and services, the entire organizational system would call for overhauling in terms of revisiting the vision, mission, and objectives of the company. Moreover, subsystems, processes, operations, communication channels must be revitalized and reinvented. It must be done in such a manner that consistent utilization and application of different structural components of the system must not breakdown and crumble, from the shocks emanating from the internal system or factors impacting as external disruptions.

Today, leadership lacks creativity, sensitivity, hope, emotional stability, perseverance, variability in imagination, an intuitive mindset, concentration, identification of characters in the environment, etc. Business cannot be run with stiffness; the conventional thoughts of mass production and consumption wherein revenue generation, profit maximization and shareholders' dividends are kept at the center of all business-related objectives. Since business lacks creative sense, management continues to run on a mechanistic approach of tackling business situations in industry. But researchers are now taking keen interest in the belief that creativity and innovation in work settings are critical factors for a congenial and learning environment. Arts can be instrumental in enriching a new leadership order in business by providing imagination, intuition, envisioning ability, self-expression, thus enabling the leader to view the larger picture without losing attention of the core aspects of business.

Arts is all about the outlet or channel of expressions. Since the field of study is extremely new, a lot of research inputs in this direction needs to be generated in order to justify the assumption. Traditionally, business views arts for decoration. Gradually, business started using arts for entertainment. A little more seriousness was observed, when business started recognizing arts as an instrument to tackle issues of working teams, improving communication channels, instilling leadership qualities among managers, introducing innovation as practice, etc. The business fraternity is really not in a position to accept the fact that art forms possess the potential to offer sustainable results, in terms of generating the creative element amongst staff and managers. Organizations are divided in their opinion to consider arts of being capable of changing the leadership approach, bringing promising changes in various subsystems of the modern organization. Giving due consideration to the way arts is being seen as an instrument, the present chapter proposes that managers and practitioner in business organizations experience arts as a strategic process of transformation through personal development and leadership, culture and identity, creativity and innovation.

In Chapter 9 titled "Service Quality and Customer Experience: The Key to Building Sustainable Competitive Advantage in Fine Dine Restaurants," the authors Gaurav Tripathi and Kartik Dave discusses how delivering excellence in restaurant services is achieved by providing high levels of service quality. Service quality is the measure of customer's perception that influences customer satisfaction and, in turn, influences behavioral intentions. Higher levels of service quality result in increased number of customers patronizing the restaurant. Service quality encompasses factors such as ambient environment, decor, staff responsiveness, cultural sensitivity, etc. Competitive advantage is achieved by offering superior quality of services in comparison to the competitors.

In this chapter, the relationship between service quality, customer experience, customer satisfaction, and behavioral intentions has been established and then tested using a customer survey. The empirical results have been validated and linked with what the restaurants are doing, for providing superior service quality levels and memorable experiences. Further, a discussion is factored on how the efforts mentioned by the restaurant management have resulted in competitive advantage and how they have been able to sustain them.

Service quality is strongly linked with financial returns. The discussion on customer satisfaction and customer retention is strongly connected with service quality models. Customers visit restaurants for experiencing pleasure from restaurant services. They may love to eat high-quality food with exotic ingredients. However, such ingredients and recipes are widely available in the markets of urban metros; hence, the high-quality food is not the only thing which the restaurants focus. In the present scenario, restaurant patronage is strongly linked to various elusive aspects. This can be the ambient environment, personalized services, and happiness. The desire to visit and revisit a restaurant is largely subjective rather than objective. It is based on the feelings evoked.

Although restaurants are known for selling food only, in reality, they are the retailers of food service experience. Service quality has two important components, technical and functional. The former is related to what the consumer receives and the later is about how the services are delivered to the customer. The physical surroundings can be used to make inference about the quality of services. Hence, it can be concluded that the service environment is the key to developing perception about the service quality. Meyer and Schwager (2007) said that customer experience encompass every aspect of consumer offering including service attribute. If positive experiences are greater than the negatives ones, then customer satisfaction is positive while it is negative when positive experiences are less than the negative ones.

The antecedents of customer experience. Are dependent upon convenience, price fairness, and quality attributes including the physical and social environment. Satisfaction is basically a judgment of the customer in which they make comparisons between the expected and actual performances from any service. Satisfaction is an evaluation of the selection made, whether it is in line with the past beliefs gained about that particular option. Behavioral intentions are important in the context of services as it caters to the sustainability of the service business in the long run. It is the surrogate indicator of the actual behavior of the consumer (Fishbein & Ajzen, 1975). Loyalty is basically all about showing preference for a particular service brand in comparison to others. This helps in increasing their business and hence account for sustainability.

The ambient settings have shown positive and significant influence on the restaurant service quality factors. The impression comprises parking areas, building exteriors, and attractive dining areas. Aesthetics are a key aspect of restaurant service quality. It includes comfortable seating, visually attractive interiors and table settings. These aspects are the tangible. The next restaurant service quality factor which is influenced by ambient settings is reliability and responsiveness. It is related to the service deliveries by the restaurant which can be based on the time they promise to their patrons, no discrepancy between the order taken and delivered and also the quick and prompt services. Empathy is one of the most elusive aspects of restaurant service quality. It is all about how sensitive are the restaurant employees toward the needs and expectations of their customers. Many of these needs and expectations are unsaid or never specifically mentioned by the patrons and hence the employees need to remain vibrant to such needs. In other words, these needs are to be anticipated. Privacy and entertainment are strongly related to ambient settings and are very significantly affected by them. In a fine dining restaurant, the consumers expect that the privacy level should be well maintained, there should not be much noise which may act as a deterrent to their experience and the music should be befitting with the dining atmosphere.

Similarly, the restaurant expects the new customers to visit and expect a full occupancy on most occasions. However, this is not the reality due to high competition. Overall, the focus is on maximizing the customer base. It is very difficult to gain new customers as compared to maintaining an existing one. However, newer customers add to the database and with the support from the current customers gaining them becomes easier. However, maintaining them is far more difficult. The focus should be on the few quality customers, who would not only provide maximization of revenues by contributing to the lion's share of the profits; they would also help in maintaining the high-quality image of the restaurant.

In Chapter 10 titled "Push for the Food and Beverages Segment to Drive Revenue Growth in Indian Hotels" penned by authors Debpriya De and Sandeep Munjal opine that the food & beverages (F&B) as a business segment is a key value proposition for the Indian hotel industry, as its potential to contribute to revenue growth is immense. Accommodation-driven revenue that constitutes almost 80–85% of the total revenue and nearly 90% of the net profit is influenced by an oversupply market. Hotels are focusing on F&B segment as one of the key drivers to growing operating revenues. This chapter probes into the new methods that the hotels are adopting to seek higher revenue contribution from the F&B segment, given the challenge of weakening ARRs (average room rate) and struggling occupancy percentages. A price-bundling strategy where F&B offers are combined with rooms to create a value deal is being utilized as a profitable strategy.

Within the F&B space, segments such as in room dining or room service, events, meeting, and conferences have the potential to drive revenue growth. New cuisines and theme-based F&B are profitable revenue generators, leading to critical sustainability. Alcoholic beverages are a strong volume growth as well as highly profitable component of the overall F&B revenue mix. In order to deliver superior F&B services, the staffing pattern and outlook of the department has undergone significant development. Young chefs are being hired as the hotels are coming up with interactive kitchens, live counters, multicuisine buffets, etc. and the guests like to see culinary innovation at display. Key hotel brands like The Leela, ITC, The Taj, The Marriott, The Park are all recruiting culinary talents Chefs. The concept cooking trend is also driving the increased demand for culinary and service staff, to manage the increasing load on the food and beverage operations, which has also grown in parallel. The market segments comprising quick service restaurants and casual dine-in formats account for 74% of the total chain market, while cafés make up for 12% with fine dining and pubs, bars, clubs, and lounges comprising the rest. The chain and licensed segment of the standalone restaurant space is expected to contribute an estimated Rs. 24,600–25,000 crores by 2018. The share of delivery and take-away formats is growing fast due to their focus on convenience. Experimentation with new formats, themes, and menus is likely to drive the growth story broadly, as suggested by experts.

In Chapter 11 titled "Culinary Innovation in Indian Hotels and Building Cost Efficiencies that Spur Profitability Growth," the author Sanjay Sharma outlines the significance of innovation as a catalyst to increase profitability and sustain success in the hospitality industry. The hospitality product is considered to be complex from its production to marketing and distribution. Innovation can only be undertaken when there is a high innovation dividend reaped, for the added cost and risk of innovation.

This study obtained data from various food outlets practicing innovation; it analyzes the relationship between culinary innovations based on services, product, and technology and its performance at the outlet level. It was found that product innovation and induction of technology are positively associated with employee turnover, their motivation, and growth. Unique selling prepositions, sales growth, competitive advantage, sales promotions, and capacity utilization serve as catalysts. Finally, it was found that culinary innovation is activity associated with higher profitability; it also helps to retain customers and has other tangible and nontangible benefits.

The leaders of organizations play a pivotal role in affecting the innovation process, majorly through their attitude and influence at the work place (Shalley & Gilson, 2004). Innovation process frameworks are treated as a roadmap from the development of food item to its menu introduction and beyond. Although using such frameworks does not always guarantee financial success, it increases the chance of being successful. Service industry innovation includes two main concepts; new product development (NPD) and new service development. The NPD caters to tangible goods, whereas NPS focuses on development of innovative service related aspects. Michelin chefs are less prone to using traditional steps which are considered as conventional wisdom in new menu development. They pay more emphasis on service staff in the restaurant due to the importance of service delivery. Moreover, leadership guidance, support, and commitment are crucial aspects in the success of any innovative product. Indian cuisine roots date back to some 5000 years and together with some other Asian cuisine, it forms the foundation and inspiration for traditional food cultures. Culinary innovation has always been at the heart of the Taj Hotels dining experience. In many instances, it has been a Taj Hotel that has introduced the city to exotic cuisines such as Thai or Schezuan. Favorite dishes from all over the subcontinent are reinvented at Masala Kraft, Masala Klub, and Masala Art with an emphasis on flavor and freshness, using lighter, healthier cooking techniques. Excellent ingredients are the starting point. As a complementary practice, the Taj chefs like to work with local farmers to obtain the local, organic products they need. Chef Manjit Singh Gill, Corporate Chef, ITC hotels has documented traditional Indian cuisine to preserve its authenticity and rich traditions. "It is not that I am against innovation," says chef Gill. "But young chefs need to understand a cuisine before they start adapting it. They need to know the roots of the cuisine and in India many of them do not" (Tyler, 2014). Chef Jerson Fernandes, Corporate Chef, Keys Hotel believes that experimentation and innovation are the key elements to culinary evolution and is a big fan of fusion cooking. At Keys Hotels, innovative food is the crux of their F&B services.

According to Restaurant India Research, 2015 was filled with food-tech innovations focused on healthy food, prompt delivery, and a structured supply chain. They researched the culinary fraternity to spot the trends that ruled the Indian palate in last 2 years including start-ups, packaged food trends, Indian cuisine with a modern twist, healthy meals, locally sourced fresh ingredients, online food ordering, meals on wheels, and sharing meal experiences on social media.

Another similar trend to increase profitability and reap the benefit of economies of scale, the Indian restaurants association of Singapore, launched Central Processing Units to collectively procure, prepare, and produce vegetarian and nonvegetarian food. A government official from Singapore said key initiatives such as the CPUs are helping businesses reap productivity gains, improve job quality and provide better service for customers and "Restaurants will gain from higher productivity." One of the process-driven aspect of restaurant is purchasing and receiving, and the resultant supply chain. The hotels are working with primary producers to reduce cost and improve quality and profitability. This development is been greatly helped by the use of technology and internet. However, on the other hand, we see horizontal integration with the supplier that supply complete range of food and other hospitality products on contract basis, such suppliers have the benefit of economies of scale to bear the pressure of inflation. However, there is a need to implement standard purchase specifications, with the help of technology.

Computerized inventory management has made stock management easier with a strong integration with accounting and forecasting systems. Technology has also changed the way we cook in commercial kitchens, use of microwave ovens, induction cookers, and cook chill methods and many other labor saving technologies have been inducted to reduce cost and increase productivity. Another concept which is gaining popularity amongst the hotels and restaurants is the concept of outsourcing. For culinary professionals, outsourcing is getting the prepared food from outside instead of cooking it in house. The consequences of ready to eat food are that one side, it saves labor cost but on the other, it reduces staff skills and training opportunity. In the past couple of years, the restaurant sector has seen great possibilities that technology has to offer and this generates opportunities to motivate hoteliers toward innovation.

In Chapter 12 titled "Events and Catering Business: Shift from Unorganized to Organized," the author Kaveri Vij aims to highlight the reasons for the unorganized nature of these industries and the influences which led toward their structuring. A change in mindset, lifestyle, and increase in disposable income has been the big influences. The latter part of the chapter addresses what are the current factors which are influencing the further growth of events and catering, as well as limiting its double digit growth.

Catering primarily refers to offering meals to people in bulk. Dating back to our old times, we had a concept of mass cooking pertaining to the large size of the families and financial constraints. Considering occasions where large scale cooking would be required, the family members would divide the cooking chores and the meals were consumed within households itself. Then, we saw a transition from larger families to nuclear families. Nuclear families having no additional help are starting to need external help to organize small get-togethers. Slowly, we saw every family has a halvai for every occasion or celebration. Graduating, we had full-fledged catering companies offering cooked food in a hygiene manner. With the restaurant industry growing and booming, every guest wanted the best of the best dishes at their events. That's when these catering companies started roping in famous chefs to head these companies. Initially, catering would have a straight buffet snacks, salads, main course, and desserts. Now live cooking stations are organized, where chefs showcase their talents for guests. Hailing to healthy options, we see the caterers now including size 0 snacks and healthy items as a part of the menu and food options.

The industry has maintained a 15–20% growth rate year on year. Catering still remains largely unorganized. We would have someone cater at Rs. 250 per head to Rs. 2500 per head. While smaller towns in the country are ridden with local chefs and small operators, bigger cities and metropolitans have seen an increase in established names in the food and restaurant space getting into the business. In the west, any catering at an event is often more expensive than going to a restaurant because it offers a premium service as opposed to our country.

With the introduction of laws, taxation and food becoming a fashion statement for each and every event, a lot of organized operators comprising international catering companies and big restaurant chains have also started taking catering seriously. Catering is no more limited to weddings and birthday parties in the country but also includes corporate events and fashion shows. Progressing, with the need of having cleaner options for food and considering other elements, we have government regulations stating the formation of these companies by having certain legal laws in place. Every company would have to be identified under certain section and apply for a license to be able to serve food. Though the industry is inching toward organization, it still remains unorganized in a lot of ways. Similar to the hospitality industry, catering companies are also labor intensive. They need skilled labor in terms of chefs. Companies have certain people on their payroll and also hire a certain percentage of labor such as waiters, cleaners, helpers, chefs on a contractual basis. However, the established players in the industry take care of these finer details and have majority of their employees on permanent payroll and offer a world of difference in their service levels.

Another factor which plays a major role in this industry is the seasonality of the industry. Though these companies are busy throughout as they cater to different sectors, the wedding season is the busiest. The challenge still remains to make this industry skill specific. Hygiene is another big challenge. Emphasis also has to be on choosing safe ingredients and preparing food within hygiene regulations. Segregation of vegetarian and nonvegetarian, cooked and raw food, dairy and bakery helps avoid cross contamination. On the bright side, the start-up costs for a catering service business are relatively lower and the premise doesn't necessarily have to be in a prime location. The catering business may be covered under the service tax and sales tax based on the annual sales turnover and state of operation. A state VAT registration may also be applicable based on the turnover of the catering business.

Events range from social events like weddings or corporate events. With the advancements in time, a term called MICE (meetings, incentives, conferences, and exhibitions) has emerged, covering all different types of events. Broadly, events can be classified as social events, corporate events, PR events, and events for a social cause. It is expected to grow at 25% annually and estimated to reach $996 million by 2015–2016. With a compounded annual growth of 14%, this industry is projected to reach Rs. 5000 crores by 2015 (Sanjay Kankaria, Director, Rachnoutsav Events Academy). Another budding trend this industry has witnessed is the emergence of wedding planners. The wedding industry in India is estimated to be worth $40 billions. As per a survey conducted by Ernst and Young, Indian families save the most for the education of their children, followed by marriages. Economic liberalization and the rise of the middle class have prompted a change in attitudes. The planners usually charge a commission from 10% to 17.5%. This means a Rs. 1 crore wedding will leave the planner richer by Rs. 10 lakh. While for most upper class people wedding budgets start at Rs. 70–80 lakh, it can go up to even Rs. 10 crores for industrialists and businessmen. Destination weddings cannot be handled without professional help, as lot of planning is required. A farm house wedding with more number of people works out more economical, however, a destination wedding is more like a fashion statement. NRIs are the biggest clients for these destination weddings.

Corporate events have been hugely affected by the economic slowdown and profits are cut greatly due to low demand. These two industries which rely on each other in a very big way need to work on acquiring the right talent pool, managing costs, and having transparency in their operations. Digital events and activation are also expected to grow significantly on the back of smart phone penetration, internet availability, and the cost efficiency. The industry must build robust policies, processes, and information systems to manage business efficiently and safely, and implement technology and automation. Double taxation, taxation across multiple states, and varying and inconsistent application of different taxes, needs to be regularized to introduce organization in these sectors. There is a need to improve the supply chain by developing quality vendors, implementing a system of vendor accreditation, and improving overall risk management.

In Chapter 13 titled "Generation Z and Specialist Coffee Shops in India—A Perspective of the Needs, Motives, and Issues of Generation Z," the author Dr. Durgamohan Musunuri explores the role of specialist coffee shops in India, and the issues this generation has vis-à-vis these coffee shops. Generation Z is defined as those born after 1990, and consequently have entered the job market or are still students. This group born after the liberalization of the Indian economy is a group of consumers who have changed the consumption patterns, experienced a wide variety of choices available in the market place, are tech-savvy and consequently no strangers to global products and services.

Coffee is not native to India and was introduced 400 years ago by a saint called Baba Budan. Baba Budan from India went on a pilgrimage to Mecca. He stopped at a street stall in Arab land for some refreshments and had a dark sweet liquid called "Qahwah." The liquid refreshed him so much that he wanted to take it back to his people in India. However, the local law did not allow anyone carrying it. Baba Budan had surreptitiously carried seven seeds strapped to his stomach and brought those seeds to India. He planted these seeds in the hills of Chikmaglur in the federal state of Karnataka, India. Thus, the coffee plant was born in India. In the ensuing period of 400 years since Baba Budan planted those seven coffee seeds, others have influenced the growth of coffee plantations in India.

The two major coffee varieties that are grown in India are Arabica and Robusta. Coffee production in India has reached 327,000 metric tons (MT) in 2014–2015 from 18,893 tons in 1950–1951. Robusta variety accounted for 229,000 MT amounting to 70% of the production and Arabica 98,000 MT making up the balance 30%. With this production, India became the seventh largest producer of coffee in the world. The per capita coffee consumption in India is 80 g/year, whereas it is 8 kg per year in developed countries. The size of the café market was estimated at USD 290 million in 2013 and is expected to grow at a CAGR of 20% and reach USD 725 million by 2018.

The concept of a coffee shop is a recent phenomenon in India. Earlier in 1980s and 1990s, coffee shops existed but were restricted to the 24-h coffee shops in luxury hotels, which were out of bounds for the majority due to very high prices. The new millennium saw the entry of specialty coffee shops into the Indian market. Coffee is now competing against tea in these cafes, especially among younger consumers. Increasing disposable incomes and a willingness to consume food and drink outside home are the reasons that are fueling the growth. Some of the major ones are Café Coffee Day, Costa Coffee, Barista Lavazza, Café Pascucci, Di Bella Coffee India, Gloria Jean's, The Coffee Bean & Tea Leaf, Starbucks, Javagreen, Mocha, Brewberrys Café, Coffee N U, BRU World Café, Cuppa Joe, Qwiky's Coffee, and Coffee World.

Coffee shops have become the hub for a multitude of people like corporate, teenagers, couples, artists, expats, etc. Coffee shops are used as a meeting place and for holding business meetings due to their ambience; thereby, coffee is not an impulse buy for them. Coffee shops as places where intimate groups of well-dressed sophisticated people are in conversation or looking into their computing devices, perched on narrow wooden benches with an unapologetic pretension. The CEO of Café Mocha points out that call centers and the consequent night shift professionals added to the people working during the day time is one of the factors responsible for the growth of coffee houses. These people need a place to socialize with other who share their interests and are of the same age (Branded Coffee Houses a Rage in India, 2005).

As regards engaging the Generation Z buyers, global brands like "Puma," "Starbucks," "Lego" are actively engaging with this generation in innovative ways. "Creative factory", a shoe-making studio, is one initiative, wherein buyers get hands-on in the creative process and could design their own sneakers. "My Starbucks ides" is another innovative method to engage Generation Z. Coffee drinkers are invited to make suggestions on how to make Starbucks products, services, or any other aspect better. The company implements 13–17 suggestions out of the thousands received every year, showing that Generation Z informs and changes large organizations. As Generation Z is very different from other generations, marketers need to refocus their efforts to engage them. By 2020, Generation Z will be making 40% of the consumers of the United States, Europe, and BRIC (Brazil, Russia, India, China) countries and 10% of the rest of the world. Another head of business operations is of the view that Generation Z are informed buyers and have the tools and techniques to compare products and hunt for the best prices. They have the power to go from one retailer to another, share information on social media, and discuss with friends before making the buying decision. This generation wants to be involved from conception, design, creation on one side to marketing and retailing on the other. Customization is the key in attracting Generation Z customers, which provides a platform for the customers' individuality and expression. Retailing needs to fundamentally change its way of engaging Generation Z.

Most of the coffee shops have a presence on the social media, which are used by Generation Z very frequently. Social media is used as a tool and vehicle to engage with Generation Z. Given the fact that Generation Z is very active on social media, this will yield benefits to the coffee shops. Looking at India and the 31 million strong Generation Z, for them bars where liquor is served, is still a taboo place to meet, and also is expensive. The taboo aspect will continue to be a force, as it is part of the culture of the Indian society that draws people to coffee shops, the demand for the products and services of coffee shops will continue to be in demand till such time the culture changes. Hence, coffee shops thrive because of the unique services they offer at affordable prices.

14.1 FUTURE PROSPECTS AND TRENDS OF THE INDIAN HOSPITALITY INDUSTRY

In this section of the chapter, we focus on the sweeping changes taking place in the Indian hospitality industry, and the future prospects and trends experts expect to witness in the next decade. There are many examples showcased in this section, on the different technology and tools being used by hotels worldwide to increase customer traffic and improve their top line revenues. We expect the Indian hotels to slowly adopt and implement these mobile and online technologies, to improve the customer experience and create repeat business.

The Indian hospitality industry has been undergoing fundamental changes in the last 5 years. Competition, changing consumer preferences, technological advances, consolidation of brands, price variations, and online distribution channels are conspicuous factors that have been the game changers in this industry. Brand India is being marketed under the different facets of cultural tourism, eco-friendly vacationing, medical tourism, religious circuits, adventure sports tourism, wildlife safaris, beach destinations, and wellness vacations. Development of micro-markets, secondary and tertiary cities are fueling the growing demand for quality hospitality services across the country. In order to capture business from foreign tourists, the influences that need to be addressed are quality of infrastructure-related developments, ease of attaining tourist visas, the country's image as a safe, secure and friendly destination, cleanliness, etc. The entry of almost all major international brands due to the lucrative Indian market with the one billion plus population, and the emergence of branded budget and economy hotels, have led to the tourism industry emerging as a key contributor to the country's gross domestic product.

Over the past four decades, the hospitality industry has witnessed dramatic changes on account of technological innovations. Business and technology have become inseparable. Speed, connectivity, and ability to reach out to the masses by employing knowledge are key competitive ingredients today. Highly customized services are the key to differentiation of product and services in the hospitality industry. "Today's 86 million Millennials, born between 1980 and 2000, hold $200 billion in spending power and represent the most lucrative market for hoteliers" stated Junvi (2015). According to Rauch (2014), this consumer segment wants to employ technology to do things others undertake manually: checking in at hotels, make up their restaurant and bar bills, and looking up places to eat, shop, etc. "High tech, high touch" Naisbitt (1982) quoted is the service, the e-tourist wants from the hotels.

The desktop, the laptop, and now smartphones have become the most important devices influencing the consumer's consumption choices. Mobile search is a key tool of marketing now. Every three in five people use mobile devices to search and 80% of local searches on mobile devices convert to purchase. With Google rolling out a new ranking factor for mobile-friendly sites, it is essential that websites are optimized for mobile searches and are compatible to viewing on all mobile devices. MakeMyTrip reported that one-third of their online monthly unique visitors came from mobile searches and constituted 24% of all their online transaction. eMarketer's forecast that the number of smartphone users worldwide will surpass 2 billion in 2016. For the first time, more than one-quarter of the global population will use smartphones in 2015, and by 2018, they estimate that more than 2.56 billion people will do so. Hence, mobile bookings will see a jump in the year and may even surpass online bookings from other devices.

Hilton Worldwide has launched their digital check-in with room selection technology, now available at more than 3700 hotels worldwide. This technology empowers Hilton HHonors members to check in via their HHonors profile on their desktop, mobile, or tablet and choose the exact location of their room and their room number observed by McLean (2015) "Unlock a whole new way to stay" Starwood Hotels is already offering a mobile room key in a number of Aloft, Element, and W hotels. Starwood Hotels is also developing an app for the Apple Watch that will allow hotel guests to use it to unlock their rooms. Just wave it in front of the door and access is granted! If the customer has a watch and a compatible iPhone, they can self-check in into their hotel room, as reported by www.nypost.com 2014, December.

"By launching the Accorhotels application for Apple Watch™, Accor is establishing itself as a leading digital hospitality player," said Romain Roulleau, Accor's SVP e-commerce and Director of the "mobile first" program as reported by Hospitalityupgrade.com (2015). "The policy is part of the group's digital plan that aims to align itself to the new mobile practices. Accor is keeping up with consumer demand by embracing the era of connected wearables and is providing guests with a value-added service before, during and after their stay." The app will be available in ten languages and works in connection with the smartphone app. In addition to promoting hotels and destinations, the app will allow users to manage current bookings. With this app, Accorhotels customers will be able to access alerts indicating that online check-in service is open, access information about their bookings: arrival date, number of nights, number of guests, receive information about the hotel's services (free Wi-Fi, parking, spa, swimming pool, etc.), access the interactive map, including the hotel's location and the local weather forecast and access the Le Club Accorhotels loyalty card details, including status and loyalty points.

Kinsella (2015a,b) points out that mobile room keys bring the following benefits to both the guests and to the hotel. The traveler can now check-in using their Smartphone and go to their assigned room without needing to stop at the front desk. This results in reduced load on the Front Desk, equates to labor savings for the hotel and frees the staff up to focus on meaningful interactions with guests that choose a full service check-in process. At the same time, those guests that value speed and convenience can choose their preferred self-check in option. We will slowly see the increased functionality of these technology platforms in Indian hotels, in the near future.

Online marketing has become essential to hotel operations. Hotel brands recognize the strength of the internet as a medium of sales and have made their websites interactive and user friendly. Several brands have launched best rate guarantee programs that promise the consumer, the cheapest available online rate on their website, as compared to those quoted by third party online vendors. Seamless integration of websites with real-time operations enables better yield management and pricing strategies. There is an increasing role of sites in the overall sales and marketing strategy of all hotel brands, and there is an increasing reliance on search engine optimization, web advertising, and e-marketing. The service provider's website also has to tap into the options of enhanced local search, to create optimized content and local profiles, manage quality citations, maps and directory listings, and deliver a seamless mobile experience across devices. Optimization of content includes features such as headers, title tags, metadata, footers with location-based schemas, and image alt-tags. A vibrant social media strategy is essential today to develop and retain customer relationships. Social media platforms such as Google+, Facebook, Instagram, Pinterest, and LinkedIn engage audience if there is focused outreach, engaging content and appealing visual media. Tracking KPI indicators such as click through rates, engagement patterns, time spent of the page, etc. helps hotels develop and showcase content of interest to their customers. A hallmark study conducted by the Cornwell University School of Hotel Administration found a 1% increase in RevPar for every 1% increase in the hotel's "online reservation score," directly equating improved ratings with increase revenues, as stated by King (2012).

In a survey conducted by Google and Ipsos MediaCT, 70% respondents claimed to begin researching online before deciding where or how they want to travel. Users are looking for smoother interfaces to identify new travel locations and make bookings. Presence on metasearch engines and OTAs is essential, with a user friendly downloadable app. Reviews from TripAdvisor, MakeMyTrip are powerful references for the consumers while making buying decisions. Google Analytics (2014) reported that "TripAdvisor branded sites make up the largest travel community in the world, reaching nearly 260 million unique monthly visitors in 2013, and more than 200 million reviews and opinions covering more than 4 million accommodations, restaurants, and attractions. The sites operate in 42 countries worldwide. TripAdvisor also includes TripAdvisor for Business, a dedicated division that provides the tourism industry access to millions of monthly TripAdvisor visitors. TripAdvisor content showcases more than 200 million reviews and opinions from travelers around the world, 3.7 million businesses and properties in 139,000+ destinations and 19 million traveler photos. 82 million people have downloaded TripAdvisor apps, up nearly 150% year-over-year." In a research study by SAS, it was revealed that a negative review, more often than not, removes the hotel from a consumer's buying decision. People are no more silent about a bad experience. Online opinions by guests play a very important role in guiding purchase behavior within their circles of influence.

The commissions the hotels pay to the OTAs can range from 15% to 30% and that causes problems in reaching the targeted REVPAR for the hotel. The reach of OTAs has risen by 45% since 2008 in spite of the fact that travelers booking directly on the website are cheaper for hoteliers. The answer is to make the hotel website more user-friendly. Patak (2014) says that having an easy-to-navigate, effective, and attractive website wherein everything from rates to rooms to services and packages are clearly highlighted is the only answer. An excellent website with all important details and strong booking engine are the key to surpassing business generated through the OTAs. According to Matur (2014) as OTA commission checks continue to rise, small, and mid-sized hoteliers are increasingly considering TripConnect as a viable platform to generate direct bookings. The aim of TripConnect is to let your hotel compete with OTAs on TripAdvisor by placing bids. It displays real-time room rates and availability. Instead of travelers booking via OTA sites, it lets them book directly from your site. Your hotel needs to have a TripAdvisor business listing to use TripConnect. TripConnect works on a bidding model, through a cost-per-click campaign. Hoteliers need to use the TripAdvisor auction platform and bid for bookings. Once you place bids, your hotel's official site icon appears as an option alongside the OTAs on your hotel's TripAdvisor page. Only if a traveler clicks on your official link and comes to your website to book, do you pay the bid price to TripAdvisor.

According to Yu and Singh (2002), one of the major challenges for electronic commerce is to forge a relationship of trust between different parties. Reputation systems seek to address the development of trust by recording the reputations of different parties. For reputation management, Tripadvisor is very effective as a credible forum. Online reviews are also displayed from Facebook, Yahoo, Yelp, and Expedia as well. Rauch (2014) suggests to hotels to use only one tool instead of different others for managing a property's reputation process. Based on his opinion, one of the means is Revinate as a complete, one-stop solution for reputation management instead of managing the process of logging into each platform and spending an exorbitant amount of time on a crucial yet time consuming aspect of the hotel industry. Engaging with guests and responding to their needs publicly through these forums can go a long way in driving future bookings to the property.

Koumelis (2015) stated that "Revinate, a San Francisco-based technology company that is reinventing the hotel guest experience, launches inGuest in Europe. inGuest brings together reservation (PMS) data and stay histories, with preferences, social media activity, and guest feedback to surface comprehensive rich guests profile on a single platform. For the first time, hoteliers can truly understand their guests and engage with them more effectively before, during, and after their stays, increasing guest satisfaction and revenue. With inGuest, hoteliers can execute precisely targeted engagement campaigns. The platform also includes a request center to establish a two-way communication channel with guests via email, SMS, and app notifications, a hotel-branded native app and a branded mobile website to streamline advance check-ins, room service orders, service requests, problem solving, concierge tips, and more." Already launched with proven success at leading hotels such as Provenance Hotels, Grande Colonial Hotel, and Makena Resort, inGuest is now available in the United Kingdom and Ireland at Macdonald Hotels, Grange Hotels, and Fuller's British Hotels, and Inns. We will witness the increased adoption of inGuest in Indian hotels soon.

InGuest contains three stages: (1) pre-stay, (2) on-site, and (3) post-stay. A live example here describes its value. For instance, the client is a female, between 24 and 35, and an active user of LinkedIn, Facebook, Twitter, and Tripadvisor.

(1) Pre-stay: "Adele makes a reservation at the Avertine Hotel. inGuest begins to fill in her guest profile with past stay information. The hotel receives an arrival report with a VIP guest list. Adele's profile shows 6 hotel reviews and high social activity with 5K Twitter followers. Adele receives an advanced check-in email and upgrades to a suite. The front desk gets an SMS and confirms with Adele. After checking-in, Adele receives a welcome SMS and heads to the bar for happy hour. (2) On-site: She uses the Mobile App to order room service for breakfast. (3) Post-stay: The hotel gets an alert that Adele has written a 5-star review on TripAdvisor. Three months later, the hotel sends a targeted email to Twitter VIPs and wine lovers. Adele makes her fifth reservation."

According to Trackmaven, "Real Time Marketing is marketing that is based on up to date events. Instead of creating a marketing plan in advance and executing it according to a fixed schedule, real time marketing is creating a strategy focused on current, relevant trends and immediate feedback from customers. The goal of real time marketing is to connect consumers with the product or service that they need now, in the moment."

Every consumer wants to be the member of the "Being Trendy" group. If hoteliers strategically place their advertisements to reflect a current event (e.g., Formula1 after party, fashion show, etc.), their service may become more appealing to guests. Video campaigns (e.g., Flip to) on social media, when done properly, are proving to be successful for hoteliers looking to generate guest engagement. Flip allows hotels to connect with guests from the moment they make a reservation and to create a unique experience upon arrival (Rauch, 2014). Gary Vaynerchuk, a well-known Internet entrepreneur and author, pointed out, "Content is king, but marketing is queen, and runs the household." Creating great content for your website and/or blog is helpful, but content alone will not drive increased hotel revenues. The importance of content for SEO, drive results and increases brand awareness, only when deploying content with an effective marketing strategy. How content is researched, put together, and distributed will separate the winners and losers in organic search moving forward. "What is your hotel's content strategy? Are you simply writing more content because you've read that it's the right thing to do? Would you create a package for your hotel just for the sake of having a package to offer? When approaching content development, create a strategy with clear, measurable goals to further the growth of your hotel or brand."

IBM quoted the following example of customizing services in the hospitality industry. A worldwide hospitality organization is using real-time execution as an important component of its overall marketing strategy to build customer dialogues, enhance loyalty, and, ultimately, increase the amount of money spent during each hotel visit. Upon making a reservation, a guest receives a confirmation email delivered in a matter of minutes summarizing his reservation with a tailored up-sell offer. Forty-eight hours prior to the visit, he receives another email listing the activities available at the hotel during his stay, as well as a promotion to encourage participation. The promotion is based on historical customer data, preferences, and predictive analysis. When the guest checks in, he receives a tailored letter summarizing the daily activities and, again, coupons to participate. Lastly, after check-out, the individual is contacted through their preferred channel to gather information pertaining to the visit as well as to encourage future visits. This timely, relevant, and optimized dialogue communication strategy has increased customer loyalty while increasing the average revenue generated per visit. The investment in a flexible and scalable real-time solution that integrates with a marketing technology platform that handles not only real-time activities but also periodic and transactional activities has resulted in significant ROI and impressive bottom-line results.

Hotels will move increasingly toward developing a customer-centric strategy, enhancing their information management systems, changing organizational culture, business processes, working practices, and the ability of hotel managers to translate their technology requirements into profitable investments. We will witness the convergence of all information systems and interaction (call center, front office system, Internet, etc.) into a central data warehouse, to facilitate information sharing across hotel touch points. A suggestion to develop a robust customer-oriented information system entails the following process. Firstly, the specification of the final guest information matrix, based on a technical audit is required with those managers who showed the highest interest in customer knowledge and a strong commitment to creating an electronic guest profile. Then the creation of a data input design easily accessible by the hotel's different touch points on permission. Finally, planning complete customer information needs of each department. Here key information is collated from different customer-facing and back end information systems and databases (CIS interface, PMS, CRS, interactive TV, yield management system, Web reservation engine, etc.) as well as from external sources, to build a consistent guest history storing different profiles for the same guest. The data center where information from different sources will be captured and standardized, and then analyzed by using on-line analytical processing and data mining techniques (Dhillon, 2012).

Traditionally, the hospitality industry is practical and technical in nature, and this deeply rooted tradition continues to have influence in the educational field. Greater emphasis is being given on practical skills by employers, and the curriculum has to become more fluid to incorporate the changing skill needs of the industry. Industry-led teachers will be more in demand, who can impart real skills to aspiring employees. The emphasis will increasingly be on meeting the needs of industry employers, with an educational mindset of adaptability of both the curriculum taught and the skills imparted that fit the employer demands. Developing a continuous dialogue and alliance with industry partners will increase as skills levels demanded become finer. Hospitality education faces differing challenges in varied regions of the world. In India, issues such as curriculum content, proper credentials of instructors, inadequate training infrastructural facilities are some of the problems that need to be addressed to, satisfy the hiring needs of the employer. We will witness further specialization of hospitality courses in fine dining, bar management, F&B specialties, housekeeping, revenue management, etc., as employers fine tune job descriptions leading to a more vocational styled education in hospitality. Hotel companies have prepared manuals detailing the procedural handling of every conceivable situation in a hotel operation scenario, reducing the reliance on age and experience. This has resulted in younger individuals taking on the helm of operations for a unit. Hotel managers have realized the difference in service levels achieved through trained staff and otherwise and have made a transition for the better. This has created a specific requirement that is currently not being catered to by most of the educational institutions across the country. There will be a rise in a crunch for good quality talent, leading to better pay packages and perks to enhance incentives for skilled job seekers. Top management support for innovation is essential to development and refinement of services. For instance, Choice Hotels conducts an annual organization wide talent review, mapping the upcoming business initiatives against competency shortfalls by senior executives. They use this readiness assessment to determine current leadership capability to pursue new business initiatives

With increasing sophistication of capital, hotel operators will be pushed to think more creatively with the stringent demand of ownership returns expected by the investors. Asset managers will act as custodians of ownership capital, who will be instrumental in making sure that operators have a more focused day-to-day operations management, thus creating value at the individual asset level. The trend of consolidation of more brands under fewer umbrellas will continue as hospitality players capture larger markets such as India, China, etc., with lodging offers ranging from luxury to economy for the customers. Capital will be deployed more efficiently for the development of the hotel industry but will remain cyclical in nature with investors who will act as asset traders and exit at a premium return. The separation between ownership and operations will continue, with growth of REIT like structures to facilitate public market investments and participation. Private equity players will acquire more assets in the budget and mid-market segments of hospitality. The next decade should witness many transactions occurring in the form of mergers and acquisitions, to take advantage of the low cost of debt in India. Formation of hospitality funds will increase due to willingness of equity players to invest in this sector. More hotel aggregators will emerge to tap the huge opportunity available, like Oyo Rooms, Vista Rooms, etc.

The MICE business is a key revenue contributor and has the potential to add to the overall development of India as a destination. HVS research reveals that convention or meetings tourism accounts for over 20% of all international arrivals globally. Till the late 1990s, North America and Europe had dominated the conventions and conference markets. The United States still holds the top spot for the highest number of meetings held. There are several other Asian countries that have successfully captured a growing portion of the MICE business in recent years. With the emergence of India as a key economic hotspot along with China, convention tourism has enormous possibilities in the country. India's growing strength in the IT arena has induced international bodies to host trade shows and conventions in the country and businesses such as bio-technology, pharmaceutical, and the manufacturing sectors are also expected to bring convention revenues to the country in the coming years. India still needs to gear up to attract large international conventions. The reason being the lack of world class convention centers in India. The Hyderabad International Convention Centre is India's only branded (Novotel), large scale convention facility. Bangalore and Mumbai are making consolidated strides toward developing its MICE facilities, to become a contender for this lucrative business segment. To increase the return on investments, hotel companies will ensure that their technology systems are prepared for global deployment. MICE bookings will increase online, wherein onsite formats, menus, room rates, excursions, etc., will be planned remotely by corporate and other global participants. The availability of a wide choice in the travel market has resulted in travelers, wanting an experience rather than accommodation. The popularity of Airbnb and Uber is a testament to this fact. The health awareness wave in India is another upsurge and brings with it a new segment of health conscious travelers. The health trend is here to stay and needs to be catered by Indian hospitality providers, bother by the small and chain players. Menus will reflect cuisine tailored to healthy options to increase customer convenience and preference. Hotels such as Ganga Kinare, an independent boutique hotel in Rishikesh, which hosts the annual International Yoga Festival held there, is a very popular experience which is much sought after. It has from over 200 participants from across the globe. Hotels must understand that enjoyment means different things to different people. Not all people want to have a lazy holiday. Organizing health-focused events and incorporating healthy menu items are ways of winning guest loyalty. India will see an increased entry of global fine dining specialty restaurants such as Jamie's from London, specialty coffee shops and a variety of fine dining options. Supermarkets will carry a variety of branded hotel food products, packaged, and sold ready to eat for retail consumers.

The Indian customer has become very price conscious and demands greater value for his money. The industry is moving toward budget accommodation without compromising on standards. More and more hotels will launch their budget versions under their own brand names, thus catering to a much larger market. Hotels will also be exploring various other avenues for monetization, like managing events, taxi services, specialized catering, event integration, etc. apart from their core business. Medical tourism is also a revenue generator which will increase with time. Serviced apartments are likely to become a major money earner. With most big cities being saturated, the focus will shift to the Tier-II and Tier-III cities in India for growth. The industry is moving toward offering better quality services and increased use of technology, to deliver lasting customer value.

KEYWORDS

- **hospitality**
- **tourism industry**
- **brand value**
- **Indian market**
- **investment opportunities**

REFERENCES

Accor Launches Accor Hotels App for Apple Watch, 13 March 2015. Retrieved from: http://www.hospitalityupgrade.com/_news/NewsArticles/Accor-Launches-Accorhotels-app-for-Apple-Watch.asp.

Apple Watch is the New Hotel Room Key, 9 December 2014. Retrieved from http://nypost.com/2014/09/12/apple-watch-is-the-new-hotel-room-key/.

Dhillon, J. S.; Joshi, M.; Verma, R. Indian Hospitality Industry: Moving Towards Customer Oriented Information System (COIS). *J. Bus. Manage. Soc. Sci. Res.* **2012,** *1*(1), 58–69.

Google Analytics. *Average Monthly Unique Users*, Q1 *2014*; does not include traffic to daodao.com.

King, D. *Cornell-study-links-hotel-reviews-and-room-revenue*, 29 November 2012. Retrieved from http://www.travelweekly.com/Travel-News/Hotel-News/Cornell-study-links-hotel-reviews-and-room-revenue/.

Kinsella, T. *Hotel Management Software—Let's Get the Mobile Phone Right First*, 26 March 2015a. Retrieved from http://stayntouch.com/hotel-management-software-lets-get-mobile-phone-right-first/.

Kinsella, T. *The Hotel Room Key Goes Mobile... What's the Big Deal? The Answer is "Choice of Service"*, 23 March 2015b. Retrieved from http://stayntouch.com/hotel-mobile-room-key-whats-the-big-deal/.

Koumelis, T. *Revinate Launches in Guest in Europe to Deliver a Breakthrough in Guest Engagement: Rich Guest Profiles*, 10 March 2015. Retrieved from http://www.traveldailynews.com/news/article/65110/revinate-launches-inguest-in-europe#sthash.gFOGtvDG.dpuf.

Mclean, V. *Hilton Worldwide Truly Opens Doors: Company to Roll Out Mobile Room Keys in 2015 at Hundreds of U.S. Hotels Across Four Brands*, 03 November 2014. Retrieved from http://www.hiltonworldwideglobalmediacenter.com/index.cfm/newsroom/detail/27701.

Naisbitt, J. *Megatrends: Ten New Directions Transforming Our Lives*. Warner Books/Warner Communications Company, 1982.

Patak, M. *Simple Ways to Overcome OTA Blues and Increase Direct Hotel Bookings*, 22 December 2014. Retrieved from http://www.hotelogix.com/blog/2014/12/22/simple-ways-to-overcome-ota-blues-and-increase-direct-hotel-bookings/.

Rauch, R. *Top 10 Hospitality Industry Trends in 2015*, 8 December 2014. Retrieved from http://www.4hoteliers.com/features/article/8736.

Sanghi, M. *6 Hotel Hospitality Industry New and Current Trends You Should Know About*, 6 February 2014. Retrieved from http://www.hotelogix.com/blog/2014/02/06/6-hotel-industry-trends-you-should-know-about/#sthash.6CmoCPKj.dpufhttp://www.hotelogix.com/blog/2014/02/06/6-hotel-industry-trends-you-should-know-about/.

Yu, B.; Singh, M. P. Distributed Reputation Management for Electronic Commerce. *Comput. Intell.* **2002,** *18*(4), 535–549.

WEB REFERENCES

http://trackmaven.com/marketing-dictionary/real-time-marketing
http://www.apple.com/watch/guided-tours/
http://www.emarketer.com/Article/2-Billion-Consumers-Worldwide-Smartphones-by-2016/1011694
http://www.tripadvisor.co.nz/PressCenter-c4-Fact_Sheet.html
https://www.spgpromos.com/keyless

INDEX

A

Agricultural tourism, 72–73
AIRIS Program, 159
Art and hotel business
  AIRIS Program, 159
  NyX Innovation Alliances Program, 159
  Unilever's Catalyst Program, 159–160
Arts-informed leadership
  and art forms, 160
    instrumental role, 161–163
  conceptual model of engaging
    employees through learning
      about learning and its relevance in business, 175–176
  in family-run business, 156
  implications of present study, 174–175
  methodology
    design of study, 166
    objectives of study, 167–169
  results and discussions
    customer feedback, 172
    focus groups, 169–171
    in-depth interviews, 172
"Asset-heavy" models, 34

B

Barista Lavazza, 305
"Black money," 28
Branded Coffee Houses a Rage in India, 308
Brewberrys Café, 306
BRU World Café, 306
Business ethics, 46. See also Corporate social responsibility (CSR)
Business travel segment, 11

C

Café Coffee Day, 300, 305
Café Pascucci, 305
Catering business
  from ancient to modern times, 277–279
  future of, 294–296
  introduction, 276–277
  market, 286
  overall analysis
    issues and challenges, 287
    opportunity, 286
  to start
    FSSAI Act, 283
    FSSAI license, 284
    human resource, 284
    inventory management, 285
    menu planning, 284
    pricing strategy, 285
    production place, 285
    sales turnover, 284
    tax registration, 284
    unique selling proposition, 285
    VAT regulations, 284
  unorganized chaos, 279–283
Coffee and India, 302
  coffee shops, 304–306
    and coffee culture, 306–309
  drinking, 303
    specialty coffee, 304
  generation X, Y, AND Z, 309–315
  production, 303
Coffee Bean & Tea Leaf, The, 306
Coffee N U, 306
Coffee World, 306
Cognitive competencies, 134
Competencies
  categorized, 134
  classified, 133
  defined, 132
  research, 132
  typology of dimensions, 133

Conceptual framework for hospitality
    industry, 130–131
Consumer behavior, factors affecting, 63
    economy, 64
    facilitating means, 66
    globalization, 67–68
    growth of youth market, 64
    mass media, 66
    social change, 66
    technological change, 65–66
Consumer shopper typologies, 315–317
Corporate social responsibility (CSR), 44
    and corporate performance, 56–57
    denotation of
        affirmative action, 46
        business ethics, 46
        community, 47–49
        corporate governance, 45
        customers, 46–47
        natural environment, 47
        supply chain, 46
        workplace and labor relations, 46
    in hospitality, 49–50
        methodology, 51
        New Companies Act, 2013 and
        Indian hotel industry, 51–52
    initiatives by key Indian hotel compa-
    nies, 55
    performance at glance
        luxury chain hotel, Oberoi Group of
        Hotels, 53
        Taj Hotels Resorts and Palaces,
        52–53
        young responsible hotel company,
        Lemon Tree, 53–54
Costa Coffee, 300, 305
Cox and Kings, 292
Culinary innovation in Indian hotels,
    252–253
    creativity, innovation, and profitability,
    254–259
    findings and discussion
        aptly app, 265
        city vs. resort hotels, 261–262
        edible rooftops, 264
        food inflation, 265–268

    food wastage, 265
    fresh, 262
    individuality of restaurants in hotels,
    263
    inventory rules, 262
    revenue management practice, 263
    slow food and sustainability, 264–265
    supplier's contracts, 264
    technological advancement, 263
    implications, 269–270
    limitations and future research, 272
    methodology and purpose, 254
    new product development (NPD), 256
    new service development (NSP), 256
    phases, 257
    process, 258
    recommendations, 270–271
    restaurants and, 259–261
    six steps model, 256
    steps proposed, 256–257
    technological development and innova-
    tion, 255
Cuppa Joe, 306

D

Department of Industrial Policy and
    Promotion, 3
Di Bella Coffee India, 305
DINESERV model, 207
DNA Entertainment Networks Pvt. Ltd.,
    292

E

East India Hotels (EIH), 19
Economy and culture, hospitality segment
    in
    agricultural tourism, 72–73
    authenticity, 70–71
    based on theme, 70
    ecotourism, 71–72
    growth of chains of hotels, 68–69
    medical tourism, 75
    rural tourism and home stays, 70
    spas/wellness, 73–75
    technology and emergence of
    e-services, 75–76

travel and tourism sector in India, 68
unconventional accommodations, 73
upcoming trends in India
    based on location, 69
    new entrants from outside of indus-
    try, 69
Ecotourism, 71–72
E-Factor Entertainment Pvt. Ltd., 292
ETAuto.com, 107
Event and Entertainment Management
    Association (EY-EEMA) report,
    288–289
Event industry
from ancient to modern times, 289–291
classified, 288
EY-EEMA report, 288–289
future of, 294–296
immunity from economic slowdown,
    291–292
in India, 288
introduction, 287
overall analysis
    issues and challenges, 294
    opportunity, 293

F

Family business food restaurants, in Surat
    city
fast food
    owners, age groups, 182–183
    profit margin (annually), 186–188
Gujarat (location-wise), 180–182
size of family, 183–185
Family-run business
leadership and decision making,
    165–166
managerial perspective of art forms in,
    173–174
participant's interest in arts form,
    189–191
Fast-food industry in India, 76–77
Federation of Hotel and Restaurant Asso-
    ciations of India (FHRAI), 5
classified hotels under, 10
Fine-dining restaurant, 197–198

Floor space index (FSI), 9
Focus groups, 169–171. *See also* Arts-
    informed leadership
findings of discussions
    with arts forms and benefits in family
    business, 192–194
Food and beverages (F&B) segment, 228
challenges on road to growth in
    revenues and profitability, 247–248
findings from, F&B leaders roundtable,
    237–246
implications and way forward, 248–249
methodology
    dependence on revenues, 233–234
    food and beverages revenue growth
    story, 230–233
    human resource impact, 236–237
    hygiene and food safety concern, 235
    pricing spin, 235–236
    technology impact, 234–235
operational function, 229
Food Safety and Standards Authority of
    India (FSSAI), 283
Foreign tourist arrival (FTA), 21
Foreign versus domestic tourists, 77
Functional competencies, 134

G

Generation Z and specialist coffee shops
    in India, 300
conclusions and recommendations,
    321–322
data analysis, 319
findings, 320–321
methodology, 317–319
Globalization, 44
Gloria Jean's, 305
Greenalls'-based original Jungle Bungle
    concept, 64
Growth story of hotels in India, 18
arrival of new brands, 19
business approaches, 19
capacity expansion, 19
challenges, 18
financial performance, 19
implications, 38–40

macro-environment at glance (*See* Macro-environment at glance, hotel industry)
methodology, 21

H

"Hard asset," 28
Hospitality
impact on global economy, 2
US hotel industry, 5
Human resources in hospitality industry, 110
demand side, 114–115
supply side, 111–114

I

The Indian Hotel Company, 19
Indian Hotels Company Limited (IHCL), 19
Indian mutiny, 300–301
Indian real estate companies with hotel investments, 29
Indian tourism and hospitality industry, 2
anomalies, 9–10
arrival of new brands, 19
average occupancy and average room rates across cities, 7–8
average room rate (ARR), 5
capacity expansion, 19
category rooms, 10
challenges facing, 127–128
current performance, 156–158
demand for rooms, 11
dynamics, 12–13
economic growth, 3
and employability, 3
epilogue and future trends, 326–351
fiscal performance, 20
future prospects and trends, 351–360
GDP growth rate, 10–11
hotel rooms in India, 6
incentives, 13–14
individual developers, 10
initiatives by Government of India, 4
numbers of member hotels at FHRAI, 5
occupancy and average rates, 6
occupancy for, 5
product, cost and quality, 9
rationale of study, 128–129
recent investments in, 3
trends, 4–6, 9–14
Indus Valley Civilization or Harappan Civilization, 300
In room Dining (IRD), 228
Integrated talent management, 131
Inter-Continental Hotel Group, 6–7

J

Javagreen, 306

L

Leadership development, 126
and art forms, 160
facilitator of inner transformation and awakening of consciousness, 163–164
instrumental role, 161–163
conceptual framework, 130–131
framework, for leadership competencies, 132–135
methodology, 131–132
phase 2, in-depth interviews with hospitality HR experts, 142
data analysis, 146–150
profile of interviewees, 143–144
research instrument, 144–145
phase 1, survey questionnaire, 136
data analysis, 139–142
profile of respondents, 138–139
research instrument, 137
rationale of study, 128–129
Leela Hotels, 19
Liberalization of Indian economy, 301–302
Luxury chain hotel, Oberoi Group of Hotels, 53. *See also* Corporate social responsibility (CSR)

M

Macro-environment at glance, hotel industry
additional room inventory, cost of, 27–28
brand owned/leased and operated, 33–34
business partnerships and approaches, 30
contributors to economy of country, 21
existing supply across major cities, 24
findings from interviews with hotel owners and representatives
relationships with managing hotel brands, 36–37
return on investment, 35–36
sources of funding, 36
franchise and joint ventures, 32–33
FTA, numbers in, 21
GDP, 21
hotel management viewpoint, 37–38
investment, 28–30
management contracts, 31–32
marketing campaigns, 21
proposed branded hotels, 25–26
statistics, 21–22
status of room supply in Indian market, 22–23, 27
Maggie noodles, 57
The Marriott International, 9
revenue management, 87
Medical tourism, 75
Meetings, incentives, conference, and seminar (MICS) segment, 97
Meta competencies, 134
Methodological triangulation, 142
Michelin chef-led innovation process, 258–259
Millennials, 64–65
Mocha, 306

N

National skill development initiative in India, vision
choice, competition, and accountability, 108
co-created solutions and forging partnerships, 109
dynamic and demand-based system planning, 107
folding, future in, 108
game-changing delivery/innovation, 109–110
high inclusivity, 107
issues and constraints
efficiency of training efforts, 117
employability challenge, 116
holistic education, 118
labor shortages, 115
lack of structured policies, 116
learning and teaching approach, 116
levels, 116–117
non standardization of training curriculum, 115
quality expectations, 118
recruitment and retention, 118
retraining cost for employer, 115
staff turnover, 118
THSC mandate, 119
trainer skill gap, 116
training potential of institutes, 116
use of contemporary technology, 116
made bankable, 108
policy coordination and coherence, 108
scale of ambition, 107
skills framework, 108
NyX Innovation Alliances Program, 159

O

"Oberoi Group," 19
Online travel agents (OTAs) for business, 89

P

Patanjali Atta noodles, 57
Percept, 292
"Pradhan Mantri Kaushal Vikas Yojana" (PMKVY), 119
Profitability, competing challenges
changes in global economy, 90–91

qualified revenue management professionals, 89–90
rise and dominance of OTA, 89
competition, 86
discussion and conclusion
    consumer expectations, 102
    distribution, 102
    pricing strategy, 101
    promotion, 102
findings
    challenges with revenue management, 99–101
    emerging opportunities in revenue management, 98–99
    existing revenue management practices, 92–97
    performance metrics and qualities of revenue manager, 98
    revenue management in lower demand and global weaker economy, 97
global business environment, 86–87
managing demand, 88
methodology, 91–92
revenue management, 87
    role of, 88–89
strategic management process, 87

Q

Qahwa, 302
Quick service restaurants (QSRs), 197–198
Qwiky's Coffee, 306

R

Real Estate Investment Trusts (REITs), 34
Revenue management, 87
    challenges with, 99–101
    emerging opportunities in, 98–99
    existing practices, 92–97
    in lower demand and global weaker economy, 97
    performance metrics and qualities of revenue manager, 98

qualified revenue management professionals, 89–90
Rural tourism and home stays, 70

S

Service quality (SQ) and customer experience, 196–197
analysis, 208–210
discussion, 210–214
hypotheses, 206–207
hypotheses testing, 225
limitations, and scope for further research, 214–216
managerial implications, 216–218
methods, 207–208
review of literature
    behavioral intentions, 204–205
    consequences of service quality on customer perceptions, 201
    customer experience, 201–203
    customer satisfaction, 203–204
    effect of ambient environment on perceptions of service quality delivered, 201
    relationship between, service quality, customer satisfaction, and behavioral intentions, 205–206
    service quality, 200–201
validity for
    all factors combined, 224
    SQ factors, 223
Services sectors in India, 2
SERVQUAL model, 202
Shloka Events, 292
Showtime, 292
Skilling India initiative, 106. *See also* National skill development initiative in India, vision
    readily employable workforce, 107
Social competencies, 134
Social media, 292
Spas/wellness, 73–75
Specialty coffee, 304
Starbucks, 300, 306
Stayzilla, 14
Strategic management process, 87

T

"Taj Group," 19
Taj Hotels Resorts and Palaces, 52–53.
  See also Corporate social responsibility
  (CSR)
Tourism and Hospitality Skills Council
  (THSC), 118–119
Trends and Opportunities report, 27
Triple bottom line (TBL) expectation, 56

U

Unilever's Catalyst Program, 159–160

W

Wedding Design Company by Vandana
  Mohan, 292
Wedmegood blog, 292
Wizcraft, 292
WOM communication, 205, 213
World online, 77–78
World Travel and Tourism Council, 3, 11
Wyndham Hotel Group, 9

Y

Young responsible hotel company, Lemon
  Tree, 53–54. *See also* Corporate social
  responsibility (CSR)